He who has begun a good work

Taking the Gospel to the Tarahumara
Indians of Mexico

Steven Real

ISBN 979-8-88540-754-0 (paperback)
ISBN 979-8-88540-755-7 (digital)

Copyright © 2023 by Steven Real

All rights reserved. No part of this publication may be reproduced, distributed, or transmitted in any form or by any means, including photocopying, recording, or other electronic or mechanical methods without the prior written permission of the publisher. For permission requests, solicit the publisher via the address below.

Christian Faith Publishing
832 Park Avenue
Meadville, PA 16335
www.christianfaithpublishing.com

Gratis Use: Text from the **NKJV, NCV, ICB, NET, The Voice, or the Expanded** may be quoted in any form (written, visual, electronic, or audio), up to and inclusive of 500 verses or less without written permission, providing the verses quoted do not amount to a complete book of the Bible, nor do verses quoted account for 25% or more of the total text of the work in which they are quoted, and the verses are not being quoted in a commentary or other biblical reference work. This permission is contingent upon an appropriate copyright acknowledgment.

Printed in the United States of America

This book is dedicated to the scores of instructors who imparted their knowledge and wisdom to us students, from Bible school through language and linguistics studies, never knowing for sure which of us would actually get out into those "fields that are ripe for harvest".

It is also dedicated to the dozens of financial supporters who for years allowed us to carry on living in both the US and Mexico, by faith exchanging some of their hard-earned finances for "treasure that will never perish": souls who were forever changed and are now sons and daughters of our loving God.

Someday you will certainly hear, "Well done, My good and faithful servant!"

Contents

Chapter 1: Life-Changing Decisions 1
    Listening to God's Voice Regarding My Soul 1
    Experiencing God's Leading Regarding My Career 4
Chapter 2: South to Old Mexico 8
    2.1 "Aye Señor, So Much Stuff!" 8
        Another Real Boy Comes into the World! 12
        Our Own House—and Motocross! 15
        Cops or Robbers? 17
        Meeting Poncho Villa's Wife 19
    2.2 *All right!* I Thought. *I Found It!* 21
        VW Mechanic Turned "Mechanico" 26
    2.3 First Trip to the Sierra Madre 28
        Spanish, Spanish and More Spanish… 28
        Survey into the Mountains at Last! 32
    2.4 An Unusual Stranger in this Strange Land 39
        Finding the Elusive Don Burgess 44
        The Wycliffe Story (Very Briefly) 46
    2.5 Not "Back to the Future"—This Was
    "Forward to the Past" 48
        El Divisadero—The Gem of the Sierra Madre 51
        Like a Scene Out of an Old Clint Eastwood
        Western 53
        "There Were Guerrillas Out Here?" 62
Chapter 3: Moving to San Rafael 68
    Hitch 'Em Up and Move 'Em Out! 68
    Wild West Shootout 71
    "Uh, Butch," I said. "I Think We're in For
    Some Trouble Here." 72
    Driving Mexico's Roads in the '80s 75

Chapter 4: Life in San Rafael..79
   4.1 Our First Week in San Rafael (January 30, 1982) 79
      Getting to Know San Rafael and Los Tascates 84
      Fun and Funny Stuff...89
   4.2 Exploring with Ticker and the Boys—
      February through March 1982 92
      Cliff and Diane Join Us in San Rafael 97
      "Where Did the Road Go?"....................................100
      "Breaker, Breaker One-Niner. What's Your
      Twenty?"..101
   4.3 The Van Goes Off the Road 103
      So Many of Our Problems Need Spiritual
      Solutions 106
      The Aerial Survey..108
   4.4 Real Child No. 3 110
      Recovery and Permission for a Trip to Chicago........114
      An Angel Shakes Me Awake in the Middle
      of the Night 115

Chapter 5: Spring Forward..117
   5.1 Now What? 117
      Suspicious Minds 118
      Broken Down Missionaries from Up North
      (I Think) 120
      Old Spanish Gold 123
   5.2 Partners: Take 3 125
      Enter Potential Partner No. 3 128
      Conversations with a Shaman................................132
   5.3 A Door Closes, Then… 139
      …There Was a Knock on the Door 140
   5.4 "See, I Have Set Before You an Open
      Door, and No One Can Shut It"
      (The Lord Jesus Christ, Revelation 3:8) 141
      All Coffee-ed Out...146
   5.5 Knowing God's Will 148

Chapter 6: Building the House in El Manzano........................156
   6.1 Getting Permission and Getting Started.................156
   6.2 "Unless the Lord Builds the House…"....................160

6.3 No More "Hurry Up and Wait" 166
6.4 Trucks, Trains, and Lots of Hauling 171
6.5 American Yelling, "Mud!" Tarahumara
 Yelling Back, "Mud!" 180
6.6 Drunk Driver and a Close Call............................189
 Visiting the Drunk Truck Driver 195
6.7 Second Floor and Roof......................................197
6.8 Home, Sweet Home! 201
Chapter 7: Life in El Manzano 210
7.1 I Couldn't See to Drive 210
 Daily Life in Our New Home in El Manzano 212
 "Interruptions"..214
 Evenings and Nights—Ah Yes! 218
7.2 Making Friends, El Manzano Style: Playing
 the "Palillo" 221
 When (Fishing) in Rome, Do (Fish) as the
 Romans Do...222
 Macaws, Rattlesnakes, and Bees—Oh My! 225
7.3 Will This House Ever Be Finished? 231
 Probably the Funniest Thing I Saw in El Manzano....231
 Enter Al and Polly Clark 235
 Tarahumara Culture Study in Earnest....................236
7.4 "The Cloud"...239
7.5 Culture Notes, October 1983–November 1984......242
 Branding Indians, Witch Doctors, and
 Which Doctors? 242
 The Spirits in the Night 249
 Things that Make Noise in the Night....................251
7.6 A Strange Encounter—Adela Sanchez................253
 Blizzard Border Trip, December 1983 255
7.7 A Christmas to Remember.................................258
7.8 Will Drs. Real and Real Please Report… 264
 Thank You! That Will Be One Chicken… 269
 Not Funny at All—Deadly Serious Actually 270
 The Snake-Bitten Tarahumara 277
 Rosa Sanchez..278

Chapter 8: Life and Ministry Roll On—1984 282
   8.1 Sweet Home, El Manzano!..282
      Our Own Airstrip 284
      God's Prep School for Culture Studies...................287
      God's Army and Special Forces.............................291
      The Battle in the Mind 293
   8.2 Help Is Coming…..295
      …If I Don't Kill Them First! 295
      The Cloud Takes No Break 297
      House Construction, Take 2.................................300
   8.3 Mom Comes to Visit or "You Can't Make
      This Stuff Up!" 300
Chapter 9: The First Believers 308
   9.1 The Gospel Brings Light!...308
   9.2 Team Teaching..312
   9.3 Spiritual Warfare, Drug Warfare 315
   9.4 Spiritual Hopelessness..319
   9.5 "Redeemed…to God…out of Every Tribe
      and Tongue and People and Nation"
      (Revelation 5:9) 321
   9.6 Off to the USA 324
Chapter 10: Furlough...327
      Stranger in a Strange Land 327
      Medical Help for Us, Ministering Still in Chicago.....330
      Da Bears!...331
      Busy, Busy, Busy...332
      New Wheels! Computer? Electricity?.....................334
Chapter 11: Back Home in El Manzano................................336
   11.1 On the Road Home Again!....................................336
      Refresher Course and a Serious Reality Check!.......336
      Almost There… 341
      There's No Place Like Home! 341
      New Realities in El Manzano: Financial Support....343
      Ticker's Hormone Treatments...............................344
   11.2 Mauro's Big Threat 344
   11.3 The Ejido Meeting and Psalm 35..........................346

11.4 The Trip to Uruachic 354
11.5 The Miracle Child 380
11.6 "Those who will believe on You…" 381
    Daily Life, Daily Ministry Fall 1986–March 1987 385
    The Lord Keeps Building His Church 389
Chapter 12: Medical Furlough 391
    Chattanooga, Tennessee..391
    In Chicago (Des Plaines, Actually) 393
    Counseling and Spiritual Warfare 394
    The Answer to Our Prayers! 396
Chapter 13: Ministry in Chihuahua
    (August 1988–August 1989) 401
13.1 Back to Chihuahua—August 1988 401
    "Da Bears" of Chihuahua 402
    You Can Take the Missionary Out of the
    Tribe, But… 404
13.2 Community Development and Politics.................411
    The Clinic in El Manzano 414
13.3 Out of Gas 419
Chapter 14: Out of Options..424
14.1 Counseling, Quote, Unquote..................................424
    My Reality Shock 426
14.2 My Father in New Mexico 429
14.3 A Lesson From the Book of Job 433
14.4 One Loss… 434
14.5 After Another… 436
14.6 …After Another… 444
14.7 …After Another..447
14.8 A Lesson about Suicide 451
Chapter 15: Life After New Tribes...453
15.1 Blessings and Being a Single Dad..........................453
15.2 Processing the Losses, Facing the Future 457
15.3 The Middle Years 461
Chapter 16: This is About <u>Him</u>...463
16.1 "He Who Has Begun a Good Work in
    You Will Continue It Until the Day of Jesus
    Christ" Philippians 1:6 463

16.2 God's Work Grows 466
    1989–2016 The New Tribes Ministry to the
    Western Tarahumara Indian People 466
    Dave Wolf and Company..468
    The Clinic..468
    1996 - Al and Polly 469
    1997 - Ticker and Dan..469
    2008 - Electricity and Cell Phones 470
    2009 - Dave Re-visits El Manzano.........................471
    2012 - Go West, Young Man!................................473
    2014- Dusty and His Family 475
    2014- Enter Cynthia 476
    2018- First Hand News from My Old Partner!.......477
    2022 From Boys to Men to Warriors......................480
    Barbara and Teodulo 482
    Don Burgess, A Marathon Running Servant
    of God 483
    A Tribute to Al Clark...485
16.3 "He Will Complete It Until The Day Of
    Jesus Christ" (Philippians 1:6) 486

Afterward 491

Chapter 1

Life-Changing Decisions

Listening to God's Voice Regarding My Soul

On the evening of March 14, 1973, I found myself in an old farmhouse in Bensenville, Illinois, twenty-some miles northwest of Chicago. My next-door neighbor, Bill Gast, had invited me again to the Des Plaines Bible Church for the Wednesday evening service. After several invitations, I finally agreed, and we were now, at about 9:00 p.m., at a college and career age Bible study group preparation meeting. Five guys, all two to four years older than me, were the leaders of this group. They were all new Christians, having only accepted the Lord within the last year.

I had been listening that evening to first a church service, then the discussions that these fellows were having in preparation for their Friday night Bible study. Although I had been raised a Roman Catholic, had been an altar boy in seventh grade for a year, attended Catholic school for over a year in junior high, and had attended catechism classes for seven or eight years, I had never heard the truths from the Bible that they were discussing that night.

One fellow in particular, Tom, a big tall fellow with reddish brown hair, started a conversation with me right before it was time for all of us to head home. He asked me if I had received Christ as my Savior. I told him I believed in God and knew a lot about Christianity, although I actually meant the Roman Catholic brand.

Tom proceeded to lay out quite clearly for me the fact that the Scriptures say in many, many places that Christ came to die on the cross as payment for our sins so that we could, by a conscious act of faith, accept God's forgiveness for our sins, and thereby become children of His. As the truths from the Bible that Tom was sharing with me were sinking in, other concepts in my mind finally began to be sorted out. For over three years, I had read a lot of books and literature on various religions of the world. The Eastern religions and transcendental meditation and what I knew through my schooling in the Roman Catholic faith all pointed to a struggle that man has with sin and our separation from God. These various religions and philosophies all had the same thing in common: we must work our way to heaven, being as good as we could be in this life, and hope that we would be accepted into an afterlife that would be blissful.

Subconsciously, I had become saddened with the reality that we could never be truly godly and thereby be assured that when this life was over, we could spend eternity with God Himself. Now I was reading, in black and white, verses from the Bible that very clearly stated that God actually had a loving plan for all of us humans who could never attain godly perfection, no matter how many lifetimes we lived. His plan revolved around Him sending His own Son to pay the price of our forgiveness with His own life so that we could be adopted into His family. I was astounded.

With Tom's encouragement and overcoming a few minutes of shyness or some sort of subconscious pride, I embraced the truth of God's message. I bowed my head, accepted God's forgiveness through His Son, and asked Christ to come into my life.

I was a senior in high school with barely three months left before graduation. Especially in the last year, I had become more restless in my spirit and unhappy with living with my parents. Since January, I had a backpack packed with basic camping provisions and had a plan in mind. Right after graduation, I was going to hitchhike and hop freight trains and make my way back out West to San Francisco to join up with my old friends there. I would leave a note for my folks but would not tell them where I was going.

By the next day, after accepting Christ as my Savior, I knew something in me was brand-new. I felt the resentment and anger toward my parents fading away. I felt a new life inside of me. My parents, too, saw the change in me. I realized later that it was the Holy Spirit of God who came to live in me and change me from the inside out. I definitely had not just "turned over a new leaf" as some people say. I had not, in a psychological step of optimism, adopted a new philosophy of life either. I had been trying those kinds of things for over three years. None of them worked.

Right away, I started attending the services at the Des Plaines Bible Church on Wednesdays and Sundays, but the highlight of the week was the Friday night college and career age Bible study group called Tentmakers. And the group was growing fast. There were between twelve and fifteen people coming when I started in March. By the end of the summer, there were between fifty and sixty. Within a month or two, after accepting the Lord and thinking ahead to what I wanted to do for college or a career, I felt a strong calling from God to not just get a job where I could earn money and become like so many others looking for financial security in this world. The transformation that God did in me, I felt, was something I wanted to share with as many people as possible. I felt that it was the most important thing in life. I asked God to give me direction as to what to do next.

I became really close friends with Bill Gast and his best friend, Gary Barrett, over the next few months. By that summer, we were camping and fishing and rock climbing and doing all kinds of other fun things together. Our spiritual lives were the most important thing to all three of us. We were learning so much attending Tentmakers. Our pastor, Craig Massey, had given the group that name because of certain disciples of the Lord, including the Apostle Paul, who supported themselves financially as tentmakers, even as they shared the Gospel all over the Middle East and Asia. We were much the same—enthusiastic disciples of the Lord who were finding our way in the world.

Pastor Massey was incredibly important to us and to so many hundreds of other people at the Des Plaines Bible Church in those years. All of us will forever praise the Lord for what a great man of God he was. Although legally blind and in his sixties, he continued to be a gracious, grace-filled, and wise pastor for a few more years before he finally retired.

Experiencing God's Leading Regarding My Career

Still not being sure of what kind of career I wanted to go into, I started at the local community college taking courses so that I could become a forest ranger. I have always loved the outdoors, but after one semester, I was absolutely certain that I should be in full-time Christian work. I had nothing against pastors, particularly since we had such a fantastic one at our church, but somehow, I couldn't see myself dressing in a suit and tie every day for the rest of my life. So I looked for a full-time job in order to save money for going away to some kind of Bible school.

A good friend from Tentmakers, Al Berntsen, who happened to be one of the guys who was renting that farmhouse where I had accepted the Lord, found a job for me at the shop where he worked. For the next nine months, I worked with Al in a company where we made Christmas and Easter displays for shopping centers all over the country. The funny thing was the president was Jewish, and the vice president was Roman Catholic. Although I'd only had one semester of woodshop in seventh grade, I was able to quickly learn enough to become a pretty good finish carpenter as well as getting training in arc welding and using an oxyacetylene torch.

Like any guy seventeen, almost eighteen years old, I was interested in the girls. I dated three or four girls from our Bible study group, then became really interested in one in particular. Her name was Dorothy, but she hated that name and went by her nickname of Ticker, which came from an attempt by her older brother when they were both quite small who was trying to say "little sister." It came out "little ticker," and it stuck for the rest of her life.

Ticker also had a strong desire to serve the Lord and knew she needed to get a quality Bible school education. She applied to Moody

Bible Institute but somehow didn't feel quite right about going there. Somehow, she found out about a place called New Tribes Institute, the Bible school for New Tribes Mission. New Tribes was a non-denominational, Bible-believing mission organization that sent its missionaries exclusively to tribal people all over the world. One day, in the fall of 1973, she told me she was starting Bible school at New Tribes in January. It felt like we were going to be pulled apart, but we stayed in close touch by mail.

In May 1974, she told me about a New Tribes missionary conference that was coming up in a month. It would be held only about two hours north of Des Plaines at a conference ground in Wisconsin. I decided to go for two days. It was a huge step in God answering my prayers as to what I should do for a career.

For those two days, I listened to numerous speakers who told their stories of working in the jungles, forests, and plains of South America, the Philippines, New Guinea, Indonesia, and elsewhere. One of the men who impressed me most was Paul Dye. He was a humble, sincere, godly man who you just knew had an amazing inner strength. He was serving as a missionary pilot in Colombia, flying in one of the most dangerous and uninhabited regions of South America. I had been fascinated with flying from a young age and, early in high school, had wanted to go to the US Air Force Academy. Paul spoke about his work as a pilot taking supplies to missionaries in remote areas in Colombia, but you could tell his heart was completely wrapped up in the missionaries that he transported and the Indian people that he flew out to serve.

Ten years later, in October 1985, Paul and some fellow missionaries would have one of the most harrowing experiences in New Tribes Mission history when they were captured by Marxist guerrillas in Colombia. His ensuing escape by air in the middle of the night is absolutely one of the most miraculous true stories you'll ever read. The book is *God at the Controls* written by Jean Dye Johnson, his aunt.

I had a couple of conversations with two of the executive board members of New Tribes Mission that weekend. I was really impressed with the organization and the men who led it. Whether Ticker had been part of the situation or not, I felt like God had shown me where

I was going to go to school! I applied a couple of weeks later and was accepted for the fall semester. A year later, Ticker and I were married.

This memoir is my own personal journey as a child of God and as a servant of God. Both of those roles are the most amazing things that can happen to a human being. What I want to relate to you in the following pages has to do with what I consider to be a fascinating trip that God led our family on, but it's really all about the enabling grace of the Holy Spirit of God. I am happy to still be a participant in His work in this world.

I hope that what you see here is how a regular human being who, along with his wife and three boys, has been blessed beyond measure with being a small part in a most amazing story. God has a very complex spiritual agenda in this world. After all, He sent His one and only Son to be the bridge between mankind and Himself, to win back to Himself a creation that He designed to be "in His own image," but which had fatally strayed away. To be used by Him in any way is a humbling privilege.

I also want to say here at the outset that I intend to be as honest as possible about my fifteen years as a student with New Tribes Mission and a missionary serving in Mexico. I believe it was necessary, with the passage of time, for God to temper in me some of the feelings that I had during several of the roughest times. God is wonderfully gracious and patient with every one of us as we learn to be transformed into the image of His dear Son. At the same time, we are absolutely human, and it is ludicrous for me or any other Christian to pretend that we do not experience the emotions of frustration, anger, or disappointment with our fellow brothers and sisters in Christ. We see the same emotions in Jehovah God in the Old Testament, in Jesus Himself in the gospels, and in the Apostle Paul in his epistles.

So from the beginning to the end of this account, I first of all admit to you, the reader, that I have many shortcomings in my own personal life. No argument, no excuses. In the pages that follow, I will share with you what it is like to become a foreign missionary—the physical, psychological, and spiritual journey. There were all the elements you might expect and then some. In addition to the victories and miracles, I will also occasionally share my personal disappointments and judgment calls regarding coworkers and even leaders. I'm

HE WHO HAS BEGUN A GOOD WORK

also certain that some if not all of you will be able to identify with me, your fellow Christian brother, who was doing the best he knew how in the incredibly wonderful and complex service of our Savior.

To be a missionary or other kind of full-time servant of the Lord is NOT an easy job nor is it done by perfect people. I would also never trade the whole experience for billions of dollars or an easier life.

Feature article in our home town newspaper, the Des Plaines Journal, Des Plaines, Illinois, July 17, 1980

When it applies, I'll fill in some of the blanks along the way about our amazingly good training to become missionaries, but for now, let's just jump right into arriving in Mexico!

Chapter 2

South to Old Mexico

2.1 "Aye Señor, So Much Stuff!"

It was August 20, 1980, when we drove over that big wide bridge between El Paso, Texas, and Juarez, Chihuahua, Mexico. We pulled our white Ford E-250 four-wheel drive van into one of the angled inspection lanes until a customs official motioned us to stop. He was dressed in dark green pants, a khaki shirt, and wore a maroon uniform cap. Having been briefed a little bit by our fellow missionaries about what I had to do, I first went inside the office with our birth certificates, truck and motorcycle titles, etc. I was requesting a six-month stay in Mexico. That was the only way missionaries for several decades were allowed to live in the country. We were issued tourist visas which had to be renewed every three to six months. After twenty minutes or so spent getting our paperwork inside taken care of with the immigration officials, now came the inspection of our vehicle and its contents.

The head customs official outside in a similar uniform but with a green cap said he would like to see what we were carrying inside the van. I slid open the side door.

"Aye! Señor! So much stuff! You are not tourists. This is not allowed."

Customs inspector on our first trip into Mexico

I explained that we were going to be studying Spanish in Chihuahua City, so we would need to set up household for a while. It really must've looked funny to him to see, on top of all the boxes and suitcases, a space about eighteen inches high, two feet wide, and three feet long with our son Dave lying on a little makeshift bed. That was the open space we had created for him after we crammed all of the worldly goods we were taking to Mexico inside the van.

Two and a half hours later, we had convinced this man and his boss to allow us into the country after we swore to them these were not items that we were taking into Mexico to sell and that we had no family there. It's quite understandable that they wanted to enforce their customs laws. I got away with just giving him a $20 tip, most of which probably went to his boss. It was the first of many such "tips" that we would give to Mexican officials. Hey, we didn't eat out, so what's a small tip to a government official every six months or so?

We drove south out of Juarez on the Pan-American highway for five hours. The difference between Mexico and El Paso, now far away in the rearview mirror, was amazing. We left behind well-groomed highways, prosperous city streets and strip malls, and were now in a country where so much was dry and brown, gravel and dirt, crowded and bustling. As we rolled into Chihuahua City late that afternoon, we saw amazing contrasts, and the pictures we took captured those first impressions on film.

A beautiful white stucco house with red tile roofs and decorative windows stood next to a stark concrete block apartment building, and next to that was an ancient adobe house with big sections of stucco missing. An old man rode his burro down a busy city street, both of their heads down, watching where they were going through squinting eyes. The burro had a couple of bags of groceries and a load of firewood tied onto his back in front of the saddle. Old compact cars and brand-new luxury sedans passed him as he stayed in the far-right traffic lane. With good directions from our new coworkers we navigated the traffic circles and soon found the mission's guest home and were warmly greeted.

The folks who ran the guest home were in their fifties and had finished raising their family many years previously. Our son, Dave, turned four years old three weeks after we arrived. Suffice it to say, he was a bundle of energy. Ticker, being eight months pregnant, and I had our hands full keeping an eye on him. I think our culture shock upon arriving in Mexico was minor compared to what the guest home host and hostess went through with little Dave. It was rather like Mr. Wilson dealing with Dennis the Menace.

We happened to arrive in time to meet all the New Tribes missionaries who were in Mexico at that time since we got there right at the beginning of the week of the annual field conference. It was a great orientation. Since Ticker needed to maintain bed rest before her delivery, which was only about five or six weeks away, I started Spanish study on my own. I had an hour of class and six or seven hours of study each day for five days a week. All of us were required to finish the entire seventy-lesson Spanish language course before we could leave the city for a tribal assignment.

We were excited about our new life, and the first major step was for us to find a house or apartment that we could rent and move out of the guesthouse. We received our income check once a month from the mission's headquarters, and it was comprised of all the individual donations that had been received by headquarters the month before that were designated for us personally. Despite having received pledges to us of about $600 per month by a variety of individuals and our home church, as I recall, our first month's check was less than

$300. It was quite a shock to see that small amount, just when we needed to set up our household.

Since a typical decent apartment or small house cost $250 a month or more, we were not even able to move out of the guesthouse for several weeks. We had to come up with some kind of plan, so we had a visit with our field chairman. The mission had rented a sizable classroom building as a school for all the children of the missionaries who were both in town and out in the tribes. There were several rooms that were not used, which were about twelve-by-fifteen feet in size. I came up with a plan and ran it by Ticker.

I would ask the field committee if we could rent two adjacent rooms at the school, and I would cut a doorway through their common wall to connect the rooms together. We would still have to go down the hall to use the bathrooms and shower that were part of the school facility, but that would make it affordable, and we could have our own place to live. The field committee agreed, and I did the work of cutting the doorway into the brick wall and finishing it off with plaster. We now had a bedroom in one room and a living room and kitchen in the other.

We arrive in Chihuahua City with Ticker 8 months pregnant

Dustin Peter arrives on October 8, 1980

Another Real Boy Comes into the World!

    We were a pretty unusual little family, even by missionary standards. I don't think anyone, before and probably since, had decided to start their missionary career by having a baby soon after arriving in their new country. Within days of our arrival, Faith, the wife of our field chairman, Paul, helped us arrange and was the translator for our doctor appointments for Ticker. We had only been in our new "apartment" at the school for several days when October 8 rolled around. That was the day Ticker was scheduled to deliver our second baby by cesarean section. We still didn't know if it was to be a boy or girl, but we were quite confident in Dr. Cesar Madrid and the Hospital Clinica del Centro.

    The C-section was to take place at about 10:00 a.m. On that day, since I barely spoke any Spanish, one of our Spanish instructors, Sue Esparza, would meet me at the hospital before 8:00 a.m., when the doctor was due to arrive. We checked with the receptionist every thirty minutes or so because, typically, the doctor would talk to the waiting father before the surgery started. But Dr. Madrid's light on the "in-service" board never came on, so the receptionist thought he still hadn't arrived. Finally, Sue had to go to teach classes, so I waited alone for news. So it happened that for the second time in my life as the expectant father I sat in the waiting room for almost three hours with no news and never had a doctor or nurse come and tell me that my wife and new child were okay.

    Knowing that the anesthesia required the delivery to go quickly so as not to adversely affect the newborn baby, I was really concerned about the time that had been passing since 10:00 a.m. But just like in Canada, where Dave had been born in a small-town country hospital, no one came out to tell me that my child had been born and was normal and that my wife was fine. The receptionist finally suggested I go up to Ticker's room and check on her. You can imagine my surprise when I walked in and saw her there lying in bed, looking really exhausted, but then she smiled!

"Well?" I said.

"It's a boy!" she told me.

"And you're both okay?"

"Yes," she said, "just really tired and the anesthesia is starting to wear off."

Ticker's recovery from the C-section went well, and we named our new son, Dustin Peter. Dave loved having his new little brother. Life living at the school was, shall we say, "different." It was a little louder than we would've liked during the day, but it was really nice outside of school hours. Then there was the fact that we had our own private open-air courtyard, quite large, where there was a basketball court and room to play soccer. A week after Dusty was born, Dave came and asked me if he and I could play soccer out on the basketball court. I went into the school's game room, looking for a ball. I went through all the soccer balls, but there wasn't a single one that had air. I even looked at some volleyballs and basketballs. Every ball had some kind of problem or other. One that looked the most promising did not have the inside bladder positioned so that the valve was lined up with the little hole in order to add more air to it.

I looked at that ball, set it aside, and said to Dave, "This one would be okay, except it's out of whack."

After a couple of minutes of searching through all the balls and telling him we were out of luck, he picked up the soccer ball with the twisted bladder and asked, "Dad, can you just put some more whack in this one?"

Dave was adjusting quite well to Mexico. He found lots of things about it fascinating. In fact, his birthday, September 16, is a major Mexican holiday. That is the date on which the Mexican revolution for independence from Spain began. There are lots of fireworks and excitement, and on the evening of his birthday, we went outside at the guesthouse to watch the fireworks. He asked what was going on. I told him they were celebrating his birthday, which, of course, produced a huge happy smile!

Kids can say the funniest things. I have some notes of the highlights that Dave has said, with one from October 23, just two months after we got to Mexico. Several times, Dave had told us, regarding

Blacks and Mexicans, that he liked the person but didn't know what to think of their color. On that particular day, Ticker went outside to find out where Dave was playing. There he was, covered with mud from his neck to his waist, hands, and arms. "David, what in the world are you doing?" Ticker asked him.

"I just wanted to be like a Mexican for a minute," he answered.

In our two-room apartment at the school Ticker set up a little table and chair for Dave off to one side of our living room, which was his very own desk, and taught him preschool just about every day. Dusty was growing well, nice and healthy and happy. Our parents' fears that we had taken their grandchildren "off to maybe die in a foreign country" were not even close to materializing. Ticker took Spanish classes as much as she could, considering she had a newborn to take care of, but I quickly moved ahead of her. We had a seventy-lesson course to complete as our primary responsibility that year, so for me, it was full speed ahead. But even though I was doing well, I knew at about lesson thirty that I needed much more—I needed to be immersed in Spanish somehow and to think in Spanish at normal speeds, not translating word by word in my head as I tried to speak or converse. I asked God for ideas, for some kind of breakthrough to help me and to help us to get more natural in our Spanish language abilities.

Dave's pre-school "classroom" in our apartment in the school building

HE WHO HAS BEGUN A GOOD WORK

Our Own House—and Motocross!

I remember those first several months vividly, as we became familiar with Mexico and Chihuahua City, the life and culture of our newly adopted country. It was also a time in which we nervously counted off how many weeks and then days were left at the end of each month before our next income check would arrive. We had to very carefully plan our spending.

In addition to the Spanish classes, I found that I could gain fluency in a lot of subjects—the sciences, politics, the economy, etc.—by buying and reading the Chihuahua City newspaper. As I recall, the daily newspaper only cost twelve cents, but as we got into the last week of the month, I had to decide how many newspapers I could buy that week. Sometimes it was only one or two. Any more than that, and we wouldn't have enough money for bread or tortillas—it was literally that tight.

After a few months of improving income, we were able to afford to rent a house. Our monthly checks had gone up a few hundred dollars as we wrote letters to folks back home, and they realized we really had arrived in Mexico and were loving our lives as missionaries. The house we found was very plain and basic and only a year or so old and was out on the edge of town. It was in a neighborhood that was still being developed and had empty lots scattered throughout it. We had great neighbors, and there was a preschool for Dave just a block or two away. Of course, the school was in Spanish, so he was able to quickly become quite fluent. I had to do my part in making us, as a family, use Spanish at home so that we would practice it in a variety of everyday situations.

In the preschool, they did not teach Dave how to ask for the salt and pepper, of course, or lots of other normal daily things we don't even think about. In fact, on his first day at preschool, an hour or two after he had started class, there was a knock on the door. Ticker opened it, and there was Dave.

"What are you doing back home, son?" Ticker asked him.

"I didn't know how to ask where the bathroom was," Dave answered.

So, yes, we had to practice lots of Spanish in the home so that we could start thinking and functioning in Spanish. Learning another language and becoming fluent in it is a hurdle and one that an amazing percentage of Americans don't really ever try or are successful at. I knew we needed to wean ourselves away from always relying on English at home, so for example, at dinnertime, I made a policy that for an hour or so, we would only speak Spanish. We had to ask for more water or for a napkin or the butter, for the beans, salt, milk or cereal in Spanish. It was vital for our progress and started to get us over the hump.

While we had lived in the neighborhood at the school, I yearned for neighbors that we could just have conversations with on a regular basis. But in that particular neighborhood, there were so many working professionals that we hardly found anybody out and about on the street in the evening. Our new neighborhood was better in that respect, and we made some good friends.

Across the street from us were Maggie and Ricardo and their two little children. Ricardo owned an office supply store in the city and, like the vast majority of Mexicans, was a conscientious and hard worker. They were friendly, and we visited two or three times a week. Still, I knew we needed better and faster progress. It's a funny thing how God will lead you into new experiences when you tell Him about your need and say, "I don't know how you can help me, but please do something!" So one day, while reading the newspaper, I saw an unusual activity that I thought I would check out—it was a motocross race.

The race was to take place that Saturday in the town of Delicias, about an hour south of Chihuahua City. It was something completely out of my realm of experiences, but it ended up being one of the best things I ever looked into. For two and a half or three hours, I sort of wandered around the motocross track, watching the races while not really knowing anything about motocross, and talked with people. Toward the end of the day, I met a family from Chihuahua City.

There were three or four brothers there with their wives and kids and their mom.

The boys, three of whom were racers, were in their twenties and early thirties. I asked them what they did for a living, and two of the brothers told me they had a Volkswagen repair shop on the north end of town in Chihuahua. I told them maybe I would stop in and talk to them sometime, if that was okay, just to practice my Spanish. They politely told me okay, but I could see that they doubted they'd ever see me again.

Cops or Robbers?

On my way home late that afternoon, I had an experience that really rattled me. I was ten or fifteen miles north of Delicias when a pickup truck pulled alongside me on the two-lane highway as if he were going to pass. But as I looked over, the fellow in the passenger seat, wearing a cowboy hat and a typical man's shirt, had a .45 caliber automatic pistol raised and waved it in a motion indicating he wanted me to pull over to the side of the road. Obviously, my heart started pounding, and I wondered what to do. I slowed down like I was going to pull over on the shoulder, and the pickup truck pulled in behind me. But when I had slowed to about twenty-five miles an hour, I stomped on the accelerator and pulled back out onto the highway.

I kept the gas pedal pushed to the floor, half expecting a bullet to blow out my back window at any moment. I looked in my rearview mirror and saw that the pickup truck was not going to be able to catch me. I got up to about ninety miles an hour, then slowed only to about eighty and kept that speed for several minutes. I figured that gave me a lot of room between the pickup truck and myself. I kept checking my rearview mirror, but I had definitely left those fellows behind. I later found out from coworkers in Chihuahua that was a common way for federal police to pull over a vehicle with foreign plates so they could check their papers and see if they were in the country legally or not. But being that far outside of town, it could've also just been some fellows who wanted to rob me. Did they not follow me and eventually pull me over because they were not cops? I'll never know.

Over the next several years, I would read about and hear of many robberies by bandits, many of them posing as cops or who actually were retired or active-duty cops, getting people to stop by waving a gun at them. Sometimes they shot their victims, sometimes not. I never quite got over wondering what would happen each time a cop stopped me, although it was usually just to check my vehicle papers.

In the cities, there is a division of traffic police, called *transitos*, who would oftentimes see our gringo license plates and pull us over on some pretense just to try to get a $20 bribe, er, fee, to let us out of a ticket.

The first time I did pull over for a cop, it was in Chihuahua City. It was in the middle of the day with lots of traffic around when a big Ford sedan pulled up next to me on my left. A large guy in a dark green shirt was waving a .45 caliber pistol out the window at me, motioning me to pull over. He had a gold badge on his shirt but no other identifying insignia on himself or his car. There were two other fellows in the front seat of the car who didn't have uniform shirts on, either, and who weren't wearing badges. I did pull over for him, since it was broad daylight with lots of people around. It did turn out that he just wanted to make sure I had vehicle papers that were in order.

Over the years, I got stopped probably a dozen times in similar ways, and only one other time did it feel dangerous. That time, it was after dusk in a poor, sparsely populated part of Chihuahua City, and the fellow motioning me over was wearing what could have been construed to be a legitimate uniform but with no insignia and no badge. He asked for my papers, but I asked him for his *credenciales* (credentials) before I pulled my papers out. He showed me a badge from his wallet, so I cooperated, but he seemed a bit surprised and perhaps impressed by me asking to see his ID. He was courteous enough, though, and after a few minutes, he let me go on my way.

After being stopped one or two times in the mountains by the state and federal police, they finally knew who we were and what we were doing there, so they never bothered us again.

Years later, in the mountains around San Rafael, I was definitely more concerned about bandits on the roads. They occasionally robbed payrolls destined for the couple of nice tourist hotels and the very few gold or silver mines that were actually making money. Robbers would also occasionally rob people on the buses that are the equivalent of Greyhound buses here in the States. In 1991, they robbed tourists on the Chihuahua-Pacific Railroad tourist train. One foreign tourist thought it was all a hoax and refused to put his camera down as he took pictures of the whole thing. The robbers shot and killed him, and tourism for a time out in the mountains took a big hit.

Meeting Poncho Villa's Wife

Our daily Spanish study was, well, daily, and study and work. We did occasionally find new things to do around town. Our coworkers, Peter and Mary Thiessen, and their children lived across town from us. One day after visiting them, they told us that there was sort of a museum just two or three blocks from their house. We decided that on our way home, we would stop in and see what it was all about.

There was a very unimpressive sign out front, which is the only way we knew that it wasn't a private home. It said something about being the home of Francisco "Pancho" Villa. The property encompassed a full city block. It was surrounded by an eight- or nine-foot tall adobe wall and, like the old traditional Mexican villas, had a courtyard just inside the big double gates. There were several trees and lots of foliage in the open-air interior. We walked inside, Ticker holding Dusty in her arms and David walking with me. A large elderly lady was sitting in a rocking chair near the entrance.

"*Que bonito el niño!*" she said as she looked up and saw Dusty in Ticker's arms. "What a handsome boy!"

In our best students' Spanish, we proceeded to talk with her and ask her about the house. Just a few feet away from where she was sitting was a big, open-roofed Dodge sedan with quite a few bullet holes in it. It reminded me of the Bonnie and Clyde car that we saw a few years later in Chattanooga, Tennessee, while it was on a tour of the US. I knew right away that it must be the car in which Pancho Villa had been killed, and of course, it was.

Pancho Villa had been quite a popular figure throughout northern Mexico during the years of the Mexican Revolution. Although initially he was in the good graces of the American government, who sold him weapons and ammunition, by 1914, he fell out of favor with American President Wilson. Desperate to show his audacity and rally help from his countrymen to the south, Villa invaded the border town of Columbus, New Mexico. Seventeen Americans were killed, which prompted the US Army to invade Mexico for eleven months, trying to capture or kill him. Mexicans are proud of the fact that after losing so much territory to the US in the 1800s, General Pancho Villa actually invaded the United States' home soil. During the search for Villa, General John Pershing of World War I fame used motorized vehicles and airplanes for the first time in combat. He also had over five thousand troops and cavalry under his command but never did catch or defeat Pancho Villa.

There were quite a few artifacts and photographs all around the courtyard, and we took our time looking at them all. No one else was in the museum that afternoon. The house had originally been quite impressive and had been part of General Villa's ranch, way out on the outskirts of Chihuahua City. But as happens in many places, the city had expanded outwards until residential neighborhoods finally actually surrounded it. After a little while of touring the courtyard and museum portion of the house, we went back to talk to Mrs. Villa, and it was then that she asked if she could hold Dusty on her lap. Boy, do I wish we had brought a camera that day!

Señora Villa was in her eighties or nineties but was still quite sharp mentally, and we had a good conversation. She apologized for how the property was rather rundown. She said, "You will see, as soon as I die, the government will come in here and fix this all up and make it a very nice museum."

That sounded sad to me. I wondered why the government didn't give her a little bit better pension right then so that she could enjoy a nicer home while she was still alive.

I did some reading later about her and her husband, the notorious and legendary general. She was probably in her late twenties or early thirties and the last of his two or three wives when he was killed in 1923. Although we visited with the Thiessens a few more times before we moved out of Chihuahua City, we never did go back and get a picture with Señora Villa. And she was right—a few years later, she died, and the government came in and took possession of the museum. The property was sealed off for a year or two and then one day was reopened with a beautiful, new, finely stuccoed wall surrounding it. It finally became a first-class museum.

Years later, living in San Diego, we used to dine fairly regularly in a couple of the big Mexican restaurants in Old Town. The open-air restaurants hired roving mariachis to play music for the customers, adding an exciting cultural flavor to the ambience. Having lived in Chihuahua, I knew how much the Mexicans idolized Pancho Villa. So when the mariachis came around to our table, I would always ask them to play a *corrido*, or ballad folk song, about Pancho Villa. They usually got requests for more contemporary stuff and love songs. But they had all learned ballads about Pancho Villa from the time they were young, and they always had one to play for us with smiles and gusto!

The treat of meeting the old revolutionary's wife at their home had been a great family outing. Now let's get back to motocross in Chihuahua!

2.2 All right! I Thought. I Found It!

Dust was flying from under the wheels of a couple of screaming motorcycles as they flew down the straight stretches of the dirt motocross track, then the rear wheels whipped and swung around on the turns. Two yellow Yamaha 125-cc motocross dirt bikes had the track to themselves, and I recognized the two riders as I got close. Tato, the taller one, was about twenty-two or twenty-three years old. Tin, short for Agustin, was a bit shorter with a neck like a bull. He was twenty-six or twenty-seven.

In trying to remember their somewhat vague, verbal directions from a couple of weeks earlier, I had followed a dirt road here on the outskirts of Chihuahua City to its end. There was sort of a grassy park area, and three or four trucks and a couple of families were scattered around. A few little kids ran among the trees, their moms close by with babies in their arms and on their hips. A fellow got up and walked over to me, smiling.

"So you found us! Good! Let me introduce you to my family." Ruben walked me over to meet his mother, first of all, a very kind-looking lady sitting at a picnic table with the younger mothers and kids.

"*Mucho gusto*," I said and then introduced myself. Ruben then had me meet his wife and kids, as well as his brothers' wives and children.

Oh boy, I thought. *I'm lucky to understand most of what he's saying. I'll never remember everybody's name, though at least I could always just call the mom Señora when addressing her. That would be easy.*

As I turned around, Ticker, Dave, and Dusty had gotten out of our van, so I told Ruben I wanted him to meet my family. He walked over with me and soon put everyone at ease. Ruben was a really congenial, warm guy, the brother in the middle between Tato and Tin.

Tato came riding over within a few minutes, the motorcycle loud, its exhaust popping as it wound around the rocks, bushes, and trees of the family picnic area. He pulled off his helmet, then his right glove, and held his hand out.

"*Hola!* You made it. I didn't know if you'd really come out here. How do you like our track?"

Over the next nine months, I'd come to love their track!

As soon as I felt I'd done what I needed to for Ticker to be introduced and relatively at ease, I took my Yamaha 175 Enduro off the carrier rack on the back of my truck and got ready to ride. I warmed up a bit by riding around the outside of the track. All I had done on a motorcycle so far was ride over a few very rough, very rocky trails near our house on the northeast end of Chihuahua City. The kick starter wasn't working, so I always had to push start the bike, but once it was running, it ran well.

Within a few minutes, I went out onto the track. My main objective was to ride and enjoy the gorgeous sunny day. My secondary objective was to not get run over from behind and killed by my new friends, which would certainly ruin the day. With that in mind, I rode well to one side of the track or off of it entirely when I heard one of them coming up behind me. So it went for the first Sunday and then a few more times when I went out to ride on those sunny Sunday afternoons after church.

Within a few weeks, though, I was pushing myself and my motorcycle to our limits. We were not in a class with the Reyes brothers. Tin and Tato were hell on wheels. But I got bolder and crazier every week, and it was a blast.

"We're going to reverse direction," Tin called out one weekend. "Only go this way," he said, indicating with a circular motion of his finger that we were going to go backwards to our normal direction of traffic. I had no idea how much fun I was about to have.

There was a stretch at the west end of the track that now—in reverse—went down into a gully, wound around a bit, then went up a long, straight incline. At the top, there was a level stretch about forty feet long, then a pretty tight left turn. The first several times I ran it, I was pretty cautious since you came out on top of the plateau completely blind. *What if someone's sitting up there in the middle of the track?* I'd wonder. If someone had fallen or stalled, or if a kid had wandered out onto the track, I'd pile into them. After a while, I realized that no rider would allow himself to sit or lie on the track in a vulnerable place like that, and the parents kept the kids far away from there and <u>always</u> off the track.

That's when it got really fun for me.

First, I learned to upshift on the way up the hill, going from first to second to third gear. Then when I shot off the top of the hill,

I would get some good air—first three feet, then four or five feet, and finally eight feet with the throttle wide open in fourth gear.

Land it straight. Rear brakes only, okay? Fast downshift to second. Now lean far over to the right as you go into the hard left turn, I would tell myself. I'd give it gas halfway through the turn, then ride the banked turns as fast as I could. Riding a motorcycle on a dirt track, you maintain balance in a completely different way than on pavement. You turn and lean the motorcycle into the turn but lean your body away from the turn to maintain your center of balance, straight above the motorcycle. If you don't do it right, the bike will slide right out from underneath you. On pavement, you lean your body <u>and</u> the bike into the turn and trust the motorcycle's tires to keep their grip.

I watched how Tin and Tato rode on the end of the track that had the moguls, which were about four feet high. For the average rider, and during all the races, you came out of a left turn, went over the first mogul in first gear, had to keep yourself from going over the handlebars on the second mogul, then came up to a nice, highly banked right turn. Then you could punch it again for a short straight stretch. But when the track was empty, like on the Sundays when we practiced, the Reyes brothers did it differently.

They came out of the left-hand turn and, approaching the first mogul, punched the throttle, shifting into second gear right before they went airborne. They would use the first mogul as a jump, flying completely over the second mogul, and landing on the backside of it. They had to brake hard and lean hard to the right to keep from flying off the track at the sharp right turn. Then they could accelerate again.

It was at that spot that I had my one and only accident. I was trying to imitate them on the moguls, and I'd learned that I could jump over the second mogul if I didn't hit it dead center but used the lower right side of both humps. So one Sunday, as I flew over the second mogul and into the hard right turn, I suddenly found myself flying off the track. I landed on my left side with the bike on top of my left thigh. The landing had also jammed the handlebars and my left hand into the ground. I lay there for a couple of seconds, wondering if I'd broken anything. "No way to know until I stand up and check things out," I figured.

I was also thinking I hoped nobody had seen me fall. As soon as I stood up with the motorcycle, I realized my left leg was completely numb, and so was my hand. So, in what must've looked incredibly comical, the motorcycle and I fell over in slow motion to the right! The next time I got up, I made myself be satisfied with just standing perfectly still for a moment. Then, as the feeling came back into my hand and leg, and I was pretty sure nothing was broken, I slowly walked the motorcycle over to the side of the track and took a break. It turned out I had broken a spoke, and it blew out the back tire, just as I hit the first mogul to start the jump. By the time I landed, I had a flat rear tire and no control.

Riding that track was the most fun I'd had in a long time. In fact, a few months later, I came really close to entering a race in the novice class. I thought I had Ticker talked into going along with me, but she convinced me in the end that if I broke an arm or leg, it would really delay us getting out to the Indian tribe. She had a good point, so regretfully, I gave up on the idea.

As if to confirm Ticker's point, the last race we attended at that track was probably the biggest field of racers in the expert class that I had seen up to that point. Soon after the race started, ten or twelve guys got jammed up in a bottleneck, and Tin and Tato crashed. Tin and most of the other racers got up and continued racing, but Tato was hurt. He had to quit the race with a broken collarbone and hairline fracture of his arm. He was in a lot of pain for weeks afterward, working in the shop with his arm in a sling. I guess it's a good thing I was saving myself for my real job which lay ahead.

Still, after all the riding I did and the races I watched, I bet I could have done pretty well.

Four of the five Reyes boys raced motorcycles. Ruben only quit because he had been in a really bad car accident in Arizona years earlier that broke his back and almost paralyzed him, so he didn't take any more chances on the motocross track. But their older brother, Rene, was nicknamed Methuselah. Methuselah was the oldest person in the Bible, and Rene got this nickname because he was the "old man" of motocross. He had been number one in the expert class in the state of Chihuahua for a few years when we moved there, and he was in his late thirties. His teenage son was an up-and-coming racer and, just a few years later, passed his uncles, Tin (number 2) and Tato (number 4), and was nipping at the heels of his dad. It was his skill and his dad's aches and pains that finally led to René stepping aside and his son becoming the number one motocross racer in the state of Chihuahua.

VW Mechanic Turned "Mechanico"

Three years previously, I had met Paul Theobald, a man at least three inches over six feet tall and on the thin side. He had a stately air about him, too, which you didn't expect for someone who was a mechanic by trade. His daughter, Kyla, was in my linguistics class in Camdenton, Missouri, at our language and linguistics institute. She was a lovely and very intelligent young Christian woman, and although I can't remember how I landed a job at Paul's Volkswagen repair shop, once I got to know him, it made sense that Kyla was so awesome. Paul was a devout Christian man, and he and his wife had raised all twelve—that's right, twelve—of their children to be humble and outstanding Christians.

For most of the year and a half that we were at the language and linguistics school, I worked on Saturday afternoons in Paul's shop. That was literally the only period of time from 1:00 p.m. to 5:00 p.m. on Saturdays that we had free from classes and work detail at the school and could work a job for pay in town. I earned $20 each Saturday afternoon and, on the way home, would use all of it, except for a couple of dollars in gas money for our week's groceries.

In boot camp in Canada, I had really gotten into being a Volkswagen mechanic, simply by owning one and not being able to afford to have anyone else work on it. It was there that I pulled the engine out of my 1965 VW van and rebuilt it. My buddy, Pete Humphreys, had a newer model Bug, which we also worked on extensively. In fact, Pete and I got so good at working on our vehicles that we could pull an engine in a half an hour, work on it, then in forty-five minutes have it reinstalled and ready to drive away!

All of that came in really handy a few years later in Chihuahua, Mexico, of all places.

At the end of that first motocross race I had gone to in Delicias, Tato had given me verbal directions, but no address, to their shop in Chihuahua. After driving back and forth on a section of the highway that led to the border looking for it, I finally spotted what had to be Tin and Tato's VW repair shop. I turned in.

"*Hola muchachos!*" I called out. "So this is your place?"

They were rather surprised to see me. I think they didn't really believe that I would come by and visit. The shop was a good-sized commercial-looking brick building with a metal roof. There were three or four bays for cars, a room with parts, and a front office. The guys told me in the course of time that they had gone up to the States illegally for several years, working a variety of jobs and sending as much money back home as they possibly could in order to build this particular building and start a business.

"So can I help you with anything?" I asked.

They looked at each other and looked at me and didn't quite know what to say.

"Look," I said. "Like I told you at the motocross race, I just need some time to practice my Spanish. I will clean parts for you or help you change oil or anything else I can do. I certainly don't want any money. I'll help you with anything I can, and you can help me with just talking in Spanish."

They were a bit perplexed, but I was sure that this was going to work out really well for my Spanish study. Soon, I was doing much, much better in understanding what was spoken at a normal speed and being able to speak at a more normal speed myself. Going to their shop two or three times a week was one of the best things I did for my Spanish study. I told Ticker and my fellow students all about it and encouraged them to try to find a similar situation to get into.

One day, I took Ticker by the shop to meet the brothers, and we were soon invited to a birthday party. Their family was so hospitable. Their dad had died several years prior, but the rest of the family was very close and fun. They also had four sisters, one of whom was one of the most attractive Mexican girls I ever saw. We had a number of visits with them which were all fun, including going to a carnival together and having Christmas dinner at their house in 1981. They became like a second family to us. The time we spent visiting with them was a huge help to Ticker, too, in her Spanish studies.

The Reyes family, with Ticker in the back row. right

By the end of the fall or early winter in 1981, we hit a milestone: Ticker finished the prescribed seventy-lesson Spanish course, and we were able to make plans to move out to the mountains.

2.3 First Trip to the Sierra Madre

Spanish, Spanish and More Spanish...

"*Vamos al mercado.*"
"Let's go to the market."
"*Muy bien. Que vamos a comprar?*"
"Very well. What are we going to buy?"
"*Quiero comprar platanos.*"
"I would like to buy bananas."

"*Quiero comprar frijoles.*"
"I would like to buy beans."
"*Quiero comprar huevos.*"
"I would like to buy eggs."
"I would like **to do anything right this minute—except this!**" Uhhh, did I just think that?

Oh my gosh, I thought. *This Spanish study is all very interesting, but I've already been through four and a half years of school with New Tribes before I even got here. And now, learning Spanish, sometimes I feel like I'm wading through quicksand.*

To back up just a little bit, it needs to be said that the brains behind the New Tribes Mission Language and Linguistics Institute, Jean Dye Johnson, was a genius. Literally. She was one of the leading linguists in the world for decades. She had been asked to be on the translation committee for the New Jerusalem Bible. Her first husband had been one of the original ten New Tribes Mission missionaries. While attempting to peacefully contact the warlike Guaica Indians, he and his four coworkers were all killed by them in the Bolivian jungle in 1943. Rather than being devastated and returning to the US, Jean continued on with the few remaining New Tribes missionaries in the firm belief that God had led her, as well as her husband, to reach the unreached tribal people with the Gospel. The organization grew steadily, adding dedicated men and women monthly and yearly.

After seeing what a challenge it was for American missionaries going to South America who needed to learn Spanish, Jean developed a language learning system that was called "situational learning." It made so much sense and was so practical, you have to wonder why no one thought of it before. Situational learning is exactly how all of us, from the time we are infants listening to language being spoken to us and around us, learn how to speak.

In the 1960s, the US military recognized the genius of the approach and asked Jean if she would develop a course for the military that they could use at their famous Monterey Language Institute in California. It was there that they taught—and still do teach—foreign languages to their officers who would be assigned to overseas duty. Understandably, Jean was flattered but declined, explaining that she had very important work to do with New Tribes Mission that could not be interrupted. She did, however, give them permission to use her "situational learning" technique, which they soon employed and perhaps are still using.

Jean was the program designer for the New Tribes Mission's Language and Linguistics Institute for many years. As the third and final step in our missionary training, I was privileged to study there from September 1978 through December 1979 and to get to know Jean personally. All of us who went to the foreign field had one semester in which part of the curriculum had to do with learning a little bit—only about six weeks—of the national language of the country to which we would be going. New Tribes Mission was operating in twenty-one countries, as I recall, in 1980. Jean's situational language learning course for each of those countries was developed by her personally. That included Spanish and Portuguese for the countries in Central and South America, Pidgin English for New Guinea, Tagalog for the Philippines, Indonesian for Indonesia, and the national language of what was then Senegal.

Even though I was learning Spanish in Mexico, using one of the most efficient techniques that was available, I have to say that at times it was just really darn tedious. So, after about two and a half months of lots of classroom study and struggling to converse pretty much everywhere we went, you can understand how I was ecstatic when our field chairman, Paul, told me that we needed to plan a trip into Tarahumara Indian country soon. We would be travelling into the very area where Ticker and I would be moving to with our new partners.

A consultant from headquarters, named Dick Sollis, would be going with us. We would be checking out the vast geographical area where the Western, or "Rocoroibo," dialect was located. The trip was planned for somewhere around the end of the first week of December and would take five to seven days. Paul asked if we could go in my four-wheel-drive van. "Of course," I said. I could barely contain my excitement. I was finally getting out of the city and out into the mountains where the Indians lived!

We had been partnered for a few months with Ken and Carol James and their family. They were really down to earth, fun, and dedicated folks from Wisconsin. With four children at the time, they had managed to raise about $1,200 per month in financial support before they came to Mexico. Unfortunately, $700 of that came from Ken's old boss back in Wisconsin, a roofing contractor. One day, Ken received a letter telling him that month's support would be the final check they would receive from him. The man and his wife decided after just a few short months that they could not continue that expense indefinitely. It was quite a shock to all of us. Ken and Carol literally only had a matter of days to pack up all of their things so as to have enough traveling money to get back up to Wisconsin.

Ticker and I were deeply shocked and disappointed. We had really gotten to love Ken and Carol and their kids. However, Ticker and I were still slated to be part of the next team to move out to the mountains, specifically to the Western Tarahumara.

We were excited about the future move, too. We had read a lot about the Tarahumara Indians in the months before we left the U.S. Their name for themselves is "Rarámuri", which means "foot runner". They have seen themselves as extremely tough long-distance runners for many hundreds, if not thousands, of years. The modern world finally recognized them as such only in the last one hundred and fifty years or so. Their endurance in their twenty four hour-long races for fun against neighboring communities is a testament to their extreme resilience in other ways, too. For five hundred years the more dominant Mexican/ mestizo population has pushed them further and further away from the fertile valleys where they used to plant their corn, beans and squash to the rocky mountain regions that they now inhabit. They have also maintained a strong social and cultural cohesion, and still speak their very grammatically complex language to this day. To live with this legendary tribe would be exciting. To share the Good News of salvation through faith in Jesus Christ with them would be a privilege. It wouldn't exactly be a dream-come-true; it would, however, be a miracle-come-true.

Tarahumara man

Survey into the Mountains at Last!

What happened was that instead of Ken going with us, Paul and his teenage son, Todd, Dick Sollis, and I would make up the group going out on this survey trip. We took our four-wheel-drive van, which was well suited for us to sleep in—far better than the steel bed of a pickup truck. We ended up traveling over seven hundred miles in five days, which was a lot of miles on the rough mountain roads of Mexico. We left at eleven in the morning on the eighth of December, heading west. The two-lane highway was well-traveled all the way to the sizable town of Cuauhtemoc, an important agricultural area in the state of Chihuahua. As we continued heading west, the traffic diminished, and we wound through low hills. We were paralleling a railroad and, from time to time, saw the freight and passenger trains that traversed the Chihuahua to the Pacific Railroad.

At the town of La Junta, which means "The Junction" in Spanish, we turned south. The rugged terrain was beautiful, full of mesquite and oak trees. The weather was clear, but as we headed south, we climbed higher into the mountains and started seeing snow on the ground. We passed through Tomochic, and the pavement finally came to an end. We could do no more than about thirty-five mph on what was pretty good gravel road. Finally, in the large town of San Juanito, another road turned off to the west, going toward Uruachic. We picked up a man who was hitchhiking and asked him about the road that went south out of Uruachic and back toward the railroad. Even though we had a map that showed a road that went that direction, the man told us there was no such road, only trails. So much for the official highway map!

We let him out and decided to go further south toward the town of Creel. We came to one sizable road that split off to the east so decided to do a little exploring in that direction. It was starting to get dark, and we needed a place to camp but kept driving for a while longer until we finally found a deserted area alongside a stream where we wouldn't be near anyone's home. It was now 8:00 p.m., and we were all tired of driving.

We got our gear out and cooked some dinner, discussing how far we had come and where we wanted to go the next day. The weather in the mountains was pleasant during the day but quite cold at night. We were in a beautiful pine-covered valley at over six thousand feet elevation that had a stream where we could get water. I learned right away, however, that beautiful or not, at night all the cold air settles into the low spots of the river and stream beds. I woke up at three in the morning with my feet so cold they hurt, even though I had a good winter sleeping bag. The temperature was in the upper twenties. After tossing and turning for a couple of hours, I finally gave up at 5:00 a.m. and made a fire. Todd was also miserable with the cold, and he got up and joined me.

That morning, around breakfast, we came up with our plan for the day. Paul knew of a Southern Baptist pastor named José Tapia who lived in Creel. We went back to the main road south and found José. He didn't know anything about any good roads to the west of Creel but told us about a large Tarahumara community named Sisoguichic. Even though there was a lot of Roman Catholic influence there, we decided to check it out. After eating lunch in Creel, we went back north for a ways to the little town of Bocoyna. There we turned to the east and, after an hour or so of twisting and bumping on the gravel road, arrived in Sisoguichic.

There was a large, well-maintained Catholic mission there that was established in 1667. It was definitely one of the oldest missions in that part of Mexico, founded as the Spanish soldiers and Jesuits looked for the rumored gold that existed in those mountains. Part of the Catholic mission there was an *internado* or boarding school for the Tarahumara children. There was also a large sawmill but no gasoline available.

We met a Mexican fellow who had studied under the Catholic mission there and later had worked in California. Paul and Dick Sollis had a good conversation with the man regarding the local Indian population, which I tried to keep up with, but my Spanish was still pretty lacking. We decided to keep heading south and east toward Panalachic.

We crossed twelve to fifteen streams and four major valleys where we saw six to ten Tarahumara families in each valley. The country was really beautiful with pine trees everywhere. In Panalachic, we learned that the Catholics had a mission school with a resident priest and some nuns about three kilometers outside of town in the hills. Indeed, it was what you could consider a Catholic stronghold. We also learned that this area was part of a very small dialect of Tarahumara and not part of the Western dialect that we wanted to explore.

We camped outside Panalachic, again next to a river and, at 7:15, left for Creel. Almost two and a half hours later, we arrived at the train station in town and asked about the train that headed southwest from there. Pastor José Tapia told us that the Wycliffe Bible translator, Don Burgess, had "planted some seeds" there. He also said that the Catholics and some Pentecostals had works there.

Tarahumara woman with baby on her back

At the train station, we were told that the railroad was temporarily shut down due to a train wreck, and we would not be able to get to San Rafael, even if we wanted to. So we went to the Tarahumara museum and bookstore that was run by the Catholic priest, Father Verplancken. It turned out to be a treasure trove of information.

Dick Sollis was very interested in visiting our New Tribes Mission coworkers in Guachochic, too, and now it looked like we would have the time to head south to see them before the day was over. We hadn't planned on doing this, so obviously, we would be arriving unannounced. Remember, all of this was before the days of cell phones, and there were barely operable landline phones in that part of Mexico. Even those were only installed in places of business or a private residence which was very well-off or had waited for months or years to secure a phone line.

Our coworkers in Guachochic were neither well-off or longtime residents. But off we headed, again on a gravel highway, for about three hours of driving down the spine of the Sierra Madre. Once again, it was a beautiful day, and we were traveling through some of the prettiest and most rugged country in North America.

Guachochic was a sprawling, rugged community in back hills cattle country. It was also close to the geographical center of the Central Tarahumara dialect. We had a great visit with Ed and Debbie Capps. They had been praying and looking for some land outside of town where they could settle right amongst the Tarahumara. They had learned Spanish pretty well and were now ready to start on their next step: learning the Tarahumara language. Marsh and Joy Milliken were their partners. Marsh was a linguist and would be creating language learning lessons for the whole team in the Tarahumara language. I did a lot of listening while Dick and Paul discussed with Ed and Marsh the knowledge that had been gained so far and the challenges that lay ahead.

At 2:30 in the afternoon, we got on the road again and headed for a sizable Tarahumara community called Norogachic, two hours north of Guachochic. Our coworkers in Guachochic had told us that there would likely be a large gathering and festivities for the feast of the Virgin of Guadalupe, who's official feast day was the twelfth of December. She was apparently one and the same as the Virgin Mary in the eyes of the Catholic Church. On December 9 and again on December 12, 1531, in the area where Mexico City now stands, she had supposedly appeared to an indigenous man named Juan Diego. She had asked that a shrine be built to her on that very spot. Since then, the Catholic Church had established a feast day for her throughout Mexico. The Tarahumara Indians were following along in that 450-year-old tradition.

Two hours later, we arrived in a large open valley which had a sizable Catholic church. It didn't appear that there were more than about thirty Tarahumara around. We walked around the area as the afternoon turned into dusk. It was dark by about six thirty. We could see trucks and cars driven by people who appeared to be from outside of the region, arriving in ones and twos, parking their vehicles here and there a short distance away from the church. We met a professional photographer from San Francisco, California, who had come just for this occasion. I think it was then that we realized what a significant time and place this was that we had sort of happened upon.

As the numbers of the native people grew, we saw that the Tarahumara women sat away from the men in their own groups. They were colorfully dressed in bright red, yellow, and blue skirts with their heads covered in scarves of black, white, or colorful prints. At about 7:45 p.m., the male dancers, called *matachines*, started to assemble with a number of musicians off to one side of the church in a spacious flat area. The matachin dancers wore long-sleeved shirts and loose-fitting and colorful loincloths which were quite different from their traditional white loincloths. They had very large scarves draped around her necks and tied up behind their heads. They also had long brightly colored fabric capes trailing down their backs.

Each one wore a headdress that consisted of four small mirrors attached to each other in the shape of a box. Each mirror was about three inches wide and five or six inches tall. Trailing from the mirrors down the back of each dancer were several brightly colored ribbons. All of them held rattles and streamers in each hand, which they shook and swirled as they danced back and forth, and round and round the dance area.

Someone pointed out to me that the Catholic priest was dancing among them, dressed the same way as all the other dancers. It was he who called out, "Look into the mirrors of the dancers' headdresses as you pray." I got some stunning pictures with the dancers framed against the pitch black night sky. After a while, the number of matachin dancers grew to about sixty. For about two hours, they danced outside of the church and then moved inside.

In the well-lit interior of the large church, the colors of the dancers' dress were strikingly impressive. The musicians played scratchy music on their homemade violins and beat drums as the dancers shook their rattles and created a rhythm with the bells that were tied in clusters around their ankles.

Tarahumara Matachin dancer at Norogachi against the night sky

There were at least 500 Tarahumara and mestizos inside the church now. We Americans stood at the back, watching in fascination. I also found myself having short conversations a couple of times with a Mexican bystander. After a few days of basically having Paul be our translator and asking all the questions on this trip, it was gratifying to use my Spanish. At the end of it all, it was still a total mystery to us Americans as to what spiritual significance the Tarahumara took away from that event. That's precisely what I would need to learn about in the future. What did the Tarahumara believe that was linked to the Christian faith? The Catholic religion had obviously added a very complex and multifaceted set of rituals to their worldview.

That first trip into the Sierra Madre was exciting and so informative for me personally. Considering all we had seen and done at the end of those five days, and having picked up some very informative books on both the language and the culture of the Tarahumara at the Catholic mission store in Creel, it looked like we would have to go much further to the west to get to the Western dialect. This trip, however, gave me and our chairman, Paul, a good idea of the condition of the roads and the distances we would have to travel by truck. It was still a big mystery, however, just exactly what the one and only road west of Creel would be like.

2.4 An Unusual Stranger in this Strange Land

A few months later, in Chihuahua City, we met a very interesting American missionary named Terry Bircham. Terry had gone to Mexico as a single man several years earlier, started sharing the Gospel with the Tarahumara in a community named Guaguachique, led a young woman to the Lord, and married her! Terry invited our family to go out and visit him for Easter, so Ticker and the boys and I went out for a three-day trip. This was their first time traveling out into the mountains. They soon got used to swaying with the movement of the truck on the gravel roads and enduring the bumps and potholes. Like me, they found the beauty of the mountains refreshing and exciting. It was a welcome change from the sprawling city of Chihuahua.

In Guaguachique, there was a large adobe Catholic church, a strong Catholic presence, and at least a couple of hundred Tarahumara who had come for the Easter festivities. Compared with the Indians at Norogachic, the Tarahumara here dressed more like mestizos, wearing shirts and long pants. Only a small number wore the traditional white loincloth or *zapeta*. On Easter Sunday, there was a group of Indian performers who dressed in a variety of clothing that they thought depicted the Jews and the religious leaders of Bible times and the Roman soldiers who arrested Jesus. Some of the men wore strange tall pointy hats, and a man who seemed to be in charge wore a headdress of turkey feathers. They had a many hours-long reenactment of the events surrounding Jesus's death.

At one point, they made a straw effigy of Judas and, after parading him past the people, tore him apart. A very tall image of the Virgin Mary, dressed in black, was carried by several women with poles on their shoulders. For the next few years, we would see similar Easter processions of Indians march around and into the Catholic churches and came to find out that they had a very mistaken view of what had actually happened to Christ on Easter week—that is, in comparison to the very clear record from the Gospels. That very confusion about the most important events of the life of Christ—his death and resurrection—was what we would painstakingly work to avoid in the future in whatever community God had destined for us to live in.

By staying for a couple of days with Terry and Maria Bircham, it was quite an eye-opener to us all to see what life was like for someone actually living in those mountains. The people were poor for the most part. Most of the houses were adobe, but there were a lot of substandard ones that were just made of ill-fitting rough sawn boards. Almost every house had dirt floors.

While we were at Terry and Maria's, I helped them butcher a large pig for our food. We did it outdoors almost on the ground, like a hunter would do it, but had the luxury of big wooden planks laid on blocks of wood crisscrossed with decades of knife cuts. A few feet away, we had drums of water heating on open wood fires for cleaning ourselves and the knives. Every part of the pig was used, and only the least edible parts were given to the skinny dogs, of which there were many.

The next day, we planted corn the Tarahumara way. You would walk through the plowed up dirt field with a four- or five-foot long planting stick. You'd poke the stick into the ground about six inches deep, drop two or three kernels of corn into the hole, then push dirt over the top of the corn with your foot and lightly tamp it. You'd repeat that about every twelve to fifteen inches, walking in a straight line back and forth across the field. It was a vivid time of introduction to what life would be like when we ourselves would live with the Indian tribe.

HE WHO HAS BEGUN A GOOD WORK

Corn field. Corn is the main staple for the Tarahumara people

What Terry had undertaken was a very brave step of faith. There were some in our group of missionaries who thought Terry was a rather odd or at least unorthodox missionary. But in the town of San Rafael, many miles and hours away from Guaguachique, I was to find out a year or so later that his Christian faith and testimony reached far beyond his own valley. Like all of us, Terry <u>was</u> unique. There's no doubt in my mind that he will have great rewards in heaven for his patient, faithful work sharing the Word of God with the Tarahumara people.

On our way back to Chihuahua City, Ticker and the kids and I stopped at the Catholic mission store in Creel that I had visited on the trip with Paul and Dick Sollis. It was quite an impressive place. A priest named Father Ver Planken, for over thirty years, had quite a wide-ranging ministry in the surrounding area. He had done all in his power to see that the Tarahumara were treated with dignity and given a respected status in society amongst the Mexican people. There were scores, if not hundreds, of really high-quality photographs that he and others had taken of the Indians. With the help of local businessmen, he had established a very successful medical clinic. The well-supplied store was popular with the tourists and sold quite a few native artifacts that the people made, thereby featuring their culture in a very distinguished manner. There were dozens of books on the shelves that described the Tarahumaras' language and culture in detail. Most of these dealt with the central dialect, which had about two-thirds of the total 50,000 speakers, but I found some information about the Western dialect also.

We took our time going through the store, and of course Dave, at four years old, was fascinated by the bows and arrows, drums, and spears. There were brightly colored serapes, belts, and scarves that the women wore. The store also had lots of pottery and baskets, the type that the people used every day in their homes throughout those mountains. It was a treasure trove and provided us an exciting glimpse into the multifaceted world of these people we were about to live with.

Back in Chihuahua City, we plugged along with Spanish study. As Dusty got a little bigger, Ticker was able to spend more time studying and was making good progress. She still had to complete all seventy lessons in the Spanish language course. We also started getting to know our new partners, Cliff and Diane S., better. They were from Chicago, a city we knew quite well. Cliff's father had been a Black army soldier who married a Japanese woman. Diane was from an Italian family. Both of them were friendly but fairly quiet and reserved.

Goats are a resilient livestock for the Tarahumara, well adapted to the rugged mountains, and are usually herded by young boys

We got together with them every week or two for an evening of dinner and games. The card game Uno was popular amongst all of our coworkers. They had a little boy named Brian who was just a little bit older than Dusty. The boys became great playmates, and we had a lot of laughs together with them.

Regarding the timing for us to move to the mountains, it was fairly obvious that we didn't need to spend months spinning our wheels in Chihuahua City waiting for the S's to finish their Spanish study. I had already been finished, so I began deeper researching of the area we would probably want to move to in the mountains.

Women carry a statue of the Virgen Mary during the Easter festivities at Guaguachique

After a lot of searching, I found that there was a company in Chihuahua City that sold very detailed topographical maps of the Sierra Madre. They were published by the Interagency Air

Cartographic Committee and were done for the benefit of the Department of Defense, Federal Aviation Administration, and the Department of Commerce. They were made using American military mapping satellites.

The 1:1,000,000 scale map was helpful to get familiar with a large area, but the 1:50,000 scale was extremely valuable for us driving or even hiking from one community to another. They were highly detailed, showing every road, a lot of foot trails, and buildings. Every house or large structure appeared as a square. A church appeared as a little square with a cross on it, and schools were identified with a flag on top. Our United States military had made these maps mostly for navigation for private or commercial pilots, and in case they were needed by our own military for some reason, but also had made them available to, in this case, Mexico.

When it became apparent that we would be moving to San Rafael, I bought two maps that showed the region all around San Rafael as well as the areas north and northwest of there. I bought two copies of each. The extra copies ended up being a really important purchase years later.

Finding the Elusive Don Burgess

An important task that I tackled was how to get in touch with a man named Don Burgess. Don had been a missionary and linguist with the Wycliffe Bible Translators years earlier and was still working on the Tarahumara language. He had moved into a small Tarahumara community named Rocoroibo several years previously and was known by many people to be the only linguist working on the Western Tarahumara dialect. The details were sketchy in 1981, but it seemed that Don had evaded or just not responded to inquiries from some other American missionaries. If that was really the case, I was told that he probably had good reason for that. He had seen far too many Americans who were gung-ho about working with the

Tarahumara, but after a short period of time, they all had quit and gone home.

It took me several attempts, working through various channels, to finally find an address for Don. Then it took two or three letters to him before he finally responded. By then, we were living in San Rafael, which I told him, and that we were going to build a house in El Manzano. He was undoubtably a very busy man, but fortunately, I finally got his attention. I think he realized that we were pretty persistent and determined, by the grace of God, to stay for the long term.

Eventually, Don wrote back to me and explained that he was still working on literacy materials for the Tarahumara. His goal was to translate the New Testament into their language, but of course, that would not do the people any good unless they could read their own language; thus, he was also developing literacy materials for them too. Don maintained a small house in Rocoroibo but was at that time living nine or ten months out of the year outside Tucson, Arizona. Over the next several years, we got to be good friends with this tall, quiet, and humble man.

We also got to know his personal story, which was quite compelling. He had been through a divorce, but Don felt quite strongly that God had led him to the Tarahumara. Due to the divorce, he could no longer continue working officially under the auspices of the Wycliffe Bible Translators organization (that exclusion was true in New Tribes, too, and many other mission organizations). For a time, he taught Tarahumara ethnology and field linguistics at the University of Texas in El Paso. He explained all of that to his financial supporters as well as his desire to continue working to get the Gospel to the Tarahumara.

As God would have it, he raised enough financial support to quit his job at the University of Texas and could once again work full-time as a missionary and translator. Then years later, he met a lovely, like-minded Christian woman, Marie, and they married.

Ticker and I visited Don and Marie in their house outside of Tucson in 1985 as we started our one year furlough. It was a fascinating eco-friendly home that was partially built underground in order to stay cool in the hot Arizona desert. It was in a development that a wealthy Christian businessman had purchased specifically for Wycliffe Bible translators. Every single Wycliffe missionary had their special resident visas revoked by the Mexican government in 1979, just a year before we arrived in Mexico. It was the result of anti-American sentiment that was sweeping through several Latin American countries at the time.

The Wycliffe Story (Very Briefly)

After having been welcomed in 1935 by the Mexican government of President Lazaro Cardenas—himself a mestizo of Tarascan Indian heritage—and granted special visas, Wycliffe had done exceptional linguistic and literacy work in many Indian tribes all over Mexico. They had done this under their contract with the government through their scientific organization, the Summer Institute of Linguistics, or SIL. Their well-planned expansion and trained personnel then started works in various other South American countries. Then, the late 1960s and 1970s saw a period of time of large-scale social upheaval in Mexico as well as in the United States. As the diehard socialists and leftists attained substantial legitimacy and power in society, mostly in the universities and in politics, anti-American sentiment swept through the country.

According to an article in the *Washington Post*, dated September 29, 1979, a four-year long "systemic study" by Mexico's National College of Ethnologists and Anthropologists concluded that Wycliffe/SIL preached a "conservative, capitalist, individualist American work ethic." It claimed the Indians were taught "obedience and passivity which has an adverse effect on their liberation movement."

Wycliffe countered that they teach respect to the local authorities and for the law and that the concept of private property and individualism was introduced among Mexico's Indians by the national government itself during the nineteenth century liberal reforms.

In the newspapers, Wycliffe missionaries were outrageously and falsely accused of working with the CIA, and there were calls for their expulsion from the country. Suddenly, one day, there was a mysterious bombing in the parking area of Wycliffe's headquarters near Mexico City. It was probably meant more as a "warning shot" than an attempt to kill anyone. It wasn't long before left-wing activists in the government successfully lobbied for the Americans' "diplomatic type" visas to be revoked. Wycliffe was given one year to turn over all installations and printing equipment, including their headquarters complex south of Mexico City, to the Mexican government.

The backlash in other countries was similar. In Colombia, on January 19, 1981, events took a horrible turn when leftist guerillas from the M-19 organization kidnapped Wycliffe missionary Chet Bitterman and demanded that SIL leave the country. Forty-eight days later, his body was found on a bus outside Bogota. The guerillas had run out of patience in negotiations with the Colombian government, and he had been executed, shot in the chest.

The moves against Wycliffe personnel and loss of their visas caused a huge upheaval and interruption of their work in scores of Indian tribes throughout Mexico. Some of the missionaries resigned or went to other countries. However, Don and many others looked for a new center of operations in Texas or Arizona as they carried on their work on an itinerant basis. They did this for months, and one day, a wealthy Christian businessman learned of their situation and purchased a large piece of property on the outskirts of Tucson. It was a huge blessing for those tenacious missionaries. Don was one of the beneficiaries.

It was in those months before we moved from Chihuahua City to the mountains that I had to get a better idea of where it was that we were going to be moving to. In that vast Sierra Madre Mountain Range, just where exactly did our dialect of the Tarahumara language extend? It turned out that it was a sweeping area of over ten thousand square miles. Within that area, there were approximately eight to ten thousand speakers of what was called the Western or Rocoroibo dialect. To get close to the geographical center of that region, we would need to travel southwest from the town of Creel. Then, almost forty miles from there, on the Chihuahua to the Pacific Railroad, was a town called San Rafael through which Don Burgess traveled on his way back and forth to Rocoroibo. That was the next place for me to check out.

2.5 Not "Back to the Future"—This Was "Forward to the Past"

I showed the results of my research to our field leadership. Cliff and I then decided to make a trip to San Rafael at our next opportunity. Late summer saw the end of the rainy season, so on October 25, 1981, with enough supplies for a three-day trip, we headed out once again in my four-wheel-drive van.

We would be going to Creel, where I had been twice by now, then would take a dirt road southwest to San Rafael. This was Cliff's first time seeing the country outside of Chihuahua. From the dry brown city limits, we headed west on the paved highway, passing through Cuauhtemoc, a large agricultural town. For eighty or more years, a sizable colony of Mennonites had lived and farmed the countryside around Cuauhtemoc. They had sprawling vegetable and dairy farms and were especially well-known for their excellent quality cheese.

West of the high desert of Chihuahua City, we were soon winding through sparsely inhabited hill country, full of mesquite and scrub oak trees. Here and there was a bus stop shelter where a small community of eight or ten ranch homes lay close by. Almost two hours from Chihuahua City, the pavement ended. For more than forty-five minutes, we drove on a wide, dusty gravel road. In places, the washboard surface was so rough we had to slow down to ten or fifteen miles an hour—and even then, it rattled our teeth. When we wondered how much farther we had to endure this brutal road, we finally came to the large mountain town of San Juanito.

Here there was everything a country dweller could need. There were ranch supply stores, mom- and-pop-owned grocery stores (of the mountain variety), truck and tire repair shops, and diners. Cliff was pretty quiet as he took it all in. Everywhere were dusty pickup trucks, flatbed cargo trucks with hay or boxes of groceries, but very few cars. The ones that were there had definitely seen their better days. The horses, mules, and donkeys that were transporting people and cargo fared far better than those cars. It was like being in a Southwest American town fifty years earlier.

I told Cliff we could eat in Creel, which had better restaurants. We pulled up to a store and each got a tall, cold bottle of Coca-Cola, stretched our legs, and got back in the truck.

Just on the far edge of town, surprisingly, was where pavement began again. It was a strange thing how the Mexican government had decided to pave that one stretch of road, but there it was, and we enjoyed every mile of it. We had climbed into mountains that were between 7,000 and 8,000 feet high, and now we were completely surrounded by pine forests, and they were much easier to enjoy as we twisted and turned through the mountains on an asphalt road. We had to be careful in places though. Although it was late morning, there had been frost or perhaps runoff from rain in places, and on the curves where the sun didn't shine, there was black ice. But in another thirty-five or forty minutes, we came into the town of Creel.

Just in the previous decade, Creel had begun to be developed with tourism in mind. The Mexican government wanted to open up the region for development, but nothing significant had changed in the previous hundred years. There had been some productive gold and silver mines to the south and west centuries before, but most of those had petered out. There were small cattle ranches in the area, as well as farmers who raised sheep and goats. So, under what was called the Gran Vision, or Grand Vision, the highway had been improved all the way from Chihuahua City. Business owners were encouraged to build hotels and restaurants for the tourists "who would come." And, of course, the Chihuahua to the Pacific Railroad was intended to be a primary means of travel. Creel was the only sizable town with halfway decent accommodations between Chihuahua City and the Gulf of California coast town of Los Mochis.

Just as we came into Creel, the pavement ended, and we bounced along at ten or twelve miles an hour on dirt streets full of potholes. Like everywhere in Mexico, Creel was a place of contrasts. The buildings were an even mix of adobe and wood with shake shingle or corrugated metal roofs. The wooden buildings were sometimes made from rough-sawn boards but also from what are called "slabs." These are the outside edges of the logs as they are first run through the sawmill. Since they're almost scrap lumber, they're much more affordable than boards. They look quite rustic, too, so were rather appealing to the tourists.

Cliff and I pulled up to a sizable restaurant that was sided with slabs. Although I tried other restaurants from time to time in the coming years, this particular one became my favorite.

Looking out the clean windows at the dirt street, we watched dogs patrolling their territory, looking for scraps of food while pickups kicked up dust on their way to and fro. We would see the occasional tourist walking past the stores, but mostly, it was just the traffic of locals going about their daily business. The restaurant's menu had all of our favorite items on it. I ordered Chile Colorado—steak with a rich, red chili sauce.

I don't remember what Cliff had, but I was about to get one of my first meals "out in the country" of Mexico that had the authentic, dried, hand-ground red chilis that Mexico is famously known for. It was one of my early favorites that had me hooked on the old Mexican way of preparing food. There is nothing like the flavor of those dried chilis hanging in the corner of the kitchen or dining room, which someone takes down and grinds for your meal right then. Fresh. Rich. "I'jole (Oh, yeah)!"

Someone pointed us toward the road to San Rafael, and we were off again. We had been told that the government had plans to greatly improve this road all the way to San Rafael. We could see that some grading had been done for a mile or two out of town, but that was about it. The road soon turned quite rough. I guess I was being especially careful with my truck because in my notes about this trip, it shows that it took us five and a half hours to get to San Rafael. The distance was just under thirty-six miles! In future years, it would normally take us two and a half to three hours in good weather. We passed through the small communities of Estacion ("Station") Sanchez, Pittoreal, El Divisadero, and Areponapuchi before we got to San Rafael.

The location of the Copper Canyon, and our future home just to the north and west of it.

This road that we were on paralleled the railroad, so there were several places where we crossed over the railroad tracks. I don't recall that we saw a single pickup truck going in the opposite direction from us on their way to Creel. The only trucks we saw were around the small towns. Even the locals were apparently of the opinion that you didn't travel that road unless you really needed to. The towns were mostly supplied by the railroad.

El Divisadero—The Gem of the Sierra Madre

There is nothing even comparable on that road or almost anywhere else that I ever saw in the Sierra Madre to the view at El Divisadero. It is a stopping place on the railroad that clings to the very edge of the Barranca de Cobre or the "Copper Canyon." Every passenger train that passes the spot, whether going east or west, stops for about twenty minutes to allow the passengers to get out and enjoy the view. The Copper Canyon has been called the Grand Canyon of Mexico. It's just about as deep but actually is not nearly as wide, which makes it more spectacular in its own way. It also has its own beauty because of the pine forests that are not only on the rim but cling to the sides and extend to the bottom of the canyon.

It's a very long canyon, but because it twists and turns with such steep sides, you can't always see too many miles either upstream or downstream. The altitude at the bottom of the canyon ranges from 1,000 feet to perhaps 3,000 feet, while the elevation of the rim is 6,000 to 7,500 feet. The top has an Alpine climate, but on the valley floor, there are citrus groves, bananas, and all sorts of tropical plants.

There was a hotel that had been there for perhaps ten or fifteen years at that time which literally sits right on the edge of the cliff. When the train stops, the tourists are free to walk wherever they would like, but most go down to a railing and a viewing area only about forty yards away from the train platform. Looking to the left, you are looking upstream and can see most of the front face of the hotel with its rock façade and stone chimney that is perhaps twenty-five feet high. Straight ahead, you're looking south at the far rim of the canyon several miles away. To the right, the canyon gets deeper as the Urique River flows toward the ocean. There are unusual rock formations everywhere. Hawks and buzzards can be seen riding the winds and updrafts of the canyon far below.

Once you have drunk in the view and appreciated the enormity of the canyon, you can walk back up toward the train station where the Tarahumara women and children are selling a variety of their handcrafted items as souvenirs. The Indians are encouraged to dress in their traditional clothing here, and that's easy for the women and girls with their colorful, multilayered skirts and headscarves. Men and boys, however, tend to dress more in the mestizo style, wearing long-sleeved shirts and long pants. Just like all throughout the Sierra, almost all of them wear *huarache* sandals. These consist of a piece of truck or car tire tread for the sole with a leather thong, just like the flip-flops that we wear on the beach. Although some Tarahumara, if they can afford it, will wear shoes or boots in the winter or for special occasions, the huaraches are their everyday dependable footwear of choice.

To look at the feet of these Indians in their huarache sandals is to have a micro view of their life and character. Their feet are weathered, tough as mule hide and oftentimes cracked and split from exposure to the elements. That's quite an accurate reflection of their very nature—resilient, independent of the white man's ways, and able to contentedly hang on to their own style, despite what decade or even century it happens to be.

The rugged, beautiful Sierra Madre mountain range

Like a Scene Out of an Old Clint Eastwood Western

Back in the truck, Cliff and I continue on our way toward San Rafael. The road winds through hills and mountains not far from the edge of the Copper Canyon. Wherever there is a decent-sized valley, large or small, there is a ranch or a community consisting of a handful of houses. Two miles past El Divisadero is Areponapuchi, a collection of several ranches and a small town. It's a strange name, and I wonder about its etymology. About 5.3 miles and fifty-five minutes later, we start seeing huge piles of sawdust alongside the road. It's a sure sign that we're coming into a logging town.

Suddenly, there it is in front of us in a narrow, long, winding valley. It's the beginning of San Rafael. I find out later that this is actually a town called Los Tascates. San Rafael is technically a mile or mile and a half further on with a railroad station, post office, schools, and where a couple of other official buildings are located. But, basically, because the two towns grew together in the middle, the whole stretch is referred to as San Rafael.

Anyway, within a few hundred yards, we see a big sawmill on the right-hand side of the road. Huge piles of logs are arranged so that a large forklift can carry them over to the saw itself. Trucks with wooden flatbeds and dual rear wheels traverse the road to the entrance, loaded ones going in and empty ones coming out. The ones going in amble slowly over the uneven dirt road, their load of logs piled from six to twelve feet high, held in place by just two chains. Most of the trucks look a bit beat up; all of them are plenty dusty. There are a few newer models, but most look to be five or ten years old or even older. Some are diesel and some are gasoline. We drive past the sawmill to check out the rest of the town.

Like everywhere else we have been in the mountains, there are humble wood houses and nice-looking adobe ones that are stuccoed and brightly painted. We pass a small medical clinic building and a few stores. The road crosses down into a creek and back up the other side, and we continue southwest on the main street. Cross streets run to the left and the right, and the streets on the right are sometimes quite steep since the mountain rises up close by. Soon we are on a section of the main street where the buildings on the left are just a couple of feet above street level whereas on the right, they are built against the side of the hill and are several feet higher.

As is typical here, almost all the men wear cowboy hats, long-sleeved shirts, and jeans. But on the right-hand side, I notice a man who is just strolling slowly on the raised sidewalk in front of the businesses, and he has a pistol in a holster on his hip. A hundred yards further on, I see another man, also taking his time walking slowly and glancing around. He has what looks like a .45 caliber pistol on his hip. Although they're both wearing blue jeans, I realize both men are wearing gray shirts. In typical Mexican fashion, this is their uniform without being a uniform. They're not wearing badges. I suppose everybody knows who they actually are. "Hey," I say to Cliff, "I bet that's the Chihuahua State Police."

As we roll down the street, it starts to feel like a scene from an old Clint Eastwood western: 'The stranger walks his horse down the main street of town, looking all around, his eyes missing nothing. He doesn't want to attract attention, but it's a small town, and folks recognize he's an outsider. Now the dusty, white four-wheel-drive van with American plates ambles down the main street, the two guys in the cab checking out the buildings on the left and on the right, trying not to stand out, but—'

Seeing a promising restaurant on the right, I find a spot to pull over and park. Cliff and I climb out, stretching our cramped legs. I half expect to hear someone say, "You're not from around here, are you, son?"

We climb up about six steep steps to the concrete sidewalk above and then a few more steps into the restaurant. It's brightly painted inside and looks pretty clean. We're lucky because it's late afternoon—5:30—which is a little bit early for dinner for most Mexicans. There are only two other people in the dining room, which is eight or ten feet above street level, so we have a nice view out the windows up and down the street. It takes a few minutes for someone to realize we're there, but when he comes out, the server doesn't have menus in his hand, just a notepad. He asks what we would like to eat. I ask him what there is. He says "Beef or chicken?"

I take it that means those are the two meat choices, and we need to tell him whether we want that in burritos or tacos or as part of a combination meal plate. I order a beef plate, and Cliff orders a chicken plate. The server disappears into the back for a moment, brings us our water and Cokes, then goes over to a half-side of beef that a couple minutes earlier I had noticed hanging in the corner of the dining room. He has a big knife and a plate in his hands and slices off a decent sized slab of meat. It dawns on me that just might be my steak.

Fifteen minutes later, he brings our food out. I had spent a few minutes wondering if I needed to be worried about whether the meat was going to be good or not. After all, it wasn't exactly hanging in a nice big walk-in cooler. As I also notice that there are no flies around, I consider how dry the climate is and think about the fact that at this altitude, about 7,000 feet, the nights are quite chilly, and perhaps this is just how they preserve their meat while it's fresh. I decide not to worry about it, since obviously, the other customers all see where their steak comes from, and this place seems to be pretty successful.

When I cut into the steak and take a bite, I am beyond pleased. This has to be the best steak I've eaten in years! I say so to Cliff as I finish telling him what my thoughts and worries had been a few minutes earlier. His meal is good too. We start off with a great first impression of the Wild West town of San Rafael.

Since it's dusk by the time we finish our meal, we decide to look for a place to sleep on a decent bed instead of camping. What we find is marginal but takes care of our needs. A little establishment a few doors down caters to visitors and traveling businessmen. They have a total of four or five single beds in two or three rooms with a nice stack of blankets for each one. We pay for the rooms and drive through town a little further to see what else there is to see. A block or two further down from the restaurant is the train station, the biggest business in town. Besides that, there are just more small grocery and variety stores with one larger government employee grocery store called Conasupo, which we were familiar with from Chihuahua City.

The next morning, we look into a lot of details about what's available in the town. We find that the passenger train rates are quite reasonable. We're not too thrilled about bringing our trucks in and out on that road from Creel so ask what the freight charges would be to put them on a flatbed train car. It sounds like a huge hassle and expense, about three times what monthly rent for a house would cost. Plus, the truck would have to be unloaded down at the sawmill where they "probably" had a ramp adequate for the job. The person putting the vehicle on the flatbed car would have to supply their own chains and ride with the vehicle. It could take one to three days from Chihuahua City, depending on what else was on the freight train. The freight trains always pull off on sidings to allow the passenger trains from the East and the West to go by and stay on schedule. Hmm, sounds like we're going to be driving that road whether we want to or not.

We find that the prices of beef and chicken are comparable to Chihuahua because they are obviously locally raised and butchered. All the rest of the food items, since they come from Chihuahua City, cost 20 to 25 percent more than they do in the city. The town has only had electricity for about three months, so most of the homes have no electric wiring running to them yet. Almost everyone uses oil lamps for light. Lamp oil is only available in small quantities and costs five pesos per liter.

In Chihuahua, it costs one peso per liter. Propane is "sometimes" available for about four hundred pesos per forty-five-kilo tank. In Chihuahua, we pay 194 pesos for the same size tank. If we want to ship our own tanks out to be refilled, which is what most people do, they're sent to Cuauhtemoc or Chihuahua, the freight charge is a hundred pesos each, and they take fifteen days, more or less, for the round-trip. That is going to make for some interesting planning on our part.

Then there is the situation regarding getting gasoline. There is no gas station. Gas is only available at the Ponderosa sawmill, so we drive down there to check it out. We're told that the supply is not 100 percent reliable. There are times when they don't get a tanker car in on schedule, so gasoline has to be rationed. You have to get into the sawmill during regular working hours, between about 8:00 a.m. and 4:00 or 5:00 p.m., but it's a good idea to miss the early morning or late afternoon hours because of the number of log trucks that could also be trying to get refueled at those times. The price isn't too outrageous, only about 10 percent more than in Chihuahua, but the process was really interesting. We go into an office and pay for the gas, which you ask for in multiples of five liters.

When we go out to fill up my truck, I learn why this is the case. The attendant fills an open ten-liter metal can with a large funnel-type spout on it from a large stationary tank. He fills it up to the top for ten liters or halfway up for five and then pours it into the filler tube of your gas tank. If the wind is blowing, it's going to get some dust in it. If it's raining, you're probably going to get a little bit of water in it. Note to self: *I'm going to have to change the fuel filter on the truck more often.*

Water, the essence of life (right before you get to make coffee with it, which to me is the "nectar of the gods"). My notes of the trip say "Town has a few water tanks with pumps that sometimes work and gravity that always works." We were to discover when we lived there, that statement said it all. The town pumped water into their own tanks, then allowed it to flow into the town water system a little at a time. You never knew if there would be water pressure or not, so just like in Chihuahua City, most houses had a water drum or large tank on a stand eight or ten feet above ground level. That tank would fill, at least partially, whenever there was water pressure which was oftentimes only at night. Then you had gravity feed into your house for your daily use. Every family had to monitor the level of their own tank and not use too much water.

As we drove around town, we could see the flexible black plastic water lines alongside the roads and streets. This is the town's water supply system. The ground is very rocky, so the black lines oftentimes aren't even buried. It's obvious this could be a problem in the winter since they would freeze and maybe even split.

Regarding houses for rent, we were told that there were a few large houses empty right at the time. Rents were about a thousand pesos per month, around $200 as I recall, so that was a good price. But when it came right down to getting in contact with the owners, that was not an easy task. One man that we found out about who wanted to rent his house was a log truck driver named Marcel. He seemed like an enterprising, energetic young man of about thirty years old. His house was located across the road from the Ponderosa sawmill on a property of about one and a half acres full of "Rome Beauty" apple trees. I'll never forget the name of those apples because of the way Marcel so carefully enunciated the words "Rome Beauty" in English. It was pretty funny. He was quite proud of the apple orchard and rightly so.

He seemed like a nice guy, honest and sincere, so I got his address so that we could stay in touch regarding our plans and the availability of the house. He was willing to move out of the house and rent it for extra income, and it was nice-looking and in good shape. It was small, with the kitchen/living room measuring about fourteen-by-sixteen feet and the bedroom about the same.

I don't remember now how we were introduced to some of the people that are in my notes from the trip, but we did get to meet some interesting fellows in a short amount of time. One was named Guadalupe Calderon who worked for the railroad. He was about thirty-eight or forty years old and was really friendly and helpful. He's the one who first guided us around town and helped us to get gasoline, etc.

It may have been Terry Bircham, whom we had visited at Easter time, who told me about a fellow named Martin Lopez. I think when we visited Terry, we knew we would be going out to San Rafael at some point, so I asked around town and finally found out where his house was. Martin turned out to be a real blessing to get to know, and we stayed in touch the entire time we lived in the mountains. He was a big, rotund log truck driver who was half Tarahumara and half mestizo. He was married to a Tarahumara lady, a cousin of Maria Bircham's, from Samachique, and had lived there for several years before moving to San Rafael. Talk about a small world!

Martin was fifty-nine years old and had accepted the Lord four years earlier through a Pentecostal preacher named Hermano ("Brother") Carpinter. The brother was a North American who lived in La Junta (where the road from Chihuahua turned south toward Creel), and he traveled up and down the railroad sharing the gospel. He had built a twenty-by-forty-foot stone church in San Rafael where he only occasionally had services. In all the time we lived there, we never did meet him.

But Martin was a really cheerful and sincere Christian believer. I visited him and his wife at his house a few times and, in the years to come, would see him out on the road, hauling logs. Whenever we passed on the road, we would stop and talk for a while. Martin had a teenage daughter named Lupe who was also saved.

Tarahumara men and their goat ride into San Rafael on a loaded log truck

It was funny that within a short time of getting to know Martin, he started asking me if I could bring him a sleeping bag from the United States next time I went. We were always pretty strapped financially when we went to the border for new visas and supplies, and sometimes, if I hadn't seen Martin for a few months, I'd figure he had probably gotten his sleeping bag by then. The log truck drivers all needed something that was warm, too, since it was very common to have to spend a couple of nights a week out in the mountains while you waited for a load of logs to be loaded onto your truck. But after we had been there a couple of years, I bought a nice sleeping bag for Martin in El Paso and brought it back. I went over to his house with it, and you would've thought I had shown up with a bag of cash. He was so excited!

He asked how much he owed me, but I was reluctant to take anything from him. They just didn't have much in this world, and I know he struggled to be able to keep his older log truck running. So I said, "Nothing."

He said, "Then take this, brother!" and he pulled this big thick blanket off the seat of his truck. It turned out to be what I consider my most prized possession made by the Tarahumaras. It was a real wool blanket, dark brown in color, with a red design through it. The Tarahumaras were making fewer and fewer blankets even back then. They raised their own sheep and spun their own wool, but it was very time-consuming. Most of the sheep were white, too, so even having a brown blanket was unusual. But the quality was so good and the blanket so thick that even though big Martin had sat on it for who knows how many miles over who knows how many years and tried to wrap up his big body in it to sleep for who knows how many nights, it was in perfect condition!

"No, brother," I said, "that is too much."

But he wouldn't take no for an answer and was so excited about his sleeping bag that I figured we both got a fantastic deal.

There was another fellow in San Rafael that we met on this same trip named Jesus Caballero. He was thirty-two years old, an excellent guitar player, and had played basketball with Don Burgess. Mexicans love basketball and most of the schools, even if they don't have enough land for a baseball diamond or a soccer field, have basketball courts. Jesus was real friendly with us, too, and was apparently a strong believer. He knew the Birchams, especially Maria's sister, Perfecta. We also met Alvaro, Jesus's eighteen-year-old brother. He had just been saved for two months.

After a day of getting to know San Rafael, we decided to go on to Rocoroibo. On the way out of town, we checked out the airstrip that served San Rafael. It was on a ridge just outside of town with a really bad road going up to it. But the airstrip was in very good shape, a little more than 0.4 miles long and about forty yards wide. It was hard packed dirt with a good approach at both ends. We were told that the Ponderosa sawmill's two-way radio could be used in an emergency to have a plane called out from Chihuahua. That was good to know about in case of an emergency.

STEVEN REAL

"There Were Guerrillas Out Here?"

At various points on this trip we had asked several people for information regarding San Rafael and Rocoroibo. I was pretty alarmed by what we learned regarding Rocoroibo. It had earned itself a reputation for sure.

The first story was told to us by a man in El Divisadero. Then we got more details from Martin Lopez and his wife and a friend of theirs in San Rafael. They told us that between four and six years previously, a group of leftist guerrillas had attacked an army patrol from Chihuahua City and inflicted heavy casualties on them. They said the guerrillas were made up of students who were angered by the lumber company exploiting the Tarahumaras. They burned a man alive after pouring gasoline on him, then burned down the sawmill that was out in the mountains. They also said a logging company pickup truck had been burned by the Tarahumaras, and the driver had fled on foot toward San Rafael. They said everything had been calm now for about four years.

Obviously, I was quite startled that something that violent had happened out where we wanted to live. Did our field leadership know anything about this? Were there still remnants of these people living out there? This was something serious to find out about, and in the next couple of years, I would get much more accurate details from people who lived out there at the time. This is what I learned:

From Don Burgess, I got the best and most accurate account. There had indeed been leftist students with ties to communists and revolutionaries from down in southern Mexico at the huge autonomous university there near Mexico City who came up into Chihuahua and other parts of northern Mexico seeking to advance their agenda. They came into this part of the mountains because they felt that any commercial operations that existed in Indian territory were certainly taking advantage of the native people. There was very little mining going on, but the logging industry was a major enterprise. The guerrillas wanted to get a foothold in a fairly remote part of the mountains where there wasn't a police or army presence, so they chose the area around Rocoroibo and the sawmill town near it called Bachámuchi.

These "students" or former students who were now bona fide leftist guerrillas, moved amongst the Tarahumara, telling them that there was no doubt the Ponderosa log company was taking advantage of them financially and was stealing land that was supposed to be theirs. They found sympathizers among some of the Tarahumara who put them up in their homes, fed them, and familiarized them with the roads and trails. One day, the guerrillas wrote a letter and delivered it to the Ponderosa log company's office, demanding a huge payment of reparations for the Tarahumara.

The logging company, of course, refused to pay, so the guerrillas soon after went to the sawmill. They were going to send a powerful message by killing the director and burning down the sawmill. By the most amazing good fortune, which we know was the grace of God, the director had left that morning in his pickup truck to go into San Rafael. But the guerrillas did burn down the sawmill and apparently poured gasoline on and burned someone else who was there, killing him.

The Ponderosa company immediately called on the state and federal authorities to come out and defend them. The army sent out a squad of soldiers who probably figured that they would be able to intimidate the guerrillas into leaving. However, the guerrillas had armed themselves with automatic weapons and ambushed a patrol, killing several soldiers. The army sent out a much larger force along with an airplane to do reconnaissance from the air. The guerrillas were hiding in the hills and using trails to evade the soldiers. A high-ranking commander went up on a reconnaissance flight one day, and the guerrillas were able to shoot down the small plane, killing everyone on board. The army now responded with a vengeance.

Soldiers went from house to house, looking for the guerrillas but also looking for their Tarahumara sympathizers. As is common in so many places in the world, the Indians were considered low-class people who barely, if at all, were entitled to any human rights. They were tortured into giving up the names of those who were feeding and sheltering the guerrillas. When the soldiers felt that they had grabbed the right accomplice, with their family and fellow villagers present, they would put a shovel into the man's hands and tell him to start digging a hole the size and shape of a grave. Then they would walk up to him, say, "So you like burning people alive? Well, now it's your turn." They would pour gasoline on him and light him on fire. As he ran away screaming, they would shoot and kill him, then have someone drag him over and put him in the hole in the ground. They did this several times until they rooted out all the sympathizers. It wasn't clear how many of the actual guerrillas were also caught and executed.

One detail that Don Burgess didn't find out about until months or years after it had occurred was the imminent danger that he had been in at one point. He had been living in Rocoroibo for a few years and had made a number of friends amongst the Indians. When the guerrillas arrived and found out that an American was living in the community, they were quite alarmed.

"Why do you let this American live here with you?" they asked.

"He says he wants to learn our language and will help us learn how to read it," they were told. "They are good people and help us with other things too," they said.

"Well, you're wrong," responded the leftists. "All Americans are capitalists. They will take advantage of you the first time they possibly can, just like the logging company does."

Very early one morning, the guerrillas got a few of the Tarahumara men together and said, "Come with us. We have something important to do." They went to Don's house. Don, his wife, and their two young girls were inside. "We're going to burn their house down with them inside," said the guerrillas. The Tarahumara refused, however, and they prevailed. Apparently, the guerrillas didn't think it was worth escalating the issue to the level of having a conflict with the Indians. But we all know that it was the grace of God and his protection that saved the lives of Don and his family.

There was a main logging road heading out of San Rafael to the north and west, and forty-five miles and three and a half hours after leaving town, we arrived in Rocoroibo. The road we were on at this point was maintained by the Ponderosa logging company. Although I would hesitate to call it a good road, it was a far cry better than the one between Creel and San Rafael. We asked directions and found Don Burgess's house. It was a small two-story sixteen-by-twenty-foot adobe house with a steep roof and large wooden shutters on the windows. We were directed to his neighbor who lives just across the small creek, José Maria. He was about forty-five to fifty years old, had a couple of small children, and walked with a cane. Upon asking him where we could camp for the night, he opened up Don's house, which was padlocked on the doors and shutters.

The downstairs was one big room serving as a dining room and kitchen with a small woodburning stove and a small gas range. The upstairs was divided in half by a bookshelf partition. The beds were foam mattresses placed on boards which were on short sections of pine logs for legs. The floor downstairs was made of rocks, and the upstairs floor was plywood. There was fabric upstairs tacked between the rafters as a ceiling. The house was humble but very functional. It felt strange to be in the space belonging to someone else without first asking their permission, but we had said that we were his friends, so I guess this was Tarahumara hospitality at its best. It was an honor to be there, so we made ourselves as comfortable as possible and had a good night's sleep.

We saw that a lot of the Tarahumara men in this area, from Creel all the way to Rocoroibo, dressed more like mestizos and not in the traditional *zapeta* or loincloth. But they did use the Tarahumara language here openly, which was a good sign that they were not ashamed of their native language. That is not always the case with indigenous peoples. Rocoroibo was pretty much at the proverbial "end of the road," and it was obvious that Don had chosen a good place to immerse himself in the language.

Out and back from San Rafael, we noted several communities off to each side of the main logging road. Again, from the trip notes:

> El Muerto—apple orchards; sits right on the road; 6 to 8 houses visible from the road. Pitorreal—2-3 houses spread out, right on the

> road. Road to the West, to Monterde—a fairly wide road with a cross near the fork. A valley, Ocóbiachi, with an airstrip on a wide mesa and several large buildings can be seen long before coming to the road that drops into the valley, which is to the east of the main road. Tierra Blanca—several small farms on the sides of the mountains to the west. La Lamita—small sawmill, is going to move within the year. Road to Ocóbiachi goes to the east. It's a smaller, narrow, downhill road. Within 100 yards is a tienda (store)/house right on the main road, the only one within an hour's drive in that area. Cerro Prieto—was a sawmill years ago; about 10 houses on both sides of the road. One road goes downhill to the northwest toward La Finca, and a few Tarahumara valleys. After going over the top of a high mountain and heading first west, then southwest, the road drops into a long, rugged valley with a few houses in it and the road goes through a stream. Sawmill Bachámuchi- the largest settlement so far. Lots of houses, log trucks, a large office building, a meeting hall-looking building. Several friends and acquaintances of Burgess's live there.

Obviously, we had to stop and ask people what the name of that particular community was if it wasn't on our topographical map from Chihuahua. It made for an interesting day of exploration.

On the main logging road each day, we saw three or four loaded logging trucks lumbering (no pun intended) toward San Rafael and about the same number going back out toward Rocoroibo without logs. We were able to go about three times faster than the empty log trucks, but the loaded ones were much slower. On both loaded and unloaded trucks, we oftentimes saw passengers riding, usually men, but sometimes women and children too. It looked especially precarious to see people with blankets or a few personal possessions riding on the top of a load of logs. I'm glad I didn't have to do that just to get to town. There's no doubt that it took some of those trucks all day long to make the trip that we made in about three and a half hours. We didn't pass a single pickup truck in those two days, only logging trucks.

In order to be thorough on this trip, we knew we had to check out the region to the north of Rocoroibo. There was a really deep canyon to the west and north where the Oteros River flowed toward the Gulf of California, and there were no roads that crossed it to the north. So our only alternative was to backtrack all the way through San Rafael, past Creel, to San Juanito where there was another road that headed west to a town named Uruachic. This took us a day and a half to traverse.

Uruachic is the seat of the *municipio*, or municipality, which encompasses an area about the size of a very large county or two in the US. It's an old mining town dating back to the 1500 or 1600s. The road was a pretty good gravel road due to the town's importance. They had a post office, telegraph office, electricity, two-way radio to Chihuahua City, and a very small airstrip. The Mexican population, or mestizos, have been well entrenched for hundreds of years in this area due to the mining. There are also a lot of cattle ranches. It seems that the Tarahumara had been pushed out of this area for the most part. They do live scattered around the region, far from town, and down toward the Rio Oteros. It seemed that there was a much better probability of finding a sizable Indian population in the Rocoroibo area.

That completed our circumvention by road of the Western Tarahumara region. We headed home to Chihuahua, our families, nice soft beds, and good home-cooked meals!

Chapter 3

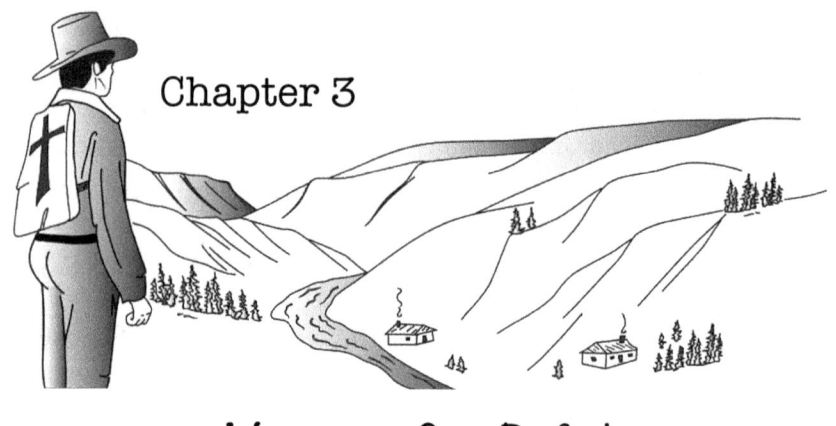

Moving to San Rafael

Hitch 'Em Up and Move 'Em Out!

Back in Chihuahua, Ticker had been holding down the fort. Even though Dave was in a Mexican preschool class, she taught him preschool in English also. He had to learn numbers, some basic math, the alphabet, and the basics for reading. Dusty was now fourteen months old and had been walking for a little over a month. Thankfully, the kids were healthy and happy. Now our next challenge would be our move to the mountains.

One of the most important things we needed for living far away from electricity was a propane refrigerator. I was enlightened by my fellow missionaries on what to look for and had searched the newspaper diligently for a couple of months before it was time to move. The best deal I found was a Servel refrigerator that was at least forty and possibly fifty years old. Servels had a great reputation for being dependable and long-lasting, despite their age. Made in Evansville, Indiana, from 1927 through 1956, millions of their propane gas and kerosene-powered refrigerators had been made for use all over the United States in rural areas before the States got electric lines and infrastructure. Many of these Servels made their way to Mexico and were actually quite valuable. I paid $700 for ours. In 1981 dollars, imagine that—$700 for a forty-something-year-old refrigerator!

The fridge was a little over five feet tall with rounded corners, just like you would imagine something that old to be. It's an interesting lesson in science to learn how they function, using propane to keep a small flame and burner going which heats up a liquid ammonia solution. As the ammonia rises into the freezer area, it is quickly cooled to quite a low temperature and pulls heat out of the freezer. The system was quite simple, but it was important to find a refrigerator with a good quality burner and lines that had not been corroded and soldered back together. I looked a few over carefully before I bought the one we had, and it served us faithfully for the next eight years.

It's only major drawback was that the freezer was quite small, about twelve inches wide and twelve inches tall by eighteen inches deep. We needed a far bigger freezer for life in the mountains where we were going to be far from the grocery store. From a scrap metal yard, I got some heavy gauge aluminum sheet material and added on to the width of the freezer, basically tripling its size. When I did the modification, I wasn't even sure that the extra space would actually stay as cold as it needed to, but it did.

Not only had Ticker and I moved regularly before and during our entire marriage, but I had moved far more than the average person when I was younger. After I was born in Phoenix, Arizona, my folks lived in the town close to my grandfather's cattle ranch for three or four years. Then my mom and dad split up when I was five, and my brother and I lived on the ranch with my grandparents for a little over two years. I attended first grade in Stanfield, a few miles from the ranch. Then Mom remarried, came and picked up my brother and me, and we moved with my new dad to Schiller Park, Illinois.

From there, we moved out to a really cool country town, Algonquin. Then my dad accepted a transfer with his company, Lockheed Air Terminal, to West Los Angeles, California. After a year or so, we moved to Van Nuys. By then, Dad was in a management position, so in the tradition of IBM and other large companies of the day, he was offered promotions on a regular basis, but they required relocating. We next moved to San Diego, California; Rochester, New York; Pacifica (San Francisco), California; then to Des Plaines (Chicago), Illinois. It was there that I graduated high school.

I had lived in nine different cities and towns and attended nine different schools by the time I graduated from high school.

Once I got into New Tribes, I attended Bible school in Jackson, Michigan; boot camp in Durham, Ontario, Canada; and language and linguistics school in Camdenton, Missouri. Between boot camp and language school, we had gone to Sanford, Florida, for one year to help the mission remodel an old hotel into a headquarters building. So after high school, Ticker and I together attended three different schools and lived in four different cities and towns. Living in Chihuahua City was the fifth. Now we looked ahead to just two more moves—San Rafael, where we would find an Indian community to move into, and finally into a house in that Tarahumara Indian community.

Whew! It makes me feel like a gypsy again just talking about it. But it was the reality of our lives. Since we had given our lives to the Lord to be in His service, I was really excited about our move to San Rafael!

* * * * *

It was a beautiful sunny winter morning as I weaved my way through the curving foothills west of Cuauhtemoc. I was moving our first load of furniture from Chihuahua City to San Rafael. Gary Johnson was helping by accompanying me and taking a full load in his Chevy Blazer. We were still on the paved highway, and there was hardly any traffic, which was nice. I rounded a curve at fifty-five or sixty miles an hour, and suddenly, right in front of me, was a big black bull standing completely sideways in the road, smack dab on top of the center line. There was perhaps a foot-wide shoulder on each side of the road and no way to maneuver past this guy, left or right, without hitting him or going off the road. I headed toward the right shoulder, stood on the brakes, and prayed I could stop in time.

Gary saw my brake lights as I entered the turn but couldn't see around the bend and down the hill. When he did see the bull, he slammed on his brakes too. About to rear-end me, though, he swerved to the left, into the oncoming lane. We both stopped no more than three feet from that dang bull! I just looked to the left at Gary next to me; he looked at me in amazement, and we both busted out laughing. That was close! If that had been at night, I'd have destroyed the front of my truck and created several hundred pounds of hamburger on the spot. Finally, that stubborn bull walked off the highway and into a field.

About eighty miles and five hours later, we arrived at my new house in San Rafael and safely delivered our two truckloads of household goods without any front-end damage or fresh beef.

Wild West Shootout

It was on this same trip through Creel that we had another unusual experience. As I pulled up to my favorite restaurant to get lunch, we could see that it was dark inside, and the door was locked. There was a typed notice taped across the doors, so I got out to read it. It was there to inform the public that the business would be closed until further notice due to a police investigation. I'd never seen something like this and was curious as to what it was all about. We found another place to eat lunch, and I asked about the notice on the closed restaurant's doors.

Apparently, just a few days before, a fugitive from justice had been spotted eating in the restaurant with a few of his friends. He had been on the run for years but eventually came back to Creel, where he had family and friends. Someone spotted him at the restaurant and reported him to the local state police captain there in town. The captain took two of his fellow officers and stationed one at the front door and one at the back to prevent the outlaw from getting away as well as to keep anybody else from entering. He walked up to the big booth where the fugitive was sitting with friends on both sides of him.

"Which of you is so and so?" asked the captain.

The man in the middle answered that it was him.

"Everybody out of the booth right now," ordered the captain.

They all began to slide out, some to the right and some to the left, with the fugitive doing the same. As he slid sideways in the booth, he reached behind his waistband and pulled out the gun that he was carrying there. He got it out so smoothly and quickly that he caught the police captain completely by surprise, then shot him right between the eyes. At the sound of the gunshot, the policeman closest to the dining room came through the door, and the bad guy shot him, too, killing him instantly. The other officer came toward the room, and a gunfight ensued. I don't remember how many died that day, but it was a really bad day for the cops. I sure was glad that we hadn't stopped there for lunch just a few days earlier.

"Uh, Butch," I said. "I Think We're in For Some Trouble Here."

It was a couple of weeks later, about six miles southwest of Creel, and I came up over a rise in the dirt road. I brought the truck to a stop. I couldn't believe what I was looking at up head.

Butch Bennet was accompanying me on this trip, the two of us in my 4x4 van. Butch was just staring at the stretch of road ahead of us, not saying anything. He was trying to wrap his mind around what lay ahead, I guess. He was, after all, a city boy from New Jersey.

For about three or four hundred yards in front of us, all we saw was a sea of muddy water. Well, that's not precisely true. There were some mounds of mud that rose up in the center of what vaguely resembled water-filled paths where trucks' tires had squished up the thickest of the mud; but basically, we were looking at a long, narrow lake thirty or forty feet wide, hundreds of yards long, with muddy water from one side to the other. I got out of the van, walked up, and looked at it closer.

The water seemed to be about six or eight inches deep in the tracks right in front of us. I could see some tree branches in the tracks about a hundred feet ahead.

"Looks like people have gotten stuck in there and used some tree branches to try to get traction," I said to Butch.

"There's no way around this?" he asked. "That's unbelievable!"

"Nope," I told him, "this is the only road." After a few moments, I decided what we'd do. "Okay, buddy. Hang on. I'm going to get a running start at this, fast enough I hope our momentum gets us through, but not so fast that if we hit some bad holes, we break a spring (I knew we had at least one and a half tons of stuff in my three-fourth-ton van). Ready?"

He gripped the armrest with one hand and the dashboard with the other, and away we went. We got about two-thirds of the way through when we lost traction and slowly, sickeningly, came to a stop.

I got out, trying to stand on the high, drier mounds of mud. I looked under the truck first. The front and rear axle differentials were dragging mud, the tracks were so deep. I reached down around the tires, trying to keep my feet out of the deepest of the water, and found that another thing previous truck drivers had done was lay rocks, hundreds of them, in the tracks for traction. We had rocks in front of a couple of tires which had just pushed themselves into parking bumpers, so I cleared them out. It was winter in the Sierra Madres, and the road here was somewhere between 8,500 and 9,000 feet in elevation. The water was freezing cold, and my hands were numb in a couple of minutes.

"I've only got one idea," I said to Butch. "Let's get the come-along out and see if we can get rolling again. I think we can reach that tree over there off the right shoulder with the extra cable."

It took us almost twenty minutes just to get into the back of the truck, dig under some boxes and furniture ("Yeah, good place to leave that, Steve!"), and hook up the come-along. I also had a three-foot-long piece of pipe I could slide over the handle of the come-along to use as a cheater bar and increase leverage.

I briefed Butch on how to put as much pressure on the cable as possible, then crank fast once I got moving, then, when he could, slip the cable off and let me go with the truck.

We tried it. I couldn't move the truck at all. I went back over to the side of the road where Butch was manning the come-along, and we cranked more tension on it and the cable. Then I realized that if I rocked the truck at all, the tension on the cable would get so bad it could snap. I pictured the cable whipping back at the truck and going through the radiator or windshield. Worse, I could see it going back and hitting Butch, taking his head off. I put the truck in park, went back over to him, and we disconnected the cable and come-along. Now I was going to try to back out.

For the next hour, we manually worked our way back through each of the two tire tracks with our hands down in the freezing cold water, straightening out the tree branches, and getting them to lay flat. We pulled out rocks that weren't flat and would stop us again. We went off to the sides of the road and added more rocks where the holes were the deepest.

Finally, before I could do anything more, I had to get my hands warm. They were so cold they hurt really badly. It was midafternoon, and the sun was getting lower. We made a small fire and warmed our hands and, leaving our boots on, tried to warm our feet. As I turned to get back in the truck, I said, "Hey, look, Butch. The water is freezing over!" Yep, there was now a layer of ice in the truck tracks.

Starting the truck back up, I rocked it gently back and forth from forward to reverse, then got some momentum going, like I'd done a hundred times in the snow in Illinois and Canada, and finally accelerated backward. Several seconds later, we were out!

Butch spotted it first, I think. There was a faint track to the right of the road that went through an area where some small trees were, and when we walked it, we could see that a few bigger ones had been cut down for passage. We got back in the van and snaked along the hillside, dodging boulders and pine trees, and soon were around the long muddy stretch. It had taken us three hours.

"What would have happened if we couldn't have gotten out of the mud?" Butch asked.

I had looked at the tracks on the road when we first got there. "I don't think anyone's been through here in a week," I said. "They know it's really bad so probably won't even try it until it dries out some. We'd have had to walk into town and try to hire someone to come pull us out with several chains and cables or something. We could have been stuck here for days."

But God…

Driving Mexico's Roads in the '80s

Most of Mexico has highways that are very much like our US Highway system—not our Interstate system but the old two-lane US Highway system that was built in the 1920s and '30s. If there's room, they'll have a halfway decent shoulder. If it's a really well-traveled highway, there will usually be four lanes. In the 1980s, we missionaries traveled not just Mexico's highways but a lot of Mexico's secondary roads as well as those other roads that were only in existence because a logging company had made them. The secondary, tertiary, and all other grades of roads below that were something else.

Some roads, like the ones which went to the Guachochic area (part of the Tarahumara Central dialect) and to the Tepehuan and Guarijio tribes, were fairly good gravel roads where you could go twenty-five to maybe sixty mph, only slowing for occasional rutted or washboard sections. Going anywhere in the mountains, however, quickly taught me to not only carry a well-supplied toolbox but also tire repair kits, a variety of nuts, bolts, and spare parts, and last but not least, a cable or chain for getting pulled out of mud or snow. This was despite having four-wheel drive. Four-wheel drive is really helpful, but you can still get—and I was on several occasions—stuck really badly.

The road Butch and I traversed southwest of Creel was finally being improved by the Mexican government. It was approximately thirty-five miles from Creel to San Rafael, and the incredibly beautiful and panoramic spot of El Divisadero was about two-thirds of the way along that section. El Divisadero was and always will be a beautiful tourist destination with a view almost like the south rim of our Grand Canyon. The Chihuahua to the Pacific Railroad crossed this entire mountain range in a northeast to southwest direction.

This road paralleled it, so for several decades, almost all supplies and people had gone in and out of the region by train. But many business owners, homeowners, and occasional travelers like myself couldn't wait for the laborious and rather expensive process of loading your merchandise in Chihuahua City and then guessing/waiting/trying multiple times to get it picked up at one of the small mountain communities' train depots. So the government was finally trying to improve this much-needed road.

For the seven years we lived in the mountains, and for thirty or forty years previous to that, that thirty-five-mile stretch took anywhere from two and a fourth to three hours to travel, depending on the weather—providing, of course, that you didn't get stuck or break down.

In the winter, the road was covered in snow and slush after a snowstorm. During and after the rainy season—basically June to early September—it could have water coursing down it or boulders or trees fallen onto it, besides the usual ruts and potholes. Often, the water in the potholes was one to two feet deep. You tried to drive on the ridges of high ground if you could safely do so without your tires sliding off the road itself. Winter or summer, driving these roads was a constant second-to-second exercise in steering to avoid the worst and sharpest rocks and the deepest potholes.

After the close call of getting stuck with Butch, I bought a fifty-foot cable, three times as heavy as the cable in my come-along, for future problems. As it was, with having to do a bit of yanking and jerking during the next few years when getting either my truck or someone else's unstuck, I had even that cable break three or four times. I always carried the tools to shorten the cable a bit and reattach the hook, too, for when it did break.

There was definitely a way you became almost one with your truck driving in conditions like that. I got to know exactly where each front tire was, and I picked my way at all speeds around holes which would jar your kidneys and send people and your gear in the truck up into the air if you misjudged. The other hazard besides potholes was rocks. Sharp rocks would cut your tires, and badly cutting the side wall of a tire ruined the tire. Having done all the work on all the vehicles I've owned since I was seventeen, I had a very vested interest in not having to repair stuff. It was inconvenient anywhere but was the worst when trying to improvise out in the middle of nowhere.

Just driving from point A to point B in the mountains in those days could be unpredictable. One afternoon, on a trip from San Rafael to Chihuahua by myself, I decided to stop and get something to eat. I had just passed San Juanito and realized how hungry I was, so I decided to do a U-turn and get some food. There was a big, flat grassy area next to a river which happened to conceal some mysterious version of silt or quicksand with about six inches of firm dirt and grass on top. As I drove onto it, the front wheels of my truck started to sink suddenly. I stopped right away, got out, and locked the front hubs into four-wheel drive and tried to back out real easy without spinning the wheels. No dice. I couldn't rock the truck out either, and when I opened the door and stepped out the next time to look underneath, the front differential was already touching the ground.

I knew it was hopeless then to get out under my own power, so I got out the tow cable, hooked it to the rear on the frame, and flagged down a passing pickup truck. Although he tried to tug me out, my cable broke twice.

An hour or more later, a big five-ton cargo truck came by. By then, without having moved for quite a while, my front tires had slowly sunken about an inch below the surface of the grass, and the whole front of the truck, frame, engine, etc. was obviously sinking into the muck! Unbelievable! I couldn't any longer even open and close the front doors, so I left the driver's door open just enough to get in and out. The driver of that big five-ton truck was more savvy than the last guy and just pulled real slow and steady, and this time, the cable didn't break. Weird stuff. I could jump up and down on the grass surface like it was a football field, but underneath, it was almost like quicksand.

Years later, close to Bachámuchi, I got the chance to return the favor for those who'd helped me. I came across a loaded log truck that couldn't get up a steep muddy grade which also had a fairly sharp curve in the middle. The truck was on its fourth or fifth try and was spinning its rear wheels, badly tearing them up. The driver backed down to the bottom of the hill to either quit or try once more. I asked him if he wanted me to pull him up. He looked at me like I was crazy but then said, "Sure."

Because I didn't have much weight in my truck for traction, I had three or four guys who'd been in his cab and riding on top of the load of logs get into my van. I hooked up my cable, put my gear shift in four-wheel low, and pulled him to the top. His truck was pulling hard, but we made it. When we stopped and I went to unhook the cable, I saw that the driver had cut his wheels sharply to the right for the first part of the grade and never turned them back straight or left for the second part. I had dragged him half the way with his front wheels sideways! That four-wheel-drive Ford van was an amazing truck.

Chapter 4

Life in San Rafael

4.1 Our First Week in San Rafael (January 30, 1982)

I'm the first one up this morning. It's cold in the house. I know the temperature outside is in the twenties or low thirties. Every single house in town has its wood or kerosene fired stove going. I look out the kitchen window as I walk across the cold concrete floor in my sock feet. There is a low-lying brown layer of wood smoke in the air, which will dissipate soon enough. But for now, it has a pleasant aroma. It has the smell of warmth.

As I build a fire in the big woodstove, I can hear the sound of logging trucks. Some are slowly heading into the Ponderosa sawmill property with their loads, having gotten into town too late the night before to unload. Others are empty, their diesel engines accelerating through the gears as they head out of town for more logs.

All the wood that I care about for the moment is in a small stack underneath the heater. On the front porch, where I brought it in from the night before, is a neat row of firewood, oak on one end and pine on the other. Pine burns up more quickly and has more pitch in it, which eventually gums up the flue pipes, so I take just enough pine to get a fire going, then put oak on it to get a good, hot, long burning fire.

With the fire started, I take a two-gallon bucket and add water to our "hot water heater"—a twenty-gallon galvanized metal trashcan with a spigot on the bottom which sits on top of the wood heater. We'll need the hot water for washing up and doing dishes in a little while.

The wood heater is a rather ugly affair. I have already put high-temperature spray paint on my list for our next trip to El Paso. But this big beast works fantastically. A coworker had shown me the design, and I made it in Chihuahua in preparation for our move since a store-bought wood heater would've cost much more, money which we didn't have. It consists of a fifty-five-gallon steel drum, lying horizontally on a framework of angle iron legs and braces. I had to look around town at the scrap metal yards to find an appropriate piece of quarter-inch-thick plate steel. This I cut to size, then cut a slit in the steel drum and slid it in, approximately two-thirds of the distance up from the bottom to the top of the drum and three-fourths of the length of the drum. I then welded everything back together and made a door in the end.

When I open the door and make a fire, the heat and flames don't go straight up and out of the flue. Instead, they hit the quarter-inch steel plate above, which is a baffle, then travel to the back of the drum, where there is a space about ten inches long by the width of the drum. There, the smoke and flames turn and rise into the upper chamber, heating the drum and squeezing even more heat from the fire. At the front of the drum is the flue pipe, and finally, the smoke goes up and out through the roof.

I hear scuffling feet and look over at the doorway to the bedroom. Dave, in his blue one-piece pajamas with the white plastic feet, is sleepy-eyed but wants to help me with the fire. I open the door of the stove, and he puts a couple more sticks in. In a few more minutes, Ticker brings Dusty into the kitchen and puts him down. He's dressed like Dave, but his pajamas are yellow. He's only been walking for a couple of months, so he shuffles noisily over to join us, his hazel eyes twinkling. I slide three chairs from the table into a semicircle next to the stove and set Dusty on one of them close to me, telling him to be careful of the hot stove. He mimics Dave and me as we stretch our hands out to warm them.

It's only our first week in this little two-room house in the mountains, but it has everything we need. I look around the room. The bright turquoise walls are so Mexican—cheerful in color and bolder than what Americans would dare to paint their houses. It's the same color inside and out, a durable semigloss over the stuccoed adobes. The ceiling is tongue and groove pine boards on top of exposed four-by-four beams. Our thirty-inch-wide propane gas range is on one side of the kitchen window that looks out toward the front yard and apple orchard with several pots and pans hanging from a wrought-iron rack above it.

On the other side is the wood grain laminate countertop that I brought out from Chihuahua City and installed, since Mexicans typically take all their cabinets with them when they move. The kitchen sink is in the middle, under the window, where Ticker has arranged dried flowers and other decorations on the wide window sill. The adobe walls are about twelve inches thick, so all the windowsills are nice and wide.

In one corner of the room is my desk, which I made while we were in language school. It's modeled after the old-style "secretary" desks with a fold-up front that is the writing surface when it's folded down. It's part half-inch plywood and part red and white aromatic cedar. The cedar is all from a scrap pile that the sawmill in Camdenton, Missouri, would occasionally put out on the side of the highway for the public to take as they willed. The desk is about three feet wide and has a two-tiered bookcase with drawers for pencils and other desk supplies. The legs of the desk are two stacks of cinderblocks that raise it up to normal desk height.

Sort of in the middle of the room is our round laminate-topped table with three chairs and Dusty's highchair around it. In the middle of the table sits our main light source, a glass oil lamp, just like those in the old Westerns. After 150 years or more, they're still the dependable standard here in rural Mexico.

Story time with Dave and Dusty by the wood burning furnace, with the "water heater" sitting on top of it.

The bedroom is a bit crowded, but the furniture fits nicely. There's the double bed I made in Chihuahua, which has a plywood base with storage underneath and a bookcase for the headboard. On top of the headboard is another oil lamp, which is the last light extinguished each night. We have a narrow, tall armoire for a closet, and next to it is the boys' bed. It's a crib on the bottom for Dusty with a bunk bed on top for David. On top of our dresser is the changing table for Dusty's diapers and clothes. There's a long, floral print curtain that divides the room in half between our bed and the boys'. The main idea is to keep the light from shining on them when we want to read in bed at night.

Ticker makes breakfast—scrambled eggs with tortillas, and a delicacy that we enjoy only once every couple of weeks: canned bacon! Looking through the stores in El Paso for canned meat, we came across canned bacon in Kmart one day. Occasionally, we'd eat Spam, usually sliced and fried with breakfast, but we tire of it quickly, always wondering, of course, what is actually in it. Canned ham is much better but more pricey. Our little freezer only allows us to have a certain amount of frozen meat, so the canned bacon is awesome!

After breakfast the house is warm enough, and it's starting to warm up outside, so I'm able to let the fire in the woodstove die down. The water in the big galvanized can on top is nice and warm, so I fill a big cooking pot with it and carry it to the sink. I wash dishes, and Dave helps with what he can. Ticker dresses Dusty for the day in a long-sleeved shirt, jeans, and shoes. Then she gets school materials out and organized for teaching Dave preschool. He's a good student and loves the one-on-one time with his mom. He knows that if he does well, he'll get to go outside even sooner to play. And, of course, that's a new adventure since he's getting to know the local kids already and that at the back of our house is a huge mountain just ready to explore.

Ticker teaching Dave pre-school in San Rafael

STEVEN REAL

Getting to Know San Rafael and Los Tascates

As we get to know our neighbors in San Rafael, they are amazed when we tell them that Dusty was born in Chihuahua City. They find it surprising that we, as Americans, had enough confidence in the Mexican medical community to have our son born here. For my part, one of the first things that I do in getting to know the town is to check out the medical clinics and find out which ones might be available to the public, rather than only to a specific government employee group, for example. Much to my delight, I find that only about a hundred yards from our house, which is in Los Tascates, is a private practice clinic. In San Rafael is another one, but neither one has a full-time doctor. However, these could be a big help if something serious were to happen to any of us that we couldn't treat ourselves.

Since pharmacies in the cities are quite common and sell a lot of medications over the counter, we have brought with us a small supply of antibiotics to treat cuts, respiratory infections, and other things. During our field medicine course in language school, we all had to buy a book called *Where There Is No Doctor*. It's an invaluable resource that covers how to treat a multitude of things from cuts to delivering babies, from treating amoeba to doing sutures. We both hope that we're never going to need it for most of those things. But we do end up using antibiotics from time to time, and they serve us quite well over the years.

While Ticker watches Dusty and teaches Dave preschool, I take care of a number of things which constantly help me to practice and improve my Spanish. We find out pretty quickly that there is often-times low water pressure, and we have to ration our water. But occasionally, there is no water for days and days at a time. At those times, word just gets passed around town that there will be water down by the train station for public distribution. I have to take a Teflon-coated fifty-five-gallon drum and have it filled from a hose on a water tower. Then I have to very securely lash the drum to the wall inside my van since the road to that end of town and back is steep and very rough. I use a hand pump at home to transfer the water to buckets and then climb up on a ladder and refill the water drum that's on the stand next to the house. After doing this once or twice, I devise a pumping system where I can pressurize the drum of water that's in my truck with air and pump the water through a garden hose up to the house's water tank.

Water, of course, is an essential part of life. Since we're not sure how clean the town water is, we always have a large cooking pot on top of the stove with boiled drinking water in it. Ticker washes laundry using a couple of large galvanized washtubs, one for washing and one for rinsing. She uses an old-fashioned washboard for washing the clothes, which is a lot of work. Although she doesn't complain, I'm resolved to find us a gas-powered wringer washing machine in Chihuahua City. Since there is no electrical wiring in our house, and electricity has only been available here for three months anyway, it's not even an option to buy an electric washing machine. Eventually, we will need a gas-powered one out in the Indian community anyway.

For showers, we've come prepared. In Chihuahua City, I bought a two-gallon galvanized bucket, attached a showerhead with a valve to the bottom of it, and we have a large nail driven into the side of one of our ceiling beams in the house. When it's time to shower, we place the big washtub underneath the shower bucket, which is full of warm water. I hang up the bucket full of warm water from the nail, and we just stand in the big washtub and bathe. Yes, water splashes around onto the floor, but that's one advantage of having a concrete floor, so we take what are called "military showers"—we get wet, turn off the valve, soap and wash ourselves, then turn the valve back on to rinse.

After a couple of months of this, however, I built an actual shower room outside the back of the house. In the cold months, we have to shower in the middle of the day when it's the warmest. But it's a nice improvement in privacy as well as not soaking a big area of the kitchen floor and not having to dump lots of soapy water out into the front yard after we've all showered.

Going to the local grocery store is one of the most interesting experiences of all. If you remember all the old Western TV shows, like *Gunsmoke*, you'll pretty much get the idea. In those old Western shows and movies, there's a long wooden counter, and the proprietor is standing behind it. The customer has to stay on the other side. There's some merchandise displayed on a few shelves, like oil lamps and dishes, coffee pots, and some basic tools. But when you want to purchase something, you tell the proprietor what you want, and they bring it out to you. You don't just go down an aisle and pick out a one-kilo bag of sugar. You ask the proprietor, and he or she brings a big nylon bag up to the front counter, where there is always a large scale, and weighs it out right in front of you and puts it into a plastic bag. Then if you want three kilos of beans, she takes the sugar back and brings the beans out to weigh and bag.

This is done for everything. A dozen eggs, a jar of instant coffee, anything and everything that you want to buy. You can't always count on the store even having a cardboard box for you to put everything in to carry home with you, so everybody brings the ubiquitous nylon mesh, reusable carrying bags. It takes me a while to even find all the little stores in town, some of them tucked away on side streets, and then weeks and weeks to figure out who has better prices and a decent inventory. Sometimes the store owners are kind of grumpy and hard to deal with. Others are only open four or five hours a day.

Although there were several little mom-and-pop eating establishments, I never thought about it until just now as I'm writing about our life there, but there was no cantina or bar of any kind in San Rafael. It seemed that if people wanted to drink, they did it with their friends at home. I wonder if it partly had to do with the fact that there weren't very many policemen of any kind, so if there had been a drinking establishment, it could've been a regular source of disorderly problems. Perhaps simply in the interest of maintaining law and order, alcohol permits just were not granted.

Although we would've really enjoyed having a church to attend to have the fellowship of fellow Christians, there simply wasn't one. Occasionally, I would hear about a Pentecostal preacher having special meetings, but it was almost always after he had left. So we had our own devotional time at home as a family each night. Seven days a week, I had story time with Dusty and Dave in the evenings. Of course, Dusty at that age could only look at the pictures, but Dave was quite interested and soaked up the stories like the smart little guy that he was.

I remember one evening that our favorite Bible storybook's binding fell apart, and the cover and pages went flying on the floor. It was a pretty good-sized storybook, running from the creation all the way through the gospels and the lives of the apostles. Dave got down and picked up all the pages and put them into a stack, and I just told him to set it aside for the time being. We had a second book which was more elementary and full of pictures that Dusty liked to follow along with. So we finished our evening story time with that one, prayed together, and the boys went to bed.

The next day, at some point, Dave took it upon himself to start putting the big storybook back together in the proper order. He worked on it for quite some time, and when I asked him to let me see it, I was amazed. He had reassembled it almost perfectly in chronological order!

There are other things for me to do these first weeks of living in this rustic mountain town that will make our lives more manageable. Along with building the shower room, I need a small shed and workshop for my tools and motorcycle. I drive over to the Ponderosa sawmill and make my first purchase of lumber. Somehow, it really makes me feel like an actual member of the community; buying lumber and building something with it gives you a sense of belonging and permanence. Looking around the big sawmill is something different and fascinating too. It's a beehive of activity with all different sizes and thicknesses of lumber being stacked under spacious open-air sheds, which only days or weeks ago were big logs on the back of a lumber truck. If not for this great big sawmill, there would be no employment or even reason for roads all the way out here in these rugged mountains.

Fun and Funny Stuff

My Yamaha dirt bike, which had served me so well in Chihuahua City when I became friends with the Reyes family, continued to be a source of fun for us. On afternoons, when the weather was dry and the boys and I needed to have some fun, I would put Dusty on the seat in front of me and have Dave on the seat behind me, and we'd go for a ride. We would head for the sawdust piles that the logging company dumped for hundreds of yards next to the road coming into town from Creel. The sawdust was in huge piles, snaking alongside the creek like a parallel road. I would ride with both boys on the motorcycle fairly slowly for a while, then I would let one off where I could watch him and take the other one for a much faster ride for fifty yards or so. We would zigzag and go up and down the mounds, laughing the whole way.

Of course, David wanted me to go faster and faster while Dusty was thrilled to just be on the motorcycle at all. It was so safe; even if we had fallen, it would be hard to get hurt going down into the sawdust. I'm sure the boys were always grateful to their Uncle Bryan for giving me that motorcycle. It's funny how you don't know where some of your blessings come from, especially when you're a kid.

"RRRoohhmm bee-you-tees" is the way my landlord pronounced the variety of apples—Rome Beauties—that grew on the property where we were living. It always cracked me up when he said it and still makes me smile today. When we were ready to move into the house, he was still storing quite a few crates of the apples there, so as he put the last dozen or so on his truck, he asked me if I wanted to buy any. I bought two crates from him and was glad I did. They were delicious. Since the house was so small, I built a back porch right off of the side door and put a roof over it so we could have a little bit of storage. We had things like mops and brooms, buckets and washtubs, and cases of Coke in the one-liter bottles that we bought in Chihuahua. We probably had three cases of bottles, some full and some empty. Next to them is where I stacked the crates of apples.

One day, I noticed that mice or rats were starting to eat the apples between the slats in the crates. I went to one of the stores and bought rat traps and set a couple one night. In the middle of the night, I heard them go off. However, in the morning, both traps were nowhere to be seen. I searched around and found that the rats had drug themselves and the traps off the porch and underneath the floor, where they then escaped entirely. *Wow*, I thought, *these are tough rats*. So then I attached a short piece of nylon line to each trap and baited them again. Again, in the middle of the night, I heard them go off, and then I heard the scuffling sound of the rats trying to escape. But, alas, in the morning, the traps were still there, but there was still not a dead rat to be found.

Time to get tough! I thought. I took some small finish nails and drove eight or ten of them into the edge of each trap in a U-shape, then cut the head off of each nail. They were going to be like the punji sticks that the Vietcong used during the Vietnam War, impaling the feet of American soldiers who stepped on them. Once again, I baited the traps, certain of my success this time. *Snap!* went the traps during the night. Imagine my surprise when in the morning, I found one dead rat in one trap but only blood on the other trap, from which the impaled rat had managed to escape! But, eventually, one by one, I managed to get all the rats.

Then, one day, in the middle of the afternoon, I walked out on the back porch, and movement caught my eye. I squatted down and saw this big rat looking at me from behind a stack of empty Coke bottles. I tried to think of some kind of weapon I had to kill him. The only thing that dawned on me was that just a few feet away, inside the bedroom next to the boys' bed, was Dave's toy Tarahumara bow and arrow. I quickly slipped into the room, grabbed it, and came back out. The rat hadn't moved. "I've got you, sucker!" I told him. At this range, I couldn't miss.

Kneeling down slowly, so as not to spook him, I slowly pulled the arrow back. I aimed it carefully right at his beady little black eyes. But I wanted to make sure that I killed him with that shot, so I pulled the arrow back just a little bit more.

Crack! went the bow as it broke in two in my hands. "No way!" I groaned. The noise startled the rat, too, and he ran behind another case of bottles. "What am I going to do now?" I asked myself. Then I remembered that I had a wrist rocket in the house. That's one of those really powerful slingshots that will shoot a big steel ball or a marble. Hoping the rat was paralyzed with fear, I went back in the house, grabbed the wrist rocket and a steel ball, and came back out.

The rat must've been figuring that this game of cat and mouse might not end well for him, so he climbed up the wall until he was just about at the height of the top row of Coke bottles. *Ha!* I thought. *That's even better. Now I can see your whole head.* I slowly drew the ball bearing back to my ear and let it fly.

Pow! The steel ball hit the top lip of the Coke bottle right next to the rat's head, and glass flew everywhere. That rat bolted for his life like he was shot from a gun. I was totally shocked and mad at myself for how I had failed twice to kill that stinkin' rodent. But that emotion only lasted for a second, then I had to start laughing at myself. Boy, did I feel like the Keystone cops of the rat hunters! That definitely could have made it on an episode of *Mexico's Funniest Home Videos*.

4.2 Exploring with Ticker and the Boys— February through March 1982

I got out the maps again and spread them on the kitchen table. I located Creel, far to the east of us. The Chihuahua to the Pacific railroad runs southwest to the coast. I found San Rafael and the Copper Canyon below that. My gaze went to the vast uncharted areas west and northwest of us, wondering how much further the Western Tarahumara dialect extended past the continental divide before the lands of the Guarijio Indians began. Then, from our previous trip to Uruachic, I knew there was a really deep canyon as deep and perhaps wider than the Copper Canyon, where no road would probably be built in my lifetime. Somewhere to the northwest of there, Tarahumara country gave way to the Pima Indians' territory.

So many thousands of square miles! "Where oh where, God, do I begin? You know where You want us to live out there. Please show me. Show me where to go," I said to Him.

That's when I said to Ticker, "Let's take a drive tomorrow and explore a bit. There are some roads that head off to the west of the main logging road going north. Let's go see where at least one of them goes."

With enough food and water for a whole day, a full tank of gas, plenty of tools in case something on the truck broke, and with the ever-present box of spare belts for the engine, tire repair kits, etc., off we went. Thirty to forty-five minutes north of San Rafael, we came to what looked like a fairly good road heading west. There were no tire tracks on it, but we headed down it anyway. Within a mile, it was apparent it was a disused logging road. As the Ponderosa company had branched off to the east and to the west of this main road, they took all the pine trees that were commercially valuable. Then, when the cost of maintaining the roads offset their income, the roads in that area were abandoned. This appeared to be one of those orphaned areas.

As we twisted and turned, every so often, we would catch glimpses of foot trails that crossed the road. Occasionally, we'd get out and walk to a viewpoint and could see houses and ranches scattered on hillsides or in little side valleys. Then we came around a curve, and right in the middle of the road was a fallen pine tree, probably twenty inches in diameter and over thirty feet long with its six-foot-tall root ball of dirt. One thing I <u>hadn't</u> brought from home was my chain saw, which I really hadn't needed to use since our old partner, Ken James, had left it with me in Chihuahua.

"It looks like we're not going any further," said Ticker, and that was my feeling, too, for half a minute. Then I had a thought.

"I wonder if I can drag that tree out of the road?" I said. I hooked onto it with my fifty-foot cable and dragged it about a foot before the tree got stubborn and my wheels just spun on the road.

Then I had an interesting thought. Maybe I could <u>roll</u> it out of our way. So I ran the cable over the top of the root ball to a spot on the backside and tried again. Sure enough, it started to roll! Once it stopped rolling, I did the same thing again, rehitching the cable on the back side. After about three times of this, there was enough room for us to drive around it!

We continued down the road for another ten or fifteen minutes, but then it deteriorated really badly due to rain and snow runoff over the years. We were as far as our four-wheel-drive van was going to take us. It was a beautiful sunny March day, and I was so happy that we were out there together—Ticker, Dave, Dusty, and me.

"Let's head back to the main road to look for another road to explore. Shoot, we haven't even had lunch yet!"

After checking out a couple of more roads and getting bounced around for what we decided was enough for one day, we headed for home, a hot meal, and a seat that didn't move around underneath us. The exploring had begun!

Although Ticker had been a great sport about it, I knew I couldn't expect her—especially when she was riding with little seventeen-month-old Dusty on her lap—to do any more of that kind of exploring. This is what I was supposed to be doing with my partner. So I tackled the next job at home that would enable me—and soon Cliff and me—to get out for some serious survey work.

Dragging a downed tree off the road. You did what you had to do, because there was not a road crew that would be coming.

I would rebuild the engine on my motorcycle.

I had foreseen the necessity of doing that a few months previously while riding on the motocross track in Chihuahua. I had noticed an unusual clacking sound in my engine when I let off the throttle. I asked Tin and Tato what they thought it was. "That is the piston slapping around in the cylinder," they had told me. "You'll need to bore out the cylinder and get a new piston and set of rings." So on the next trip to El Paso, I had bought everything I needed and brought it to San Rafael with me. At least the parts salesman at the Yamaha dealership had told me I had everything I needed. But when I went to install the new cylinder onto the engine block, there was no gasket to seal between the two. After driving all over San Rafael, looking for gasket material with every mechanic I could find, I had a crazy thought. What if I used the heavy gauge aluminum foil that Ticker had in the kitchen? If I torqued everything down tightly, and the surfaces were perfectly flat, it just might work. You know what? That aluminum foil gasket held up for many, many hours over the next couple of years before I finally sold the motorcycle!

It was about this time, the end of April or so, that Ticker told me she was certain she was pregnant. We were both thrilled! Okay, we were both thrilled and had a lot of thoughts running through our minds as to what it would be like to have a new baby just about the time we were moving into a much more primitive location—an Indian community. We had trusted God in a lot of other situations. No reason to stop now.

Knowing how rough the roads were on my truck, I decided to start checking out some of the off-the-beaten-path areas by motorcycle. I went back to the roads that Ticker and I had explored, but now I was able to go further down them. Of course, the thought was always in my mind that if I found a community we wanted to live in, we would have to maintain the road ourselves. However, just knowing how many Tarahumara were back in those mountains was the most important thing at this point.

I made a few day trips out, just taking some snacks and water. I checked out several roads, talked to a few people about how many families and ranchos were further down the road or the trail I happened to be on that day, and started getting some good information about communities we would want to hike into. About this time, I needed to make a supply run to Chihuahua City. We had already sent a few letters to Cliff and Diane about San Rafael so we could stay in touch, but it would be a great time to visit with Cliff in person and tell him what I was finding out.

After the long nine-hour trip into Chihuahua, I sat down to dinner with Cliff and Diane. I told them how great it was to finally be exploring the areas outside of San Rafael. Diane seemed really interested, but much to my surprise, Cliff was less than excited. Although he and Diane were scheduled to move out in another month or so, here he was, feeling left out. I was quite taken by surprise. Instead of expressing enthusiasm, he was feeling something quite different which I did not understand. In fact, it was such an issue for Cliff that the next day, he called up one or two of the members of our field committee. They said they wanted to meet with me while I was in town.

"Steve, you have to understand that Cliff wants to be part of the decision-making process. That's perfectly reasonable, since you are partners," I was told.

"Well, I completely agree," I told them. "I'll just find out how to get to these communities, and Cliff and I will go together."

"No," I was told, "you need to wait for Cliff to get there."

So no more trips to even check out roads? Seriously? This was a strange development. I was now relegated to a role of waiting for several weeks until the S's finished their Spanish study and got settled into their new house in San Rafael. Knowing that I would have a lot of time on my hands, I thought about what to do with it. I went to some bookstores in Chihuahua and bought books on literature, science, etc., in order to get more fluent in Spanish on a variety of subjects. But I had a nagging feeling that this directive from the field committee members to essentially go back to San Rafael and find something to do for the next month or two while I waited for the S's was a foreshadowing of things to come.

STEVEN REAL

Cliff and Diane Join Us in San Rafael

During the next couple of weeks, an amazingly positive development was that I was able to find perhaps the only house for rent at that time in Los Tascates or San Rafael, and it was right next door to our house! So the S's did actually get moved out in April. We helped them get settled, had to build an outhouse for their little house, showed them the stores and other essential businesses around town, and otherwise made this new beginning for them as easy as possible.

As missionaries, we were in the people business. I personally have experienced years of being a shy and not very outgoing person, especially in high school before I became a Christian. A major development in my own person and personality was that God gave me His new nature, and the old nature with its uncertainty of where I fit in the world was replaced with a solid, hope-filled sense of confidence. One day at a time, then a month at a time and a year at a time, we advanced through our walk with the Lord. From our home church, to the churches we attended in the five and a half years of our training with New Tribes to become the Lord's ambassadors, God was preparing us to go to some place that His message had not yet gone.

This gave me joy and optimism, and I rather expected to see a similar spiritual energy in the lives of my coworkers. We all had our personal hurdles to overcome, so we weren't always sitting around during our social times with big smiles on our faces. But the fact that we felt led by God and had accepted the job of being missionaries necessitated that we made people—and communicating with those people—an essential part of our lives. Despite the S's path through the training program, a year of living in Chihuahua City in order to become fluent in Spanish, and with the added advantage of also being a linguist, mostly what I saw in Cliff was a person who wasn't exactly sure how he'd gotten to this point and was deeply threatened psychologically by the next steps.

Once they were settled in and familiar with the mountain life, I expected Cliff to get much more interested in the survey work of the Tarahumara communities, which was the most important thing on our agenda. Instead, with him living right next door, I saw Cliff's shyness and insecurity in not being very good with the Spanish language become real obstacles to moving forward with our work. It's not that I didn't feel for him; I, too, had gone through those painful months of struggling to communicate in a foreign language and knew what it felt like. But to stop trying and trying hard was to surrender. We had all been through Bible school, boot camp, and language school. In addition, Cliff and I had both spent an extra year in the intensive linguistics program.

Now the S's had just finished a full year of Spanish study in Chihuahua City. All of these years of preparation were meant to equip us to swim and not sink in the ocean of being foreign missionaries. Treading water or sitting at home, speaking English with our immediate family every day, was not going to help us navigate that ocean and reach our destination. If speaking Spanish was too much for Cliff to manage psychologically, learning the Tarahumara language would be completely out of reach.

In the first several weeks that they were in San Rafael, Cliff and I made one or two trips out into the hills for a day at a time in either my truck or his. But he soon saw the practicality and the economy of going by motorcycle for our initial survey work. He and Diane had to go out to El Paso for new visas in June, so he decided to come back with a motorcycle so we could travel together that way. What he brought back was a Harley-Davidson 125-cc dirt bike. I didn't even know Harley-Davidson <u>made</u> dirt bikes. He got used to riding it around town, and we had to work some bugs out of it. But after a week or two, he agreed that he was ready to head out into the mountains and see how he and the bike would get along.

Our first trip was to be a long day trip, and we packed only water and some food. I led the way for a couple of miles, checking over my shoulder to see that Cliff wasn't too far behind. But it's not fun being the guy who's eating someone else's dust. He stopped a couple of times, and then ended up lagging so far behind that I had to turn around and go back and look for him to make sure he was okay. So I told him we should trade, and he led the way. We would go until we saw what looked like a good-sized road on our left, which was the road that Ticker and I had taken in the van that went west until it petered out.

Cliff was not the athletic type, so he was struggling a bit with maintaining control of the motorcycle. On a curve in the road, he lost it and fell, the motorcycle sliding out from under him. He scraped up his hand and got some gravel in the cuts. We washed it off, but I could see the pain was getting to him, so we turned back toward home.

It took a couple of weeks before he felt ready to go try it again, but this time, we decided to make it a two-day trip and had backpacks with more food and water. But only three or four miles from town, he fell again. He said he couldn't go on, so again we aborted the trip and headed home.

A pattern was setting in that made me increasingly unhappy. It didn't matter if it was a trip out on the motorcycles or if I suggested we just take one of our trucks to go check out the Tarahumara communities. Cliff always had an excuse as to why he couldn't go. The excuses always revolved around his children and their health. We both knew that Diane was excited to see our progress toward moving into a Tarahumara community, and she was always in pretty good health. But each time I suggested to Cliff that we should set a goal to go back out for a survey trip in a couple of days, he would invariably say, "Let's wait another week. Little Brian has a runny nose, and I'm afraid it could turn into something more serious."

"But Ticker and Diane are here and can take care of that," I would say.

"No," he would say. "My first priority is my family, and I need to be here."

Yep, it was hard to argue that your kid might be sick, and it was impossible to say that your family is not your first priority. So there I was, boxed in for another couple of weeks. One delay of a week always was followed by a second or third delay. I was finding this "partnership" to be more like wearing a ball and chain.

"Where Did the Road Go?"

Finally, after two or three months of delays and excuses, we headed out again, prepared for a two- to three-day trip. This time, we got far down one of the roads to the west. The road dropped into a creek bed and seemed to disappear. "Where did the road go?" Cliff asked as I pulled up behind him.

"Down the creek, I think," I replied. "Let's go see."

The creek was flat and about ten feet wide at this point, with six or eight inches of water running through it but passable. Sure enough, after a hundred yards, the bulldozed road climbed back up out of the creek and continued along a hillside. We drove until the road pretty much ended, and we could see a community of several houses a few miles away in the distance. We had been descending in elevation for a while, so the vegetation had changed a lot. The pine trees were much shorter and rather sparse. There were a lot more oak trees in this area. The hills were more covered in grass and brush than anything else.

We saw a very distinct foot trail heading in the direction of the distant group of ranches, so we found an especially dense area of undergrowth and stashed our motorcycles there. We headed off with our backpacks and sleeping bags for our first real trek into a remote Tarahumara community.

The trail we were on led to a community named Apórabo, according to a Tarahumara man I had talked to briefly on one of my solo trips a few months earlier. The trail would appear to be well-traveled in places, and then deteriorate into a network of rabbit trails that apparently interconnected small ranches. The terrain was really rough in spots, and at one point, we lost the trail entirely and ended up in a steep-sided creek bed. Through the trees ahead of us, we could see a vast grassy hillside with a wide trail on it.

Rather than backtrack to some random trail, we decided to keep descending through this canyon. At times, we had to take off our backpacks, then one of us would climb down the rocks, and the other one would lower the backpacks down with a rope. Just as we climbed out of the canyon half an hour later, I heard a screech a few feet away from me. I looked up, and a gray fox was staring back at me from the top of a rock. This was the most exotic animal I had seen up to that time while hiking out there in the mountains. Apparently, we had gotten too close to this fox's den, and it was trying to scare us away.

One of the main things we discovered on that one and only trip for Cliff and me into the back country was that it was going to be hard to find people who were willing to talk to us. These folks were really pretty isolated. We learned that the other small communities in the area were named Baquivo and Ochaivo. We hiked up onto a large rounded hill, the closest thing to a mesa that we had come across. On top of it was a large Catholic church which I would guess was a hundred years old, perhaps older.

We learned that the local priest only came out once or twice a year for services. Nobody said from where, so I assumed from San Rafael but perhaps from even further away. Now that was good to know. Cliff and I spent two nights out there sleeping under the stars. We tried to estimate how many ranches and people were in an area of an hour to two hours walking distance. It was the closest we had seen to a "concentration" of Tarahumara on the west side of the main logging road.

On the third day, as we hiked back toward the motorcycles, I looked back from a hill and tried to imagine us living out there—Ticker, Dave, Dusty and I, and the new baby. It would be really tough to be out there without a vehicle, and I didn't see any way we would ever get a road built that far from the main road. Still, something told me I needed to come back out here again.

"Breaker, Breaker One-Niner. What's Your Twenty?"

Some time that summer, I believe, is when we first got our two-way radio so that we could stay in touch with the folks in Chihuahua

City a lot easier. It was called a single sideband radio. The antenna for it was an interesting arrangement. A coaxial cable, like what we still use today for cable TV, ran from the radio to the outdoors, where there was a splitter. A coax cable has two wire components: the center copper wire which is shielded with special insulation, and the outer wire, which has the screw on connector attached to it. At the splitter, a thirty-foot long piece of solid copper wire, about 12-gauge in size, was connected to the center wire, and another thirty-foot long piece to the outer wire. This sixty-foot long "antenna" had to be hung from two high poles or trees or something equivalent and placed perpendicular to the line of sight to Chihuahua City. One side of the antenna was for transmission, and the other side was for reception. Amazingly, even strung from our house in San Rafael between the roof and the tallest pole I could find, and although we were down in a valley, we were able to get reception from and transmit to Chihuahua, which was over two hundred miles away.

Our field committee had gotten permission to use the radios from the Mexican government, which was required by law. We were only able to use them on the condition that we spoke entirely in Spanish. Also, we learned that the best time for transmitting and receiving was in the early morning hours. So at seven o'clock each morning, each one of the stations in the mountains turned on their radio, and we all reported in. At the time, there were only three tribal locations—Baborigame, where the Tepehuan team was located; Guachochic, where the Central Tarahumara team was; and us in San Rafael, the Western Tarahumara team.

It was a great idea to have these radios. Any sort of emergency could occur at any time, and that family's or team's only recourse had always been to get in their truck(s) and drive to where there was help. At least this way, if someone were sick and getting worse or got seriously injured, we now had a chance to let the folks in Chihuahua as well as our coworkers in the mountains know about it, although we only talked once per morning. Later, we did have some situations crop up where we arranged for extra radio contact times for a specific emergency situation This was especially helpful if we had to ask for an airplane to come in and take someone to Chihuahua. But we also had to learn the hard way that once the air temperature got warmer and the winds picked up in the midmornings or later in the day, reception became difficult or impossible. Thus, we started our days with a 7:00 a.m. radio check-in from each tribal location.

4.3 The Van Goes Off the Road

"Well, would you look at that!" said Cliff. "That looks like a 'Working on the Railroad' song by Charlie Daniels or Willie Nelson."

We had just come around a curve in the road, and two hundred feet in front of us, twenty-five or thirty men were manually changing the railroad tracks. But this was not a section of the railroad that just paralleled the road we were on. Rather, at this very moment, they were changing the section where there was a road crossing.

Every six to ten weeks, Cliff or I had to make a supply run to Chihuahua City. This wasn't any fun, but the most crucial thing that we could not easily get in San Rafael was propane gas. So once we knew that we only had a couple of weeks of gas left for our stoves and refrigerators, and if we did not already have a scheduled trip to the border for new visas or other business, we would have to make a trip to either Creel or Chihuahua. The forty-five-kilo tanks were big, too, over four feet tall and weighing about 120 pounds full. They didn't fit very well in Cliff's Ford Bronco, so one day that summer, we took my van with several empty tanks and headed for Creel. The railroad foreman came walking over to me to talk, so I got out to ask him how long this might take.

"Hard to say," he said. "We just got the rails nailed to the new ties and still need to put all that gravel back on so that you can drive over the tracks."

That was for sure, I thought. The underneath side of my truck would surely get hung up on those railroad rails, and I wasn't going to take that chance.

For the next forty-five minutes or an hour, Cliff and I had to just watch as the men worked like ants on a whale carcass. When they had shoveled four or five inches of gravel on top of the railroad ties, a fellow appeared in front of me, waving his arms.

"Go ahead across now," he said. The gravel still didn't come to the top of the wooden railroad ties, and there really wasn't much of a slope where the roadbed should be, so I showed him where they needed to put some more gravel.

I started up the truck and gave it a try, but it was obvious I was going to get stuck on top of the railroad tracks, so I backed up. Unfortunately, this railroad crossing was at a sharp left-hand turn in the road. As I backed up, I could see I was pretty close to a drop-off on the right-hand side of the truck. I still needed to back up another six feet or so for the men to continue putting gravel down as a ramp to get over the railroad tracks.

I could see the right rear corner of my truck in the mirror, but I couldn't see the right front wheel and how close it was to the edge of the drop-off on that side.

"Hey, Cliff, come over here and give me a hand, please," I said. We walked up in front of the truck, and I showed him my predicament.

"I can't see that right front wheel when I'm in the truck, so all I need you to do is keep an eye on that wheel for me. Signal me if it gets too close to the edge. I'll be going slowly as I back up."

He nodded his head in agreement, and I got back in the truck. The foreman came over and stood by Cliff, wondering what we were talking about in English. Then as I backed up very slowly, he, too, stood there in front of the truck, watching me. I was especially concerned because that edge of the road had been built up using an old steel railroad rail to hold the dirt back, and the edge of the road went straight down about four feet from there. It wasn't sloped at all like a dirt bank normally would be.

I backed up about three feet, got out, and started to walk around the front of the truck to look at that wheel, and both Cliff and the foreman with their hands up motioned me back and said, "Go ahead back, back." So I got back in the truck and started slowly backing up a little further. I hadn't even gone two feet when there was a sudden *thunk* sound, and the right side of the truck dropped a foot and hit hard. I was still looking straight ahead into the eyes of both Cliff and the foreman, and all of a sudden, they were waving their arms and yelling, "Stop! Stop!"

No s———t! my mind screamed. I had the most sickening feeling wash over me. The wheel had gone off the edge of the road, and the front differential had hit the railroad rail. As soon as I heard it hit, the front of the truck also started sliding to the right, metal grinding on metal.

Have you ever been in an accident and you can remember how everything unfolded as if in slow motion? That's exactly what started happening as soon as the right-hand side of the truck dropped down.

"My truck is going to roll upside down off the side of the road, and there's nothing I can do about it! Those freaking idiots!" Very "un-missionary" like, a string of profanities ran through my mind in mere nanoseconds. Powerless to do anything, I hung onto the steering wheel fiercely, bracing for the truck to go upside down and onto its roof.

With a solid jolt, all of a sudden, it stopped sliding. The front differential had hit the steel rail just in time. The truck was leaning at a crazy angle. Once I realized it wasn't going to go over the edge, I knew I had to get out, and I didn't dare move quickly.

I opened the driver's side door slowly and carefully, which was really hard since it was at a huge upward angle. Even as I got it open, I prepared to jump in case the truck started moving again. Guys came running over and helped hold the door open while I got out.

"I told you to watch that side of the truck!" I exploded at Cliff. "Why did you let me back right off the side of the road? All I asked you to do was watch that wheel!" I was furious, and even though nobody else there spoke English, they had a pretty good idea what I was saying.

Cliff, sheepish as always, really had nothing to say. I walked around the truck to see what we were going to do now. The wheel was three feet or so above the ground, hanging out in space, so we had a lot of work to do to get even a jack underneath it. I calmed down after a few moments. I looked around, and the solution occurred to me.

"We need to build up a platform underneath the wheel on that side of the truck," I said to Cliff. "Let's start dragging those old railroad ties over here. We're going to need twelve or fifteen of them at least."

The anger I was feeling fueled my body for the next couple of hours as we built up a platform underneath the right side of the truck. Every time I stepped back and looked at the crazy angle at which the truck was leaning, I couldn't believe this had happened. The truck was still extremely close to the tipping point. I prayed it didn't go over once we got around to jacking it up.

The railroad crew continued on with their job, filled up the railroad crossing with gravel, and continued down the tracks, changing railroad ties and rails. Cliff and I built a platform almost three feet wide and three feet high out of old railroad ties to create a path for the truck's wheel to back up on. Eventually, we were able to put the jack underneath it. "Stay back, Cliff, while I lift the truck with the jack. It could slip, and we don't need two of us to get crushed."

Little by little, I lifted the truck. We put more wood and railroad ties underneath it to support it, and after about three hours, I was ready to back up again.

This time, I didn't even ask Cliff for his help. I didn't trust him anymore, at least not right now, so I just calculated my turn radius, held the wheel steady, and backed up slowly about 2 feet. I got out and looked for myself, then continued backing up until the truck was back on the road. Cliff was apologetic, of course, and felt terrible, but it would be hard for me to trust him with something really important again for a while. It was just another incident in a long string of events in which he did not seem terribly attentive or involved. I had a lot of thoughts going through my head on how to work with this guy as my partner, but it wasn't easy to sort them all out at the moment.

So Many of Our Problems Need Spiritual Solutions

Psychological problems, like ego or anxiety, are also spiritual problems. Emotional problems, like anger or fear, are also spiritual problems. There are also many physical issues that can be dealt with on a spiritual basis. All of us as human beings have to deal with a variety of these things. It's just part of human nature and a result of living in a world that's been corrupted in so many ways. But the Lord tells us that we don't have to be subjugated by the weaknesses and corruption that are in this world. We don't have to let our backgrounds and our baggage hinder us from being who and what God wants us to be.

The Apostle Paul tells us in 2 Timothy 1:7, "For God has not given us a spirit of fear, but of power and of love and of a sound mind." In fact, in 1 Corinthians chapter 1, Paul talks about how "God has chosen the weak things of the world to put to shame the things which are mighty...that no flesh should glory in His presence." Also, he says in chapter 2:

> **And I, brethren, when I came to you, did not come with excellence of speech or of wisdom declaring to you the testimony of God. For I determined not to know anything among you except Jesus Christ and Him crucified. I was with you in weakness, in fear, and in much trembling. And my speech and my preaching were not with persuasive words of human wisdom, but in demonstration of the Spirit and of power, that your faith should not be in the wisdom of men but in the power of God.**

Paul admits that he had weakness and fear and trembling. Having those things is not what makes us ineffective for God. Letting those things become giants in our minds and saying that we cannot defeat them are what make us ineffective for God.

Paul had to communicate the Gospel in different languages and in a variety of cultures around the Middle East. He endured situations that were dangerous, life-threatening, and completely out of his previous realm of experience. But he depended on God to get him through each and every one of them. His goal was to be faithful to the calling God had placed on him, to take the Gospel to the Jews first, and then God directed him to go to the Gentiles.

There were several lessons for me to learn from my experience of having Cliff as a partner. Perhaps first and foremost was that I wish I had known how to encourage him to give over his fears and sense of inferiority to the Lord. I'm sure I could have prayed for him more. He needed to trust God more vigorously to become fluent in Spanish and to get over his shyness around our Mexican neighbors. He needed to trust God to take care of his kids and family while he was gone for just two or three days. I don't remember specifically how I entered into the conversations with him on these or other subjects. But I do know that it was essential for us, both him and me, to face those issues head-on.

I wish I had been more mature in my Christian life and known how I could help him bear his burdens. When our fellow brothers and sisters in the Lord help us do this, we either: (1) see the issue clearly and work through it; or (2) begin to refocus on our life goals, which may make us move on to something different; or (3) we refuse to change and are therefore forced to change, like getting fired, for example, which can involve shame and trauma. Perhaps through our conversations with them, and perhaps to a great degree in their own discussions, Cliff and Diane were moving toward number 2.

The Aerial Survey

A month or so after getting back from that supply trip, realizing that it would take us quite a while to check out every Indian community to the northwest of San Rafael, we decided to do an aerial survey. Of course, we called on our good friend, Dave Wolf, of

Calvary Missionary Fellowship up in Arizona. Dave had been flying our New Tribes missionaries around for a variety of reasons for well over a year by that time.

The Tarahumara have been pushed into some of the most remote and inaccessible terrain in all of Mexico

Dave met us at the airstrip in San Rafael one beautiful, clear day. You know what? We actually had a lot of beautiful clear days living in the Sierra Madre! So, on another one of them, we climbed to an altitude about 1,500 to 2,000 feet above the ground and flew north, keeping the main logging road in sight. Over Apórabo and Baquivo, we could see that there were indeed thirty or forty ranches scattered in an area of perhaps fifteen or twenty square miles. Continuing north, we saw other smaller communities. Then we got to the point where the main logging road turned west, but we flew on further north. We did a big circuit and could see quite a few homes and ranches as well as a school down there. In my notes, as we circled over this particular area, I wrote "large Indian community." Later, I would find out that this was El Manzano.

As we headed back south, Dave asked us about the community to the east of the road that had a lot of homes and a really nice long airstrip. I told him, "That's Ocóbiachi. There's a big Catholic church and Catholic presence there. We think it's a good idea to avoid living there and try to get into a Tarahumara community where we won't be butting heads with a Catholic priest."

The aerial survey helped us in a couple of hours to find clusters of ranch communities it took days to find by hiking in.

"Well," said Dave, "that's a really nice airstrip for me to meet you at once you move out from San Rafael. We'll have to keep that in mind." And Dave was right. I would use that airstrip a couple of times in the not-too-distant future.

4.4 Real Child No. 3

Ticker's pregnancy with Dusty had been problematic, so we were not going to take any chances with this current one. On a trip to Chihuahua in September, our new doctor, Dr. Nesbitt, determined that the baby would be ready to deliver about the third week of November. He would not take a chance on a natural delivery but would opt for a C-section. After the two C-sections that Ticker had had, there was a significant amount of scar tissue built up, so another C-section was the best option, in his opinion. He had also detected that Ticker had a hernia that needed to be repaired. With this many surgeries behind her, Ticker and I prayed about whether or not to have her tubes tied to avoid another pregnancy. Should this be our last child?

We asked God for guidance. We were also aware of the theory that, when a woman has her tubes tied, it can affect her normal hormonal cycles. There was even speculation at the time as to whether or not having the tubes tied could contribute to hormone problems or even ovarian or uterine cancers. These were things that were difficult to investigate in the days before the Internet. We had to rely on printed publications and information from doctors and friends of ours.

In order for Ticker to not have to travel at the end of that last trimester, we arranged for her to be at the mission's guest home in Chihuahua City for the last six weeks of her pregnancy. When she had been pregnant with Dusty, her spotting had happened while we were driving and visiting family on our way to Mexico six weeks before the delivery. This time, she would get some good bed rest and not even have to travel into Chihuahua City on the train so close to the end.

Ticker, Dave, Dusty, and I all went into Chihuahua in time for Dusty's second birthday, October 8. Ticker took Dusty on the train from San Rafael since it was a pretty smooth means of travel. Dave and I went in the van. After getting Ticker settled into the guest home with all the clothes and personal items that she would need for the next six weeks, I bought supplies, and Dave and I drove back out to San Rafael. Dave would be my little buddy for the next four weeks while his mom rested up for the big delivery.

Even more than a kid in a candy shop, Dave's blue eyes lit up. He had taken a liking to rocks in a big way. Every time we went through

Creel, he wanted to stop at "the rock store," which was Father Ver Planken's store and museum. We were both fascinated by the colors and strange layering, crystallization, and other features of rocks. So when I told him we would stop there again, he was excited. We ended up buying quite a few different rocks over the next few years, giving them to each other for birthday and Christmas presents. I still have a nice collection of them. On our way back to San Rafael, we once again enjoyed a long visit to "the rock store." I probably bought another book or two that I didn't already have on the Tarahumara. I was definitely still going to be tied down to a lot of time at home with Cliff so unwilling to get out into the Indian communities.

The delivery of the baby would be at the Clinica del Parque, which I think was the biggest hospital in Chihuahua at the time. After a couple of ultrasounds, the technician and doctor still believed that the baby would be a girl. They had told us this before regarding both Dave and Dusty, since it seemed all three of them were shy and were hiding the view of their private parts from the ultrasound techs and the doctors. The determination, "80 to 90 percent accurate," that they would be girls, was then based on their heart rate. Apparently, girl fetuses have a faster heart rate than their male counterparts. Those were years in which an ultrasound looked pretty darned fuzzy to me, kind of like when the Hubble space telescope was broken and looking at the images was a big waste of time. I also wonder if medical science has since then revised its range of heartbeats to be more accurate. They were way off "80 to 90 percent accurate," since they were 100 percent wrong about all three of my boys!

November 26, 1982, the day of the Caesarian section, started off normally enough. I was now plenty fluent in Spanish to not need anyone to accompany me as I had when Dusty was born. The doctor and nurse had given me a ballpark time when Ticker would be going into surgery. It turned out to be a pretty busy day for the maternity ward. There were three or four other fathers there in the waiting area with various family members, all looking forward to the news of their new babies. I knew there would be a recovery time for Ticker that was different for a woman delivering naturally. Still, the appointed time came and went without me hearing a word from anybody. Naturally, I started getting rather nervous.

Anything could go wrong with a combination of the C-section, hernia repair, and her tubes being tied. But why didn't they at least come out and tell me that the baby was delivered safely once that part was complete? I suppose I had to wait for the doctor himself to finish everything. Okay, I just needed to be patient and trust in the Lord. Then I noticed that right there, next to our waiting area, was an elevator that would occasionally open up, and an infant in an incubated bassinet would be rolled past us on its way to the nursery.

Finally, I started getting up and walking over to each one of the mobile bassinets/incubators, hoping to see my baby. This was crazy, like waiting at some huge department store, sitting around with several other people, and waiting for a clerk to call your name so you could load up your new refrigerator. After looking at the names on two or three new arrivals, another infant came off the elevator, and a tag on the outside of the incubator simply said, "Real—Hombre." The word *hombre* means "male." Yes! I was ecstatic! I had another son, and he looked quite healthy. Then I had to go looking for a doctor or nurse to find out if Ticker was okay. I was finally told that she was in recovery and was doing fine. Thank the Lord! It was a great day again, after all!

A doctor or nurse never did come out and tell me about Eric's delivery or that Ticker was doing fine. I was 0 for 3 in the "Congratulations, Mr. Real, you have a healthy new baby!" department. No problem. That game was over, but I had won! Three home runs!

HE WHO HAS BEGUN A GOOD WORK

Dave holds his new-born brother Eric

Recovery and Permission for a Trip to Chicago

Ticker's recovery went well. Of course, that's easy for me to say. I wasn't the one who had been sliced and diced and sewn back together. Obviously, it was more painful even than a regular C-section, but she was tough. Perhaps it was because we now had access to a telephone, being in Chihuahua City for a while. Perhaps it was just a brainstorm on her part or an idea from one of Ticker's family members. But the thought occurred to someone that maybe the field committee would allow us to take a little time for a short vacation since we were getting close to Christmas.

After about two and a half weeks of her recovering at the guest home in Chihuahua, we asked if we could go up to Chicago for Christmas, which was now only about ten days away. We didn't know what to expect. The executive and field committees both knew that the proximity to the US could be a problem in a few ways, not least of which was that every missionary going to Mexico might feel like it was a fairly easy drive to just "go home" if things got tough. And things will inevitably get tough living the life of a missionary sooner or later. The temptation to not stay in the country of service continually for the customary five-year period, too, would always be there.

However, they granted our request. We made the trip in three long days and had a great Christmas with Ticker's family in Chicago and with mine for a few days on our way back through St. Louis, Missouri. Our families were obviously very excited to see the newest little addition to the family, but this was also the first time they would get to see Dusty. After two years and four months away from them, Dave was excited to see his cousins and aunts and uncles and grandparents again.

By the time we got back to San Rafael, Ticker had been gone for just over three months. With just the trip up to Chicago and back since delivering Eric, she had traveled over four thousand miles on the road. The previous three months had been unusually disruptive for all of us, and Ticker was especially exhausted. Now we were settling down for the next phase of our work, which was to decide on an Indian community to move into. And there was an additional new twist.

While we were in Chihuahua City with Ticker recovering from the delivery, out in San Rafael, Cliff and Diane had been doing some soul-searching. They had come to the conclusion that tribal missionary work was not for them. They advised the field committee of their decision, packed up all of their things, and planned on going back to Chicago. When they arrived in Chihuahua City, they sat down for conversations with the field committee members. They were encouraged to consider working in Chihuahua in support work, where there were needs in the school for missionaries' children and for a new bookkeeper on staff. So it was that they made a decision that was best for everyone involved. I was glad that they would still be involved in helping all of us in the tribes. I hoped that they would be happy in their new work.

HE WHO HAS BEGUN A GOOD WORK

An Angel Shakes Me Awake in the Middle of the Night

We had only been back in our house in San Rafael for ten days or two weeks. It was the middle of the night when all of a sudden, it was as if someone had shaken my shoulder. I opened my eyes and saw that the kitchen light was on. For some reason, I was instantly wide awake. I got up and went into the kitchen, where Ticker turned to me with a strange look in her eyes.

"What's wrong?" I asked her.

"I'm not sure," she answered. "I feel awful about myself, about life, about everything," she said.

I hugged her, and we sat down and talked for a while. She said she even felt suicidal, which of course shocked me deeply. My mind searched for reasons. I didn't get it. We had a brand-new, awesome, healthy son. We had just come back from seeing lots of family and enjoying a great Christmas holiday. It should have been comforting and refreshing. But I immediately thought of all the traveling we had done and felt that we had overdone it. I had heard about the "baby blues" that some women experience after childbirth. She hadn't felt like this after Dave and Dusty had been born, though.

We talked for a while before we went back to bed. I assured her that I was there to help her with all the tasks around the house and taking care of the boys. There were no other priorities higher than that for me. That made her feel a bit better, so we went back to sleep and agreed to talk about it more in the morning.

It was a delicate thing, talking about her feelings and where they had come from. She did agree that she was exhausted physically and emotionally. We also talked about whether this could be a result of a change in her hormones, since she had had her tubes tied. But, of course, it was a mystery to us. Neither of us felt that we could take a good guess at what was going on medically. Like everybody, we felt that we had made the best choices possible with the information we had at the time. So we had to trust the Lord for her to recover her strength completely, and we went on with our lives.

Once again, we had no partners to have fellowship and prayer with. The path ahead for finding a community to move into would be mostly between us and the Lord and in consultation with the field committee, of course. But we had each other, and that was a lot! And so began an important new chapter in our ministry.

Chapter 5

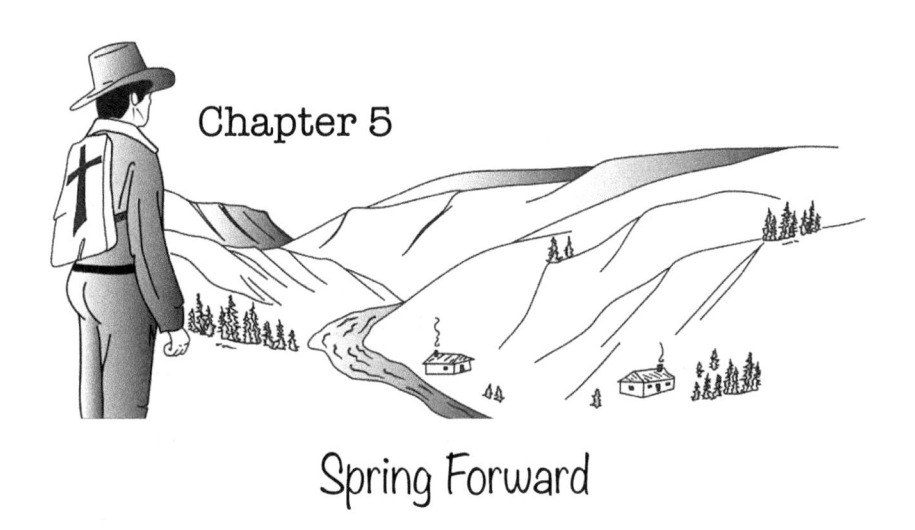

Spring Forward

5.1 Now What?

The weeks and months following Cliff and Diane's departure became a crazy blend of emotions, unexpected events, new options, and very important choices.

Who in Chihuahua City would potentially be our new partners?

Were we going to have to wait again for months and months on end before we could move to a Tarahumara community?

Did I have a good relationship with the field committee? Or did they think I had contributed to the S's discouragement?

How was Ticker doing? Was she feeling better? Or was something of concern going on with her body and hormones?

Enjoying the new addition to our family, Eric, was our biggest delight. He was healthy and happy, and his brothers absolutely loved him. I was anxious to get back out to survey the Indian communities, but it was really important right then to have our family life stabilized as a top priority. I was actually quite happy to be home, helping Ticker on a daily basis. I wanted to see her get back to 100 percent with her health. Life in San Rafael was quite manageable on every human level. Still, we had been in town for several months now, waiting for the S's to get up to speed and into our tribal ministry. The delays to moving on in our ministry were really beginning to wear on me personally.

STEVEN REAL

Suspicious Minds

———ɯ———

You know how you sometimes have a sixth sense that something is out of balance in your world? That's how I felt in the spring of 1983. We had told all of our friends and neighbors in San Rafael that we were going to move out to an Indian community and teach the Bible to the Tarahumara. And yet it seemed that all we did, month after month, was live in our house in this little out-of-the-way town in the mountains. One day, I somehow ran into the director of the Ponderosa sawmill, by far the biggest business in the whole area. Besides the two or three medical doctors, he was definitely the most educated and worldly wise man who lived in town. I always tried to have intelligent and personal conversations with people like him in order to be a good Christian witness. So I decided to ask him over for dinner, and it turned out to be quite an enlightening experience.

After some small talk for a while, he asked me just what it was that we were doing there in San Rafael. We hadn't started a church, had we? With a tinge of embarrassment because we still had not progressed very much visibly in our stated goal of moving into an Indian community, I once again told him that it was our purpose to teach the Tarahumara people about God. However, I could tell from his demeanor that there was something much bigger on his mind.

He asked me if I read the newspapers and followed the news. I told him that I had read the newspaper almost every day when I lived in Chihuahua City. I enjoyed the news quite a lot, and it helped me to understand what was going on in Mexico and helped my Spanish language abilities tremendously. But there was no way to get a newspaper here in San Rafael.

He told me that there was significant speculation in the media right then about certain Americans living in Mexico. "It's being widely discussed that there are CIA agents posing as teachers and other professionals throughout the country who are keeping an eye on political developments here in Mexico," he said.

I was shocked. So that was it. He wanted to confront me, although quite politely, about what my true role was there in San Rafael. I knew that there were many Mexicans who were suspicious of Americans throughout the country and, mostly, their suspicions revolved around political intrigue. America had "purchased" about half of Mexico's national territory, under duress, in the late 1800s, and many Mexicans were still incredibly resentful of that. There were also strong undercurrents of Marxist and socialist philosophies in modern-day Mexico, evidenced by the leftist guerrilla uprisings just the decade before. I could see the suspicion in the director's eyes and knew I needed to give him a better answer.

"Well, I assure you," I told him, "that I want nothing to do with politics. I have no idea what the CIA is really like, and I don't really care. I have taken a vow before God to do His work, and I'm very content doing that. I've had a few months of our plans being interrupted because of our partners leaving, which has been rather frustrating for me. But I can assure you that my wife and I want to get on with our work. It now looks like we will be able to push forward with finding a Tarahumara community to move to on our own."

He told me how easy it would be to learn the Tarahumara language because it "only has five or six letters in the alphabet, and maybe a few hundred words."

I know I didn't laugh at this because it was a serious subject, and he was an educated professional. I proceeded to tell him that I had linguistic training and could assure him that was not the case. I asked him if he knew of anyone who had learned Tarahumara when so many Mexicans have lived amongst the Tarahumara for almost three hundred years now. He said he knew of a couple of Mexicans who knew a few phrases, but that was about all.

"That pretty much says it all," I told him. "So many people think that their language is simple and simplistic, but it is far from it. It will probably take me twenty years to become fluent," I said. "As a matter of fact, Tarahumara does, actually, have a simpler alphabet than either Spanish or English, but as is the case with languages all over the world, that is an absolutely certain indication that it will have a very complex grammar structure." I showed him just a little bit of the books that I had purchased on the Tarahumara language, but I could see he wasn't terribly interested in them.

"And you're quite certain that they have a soul?" he asked me. "I understand that they are a little bit lower on the evolutionary scale than those of us who are of European descent," he said, "although they are more developed than the animal kingdom."

Again I was shocked, but it was a point of view that I had heard about before and knew that sooner or later I would be having this conversation with someone. Still, for such an educated man and his wife to hold these views in the late twentieth century was astounding.

After they left, I felt once again a sense of urgency to get on with our job. Not only did we have the commission from the Lord Jesus Himself to take His Gospel to the Tarahumara people, but there were obviously eyes on us, and it wasn't helpful that we looked as if we had no urgency to pursue our goals.

Broken Down Missionaries from Up North (I Think)

A couple of weeks later, we had a most unusual visit from three American men from Arizona. They drove up to the house one day in a four-wheel-drive crew cab pickup truck and asked if I was Steve Real, the American missionary. I told them that I was and asked who they might be.

"We're missionaries from a church in Arizona," said the most senior of the three. "We're doing an exploratory trip to see what kind of missionary work is going on down here. We were told that you're planning to evangelize the Tarahumara Indians."

"Well, you were told correctly," I said. I asked them about their spiritual beliefs, and it seemed that they were from a Bible-believing church. We talked about where we were hoping to move to, etc., and had a good conversation for an hour or more. It was getting close to dinnertime, and they asked where they could get some food. They didn't want to impose, and it was rather at the last minute for Ticker to try to prepare something for them. So they said they would go into town and wondered about a place to sleep for the night.

I told them about the questionable accommodations in town, where they may get bedbugs, but at least they would be indoors. They asked if there was a place that they could just camp for the night. Since the S's had left, the house next door was still empty, and I told them they could camp on our property or next door if they wanted to. We were able to offer them water and a hot shower. So they went into town, got dinner, and came back a while later and set up camp for the night.

The next morning, Ticker prepared coffee and breakfast for all of us. The youngest of the guys was probably in his late thirties, perhaps early forties. He told me that he had been a DEA agent who had to retire early with a disability. He had spent many, many days doing stakeouts sitting in a vehicle, and it had resulted in him getting bad circulation in his legs. It sounded feasible, I supposed. Then he asked me if I had heard of an American in that part of the mountains called El Guero: "The White Guy." Apparently, he was an American drug dealer that was working somewhere in our general area. I told him that I had not and asked a little bit about his age and a physical description. I said I wanted to keep an eye out for someone who might show up someday or could be a threat to us.

After an hour or so, the guys all got packed up to leave but then couldn't get their truck started. They were obviously upset and a bit embarrassed as they started looking for the problem. They pulled off the air cleaner and checked for gas in the carburetor, cranked the engine over and over again, but it wouldn't start. They got out a toolbox and started checking spark plug wires and the spark plugs themselves. After a little while, the battery went dead, and I started charging it from my truck. Once it was fully charged, they tried a few more things but couldn't get their truck to start. I asked what I could do to help, but they said they didn't want to bother me and continued to go from one thing to another under the hood, looking for the problem. I thought about asking them if I could just jump in and help them figure it out, but they seemed to be mechanically inclined, so I let them do their thing.

Around noon, they asked if there was an auto parts store in town which, of course, there wasn't, but I told them where they might be able to find a mechanic who could help them out. They didn't want to bother me any further, and I was studying Spanish and Tarahumara, so they walked into town and came back with a used distributor for their truck. Still, the truck wouldn't start.

Finally, it was late afternoon, and they were just about at their wits end. They decided that the problem was a condenser and a coil, which they couldn't get there in San Rafael, so I told them that I could try to order it from Chihuahua City for them the next morning when we talked on the radio.

They camped again that night, and in the morning, I got Peter Thiessen on the radio. He would purchase the parts for them, drive them down to the train station in Chihuahua, and put them on a rush order to us so we could get them on the afternoon train.

I went down to the train station with the youngest of the Arizona missionaries. As we drove back to the house, he said to me, "Did you notice how those soldiers were looking at you and me?"

"No," I said. "Why?"

"Well, they were looking at my boots. I never thought about the fact that these are military issue boots. I wore them while I was in the DEA, and they just seemed like good tough boots to bring with me on this trip. I hope that doesn't create some kind of suspicion about you." It didn't create a bad situation for me right then but was an incident that gave me some good insight several years later and probably helped keep my son, Dave, and his wife from danger.

The parts that we had ordered from Chihuahua City did not solve the problems with the truck, so I finally told the guys I would like to look at it. It didn't take me too long to find that the distributor cap was shorting out through the center shaft, an unusual situation, so I ordered a new one of those over the radio the next morning. The poor guys from Arizona had to camp out one more night! It actually turned out to be a blessing for us to have some American company, and it was the Lord's way of taking care of them with an imminent mechanical breakdown of their truck. If that part would have shorted out a day or two later, with them having no way to order a new part, who knows where they would have been stranded? So, yes, God works in mysterious ways! There are reasons for what we see as delays so often in life.

Looking back on that experience, I will always wonder if they were indeed missionaries as they stated. Less than two years later, a US DEA agent was kidnapped, tortured, and killed in Guadalajara in a drug cartel attack that became a major international incident. We had no idea at the time that the drug trafficking in Mexico was increasing exponentially year over year. Looking into the organization of the drug cartels and how to shut them down had become a major effort on the part of the DEA. Were the Arizona "missionaries" really what they said they were? Or were they an undercover scouting operation sent to check us out as well as the drug operations in northern Mexico? I guess I will never know in this lifetime.

The story of what happened to Kiki Camarena, the DEA agent who was killed, is a shocking one. The subsequent documentaries attest to how widespread the corruption of Mexican officials was becoming during that time. The Lord kept us very safe from the dangers of those drug traffickers, dirty cops, and corrupt politicians the whole time we lived there. He had a greater purpose for us—to build His church—and He was not going to let the gates of hell prevail against us!

Old Spanish Gold

A few weeks after the fellows from Arizona had left, I went down to the train station to pick up my mail. As usual, there was a small contingent of soldiers at the station. They were the de facto police force in several places along the Chihuahua to the Pacific railroad. As I was going back to my truck, an army captain walked over to me.

"Excuse me," he said, "I wonder if I can talk to you about something that has come to my attention?"

"Certainly," I said. "What might that be?"

"I'd rather talk about it in private," he replied. "Would it be okay to talk with you at your house?" he said.

"Of course," I replied. "I'm on my way back home right now."

"That would be perfect," he said.

"Do you know where I live?" I asked.

With a sly smile, he answered that yes, he did. "I will be there in a few minutes," he said.

Just a few minutes after I got home and told Ticker about the conversation, I heard his pickup truck pulling into the yard. I opened the door and invited him in. The soldier with him stood outside the door with his back against the house and with his automatic rifle in the ready position across his chest. I will say it looked a little disconcerting as I closed the door and invited the captain to have a seat. Ticker served both of us coffee.

"I'll get right to the point," he said. "I've had reports that you have bought some old Spanish gold from a Tarahumara man," he said. "You know that that gold is the property of the Mexican government, don't you?"

I was astounded to say the least. "Captain," I said, "I have never bought anything like that from a Tarahumara man or anyone else. I'm not sure who's telling you such things, but I can assure you it is not true. So who is this man who supposedly sold it to me? I think he is the one you need to be talking to."

"I've only been told that he is an older Tarahumara man," the captain said. "But the gold is in the shape of a brick which is how it used to be transported. Much of this gold was stolen during the mining days and has been hidden in caves throughout the mountains. Sometimes the Tarahumara find it and try to sell it. It belongs to the government and must be returned. It is illegal to have it in your possession."

"I can absolutely assure you, Captain, that I don't have anything like that in my possession. In fact, I give you my permission now or at any time to search my entire house and my truck. A few months ago, a Tarahumara man came to me and said he knew where there was an old gold mine and wanted my financial help so that he could start digging the ore again. I'll tell you what I told him: you could show me 'fool's gold' or any kind of a chunk of metal, and I would not know if it were gold or not. Plus, I'm not the least bit interested in going into a hole or a tunnel in the ground. I came here with my family as missionaries to teach the Tarahumara about God. If I wanted to earn money, I would've stayed in the United States."

The captain had been listening and looking at me intently up until this point. Now his demeanor became relaxed. "Well, I suppose it could be a rumor," he said. "We have not been able to find this Tarahumara man to question him ourselves."

"I'm not surprised," I said. "I've never had a conversation with anybody like that, but if I do, I will actually come and tell you about it. I'm familiar with the history of these mountains and the old gold and silver mines that were here. And I guess there are a few small operating mines still in business, but as I said, I have no desire to work in a hole in the ground!"

The captain thanked me for my time and left. And I was left wondering who would pass on such a rumor to the army.

5.2 Partners: Take 3

—⁂—

> **Without faith, it is impossible to please Him. (Hebrews 11:6)**
>
> **Now the just shall live by faith. But if anyone draws back my soul has no pleasure in him. (God speaking in Habakkuk 2:4 and Hebrews 10:38)**

That was pretty much how I felt about my previous partner who "drew back" from the job ahead of us. No pleasure. If we can't sense and see the faith in our coworker or partner, then how can we possibly have spiritual fellowship when in their presence? That's especially true when there is hard work and sacrifice involved. We definitely can and do experience the spiritual pleasure—joy—in our one-on-one relationship with the Lord Himself. He sustains us and personally lifts us up numerous times throughout the day, month after month, and year after year. However, if we are yoked together with a coworker who has no spiritual vitality, it will sap our own spiritual strength. Yes, quenching the Holy Spirit does have consequences.

A combat soldier can endure countless hours, days, and even months of hardships and bloody life and death clashes with the enemy when he knows he is pursuing victory for his clan or country. With camaraderie and repeated conversations with his fellow soldiers about their common and "noble cause," their spirits are refreshed and renewed, and their bodies can endure enormous punishment and privation. But then there is a real thing called "drawing back." It is a human tendency—and a spiritual surrender—which is timid about the risks ahead and entertains fearful imaginations about failure and embarrassment.

Speaking through Moses and Joshua, God told His people, "Be strong and of good courage; do not be afraid nor be dismayed for the Lord your God is with you wherever you go" (Joshua 1:9). In the first two chapters of Joshua, we see that the admonition to be strong and of good courage was not a shallow, humanistic war cry that initiated a hasty, foolish rush to action. At God's direction, Joshua then commanded the Israelites to "prepare provisions" for the coming march and battles. Next, God's strategy involved sending out spies into the promised land, psychologically preparing His people to defy the odds, and prepare themselves to see amazing miracles on a scale even beyond what their parents and grandparents had witnessed.

All of this was designed specifically by our all-knowing God to give rather weak human beings the step by step, attainable-by-faith spiritual victories that He so very much wants us to have!

New Tribes Mission provided us with an amazingly comprehensive training program for the challenges that lay ahead of us. Bible school gave us the initial spiritual training, boot camp gave us interpersonal and cross-cultural training, and finally, the language and linguistics institute gave us the skills to tackle the new languages we would have to learn. Numerous individuals and churches gave us financial support, many sacrificing and investing in us for months and years. So to draw back just as we entered the battlefield or the harvest field struck me as both sad and pathetic.

Those of us on the front lines owed so much to so many. Numerous instructors had taught us for literally thousands of hours, not knowing how much of their effort was working and penetrating the minds and hearts of the students who were watching and listening to them. There was an amazing attention to detail in developing the curriculum for cross-cultural communication of the many truths that are in the Word of God. For those of us who were directed into the intensive linguistics training, although not part of an accredited institution, we attained the equivalent of a bachelor's degree in linguistics. In fact, with its six-week analysis of the Cherokee language while we lived temporarily in Jay, Oklahoma, it had more actual field experience than almost any university program in the nation.

It wasn't just outstanding schooling and training that made us so well-prepared for what we were about to do in the Tarahumara tribe. We also had financial help from many dear Christian brothers and sisters. Sure, like Christians all over the world, some of them thought, *I could never go overseas, learn a foreign language, and be a missionary* (yes, many of them could have). But all of them made a commitment to the Lord and His kingdom to faithfully send us a portion of their hard-earned money because they loved Him!

The Lord has saved every born-again believer, including Ticker and me, and all of our coworkers from an eternity in hell, separated from Him. Thanks to His amazing love, we are now on a journey to a promised home in heaven to be with Him forever! We have the invaluable parallel lesson of how, thousands of years ago, the Lord saved the nation of Israel from slavery in Egypt and started them on a journey to their own promised land. Moses got them to the border of that "promised land;" his successor, Joshua, led the people faithfully in taking possession of the land. But not many years after his passing, the Israelites strayed from the Lord. However, God had a humble man in mind who would become an important leader for His people.

While threshing wheat in a hidden location, the Angel of the Lord came to a farmer by the name of Gideon. He said, "The Lord is with you, you mighty man of valor!" Gideon basically said, "Huh? Who, me?"

Then the Lord turned to him and said, "Go in this might of yours, and you shall save Israel... Have I not sent you?" (Judges 6:12–14).

Gideon did not want to be presumptuous, so he asked God for signs that he really had been chosen for a special mission by the Lord Himself. The Lord honored those requests because they came from a place of genuine humility and reverence for the one true God, and He gave Gideon more than one sign to encourage him onward.

In New Tribes Mission, after getting through all of the training and past the obstacles put up by the devil and the world, you would think that all of us knew—like Gideon had learned—that we were very much in the Lord's will on a mission that He had given to each of us personally. So when I would see one of my fellow missionaries balking at taking the next steps in our journey of ministry, I was genuinely perplexed but also saddened. After all, not only did those tribal people need them—I needed them! Ticker needed them. I wanted a "mighty man of valor" fighting alongside me!

Enter Potential Partner No. 3

In March of 1983, our field leaders in Chihuahua City decided that one of the next recently arrived missionaries should come out to visit us to consider being our partners. So it was that Mark Stivers came out on a familiarization trip for a few days without his wife or kids. He seemed like a real upbeat go-getter, and we had a great time visiting for a day or so while he stayed with us. Mark wasn't shy; in fact, he was pleasantly outspoken. He had come prepared to take a hiking trip with me to the same area that Cliff and I had last gone to together.

Physically, Mark was a lot like me. About five feet nine, with brown hair and a slight physical build, he was in good shape. We packed some lightweight food for camping, water, coffee, and a mess kit, camera, and a notebook and we headed out right after breakfast in my four-wheel-drive van. About two hours later, we got as far as we could go on the old deteriorated logging road that stopped short of Baquivo. I locked up the truck on the side of a small meadow and hoped nobody would bother it while we were gone. Country people out there seemed to be very respectful, so it wasn't much of a worry.

It was a beautiful sunny spring day when we hoisted our packs and started walking in the direction of several Tarahumara ranches. Since I had been there briefly with Cliff, I had a little better idea of how to navigate our way through the hills and gulches ahead of us. Still, it was constantly a guessing game to decide which of the faint trails to take. Some crisscrossed the grassy rolling hills where shepherd boys took their herds of goats to feed during the day. Others were traveled by only a few dozen individuals a few times per year when they walked out to hitch a ride from a passing logging truck on the way to San Rafael. But I knew the general direction we were heading, so we regularly climbed to the top of any small ridge or hill to get our bearings and stay on course.

Within a couple of hours, we came to a decent-sized adobe house where I saw a man moving around outside. It was really important in this area and culture to not frighten a woman by coming up to talk to her unannounced. It was much more appropriate to find a man who was willing to talk to you. The house we came to was a little larger than most, half of its roof being beat-up galvanized metal and the other half pine shingles. The man himself was probably in his early forties, dressed in a dusty blue blazer with a white shirt underneath, and wearing gray bell-bottom pants.

"*Kwira* (Hello)!" I said to him as we approached his yard. A male friend or family member sat on a crude wooden bench just a few feet away on the outdoor porch. After a few sentences of greetings, I told him we had come from San Rafael to visit his community. We were there just for a day or two and wanted to know how many Tarahumara people and ranches were in the area. Like most Tarahumara who are meeting outsiders for the first time, this fella was real quiet and didn't have much to say. After a few minutes, he suggested that we talk to another man, who was the local *gobernador*, and indicated by pointing which direction we should go. I don't remember now what this other man's name was, so I will just call him Juan.

There were generally three types of people that were the most informative and willing to talk with outsiders. They were either past or present officials like a *gobernador*, or governor, a *comisario*, or sheriff, or a *brujo*, or shaman or witchdoctor. A *gobernador* was a man who was the equivalent of a small-town mayor, recognized primarily by the local Tarahumara and mestizo (mixed blood) population. The *comisario* was elected by the local populace and was the government-recognized local constable. He was empowered to enforce the law if and when that became necessary. The brujo (pronounced brew-hoe) was a powerful local spiritual person. He had power and influence that varied a lot from person to person and place to place, but oftentimes, it was quite significant. He was seen as having a verified connection to the spirit world and could use that connection for either good or ill. Oftentimes, they used it for both. In that rural and animistic culture, no one took a brujo (or bruja, if it was a woman) lightly.

The fellow in the blue blazer pointed us in the direction of a ridge that was quite a ways away to the south. We thanked him, then started down a trail that dipped into a couple of gulches, then up the other side toward a plateau that was a few miles away. It was a beautiful sunny day with good visibility, so it was a pleasant hike. Still, it wasn't until dusk that we finally arrived at a house that we hoped was Juan's.

Steve talks with a Tarahumara man as he and Mark hike into the Baquivo area

Dogs barked as we got close, and a man emerged. He was about fifty or fifty-five years old and of typical Tarahumara build—five feet seven or so tall and, like someone who worked his fields, not heavy set.

I asked if he was Juan, the *gobernador* of the area, and he said that yes, he was.

Under different circumstances, I'm sure he would have invited us to have a cup of coffee with him, but since it was rather late, he instead asked what he could do for us. I answered that we had come to learn about the communities of Baquivo and Ochaivo since we had never been there before. I told him we had been walking all day and did not want to impose on him, so we could talk more about it the next day since it was getting late.

He asked if we wanted a place to sleep for the night. "Sure," I said. It was far enough into dusk that it would soon be hard to see. Juan went into his house and rustled around for a couple of moments, then came back with a few sticks in his hand. It was *ocote* or the sap-filled "lighter pine." He lit two pieces, one for me and one for himself, and then he led us down a trail as we held out the blazing miniature torches to light our way.

Perhaps 150 yards away, we came to a very solid-looking stone and adobe building. Since it was dark by now, I couldn't get a very good look at the whole building, but Juan opened the door and showed us into what was apparently his guesthouse. It had a clean dirt floor and, thankfully, a woodburning stove, the country-style half-barrel, with a small wooden bench nearby and plenty of firewood. That was especially welcome, since the nights in March were still pretty cold, and I guessed we were at about 6,000 feet elevation.

Juan helped us to get a small fire going right away, which was good for both the heat and the light. He asked if there was anything else we needed for the night, and I thanked him and told him that we would be just fine. He said he would see us then in the morning, and he headed back to his house. We opened up our sleeping bags on the floor and got comfortable. I made a couple of small cups of coffee for Mark and myself. It was not even 8:00 p.m., so we weren't ready to go to sleep quite yet.

Mark had only been in Spanish study in Chihuahua City for two or three months, so he understood almost nothing of what Juan and I had been talking about. I took the opportunity now to tell him everything I could remember. Pretty tired from our day of walking through the mountains, we finally went to sleep.

I woke up two or three times that night and, in the predawn hours, hearing a strange thumping sound. I would lay there awake, and when I heard it again, it felt like it was coming from the ground underneath us. I could not figure out at all what it might be.

We had brought sandwiches for our first day out but also had beef jerky and trail mix, plus soup. When I made these trips, we also carried only enough water for the first day, then had to find a spring or ask the locals where one was. If we were stuck using creek water, we always boiled it before drinking it. I could always go a long ways, though, on a couple of cups of coffee and a few handfuls of granola and beef jerky. That morning, we got up early, made a fire, and had coffee with granola and oatmeal, brown sugar, and powdered milk.

After a little while, our host came around. He had seen the smoke from our fire and knew we were up. We packed up our sleeping bags and food and went outside with him to talk.

Conversations with a Shaman

Juan took us around to the other side of the rock, adobe, and log shelter we had spent the night in, and now in the daylight, I could see a door open on the opposite side from which we had spent the night. The building was roughly square with the backside made up of tightly joined pine logs. Our side had been rectangular so was only half of the building. Although it was now empty, through the open door, I saw what looked like a barn floor. I surmised that the noise I'd heard during the night was a herd of goats that had been penned in on the other side for the night. There hadn't been the telltale odor of goats in the guest room, so I surmised the wall was really tightly caulked. Coyotes were a major and constant threat to all goat owners, so it looked like Juan had provided a far better place to keep his animals at night than in a corral, depending only on a dog or two to fight off the coyotes.

We walked a hundred yards or so toward the north where there was a nice open view of the grassy hills that we had come down through the evening before. Juan sat down on the ground, and we followed suit.

"So where do you come from?" he asked.

I told him that we came from San Rafael. "No, I mean before that," he said.

"We lived in Chihuahua City," I told him.

"You didn't come from the north?" he asked. *Del norte* or "from the north" usually meant from north of the border, which simply meant from the States.

"Yes," I said. "We came from *el otro lado* (literally the other side, meaning of the border with the US)." But it turned out he and I were not actually talking about the same thing.

"No, I mean from far to the north," he said.

No one had ever asked me that before, so I asked what he meant.

"Well," he said, "one day, I came out here to my fields, and two men came out of the sky from the north. They came right here, to this hillside in front of us, and came to visit me."

"Do you mean in an airplane?" I asked. I knew of the big abandoned airstrip at Baquivo and thought he meant that by saying "out of the sky."

I was starting to get a strange feeling about where this conversation might be going, but I decided to pursue the most plausible line of reasoning for the moment.

"Were they engineers or something?" I asked. I knew that there were men who went out into the mountains looking for either gold or silver deposits, and then on rare occasions, there were government employees who were doing geological expeditions or mapping the terrain. These were all referred to as *ingenieros* or engineers. Even though they rarely went to places as remote as where we were, they also usually never stated their real purpose for being there, keeping it confidential.

"No," said Juan, "they appeared in the sky and came right down to earth, right over there," he said, pointing to the hillside in front of us. "They were dressed in white clothing, very bright. They visited for a few hours and said they knew about me. After a while, they told me they were going to leave, so I decided I wanted to see if they could help me before they left. I needed another source of water close by for my house and the animals, so I asked them where I should look. They showed me a spot on the side of that hill right there. After they left, we dug down, and I found some water. It dried up after a few months, though. I was wondering, are you able to see water under the earth too?"

I told him that, sorry, I could not. I did, however, now realize that I was talking with a man who had seen some kind of spirits. Angels?

"Then the men started walking away, and all of a sudden, they were gone. They say you can sometimes travel very far, very fast. Have you done that?"

I told him that no, that I'd only done that in an *avion*, an airplane.

"Okay," I said to myself. "Now I know I'm talking to a fellow who is probably a shaman." I didn't want to interrupt what he was going to say next, so I didn't even try to start translating for Mark. I looked over at him, and he was pretty much oblivious as to what was going on. That was probably a good thing for now.

The Tarahumara man indicated we should follow him, so we walked on for several more minutes. The terrain was rugged and beautiful. We were on high ground, overlooking extensive grassy slopes, grazing areas for his animals. He stopped on the side of a hill, looking toward a wooded mountainside on the opposite side of the very deep gulch in front of us. We all sat down again.

"Another time, I was out looking for one of my cows that had wandered off, and I was afraid of it getting killed by coyotes. I headed off to where I had last seen it and was prepared to stay out all night. I had taken a blanket and matches and food. I made a fire after dark. That will usually keep the coyotes away. Eventually, I fell asleep, then around two in the morning, I woke up. I sat up and looked across the small canyon there," he said, pointing, "and saw a bright light. It was the size of a small campfire, maybe a lantern, but very white, almost blue. I watched it for a while but didn't see any people, just the light. The next morning, I went over to see what it was, but nothing was there. No burnt wood from a fire, no tracks from people. I still don't know what it could have been. What do you think?" he asked me.

I told him that I didn't have any guesses. I suppose I wasn't impressing him much with my lack of contacts with the spirit realm. Of course, my mind was thinking of UFOs or what I knew from the Scriptures of the spirit world. But this was a time for me to learn about the Tarahumara people and their beliefs, so I didn't volunteer anything about my worldview.

Juan continued, "So after that, I realized I could see things others can't. I guessed I was a *cuandero* (witch doctor with healing powers). People come to me now for help with problems or sickness. Sometimes I am able to help them too."

Mark had been politely quiet and impassive for perhaps an hour and a half while Juan and I had these short conversations, which were occasionally interrupted by other more mundane subjects. From time to time, I stopped to ask him in English, "Are you understanding much of this?"

He would just shake his head and say no.

"You won't believe what he's telling me," I said. "I'll tell you all about it later."

"Another time, I had a vision that there was water in a certain spot over there," Juan said. "So I started digging but couldn't find it." In these mountains, water could sometimes just come to the surface where it hit a rocky escarpment under the soil. Sometimes a spring would continue producing water for a short period of time and other times for years. But as a farmer, you wanted a steady, reliable source of water for your animals.

Juan continued, "So I decided I needed to know where some water really was. I decided to go off into the hills by myself."

Again, I could tell this was going to get interesting.

"I went over on the side of that hill," he continued, indicating another not-too-distant pine forest covered hill. "I stayed over there for two days."

He hesitated, and I think he was possibly struggling with the terminology in Spanish to describe his experience. I knew the feeling.

"I had gone to sleep and was having dreams. You never know about wild animals when you're out in the woods, you know? There are sometimes wolves and even mountain lions."

"Are there still bears around here?" I asked. I knew that bears figure prominently in the old Tarahumara folktales and were considered a spirit connection between man and the Tarahumara gods.

"No, no bears. Not for a long time. Have you seen bears?" he asked.

"Not around here," I answered. It was an open-ended statement, though, I realized. I had indeed seen bears. Did he wonder if I had talked with bears somewhere else? The conjecture couldn't hurt where this conversation was going.

"Anyway," he continued, "I woke up, and it was probably two or three in the morning. I had a fire going when I went to sleep, but it had gone out. There I was, just thinking about having a fire, and suddenly, off on the edge of my clearing, where there wasn't even any wood, a fire started. A good-sized fire too. Like the time before, though, in the morning, there was no sign of fire at all. I saw fire over there one more time after that and the tracks of a wolf." He let his words hang. I had no response, only silent amazement at this man and this conversation.

I made a mental note to myself: *Find out how or if the wolf figures in their supernatural beliefs.*

Since I couldn't help him find water, our conversation turned to more mundane things. My mind and senses were still electrified as we turned to walk back to Juan's ranch and to the trail which would take us back to the truck. With Juan several steps ahead of us, I started translating a bit of the conversations to Mark. He looked at me in amazement. I knew he had lots of questions, and it seemed to me he was about as awestruck as I was.

Soon, Mark and I thanked Juan for his hospitality and said our goodbyes. In many places, the trail was wide enough for us to walk side-by-side, so I related to Mark the details of all that Juan had said. He was quite startled, and I had goosebumps all over again telling him about it, as did he.

In coming years, I would hear many times of Tarahumaras and mestizos seeing small, unexplained lights in the hills. They were almost always off the trails, just on the side of a mountain, or down in a creek bed. I still have no idea what they could have been.

Since we were so far out in the hills, we decided to make a big loop through Ochaivo and the surrounding ranches. There was a really massive church on the mesa of Baquivo. It seemed quite unusual to me for being so far away from any town. Some Padre must have really done some smooth talking to get the Indians to make that many adobes and build something that tall. It had the typical two and a half to three feet thick walls that you see in churches in much bigger towns and stood about twenty-five feet high at the peak of the roof. The walls had been reinforced up high with big steel rods and turnbuckles. There was even stained-glass in some of the window openings.

We were told by a local Tarahumara that the priest visited once a year, perhaps twice at the most. We also noted that there was an airstrip on top of a mesa nearby, although it was fairly old and not usable without some repair work. It was fairly level, too, with a good approach. That combination was hard to find in this part of the world.

As we looped back to where we had left the truck, I realized that there wasn't really a large enough concentration of Tarahumaras for us to live in this area. Yes, the people would gather at the church by walking from as far as a couple of hours away when the priest came to visit and perhaps for other religious holidays. But those gatherings were bound to be rather infrequent. If we were to live here, there were probably only ten or twelve homes within a one-hour walking radius. Certainly, there were other Tarahumara ranches scattered further throughout the mountains, but not very close to Ochaivo and Baquivo.

Steve overlooking the Ochaivo mesa

Both from hiking as a kid, but especially from gleaning excellent cowboy knowledge from the Louis L'Amour Western novels that I read, I had learned that you didn't want to just keep your eyes moving ahead of you when you were in unknown country. You needed to look behind you frequently too. Both in the old West, and certainly here, too, it was important to see if you were being followed. But the much more important reason to keep looking back was to remember what the terrain was going to look like when you started heading back to where you had come from. You needed to make sure you distinguished one peak from another, remember whether your trail had come up out of this particular gully or canyon or the one next to it.

There was often a myriad of trails that looked fairly well-traveled, only to peter out at the bottom of a gully into nothing but wild animal trails. And we certainly didn't want to come back to a spot where we thought we had left the truck, shocked to find that it wasn't there when it was actually only a few hundred yards away in a similar looking spot!

Late in the afternoon, we found the truck just fine, got back to our house exhausted, but I was very gratified by what I had learned. Most of all, I was really amazed at having met and talked with a shaman! Mark still had a couple of days left in his schedule to be with us, and as we sat around talking for the next day or two, it was interesting to see the change in him. Whereas before he'd been gung ho about getting as many of us missionaries out to the tribes as possible, now he started talking about how what we really needed were Mexican national Christians to get out here and do the job! Over the next several months, that became his mantra back in Chihuahua City.

Then, as they got closer to finishing their Spanish study in Chihuahua City, one day, Mark and his wife packed up their truck and headed back to the States. We never did find out exactly why they decided to leave. Once again, Ticker and I were left without the hope of partners anytime in the near future.

One very interesting thing came out of our interaction with Mark, however. Just as I was reflecting on how he had been another promising tribal team candidate who had bailed on the job, his parents started supporting us financially. And writing letters. Really encouraging letters! They thought we were about the bravest, most dedicated young people they had heard of. They knew that we were going to go into a tribal community soon without even having partners but had no doubt that we could make it if anybody could. All of that apparently started with Mark singing our praises. Amazing! And encouraging!

Although I would've loved to have had Mark as a partner on our team, the Lord did add his parents to our team. That turned out to be a blessing to us for the next several years.

5.3 A Door Closes, Then...

They say when God closes one door, He opens another. God had definitely closed the door for having the S's as our partners.

Neither we nor our field committee members knew exactly how we should proceed in the short term, but in their communications with us, it somehow became apparent that we should continue moving forward, looking for a community to move into. Soon after Mark came to visit, we all knew that the Stivers would not be joining us anytime soon since they still had several months of Spanish study ahead of them. I think the field committee also came to the conclusion that Ticker and I would ultimately be making the decision on which Tarahumara community to move into and that I had been stalled in pursuing that decision for long enough. I was excited to see how God was going to lead us.

...There Was a Knock on the Door

Late one morning, a couple of weeks after Mark Stivers had left, there was a knock on the door of our house. I opened it to see a well-dressed Tarahumara man. He was around fifty years old, of medium build and height. He was dressed in as nice a set of clothes as a country person could reasonably acquire. He had on black dress trousers, a white shirt buttoned up to the neck, a black blazer and, although they were dusty, shiny black dress shoes. There was also one unusual thing about him. He was wearing a white neck gator, and after he greeted and started speaking with me, he pulled it up over his lower lip. I had never seen anybody do something quite like that, but I presumed he had either a physical defect around his mouth or perhaps something like a cold sore that he was embarrassed about.

This was actually the second time this man, Mauro, had come to the house. Six or eight weeks earlier, he had come by and said that he understood that my partner and I wanted to move into a Tarahumara Indian community. He told me that he was the Tarahumara governor of a community called El Manzano. It was north of San Rafael about two and a half or three hours by pickup truck. At that time, I had thanked him for coming by but told him that I was going to be visiting some other communities closer to San Rafael.

Now that I had visited Baquivo and Ochaivo, I was definitely interested in visiting El Manzano. I asked him if he would be there a couple of days later, and he told me he would. We agreed on a date, and I told him I would try to be out there by noon. When I closed the door and he left, I felt an excitement and optimism I had not experienced so far.

5.4 "See, I Have Set Before You an Open Door, and No One Can Shut It" (The Lord Jesus Christ, Revelation 3:8)

It was about thirty-eight miles from San Rafael to the valley community of El Manzano. It took about two and a half hours to get there. Mauro had told me where to turn right, north off the main logging road, where there were three or four houses at a place called Cerro Prieto. A mile or two further along, the road clung to the edge of a steep gulch with an almost vertical drop off on the left-hand side of about three hundred feet. This particular logging road was in pretty decent shape and continued snaking north and downhill.

A couple of miles further, I came to a cluster of five or six houses on both sides of the road. I stopped to ask directions and was told this place was called San Miguel. Yes, I was on the right road to El Manzano. At a fork up ahead, I was to go straight to get to Mauro's house, even though the main road went to the right.

The road down to Mauro's house degraded a bit. Soon I was down at the bottom of the steep gulch I had been driving alongside of with the road meandering back and forth about thirty feet above a pretty creek. As the road and creek flattened out, a decent-sized valley opened up in front of me. The largest of three houses was straight ahead, and it looked like the road ended there. I pulled up to the sound of several barking dogs and turned off the engine. Mauro, a woman I assumed to be his wife, and a couple of young boys came out to greet me.

"*Kwira!*" he called out, smiling as he walked over to me. We shook hands, and he introduced me to his wife and two of his sons.

"You have a nice place here," I said as I looked out on a really wide and long corn field. His ranch was at the bottom of a curved valley, and only a couple of hundred feet away was a small Catholic church, its weathered wooden cross high up on the peak. To the right, the valley sloped uphill, and I could see a few more houses with their cornfields nearby. Perhaps a mile above those, I could see what looked like a long adobe building. A school perhaps? Several more houses and cultivated fields were on both sides of the valley. This was indeed a sizable community.

"Come in, come in," Mauro said. The adobe house was neat and clean with the dirt floor freshly swept and a fire going in the stove. The stove was typical for these mountain communities. It was made from a fifty-five-gallon drum cut in half so that it was now a little less than two feet tall. The top flat end served as the cooktop, and the bottom was set into a raised dirt platform that was about eight or ten inches above the floor. There was an opening in the front about fifteen inches wide and twelve inches high, cut out so that firewood could be pushed inside the drum. At the back edge of the cooktop, there was a six-inch in diameter stovepipe for a flue that took the smoke out through the corrugated metal roof. The house had only a few small window openings, perhaps two-by-two feet, with simple wooden shutters, no glass. They were all open at the moment to allow the warm daytime air and a fair bit of sunlight in. The door, barely six feet high, was made of tightly fitted one-by-eight boards and was held open with a rock. Outside, three or four skinny dogs paced back and forth, sniffing the air, obviously trained or conditioned not to come inside.

"Please, have a seat," Mauro said as he motioned to a wooden table and chairs. "Would you like some coffee?" he asked.

"Yes, please," I answered. With water that had been heating on the stove, his wife made a cup of Nescafe instant coffee and put a bowl of sugar, an opened can of condensed milk, and a spoon in front of me. The simple wooden table was covered with a very nice, new, colorful plastic tablecloth. Mauro sat down across from me with his own cup of coffee. His wife stayed several feet away against the wall, smiling shyly, with her gaze mostly averted out of politeness but ready to serve us.

I've loved coffee since I was a teenager, and this was nice and strong. After several minutes of introductions of his wife and children and some polite small talk, Mauro asked me if I would like to see two potential house sites.

"Of course!" I said.

We walked over toward the creek that I had just been driving parallel to, and Mauro indicated a piece of land that was a couple of hundred yards away from his house and against the hillside. My thought was that it was a bit too close to him and the other houses. I guess he could see that I wasn't too excited about that particular spot.

"There's another place you could build a house," he said. "It's just a little further away."

"Let's go look at it," I said. We walked across the creek and up the backside of a pretty steep hill, zigzagging our way to the top. There was barely the faintest sign of a trail here. As we got to the top of the hill, which was probably 250 feet above the floor of the valley behind us, I saw some clear land with small patches that had once been fields. There was a small adobe building about ten-by-twelve feet with just a door, not even a window. It had a shake shingle roof which looked to be in decent shape.

Now this piece of land has some nice potential, I thought. Walking back and forth across the parcel, I saw that there were views to the north, south, and east for quite a distance. There was a fairly tall ridge a couple of hundred feet to the west, and it appeared to be perhaps two hundred feet high.

Looking south, the direction that I had driven in from, I could see some of the houses at San Miguel and a short section of the logging road up there. To the southeast, about a mile away, a tall mountain rose up seven or eight hundred feet above where I was standing. It was mostly covered in pine trees, but I could also see a different variety of tree in a large oval patch up there. I was to find out later that they were elm trees. To the northeast, I could see the upper part of the El Manzano valley where the school and several scattered ranches spread out across the sides of the hills. Looking due north, there was a wide cut in the mountains. Apparently, the creek that was below us continued to flow in that direction until it met up with the much larger Rio Oteros.

"I like this spot!" I told Mauro. "Whose house is that?" I asked him.

"My brother Ignacio wanted to live up here and farm, but the soil is really poor for corn. Then my oldest son thought that he might want to live up here, but he chose to live down by us because of the road. He drives a log truck for a living, and it's a lot easier for him to live right next to the road."

That made me wonder how I would get a road up here. Looking at the terrain, I couldn't see a real good way to put in a road.

"How would you put in a road to get up here?" I asked Mauro.

He thought about it for a moment and then said, "We can do it by hand with several workers. There's also the possibility that a bulldozer that the Ponderosa logging company uses to fix the old roads and put in new ones will be working near here soon. Perhaps you could hire that crew. They could cut a road from the creek with probably just two switchbacks to get up here," he said.

We walked over to the edge of the hill that overlooked the creek below. I could picture what he meant as I looked down. With two switchbacks in a distance of only about two hundred yards, a road could reach the top of this hill. Then I could hire the same bulldozer to level a site for the house itself. This was getting exciting to imagine!

"I think I'd like to bring my wife out here to look at this," I told him. "I would like to see what her impression is too."

"So this land does not belong to anyone now?" I asked him.

He hesitated for a moment before assuring me that it was all *ejido* (pronounced eh-hee-doe) land. That meant that it was owned by everyone but no one. It was open land under the jurisdiction of the local cooperative of people who had settled in the area generations before.

"So I would just need to get permission from the *ejido*?" I asked. I already knew that would be the procedure we would want to go through. It would be a bad idea to borrow or lease land from a private party. Like anywhere, a property owner could either later be offended by the Gospel or get greedy and demand bigger and bigger payments for the land, leaving the missionary in a hopeless situation. Our field leaders were well aware of this too. In all the tribal areas that we were going into with missionary teams, there was plenty of empty land that was controlled by the different ejidos.

"Yes, that would be the thing to do. I can speak on your behalf to the ejido," he said.

"That would be great," I said. "We would want an agreement that would allow us to live here for perhaps twenty-five years so that we can learn the Tarahumara language well and teach the people about God. It will probably take that long."

I looked in every direction one more time from the top of that hill before going back down to Mauro's house. The beauty and tranquility up there was amazing. It was rather rugged terrain, with a bit of a saddle across the hilltop, which was about two hundred yards long and fifty yards wide. With a bit of work, it had the potential to be a great place to live. Yes, I had a good feeling about this place.

Back down at Mauro's house, we talked some more and, of course, had another cup of coffee. That was the local people's favorite way of showing you hospitality—a cup of coffee with sugar and condensed milk.

Mauro went into his businessman mode now. "All you have to do is tell me how big you would like the house to be, and I can have it built for you," he said. "You could build it out of either logs or adobes, but adobes are a lot warmer in the winter. I have people here who could make the adobes and cut all the beams and rafters for the house. Then we can even get a truck to bring out the metal roofing. I think we can get it built in just a couple of months," he said.

I hoped that the amused smile that popped up inside my mind did not show up on my face. Really? I would let a guy build my house who probably didn't even own a level? There was nothing on these mountain houses that was terribly straight, plumb, or square. It would be kind to say there was quite a range in the levels of talent when it came to their construction abilities. I imagined that there might be a couple of people in the community who owned a four-foot level, and hopefully your adobe mason was one of them. Or maybe your carpenter could borrow or rent a level, but I certainly wasn't going to take a chance on that. *No, I thought, I believe I will have to be in charge of the construction.* But I wasn't going to say that outright to Mauro.

"We'll have to talk about that when the time comes," I said. "First of all, I'd like my wife, Dorotea, to visit here." I also knew that I would have to make sure that there was a significant number of Tarahumara speakers in the area. Mauro had told me that his family all spoke Tarahumara, but I wanted to visit around the community a little more too.

Back in San Rafael, I described my trip to Ticker in detail. She was my one and only partner, and we would be making this big decision together. I was certain God would give us His guidance. He had already guided us away from certain people and places. Once again, we would trust Him to give us direction and a positive sense of His will.

All Coffee-ed Out

A week later, Ticker and I got Dave, Dusty, and Eric comfortable in the van and made the trip together. I think we decided to go on a Sunday and that I had told Mauro that would be our plan because during the week, a lot of the men were out working and not at home. On Sundays, families pretty much stayed at home and rested up for the week to come.

Once again, I drove down to Mauro's house, but this time, another one or two of his sons were at home. We went inside the house and had coffee as Ticker talked with Mauro's wife, and Dave met and talked with Mauro's sons. Dave was quite good with Spanish and soon was outside exploring with Mauro's boys, Dusty following along close behind him, checking out the chickens and the baby goats and everything else that interests boys on a farm. Ticker had to keep Eric close at hand, basically on her lap so he wouldn't get too extraordinarily dirty crawling on the dirt floor. She was fairly successful for the first hour or two and then just had to chuckle at how dirty he got and the thought of how she was going to get his clothes clean again.

"Let's go over to my brother Ignacio's house," said Mauro. So off we went to meet him and his wife and their children, who ranged in age from a two or three-year-old to a couple of kids in their late teens. Again, there were introductions all around, shaking of hands, and the table was set with coffee for everyone.

Since it was Sunday and everyone knew we were coming, there were also cookies and other treats set out. These folks had very little in the way of earthly possessions, but they were eager to entertain, and apparently, it was a great delight for them to meet strangers like us.

From Ignacio's place, whose nickname was Nacho, we walked further up the valley on the dirt trails that linked all of the homes one to another. Sometimes there was a rock wall with steps up and over that had to be negotiated, other times a split rail fence with a gate in it, but we made a circuit of a few of the houses there in El Manzano. With just a few exceptions, we were invited in for coffee and a snack, and around lunchtime, someone served us beans and tortillas with goat cheese. I don't remember if we had water anytime over the course of those three or four hours, and of course, we were somewhat concerned about cleanliness and the quality of water at the time. But we certainly drank a lot of coffee. Ticker took milk in her coffee but no sugar. But I've always drunk my coffee black, and I like it fairly strong.

Suffice it to say that I got "coffee-ed out" by the end of the afternoon. I know that I had seven or eight cups by the time we left to head home. I'm pretty sure I didn't get to sleep easily that night!

Ticker and the boys were the great attraction of the day to all the folks we met. Dave loved meeting new kids and exploring around their houses with them until it was time for us to move on to the next house. Dusty, with his reddish hair, freckles, and light complexion was quite the novelty. Eric had dark hair but a light complexion, too, so every single woman and teenage girl would say, "Ahh, what a beautiful baby you have!"

It was quite a great visit, getting to know the folks in El Manzano for the very first time. We talked with them about their families, what the men did for work, and whatever else we could ask about tactfully to get a feel for the life of the community. We left in the middle of the afternoon and began that two-and-a-half-hour long, bumpy, and rocky drive home on the logging roads. It was the first trip of many, many more to come.

That night at home, after putting the boys to bed, Ticker and I sat down together and began to pray to the Lord regarding what seemed to be an open door in El Manzano. We both were very encouraged by what we had seen and experienced. Over the course of the next few days, we came to feel very strongly that it's where God wanted us to be.

5.5 Knowing God's Will

This is probably a good point in our personal story to discuss in a little bit of detail the subject of knowing God's will for our individual lives. When I say "knowing God's will," what I'm actually saying is what I think every Christian wonders about on either a few big occasions or in hundreds and perhaps many thousands of situations over the course of our lives here on earth. When we truly want to know if we should make a certain decision that is really significant or when we're at a difficult crossroads in life, if we genuinely believe that God has a plan for our lives, then we ask Him what His will is for us.

Ticker and I had mostly been in a community of dedicated Christians for nine or ten years by this time. We had heard people talk about "God's will" hundreds of times, especially as we progressed through our missionary training. Both we and our fellow students came to points in time where we wanted to know what God's will was for us regarding the next steps we should take. For example, after Bible school, we wanted to know if we should apply for a certain one of the seven boot camps that New Tribes Mission had around the country and in Canada. As we progressed through boot camp, which was three semesters for us, we assumed that we would be heading for language and linguistics school at the beginning of the next semester. But then New Tribes asked for volunteers from the various schools to go down to Sanford, Florida, for a few weeks or the entire summer, if possible, to help get the new headquarters building remodeled.

Headquarters was being moved from Waukesha, Wisconsin, into a massive building that had been a very large hotel built in the 1920s and needed significant renovation. So there were a couple hundred of us who asked to know the Lord's will regarding pitching in on that project. Ticker and I ended up spending not just the summer but an entire year working on that renovation project because of the huge need for manpower.

It was also at that point in time after boot camp that many folks in the training asked God to "know His will" regarding the next significant step of going on to language and linguistics school. A large number felt in their hearts that tribal missionary life was not going to be the area of ministry for them personally, so they dropped out of the training.

As we started our studies at the language and linguistics institute, the staff asked us to decide on the country that we wanted to go to serve in. At that time, the fall of 1979, New Tribes was in twenty-one or twenty-two countries around the world. In addition to taking a field medicine course, continuing studies on cross-cultural communications, and a few other subjects, the primary objective in the first semester was to get at least six weeks of an introductory course in the national language of the country to which we would be going. For most of Latin America, that was Spanish, for Brazil it was Portuguese. It was Indonesian for Indonesia, Tagalog for the Philippines, Pidgin English for New Guinea, and other languages for the countries in Africa. So it was a significant time for all of us to pray and ask God to either decide for the first time or to confirm in our hearts which country we felt He would have us to serve in.

Ticker and I had been leaning toward going to Indonesia due to the huge number of tribal groups (approximately seven hundred) in that country. But interestingly, shortly after we were asked to make a commitment on which national language class to take, a fellow named Marsh Milliken came and spoke to us about the need for linguists in the tribes in Mexico. New Tribes had only recently begun working in Mexico, perhaps a year or so earlier. As he and the field leadership quickly determined, the native languages of Mexico are amongst the most linguistically difficult in the world. In fact, the largest concentration of diverse dialects and languages is in a two- or three-hundred-mile radius of Mexico City.

When we first arrived at language school, we were told that we would be needing to make a decision within a couple of weeks regarding the national language course, but we were also given an aptitude test for linguistics. The staff and curriculum required that they know how many potential linguists were in the incoming class as soon as possible. Just like some people have natural abilities in art or mathematics or public speaking, a certain percentage of the population—and I believe we were told it's about 7 percent—has a natural ability for analyzing the components in languages. Thus we were given an aptitude test, and the results were made known to us several days later. If the test results showed that we had an aptitude for linguistics, we were basically told, "Congratulations! Please be prepared for an additional year of time here at the institute. You will be taking an intensive course in linguistics, which will be of immense value on certain teams in different parts of the world. The tribal language where you are going probably has no written materials that will help you to learn the language, so you will be the team member responsible for not only learning the language but making language learning lessons for yourself and your teammates."

The test results were something that we were informed about with the assumption that we would agree to take the extra twelve months of training. But also being practical, the mission leadership realized that when the linguist was a mother with two or three children, perhaps planning on having even more, the couple would be consulted about whether the woman would really and truly be able to apply herself to doing the very focused and tedious work of linguistics in the tribe. In general, those women were exempted from taking the course, unless they really felt that was a job they would be happy and willing to do.

The norm in every tribal location was that the mothers would homeschool their children until the beginning of second grade, usually as a team with their partners, and the leadership did not want these mothers/linguists to be either overwhelmed or to sacrifice the good of their families for the job of linguistics. The rest of us were considered to be future linguists!

Apparently, God had given me an aptitude for linguistics. So it was that just a week or two later when Marsh Milliken came to appeal for future workers for Mexico, he had a special session talking with just the future linguists. He knew that most of us had been gravitating toward a certain country in the world in which to serve and that going to a country like Mexico had never even entered into our minds. The field of Mexico was going to have challenges unlike other countries where our missionaries served. If an individual or a family felt like the struggles they were having serving the Lord partway around the world were overwhelming, they would have to make a major financial decision to all fly home and start their lives over again. From Mexico, they just needed several hundred dollars for gas money, and they could drive home.

So the message from Marsh was unique and clear: please consider the unusual need that we have for linguists in Mexico, but also please consider carefully whether God wants you to serve Him in Mexico. Just like in any country, the field leadership did not want a high rate of attrition.

Once again, Ticker and I took the time to ask the Lord for His specific guidance regarding this major decision. I know psychologically it was a change in thinking, but neither of us had really felt strongly previously that He wanted us specifically in Indonesia either. After a few days, we felt the peace from God in responding to the call to Mexico. We told the appropriate staff members and became new enrollees for the six weeks of Spanish study that would soon begin.

In the Old Testament, we see numerous examples of God instructing His people regarding what to do at a certain point in time or them experiencing a major victory perhaps, and He tells them to build a monument at a certain place to remind themselves and their future generations of what transpired there. The monuments were not supposed to be fancy. In fact, God said not to even make them out of "hewn stones." He preferred that they be natural and unpretentious. The important thing was that they were a marker regarding a time and place where God specifically intervened and gave guidance.

As modern-day Christians, we are instructed to also remember to build a durable "monument of stone" regarding how God has intervened and guided us in so many ways, both large and small. Those times are extremely important to be able to look back on. There will absolutely be factors that could cause us to quit serving Him: times of boredom or complacency, perhaps intense spiritual warfare, temptations to pursue better (according to the world's standards) financial stability, or any number of other ways in which we might compare ourselves and our progress through life to other people.

God has His custom-tailored way of guiding all of us through this life, and oftentimes, it's a very winding road. But He absolutely wants us to remember some important times when we needed Him to give us specific guidance. He does not want us to turn back from following Him in faith for any reason whatsoever, and that is true for however many years He gives us to live on this planet.

Of the hundreds of times that I have heard my fellow Christians say, "The Lord encouraged me by _____ (insert a verse or a sign), so I felt that it was God's will to do____ (insert do a good deed or talk to so-and-so," I readily admit that I wish I had that feeling more regularly in my life. That can be a readout of our sensitivity to the leading of the Holy Spirit. But I also have heard many Christians say, "I feel that God is leading me (or us) to go do something different now," and that was oftentimes when they were quitting New Tribes Mission.

I truly don't want to be unkind, harsh, or too judgmental regarding my fellow Christians, anywhere or at any time. That can be hurtful to them, to me and to God's purposes for all of us. However, when you watch somebody struggling with certain difficulties, like learning a foreign language or not getting along with a fellow Christian, and then they decide to go in a different direction, I think it is oftentimes a human decision to leave, not a spiritual one.

I know how many thousands of times in my life I have needed God's help to get through a myriad of difficulties. Sometimes they are interpersonal and sometimes they are temptations or shortcomings that are entirely personal with me. Every single time, I believe God is willing and able to work with me through the guidance of His Holy Spirit. But whether or not I have spiritual victory, and then from that moment on live in a way that is pleasing to Him is dependent upon whether I want to abide in and obey Him.

Since we have a flawed human nature but also have the indwelling Holy Spirit who is willing and able to make us more like Christ, it is a moment by moment or hour by hour, day by day process that will last our entire lives. But that's okay! We really and truly do have the everlasting, eternal God living in us and with us! That is the good news (the gospel of John, chapters 14–17).

How do we know if something is the will of God? Well, we certainly know that a decision cannot contradict what He tells us plainly in his Word, like disobeying the Ten Commandments, for example. And we also know that if we do not read His Word and otherwise expose ourselves to His Word regularly and daily, we will essentially be plugging our ears to what He would have us to hear from Him. But assuming that we are staying in a close relationship with Him, I think each of us can hear His voice in different ways. I know that for many years, I personally have relied on the truth of a couple of passages of scripture.

The prophet Elijah was one of the most outstanding men in the Old Testament. In 1 Kings chapters 18 and 19, God used Elijah to initiate a major display of his power against the four hundred fifty false prophets of Baal and the evil king, Ahab, and his queen, Jezebel, who were aligned with them. When all their false prophets were killed, Jezebel swore in her anger to have her vengeance on Elijah. He fled for his life into the wilderness. Elijah prayed fervently for the Lord's protection and His guidance.

The Lord answered him by telling him to go stand on a mountain where "He (God) passed by," and immediately, there was a powerful wind which tore the rocks in pieces, followed by an earthquake which was then followed by a fire. But after all of this pandemonium, we read in 1 Kings 19:12–13, "And after the fire a still small voice. So it was when Elijah heard it…that he went out and stood in the entrance of the cave."

What then follows are specific instructions from the Lord to Elijah. Elijah was a man who had regularly heard the clear and plain voice of the Lord regarding his mission in life and the words he was to say. But at one point, God chose to cause a huge, noisy, and powerful commotion, then to begin to speak to His servant in the most quiet and subtle way: <u>"a still small voice," (1 Kings 19:12).</u>

I think today we very commonly have to deal with the commotion and noise of this natural world, including human beings, which would distract us from hearing what God is saying to us. So I think we have to regularly ask Him for understanding of His will and then listen for that still small voice. His comfort and guidance will no doubt follow, especially in light of the facts of what He told the disciples (and through them, said to us) since the Holy Spirit had been promised to live in them and provide guidance for them.

There is another verse that gives me spiritual guidance also when I don't seem to be hearing a voice from God. It is found in a psalm of David which is replete with so many spiritual, psychological, and emotional overtones, i.e., real life. <u>In Psalm 32, verse 8, God says through David, "I will instruct you and teach you in the way you should go; I will guide you with my eye."</u> Then the next verse so graphically adds to the explanation: "Do not be like the horse or like the mule, which have no understanding, which must be harnessed with bit and bridle, else they will not come near you."

If you've ever been around horses a lot, you know that they are powerful but sensitive creatures. Whether when they are young or a bit older, in order to be in a friendly and useful relationship with man (yes, think God and man here), the horse's wild spirit needs to be tamed. That certainly does not mean that they will no longer be happy. What it does mean is that the horse will from that point on be well-fed and cared for, appreciated for his strength and unique ability to work with the man or woman he is now bonded to.

So David is saying do not be like the untamed brute horse or mule which "has no understanding" and must therefore be guided by force, yanked around. Rather, God tells us to be guided "with my eye." That means we must be looking Him in the eye or be side by side with Him in order to see what He is looking at. What a concept! As a trainer works with a horse, he first of all walks him around in a small manageable area, looking the horse in the eye so that they bond. Soon, the horse can see that the man is patient, giving direction, and has a purpose in mind for everything that he is doing. The horse learns to trust the man, and soon, his great strength is being used for a greater purpose. How much that is like a servant of the Lord who aspires to do great things! Rather than trust that He will "yank" us around into doing His will, how much better to be perhaps side-by-side with Him, and when we ask Him what we should do next, we follow His gaze?

Back to how all of this relates to our journey as missionaries at that point in time: within a couple of days of our visit to El Manzano, Ticker and I felt that's where the Lord was looking, and His guidance was to have great significance for the future.

Chapter 6

Building the House in El Manzano

6.1 Getting Permission and Getting Started

First things first. I knew from the work that our other missionaries were doing in different tribes that we needed permission to live and operate there in the mountains from what is called the ejido.

Ejido (again, pronounced eh-hee-doe) essentially means "common" in Spanish. The national government had divided most of the land in the country into thousands of ejidos, and that land was owned in common by the legally recognized residents of the area. Those residents are called *ejidatarios*. What we would need to do before ever assuming that we could begin to build a house in El Manzano was to attend a meeting of the ejido that had in attendance a majority of the voting ejidatarios, where I would make a statement regarding our desire to live in El Manzano. I would present to them the fact that we only wanted to live for a certain number of years amongst them so we could learn Tarahumara and teach the people about God. They also needed to know that we would not be starting any kind of a business, thus eliminating any ideas or fears regarding us taking financial advantage of them in any way or having a secret desire to get into silver or gold mining, for example.

Mauro would be our sponsor, of course. He would be making a statement to the ejido assembly as the governor of the community of El Manzano, which would carry a lot of weight. I prepared a statement and made sure I had all the right terminology in place during the days leading up to the meeting. This would be my first legally binding and official piece of business in Mexico. It was a big step of faith, and of course, Ticker and I asked God for His guidance and help. Since the trip in the truck was a rough one, and men usually took care of this kind of business on their own, I would be driving out there from San Rafael by myself.

On the designated day, and the ejido meetings were always on a Sunday, I left really early from San Rafael to drive to El Manzano. At Mauro's house, I picked him up along with several other passengers. My four-wheel-drive van had bench seats in the back and could reasonably hold a total of ten people. However, that was never the normal number of people that would ride with me. On that day, and many more occasions in the future, I would open the side door of the van and let the people themselves decide how many more they wanted to let in. Oftentimes, it was closer to fifteen or eighteen people that would pile in!

The ejido meeting took place in a building that had been built just for that purpose. The building somewhat resembled a high school gymnasium with two side walls that were about ten feet high and end walls that went up to a peak of eighteen or twenty feet. At one end was a stage that was three or four feet above the floor, perhaps ten feet deep, and extended the width of the building. On the far right-hand side was a set of steps that went up onto the stage.

When we arrived, there were over a hundred people, mostly men, milling around inside the building, talking with each other. Dozens more were gathered outside in small groups. Although many, like Mauro, had on their Sunday best clothing, it was my first time seeing a great cross-section of the people from the surrounding communities. Almost everyone was wearing huarache sandals, made from the treads of car or truck tires. Some of the men had their straight black hair cut short, while most of them wore it rather long, and some had it quite long, tied with a headband. The women tended to gather away from the building itself in smaller groups with their friends and the children.

It was noteworthy that when business was to be conducted, like for this ejido meeting, almost all of it would be done by the men. Soon, a group of six or seven men went up onto the stage and sat down in a semicircle around a table. One man stood up and announced that the meeting would now officially begin.

The first order of business had to do with proposals from the Ponderosa logging company regarding wages for paying laborers to work on maintaining existing logging roads and starting a couple of new ones. Two representatives of the Ponderosa logging company stood at the front of the stage, fielding and answering questions from both the ejido board and the members of the public. There was no PA system, so anyone who wanted to hear what was going on and be part of the negotiations had to make their way to the front of the room to hear and be heard. Statements and conversations were generally calm in nature but at other times got a bit tense, perhaps even heated. Watching all of this, I wondered what the discussion would be like when it was time for me to make my presentation.

After an hour and a half or more, it was finally time for the next item on the agenda. Mauro and I were summoned and went up on the stage. He spoke first while I stood a bit to one side of him. Like the rest of the people there, I was dressed in my Sunday best—tan Levi jeans, a long-sleeved button-down shirt, polished cowboy boots, and my freshly brushed felt cowboy hat.

"There is an American here with me today that I want to introduce to you," he said. "He would like to live in El Manzano, and we have invited him to do that. I will let him tell you more about his wishes."

I walked over toward the semicircle of ejido officials and mostly faced them but partially faced the crowd of people below. A couple dozen people had pushed their way within hearing range of the stage, including all of the residents of El Manzano that were present.

"Good afternoon," I said. "My name is Esteban Real. I am a missionary and am living right now in San Rafael. The organization I am with is interested in teaching indigenous people about God in their own language. We are not from a specific religious group. We teach about God straight from the Bible. It is my desire to learn the Tarahumara language and teach people in this area about God in the Tarahumara language. Since this will take a few years, we would like to build a house in El Manzano. We have our own finances to live on, so we are not interested in and will not be involved in any kind of businesses here. We are only interested in having a small piece of property on which to live while we learn the Tarahumara language and then teach people.

"We have been invited to El Manzano by Mauro Sanchez, the governor there. We like the community, and he has shown us a piece of land where we could build. We do not want to own the land, we just want permission to live there and use it for twenty or twenty-five years. Anything we build on it, and any improvements we make, will go back to the ejido when we leave.

"Our mission organization always has at least two families as a team, so we hope to have another family join us in the next year or two. They will only want the same thing: a site to build a house on where they can live for several years, and everything will be returned to the ejido when they leave also. I would like to ask your permission today for the ejido to grant us the use of this parcel of land for free."

The ejido board members asked Mauro and me a few questions, including whether anyone else had a claim to the land. Mauro assured them that no one did. After a few minutes, they were satisfied with our answers and put it to a vote by the ejido members.

The vote was done verbally and by raising of hands. There had been a quorum officially recognized before the Ponderosa log company's business had been presented, and most of those people were still there and voted overwhelmingly to allow us the permission we were asking for. In fact, there was no dissent whatsoever.

We had reached our first milestone in living amongst the Tarahumara! Praise the Lord!

My heart rejoiced, and the unconscious tension in my body and mind melted away. A couple of members of our new community of El Manzano came up, smiling, and shook my hand in congratulations, although we barely knew each other. Before we could leave to head back to El Manzano with all of my passengers, the ejido's secretary typed away on a manual typewriter (the closest electrical power was way back in San Rafael or far across the Rio Oteros canyon in the municipal seat of Uruachic), and handed me my officially stamped and signed copy of permission from the board.

I had also prepared a written document with a copy for them and for us, stating exactly what I had verbally presented to them. It was basically an open-ended lease that was between us as members of Mision Pro-Indigena, the official incorporated organization that was New Tribes Mission in Mexico, and the ejido. I knew it had to be as much akin to a legal document as possible, having learned from our coworkers in the Central Tarahumara dialect near Guachochic not to trust a verbal or handshake agreement.

As we drove back on the winding, dusty, and rocky road to El Manzano, Mauro and I discussed the next steps. I would come back out in a few days and talk to him about getting materials for the house that the local people could make. I dropped everyone off in El Manzano and, almost fourteen hours after leaving home, was back in San Rafael with Ticker. It had been a really long day, but sitting around the table with the boys and her in the light of our kerosene lamps, I felt like a new man!

We were about to jump into the Tarahumara community where God had opened the door!

6.2 "Unless the Lord Builds the House..."

they labor in vain who build it. (Psalm 127:1)

Just like in everything else I had done in life to that point that was of any importance, and all that was to follow, I definitely needed the Lord's help.

By this time in life, I was a pretty good finish carpenter, but I had never built a house. I knew I would be building one in the tribe someday, so I had paid attention to all the building techniques I could observe during our short time living in Mexico, both in the city and in the country. The log houses were not as warm as adobe houses and required a lot of really large diameter trees that could be cut from good sized forests.

Out where we would be living, the only big trees that were allowed to be cut had to be gotten with a permit from the government. Those permits were only given to the logging companies unless someone had a lot of trees on their own private land or had some government connections. Anyway, adobe was much warmer in the winter and cooler in the summer, so we planned on building using adobes.

During the weeks and months in which I had been delayed, waiting for Cliff, I had drawn up a house plan that I thought would be practical. It would be a two-story house, with the living room, kitchen, bathroom, office and guest room combination on the first floor, and the two bedrooms on the second floor, so the house would be roomy but without a big footprint. The bottom floor would be about 800 square feet. The two bedrooms upstairs would be located under the center of the roof with the hallway and closets against the eaves on each side of the house. Essentially, it would be a one and a half story house so that it wouldn't be excessively tall either.

I would have adobes made that were twelve-by-eighteen inches and four inches thick. On the first floor, the adobes would be set sideways, so the walls would be eighteen inches thick for the strength needed to support the second floor. On the upper floor, they would be set long ways, so those walls would only be twelve inches thick. The rafters would be pine poles about four inches in diameter. On top of those would be one-by-four purlins and a galvanized metal roof. The ceiling of the first floor, which was also the floor of the bedrooms, would be one-by-six tongue and groove pine boards.

Although we would initially use the woodburning stove that we had in San Rafael for heat, I wanted to heat the whole house with a fireplace. I knew I would love the ambience of the fireplace, but I also had to come up with an idea on how to heat the second floor efficiently. I really, really did not want the bedrooms to be cold in the winter. We had just finished living in San Rafael for the second winter and knew how cold the mountains could get. In El Manzano, we would be at roughly the same elevation—7,200 feet.

On my next visit to El Manzano, I met right away with Mauro to talk about the building process. Although he had the idea that he would like to be our general contractor, I had a very different plan in mind.

Sitting across the table from him with the usual cups of coffee, I began to ease into the specifics of what I had in mind. As was Mauro's natural temperament, he would only look me in the eyes for a few moments and then avert his gaze as we talked. Again, sensing that he was not totally honest and above board actually helped me to take control of the situation and start clearly into this new conversation.

"Thank you for offering to be the contractor," I told him. "But I think I will be able to build the house with the help of folks here and some of my friends from Chihuahua City. What I really need your help with is to get all the materials together. I think the first thing to plan for is getting adobes made. That might take a while, right?" I asked him.

I could tell right away he was rather disappointed. I think he saw big dollar signs being pulled away from his grasp. After trying one more time to convince me to let him build the house, and I wondered whether he had made promises to his family and neighbors regarding them getting a piece of the pie, he acquiesced.

"Yes," he answered, looking down at the table. "You will need to get adobes made before the rainy season starts. That is only about two months away."

"Who around here can make adobes?" I asked.

Apparently, that wasn't a very lucrative or prestigious job, so he didn't volunteer to do it himself or even to have his sons do it.

"There are two fellows I can think of who might do it," he said. "How many adobes do you need?" he asked. I told him I had estimated about 2,500, and they would be twelve-by-eighteen inches and four inches thick. He could see that I had been planning this part, so he said he would find someone and get them started as soon as possible.

"What else do you want?" he asked.

I had come up with a list of beams that I needed to hold up the second floor, a big post, and the rafters which could all be cut from trees in the area. I asked him if that was all possible.

"Yes, we can do that," he replied. "My sons and I will get started on that right away. Can you bring us a sharpening stone for an ax? Mine got lost not long ago." I didn't realize at the time that even getting that much wood cut from rather small trees might create a problem with the local government logging officials, and he never mentioned that it could.

"I will also need a lot of sand and gravel for the foundation," I told him. "Is there sand and gravel nearby?" I asked.

"We can get it out of the creeks," he told me. "You'll need to bring a couple of dozen gunnysacks," he told me, "and I will find some guys to fill them up for you."

At this point, I was feeling really grateful that this part of our relationship was getting off to a good start. It had been rather apparent to me from the second time that Mauro came to invite us in San Rafael that there was probably a financial ulterior motive in his invitation that involved some kind of benefit to him eventually. I was hoping now that he was able to see that being the middleman for materials might not be as lucrative as being the contractor but still had its prestige. The more we talked, the more he seemed to be interested in getting involved in the project. I was really pleased with that.

"One big thing I have to figure out is how to get a road up to the top of the hill where the house will be," I said. "You had said that it could be done by hand, but that seems like it might take at least a couple of weeks and a lot of workers," I said.

"I just found out the other day that there is a bulldozer and crew coming out here to fix a road soon," he said. "If you tell them you want them to do the road for you, I think they would do it."

I was absolutely amazed! How incredible the Lord's timing was! That had been a major issue for us so that we could get materials up to the house site, let alone the fact that we needed a road eventually anyway.

"So it's a Ponderosa bulldozer crew?" I asked. "Do I need to get authorization from the sawmill to hire them? And who would I pay?"

I could imagine the process taking weeks or months, and now I was anxious to get started.

"No, no" he said. "I will find out exactly when they're coming here to the valley, and you can pay them directly."

"How much do you think it will cost?" I asked. I braced myself for a big shock, but he told me a price that seemed far too low. He said that I could talk with the head of the crew, Manuel, in the next day or two.

After going over the basic prices for adobes, beams, rafters, and sacks of sand and gravel with Mauro, I was pretty pleased with the way things seemed to be progressing. We certainly didn't have much money in the bank, but all of this seemed pretty affordable for the moment. I had no doubt that God would make a way for us.

Now that Mauro and I had talked about a lot of the details, and I had agreed to the prices and gotten the ball rolling, I headed back to San Rafael with a solid plan for how to proceed. Ticker and I talked it over, and it was obvious that I needed to be able to stay out on the property for a few days at a time. The five-hour round trip was pretty good at beating up both me and the truck. We made a list of things that I would need for camping out there: food, our camping stove, jugs of water, sleeping gear, etc.

On the next trip a few days later, I met Manuel for the first time. It turned out that he was our local community sheriff or *comisariado*. Manuel was either Mexican or mestizo, not Tarahumara. He was probably in his mid- to late-fifties with barely graying hair. He had a slightly sagging lower lip and eyes and drooping shoulders, signs of a man his age who had worked hard for a living. He also spoke simply and directly. I sensed a good and honest heart. He was not the bulldozer operator, but he was the senior fellow on the team and was actually the one authorized to use dynamite.

Apparently, the crew had a good deal of autonomy under the Ponderosa logging company in performing their work. In hindsight, I think the company knew that they would be doing side jobs once in a while and therefore getting paid on the side, too, but that was one of the perks of their job. Besides, there were literally no wealthy people out there in the mountains requesting something like we were.

Our need for this short section of road was a rare thing indeed and simply provided some much-needed extra money for the four guys on the crew.

Manuel told me when they expected to be finished with their current road work, so I was out there the following week, prepared to pay them in cash. It took them four days to cut the road from the creek up to the top of our hill. They had to drill into and dynamite two really large rocks, which was exciting to watch. Then on the last day, they had the house site leveled for us. The site was almost on the top of the property with a cut out of the side of a hill which had a pretty large oak tree and a couple of nice big pines on it, leaving a fifteen-foot knoll to the east, blocking a portion of our view in that direction. Standing on top of that small hill, I could look north and west and see the entire El Manzano valley. Later, the top of that hill became my own personal retreat and meditation spot.

In the end, the four days of bulldozing, diesel compressor drilling, dynamite, and four men's labor only cost us about $900! It would've cost more than ten times that in the States. God was taking care of things for us before we even knew we needed to ask! Such is our awesome God!

The bulldozer grades the house site. I had them leave a knoll next to the house site, which later became a personal place of prayer and meditation for me.

6.3 No More "Hurry Up and Wait"

———〰———

Slightly more than four months had passed since the S's had left us in San Rafael. It had been only a month and a half since Mark Stivers had visited us with the remote prospect of them becoming our partners. But as God would have it, now we were pressing full speed ahead to build our house.

Ticker and I talked about how best to proceed with the construction project. We both knew quite well how rough traveling on the logging road between San Rafael and El Manzano would be for her and the boys. The little adobe shack on the property really wouldn't be very comfortable for all five of us to live in for more than a couple of days, let alone a few months. Right away, I would be needing to take a number of tools out to the house site, and that would also cut down on room in the back of the van. So we decided the best thing would be for me to go out to El Manzano for four or five days at a time while she and the boys stayed in our house in San Rafael. I could set up a kitchen with our camping stove in the adobe shack and sleep on the bed in the back of the van. The idea of converting the van into a camper van while in Chicago over two years previously was now going to pay off in a fantastic way!

From down at the creek in El Manzano, where I had been previously camping, I drove up our brand-new road to the top of the property to spend my first night. I built a campfire next to my van and thoroughly enjoyed looking up at the incredible starry sky. I thanked God for bringing us so far on our mission to reach the Tarahumara for him. I knew there was a lot of hard work ahead, but I thoroughly reveled in where we were at that moment. I missed Ticker and the boys who were back in San Rafael. I couldn't wait for them to get out here and see our new house site.

The next day was a beautiful sunny April morning. Nacho, Mauro's brother, came up to meet me shortly after I had breakfast.

"Did you bring the molds for the adobes?" he asked me.

"Yes," I told him and got them out of the truck. We walked a few feet over to where there was a low spot, a sort of saddle on the property. This was where Nacho and his sons had made their own adobes for the little ten-by-twelve-foot house. That and the surrounding half acre or so was also where he had tried to grow corn for a year or two before giving up on it. It turned out that the soil was too poor to support corn. There was an area about ten feet wide and twenty feet long that had grass growing in it and a mushy wet area in the center. The rest of the property was quite dry.

"See this area?" he asked, gesturing toward it with his hand. "This isn't really a spring that produces enough water for drinking or anything, but it will be just enough for me to start making adobes. You're going to need to find a way to get water up here soon, though, for me to make a lot of adobes. This water will probably dry up in the next couple of weeks." Apparently, it was just surface water that came out of the hillside after the winter's snow had melted, seeping out of the mountain next to us, and disappeared by sometime in May every year.

"Okay, I'll figure something out. I'll find a way to get water up here for you by the time I come out again in the next week or so," I told him. I certainly didn't want to haul fifty-five-gallon drums of water up from the creek, so I would need to bring a water line and run it from somewhere way upstream to the property here. Nacho had told me that when he lived here, he and his wife and kids had to bring buckets of water up from the creek on the trail that ran where we had cut the road. I couldn't imagine how hard that must've been. That was a really steep trail and about two hundred yards long.

Looking south from the house site, which was the upstream direction, there were no ranches or neighbors as far as I could see all the way up to the little cluster of houses called San Miguel, well over a mile and a half away. I figured the best thing for me to do was to find a spot off to one side of the creek where there was a seepage, and I could dig into the hillside and create a small water tank. We would need drinking water for our house, and I knew we could not count on creek water being clean. But when water seeps through rock and sand off to the side of a creek, it usually filters out most impurities. The water quality could still be compromised, so before I could count on it being of drinking water quality, I would definitely have to plan on getting a sample tested when I went back to Chihuahua City. I left Nacho to work on making adobes and headed up the creek bed with a shovel and a level.

I knew I only had to get to an elevation that was about fifty feet above the house site so that gravity would cause the water to flow down the hill and then up to the house. With that in mind, I had brought a two-foot level with me. Once I found a suitable spot for the water supply, I would use the level and sight across it with it aimed back toward the house site. There would be places where the water line would dip down, following the terrain, but once water was flowing, it would rise back up and flow out at our property.

For about an hour, I walked up the creek bed and searched the banks on both sides for a suitable place to start digging a waterhole. There was an awful lot of rock and not much in the way of damp soil or any small springs feeding the creek in that whole area. All of a sudden, I heard a voice and looked up from my work.

"Hello!" the fellow said. He was rather tall and a bit slender for a Tarahumara, so I suspected he had a bit of mestizo blood in him. "What are you looking for? Can I help you?" he asked. He had apparently been watching me as I worked my way uphill along the creek bed. I guess his curiosity got the best of him, and he had come to meet me. We hadn't met before, I don't think.

"My name is Teodulo," he said. "I live up there in San Miguel."

"*Mucho gusto*," I said. "My pleasure. I'm Esteban." He already knew who I was, of course. "I'm looking for a place where I can run water up to my property," I told him. "I'm going to need water at the house, plus I need to get some water up there right now for making adobes."

"Well, this water won't be good for drinking," he said. "If you want, I can show you where there is a spring on that hillside over there," he said, indicating the side of the mountain a few hundred yards away and to the east.

I pondered his words for a few moments while I considered the two scenarios. I could run a water line fairly directly toward my house from here, but if the water wasn't good for drinking, it wouldn't be of any value in the long run. I guessed I might as well take a look at the spring he was talking about.

"Sure," I said. "Let's go look at it."

Teodulo led the way. We climbed up the bank of the creek, crossed the road that went down toward my house and Mauro's, and started walking across the shallow incline of the hillside across the way. The further we went, the more I got skeptical because of the distance we were getting away from my house. "Just how long is this water line going to be?" I asked myself. In places, we walked over soil and small rocks; in other places, the ground was basically just decomposed granite. Finally, we came to a spot on the mountainside with lots of decent soil and trees around and a big patch of wet earth with a nice-sized spring of water flowing out of it. The water only flowed about ten or twenty feet and then seeped back down into the mountain.

I looked at the indentation in the ground where the water came out. It was about the size of a large washtub with gravel and sand in and around it. That was a good sign. It seemed well flushed out, so it apparently flowed fairly strongly.

"Does anyone own the land around here?" I asked him.

With a chuckle, he said, "No, no. No one is interested in living in this area. There's no place to plow for growing corn. This is all just ejido land and doesn't belong to anyone."

"So this spring doesn't belong to anyone?" I asked.

"No," he assured me again. "Once in a while, the goats or wild animals will come drink from this spring, but it's too far away from the logging road and other trails for anybody to even use it."

I went a few feet away to a large rock, and using a few sticks from the ground, I set my level on top and got it level. Squatting down with the level aimed at my house site, I could see that this spot was about thirty to fifty feet above the little adobe shack on my property. Wow! This just might be what I needed.

I dipped my hand into the water and sipped a handful. This was really good-tasting water!

"Does this water flow year-round?" I asked Teodulo.

"Yes," he assured me. Even during the winter, it didn't freeze over. I put my shovel into the basin of water, stirring up a bit of silt and dirt. I watched as within a few moments, the spring had flushed itself clean again. Yes, there was a pretty good volume of water coming out of it.

I was excited! This was going to be a far better source of water than alongside the creek. Sweet, clean mountain spring water. What more could I ask for? Once again, I lifted my heart in praise and thanks to the Lord who was taking care of my every need.

"Thank you so much for bringing me up here!" I said to Teodulo. "This is going to work out great!" I told him. He had a big smile on his face too. I think it really made him happy to be of help to me, the new guy in the neighborhood.

That was how I met Teodulo, one of my closer neighbors. He told me a little more about himself that day. He had a small store in his house right there on the road at San Miguel. So that explained why I had seen people hanging out there once in a while when I drove by. On the end of his house was a room with a pair of wooden shutters and a small countertop. Inside the room was a modest supply of sugar, beans, jars of Nescafe coffee, and a half dozen other things that people needed the most. His store was the only one in the area. You had to go almost an hour's drive to Bachámuchi or almost two hours back toward San Rafael to the little roadside store above Ocóbiachi to find any of those items. And that was pickup truck driving time. You had to multiply that by three times when riding on a logging truck, which was the only transportation for all of these folks here in El Manzano.

Our neighbor Teodulo plows his rocky corn field with oxen. To the upper right side of the photo, over a mile away in the distance in the cleared area, is our house.

Teodulo also told me that day that he was a carpenter. He said that if I needed any carpentry done, like making doors or something along that line, that I should come talk to him. We walked back down the hillside and parted ways at the logging road. Now I had to plan on how to get that good water over to my house.

6.4 Trucks, Trains, and Lots of Hauling

Three years earlier, I had bought our 1976 Ford E-250 four-wheel-drive van. Our 1965 split windshield VW van, which we had bought in 1975 right before we got married, had been a great vehicle during our last years of New Tribes training. I had bought two VW vans and put the camper interior from one into the other, which had a better body and engine. When we decided at the end of our language and linguistics training to go to Mexico and knew we needed a four-wheel-drive vehicle, it occurred to me that a four-wheel-drive van could be much more practical than a pickup truck. I knew that, eventually, we would be building a house in one of the tribes down there, so having a vehicle that we could sort of live in while we built would be really handy. Thus, I sold our dear old VW and bought the only four-wheel-drive van that we could afford in the entire Chicago area and made a camper interior for it.

It started off its life as a cargo van. I insulated the walls with fiberglass insulation, installed quarter-inch paneling, and found a design that was used in lots of RVs for benches and a table which could be converted into a bed in the back. The ceiling was quarter-inch plywood with low pile carpeting glued to it so it was quiet on the highway. The floor in the rear was also carpeted, and the floor in the front was sheet vinyl. I also found a used van rear seat which could be bolted to the floor for when we were traveling with the kids, then removed for carrying cargo. For the previous two years, I had used it for moving us to San Rafael and transporting supplies several times from Chihuahua City. To protect the walls and floor, I had bought and cut to size one-eighth-inch thick tempered Masonite panels, which were really durable. I was now about to use it a lot as a cargo van.

Since San Rafael was a railroad town, we were going to be able to take advantage of having quite a few things shipped out to us by train. Our coworker in Chihuahua, Peter Thiessen, had as part of his job description being our "supply guy." That generally meant that those of us in the tribes could write him a letter if there was sufficient lead time or ask him via our morning radio check-in if the item was urgently needed to purchase something for us and arrange to have it picked up or sent out to us. We all had to be careful not to overwhelm him with requests, but his help to us in the tribes when we were so many hours away by truck was huge.

One of my very first orders for him was seven hundred meters of what we called "ranch line." That was the half-inch diameter ABS plastic water line that was used all over the mainland on ranches and farms for water lines to livestock watering troughs, and it's what supplied water to all of the rural towns in the mountains of Mexico. It came in hundred-meter rolls that were about three feet around.

I had paced off the distance from the spring that Teodulo had shown me, down the side of the mountain, across the creek below the house, and up the other side. I planned on having a water reservoir of some type about fifty yards from the house on a small hill, which was high enough for a gravity feed to the house itself. I also ordered a couple of sacks of cement from Peter, and a week later, they arrived by train in San Rafael.

The first order of business at the spring was to pour a small concrete water catchment tank in the ground. That meant I had to carry a couple of sacks of sand and a half sack of cement to mix into it across to the other side of the mountain from the house site. I also had to carry a pick and shovel, boards, and hammer and nails with which to make a form and several feet of water line to temporarily divert the water away from the tank while I was making it. It took a few trips to carry all of that across to the other side of the hill, and it was exhausting. I was twenty-seven and a half years old, in pretty good shape, but that first bit of physical labor was one of the harder things I had done in quite a while.

Our house in El Manzano was at almost the same altitude as our house in San Rafael—7,200 feet elevation—and it took a couple of weeks to get used to doing daily physical labor at that altitude.

After the concrete of the water tank had set up for a couple of days, I went back across the mountainside with the rolls of water line. I buried the line only about four to six inches deep so that animals wouldn't step on it and split it, but in a few places, it went across rocky escarpment, and there was no way to bury it. I just had to try to pile rocks against it on each side to hold it in place and protect it a bit. The sections were joined by doing what the Mexicans did in the rural towns: about a three-inch-long piece of copper tubing was pushed inside each section, and then it was securely wrapped with strips of rubber inner tubes and tied. I used hose clamps on the lower elevation, higher pressure, connections.

After about a two-hundred-foot drop in elevation, I got to the creek below our house. It was there that I had the difficult task of having to figure out how to suspend the water line over the creek and across to the other side. The solution fell in my lap, or more accurately, appeared at my feet one day. I had been walking along the hillside next to the logging road that came down from San Miguel and saw a real heavy gauge galvanized wire lying on the ground. It was partially covered in dirt from erosion of the soil from the rain and snow. I asked Mauro about it, and he told me that several years earlier, the government had tried to run a telephone line down into El Manzano. The project didn't work, and it was never completed, so they just abandoned the line and left it lying on the ground.

Apparently, there were thousands of feet of that line laying alongside the road in various places, and I could help myself to whatever I needed. So I pulled and yanked and managed to salvage about eighty feet of the wire.

After trenching under the logging road, I brought the water line to the side of the creek bed. The creek would flood and get several feet deep during the summer rainy season and with snow runoff in the spring, so I had to suspend the water line far above that level. I spotted two good-sized pine trees that were on opposite banks of the creek and would not be in any danger of falling for the next twenty years, I hoped. I secured the wire around the base of one tree and then did a spiral wrap of the wire around my water line for about fifty or sixty feet and then secured it to the base of the other tree. That kept it suspended and safe from breaking, even if small tree branches were to fall on it.

From there, the water line went a couple of hundred feet up the hillside towards the house. For the time being, Nacho would be needing the water for making adobes, so I would just let the water flow down the backside of a little hill where it wouldn't erode my property.

After I had run the water line and made all the connections between the seven hundred-meter rolls, I went back up to the spring to make the final connection. This was the moment of truth. Would there be enough pressure from the downhill fall to push the water up the other side to the house?

As I went down the side of the mountain, I would occasionally stop and listen for the water in the line. I still hadn't buried the line in the shallow trench I had made. I could hear it trickling through the line. I went up to the house site and waited for the water to come out. Ten minutes, twenty minutes, and still no water. *Oh no*, I thought. I went back down to the creek and disconnected one of the joints. Water was gushing from there! I went uphill toward the house and disconnected another joint. Hot air gushed out, and finally, the water started flowing.

I reconnected the joint and jogged up to the end of the water line, hoping and praying the whole way. Yes! The water was finally flowing! There had been an airlock that had to be released, and I finally had sweet mountain spring water at the house site!

Nacho had been making adobes for several days by now but was only able to make thirty or forty per day because of the lack of water. He had dug a small pit where the water seepage spot was so that he could dip a bucket into it for making mud for the adobes, but at that rate, it would take months to get the 2,500 that I needed. Now he would be able to make a hundred or more each day. That would basically be his limit anyway since he had to spread them out on the ground to dry. He told me he would get one of his sons to help too so that he could stay on schedule for me.

"When will the rains start?" I asked. Up to this point, there had only been an occasional rainstorm every few weeks. This was a pretty dry time of the year, and the Tarahumara, like any farming culture, were acutely aware of how much their sprouting corn plants needed the rain.

"On the twenty-first of June," he replied.

I was rather struck by the precision of the date. "Really?" I asked. "How do you know that?"

I was about to learn a new tidbit of information, Native American science a la Catholic Tarahumara beliefs. "That is the Dia de San Juan," he told me matter-of-factly. It took me a few moments to figure out what he was talking about. *Oh yeah, the Day of Saint John. As in John the Baptist, the saint associated with water! Interesting.*

"And that is why everyone who is born on June 21 is named Juan," he told me.

"So the rains start exactly on that day?" I asked.

"If not, then a day or two before or after," he replied. Now that was faith.

Well, now I had a pretty darn good date only a few weeks into the future by which I better start building the walls of the house! Once the rain started, it would be almost impossible to have adobes drying once they were spread out all over the ground.

I had already spoken to our field leadership in Chihuahua City regarding anyone who might be able to come out and help me build the house. I had also put out the word with Mauro that I needed some guys to help me dig the footings and collect rock for them. I had asked him about getting sand and gravel, too, for the footings.

"Bring out thirty or forty gunnysacks," he told me, "and we will get sand and gravel out of the creek and fill them up for you."

All of that work got underway in earnest. I took a couple of picks and shovels out to El Manzano with me on my next trip, and I had two or three local fellows digging footings for me that were about a foot deep and two feet wide. From all around the property, we carried rocks in the van, in a wheelbarrow, and by hand. Someone would bring word to me that there was a new load of sand and gravel in sacks alongside the main creek or by a side creek, giving me approximate directions, and I would head off to pick them up in the van.

HE WHO HAS BEGUN A GOOD WORK

Local fellows filled dozens of gunny sacks with sand and gravel for the footings, concrete floor and stucco for the interior walls. Often times I had to back down into the creek bed to pick up the sacks.

Peter would send twenty sacks of cement at a time out from Chihuahua City on the train. Twenty sacks was a pretty good load for my van—1,800 pounds plus all the other supplies bouncing over those rough roads. After the first shipment, when a fair number of the sacks broke open while being loaded and unloaded, every sack had to be put inside of a gunnysack for strength. When I brought the cement out to El Manzano, it had to be stored in the adobe shack so it would stay dry.

Meanwhile, Nacho would stack the adobes on the ground nearby on edge in several piles after they had dried sufficiently in the sun for two or three days. They had to be covered with plastic to keep the dew off or in case of a sudden rainstorm.

Every four days or so of working on the house site, I would head back to San Rafael to be with Ticker and the boys. That was such a welcome break for me, and I know it was for her too. I finally got much better meals, and she got some much-deserved help taking care of the kids. Dave was seven years old and a big help to her with his brothers, but he was still a very active guy who wanted to play with all the local kids and was sometimes hard to keep track of. He and his buddies would climb up the side of the big hill, which was actually a small mountain that was right next to our house in San Rafael.

Someone had named the mountain La Luna, "the moon", because of the strange rock formations up there. Dave described them to me, but I was so busy at the time that I never did get a chance to climb the mountain and see what they looked like. Apparently, there were places that looked like craters, and there may have even been caves.

I had no way of communicating with Ticker for days at a time, of course, when I was out at El Manzano. We talked at one point about trying to get another radio like the one we talked to Chihuahua City with each day, but they cost several hundred dollars and required a special permit from the Mexican government. When I was gone with the van, too, Ticker had to walk to one of the little stores in town when she needed groceries. They weren't too far away—a quarter mile to a mile—but that wasn't the easiest trip to make with a seven or eight-month-old baby, a two-and-a-half-year-old toddler, and a seven-year-old who wanted to chase after stray dogs along the way. All of this was while walking along the dusty and rocky shoulders of the dirt streets. However, Ticker did get to know several ladies in town and even started having some of the Christian women come over and visit regularly. That was great for her companionship and to be able to converse in Spanish and get much more fluent.

The folks in Chihuahua City did their best to find some guys to come out and help me with the building. Once school was out at the beginning of June, a couple of the older high school boys came out, and they were a big help. Shane DeMarce and Todd Wyma came out on the train, another great convenience at the time. It was about a nine-hour trip on the train from Chihuahua City to San Rafael, and it got in about 4:00 or 4:30 each afternoon. I would pick them up from the train station, we'd spend the night at our house, and head out early in the morning for El Manzano. Of course, I needed plenty of extra groceries to feed those guys!

Inside the adobe shack where we had our kitchen set up, I was also able to rig up a mattress on a low platform for one guy, and the other would sleep on the van seat. I always got to sleep inside my van! That is until Butch Bennett came out with his wife, Pat, for a few days.

Butch and Pat had only been in Chihuahua for a couple of months and were in Spanish study. To break up the long tedium of language study, the staff liked to give folks a break so they could take a trip out to one of the tribal locations. Since I needed all the help I could get, the Bennets came out together. It was going to be a different sort of trip having them, however. It would've made a bit more sense for Pat to stay in San Rafael with Ticker, but she and Butch both really wanted to see the Indians in a tribal location. Logistically, it would have been crazy for all of us to have tried to go out there for a week and work. Ticker really needed the conveniences of the house in San Rafael, and we would have needed a big camping tent just for all of us to sleep out there. So she and the boys stayed in town, and I drove Pat, Butch, and Todd Wyma to El Manzano in the van with a bunch of supplies.

For the first time, I had to sleep inside the adobe shack at night so I could let Pat and Butch use the bed in my van. I got my first taste of what it was like to sleep in that shack. We had been having a problem with mice coming in at night since I first took food out weeks earlier. I'd gotten pretty good at storing our food in Tupperware and other containers that they couldn't get into easily, although they did start chewing up the corners of the lids. But I won't forget how hard it was to get a decent night's sleep in that shed.

Not long after we would turn the lights off and lay down to sleep, the mice would come in from outside, climbing up the rough adobe walls. They would start scurrying back and forth across the top of the wall, which was open between the rafters and the roof. You could barely hear their feet, but they were also constantly knocking off little tiny pieces of mud or gravel from the adobe bricks, which would fall down on top of the boxes of food and clothes and even the bed that you were sleeping on. I had taken my BB gun out there, so with a flashlight in my left hand while gripping the stock of the gun, I started to reduce their numbers. Once I could make out approximately where they were in the pitch dark, I would switch on the flashlight with my left hand while aiming toward the sound with my right.

Usually, the mouse would freeze in its tracks and you could see his two beady green eyes looking back at you for at least a second or two before he would take off again. I would have to focus my own eyes quickly, too, before I pulled the trigger. After the first night or so, I got a lot better at hitting them with my first shot. One night, I got seven mice! The other trick was finding their dead little bodies in the morning where they had fallen down amongst our supplies inside the shed so I could throw them outside.

6.5 American Yelling, "Mud!" Tarahumara Yelling Back, "Mud!"

With the rainy season upon us, the house walls go up

With two or three helpers, I had dug the footings, picked up several truckloads of bagged sand and gravel from alongside the creeks, and gathered tons of rocks. I had taught the Indian and mestizo helpers how to mix the dry sand, gravel, and cement in the right proportions, then how to add water to the right consistency, and we finished the footings in a few weeks. The piles of adobes that Nacho and his sons were making grew bigger and bigger.

The weather remained beautiful, with only an occasional rain shower through May and most of June. As it got closer to the twenty-first, the Dia de San Juan, clouds would build during the day, but it still didn't rain. The temperature would be in the sixties at night and in the eighties or close to ninety during the day. We moved hundreds of adobes only fifty to a hundred feet from where Nacho had piled them to spots where they would be close at hand for building the walls of the house. The guys could move only two or three in the wheelbarrow at a time, so we started stacking them inside the doors of the van and driving them to their new spots which moved them faster.

It was as we loaded and unloaded the adobes once or twice that we started finding that a lot of them would break in half. It turned out that a sizable area of the soil where the guys were making the adobes did not have enough clay in it. It had too much decomposed granite which doesn't harden into a good adobe brick. We set aside hundreds that broke in half or into thirds that couldn't be used at all, and it started to be obvious to me that the second floor might have to be framed out of wood.

At the end of June, we went to Chihuahua City for doctors' appointments for Ticker and Eric. Paul and his son, Todd, came back out with me in the van on July 2. Paul and I talked for a couple of days about any future partners and how we were going to proceed with the construction project. On the fourth, he went back on the train to Chihuahua City, but Todd stayed out to help me.

I had bought a whole bunch of two-inch-thick and twelve-inch-wide pine boards to make the door and window jambs for the house. Since it came straight from the sawmill, it was actually two full inches thick and twelve inches wide and was rough sawn! I had to plane it all by hand. That took hours and hours and created big piles of curly shavings on the ground at your feet. Every couple of hours I would have to stop and re-sharpen the blade of the plane with a stone by hand. We were going to need all of those door and window jambs as the walls went up, and I had some help on the way!

On the seventh of July, Ticker and the boys, Todd's sister, Star Wyma, and Butch and Pat Bennett all arrived in San Rafael on the train. The next day, Todd, the Bennetts, and I drove out to El Manzano in the van, and Star stayed in San Rafael to help Ticker. I don't remember how I sent it, but on the thirteenth of July, Ticker wrote a note on our calendar saying that I had sent a note, and the walls of the house were three feet high and the doorjambs were in. I suppose I sent it with a log truck driver who came through El

Manzano that I was visiting with, so it must've been Mauro's oldest son. He had the only log truck in the area at the time and was the only one who would've come down to the end of the road.

On the sixteenth, I drove us all back to San Rafael so that the Bennetts, Todd, and Star could all take the train back to Chihuahua City. We had gotten a lot done, almost a whole week of work, and now the walls were up to six feet high!

This time, I went with them on the train to Chihuahua. Butch wanted to come back out and help me for another week and wanted to bring his truck out this time. We bought a bunch of supplies and returned on the twentieth to San Rafael. I needed to accompany Butch in his truck so he could find his way back to San Rafael on the mountain roads when he got past Creel. It was a dangerous trip in a couple of ways, so it was always wise to have two fellows if possible.

Accompanying Butch and me on this trip was Shane DeMarce, the tall, strapping son of Terry and Del DeMarce. Like Todd Wyma, he was looking forward to a little bit of adventure and a chance to get out of Chihuahua City for a while since school was out for the summer. Rounding out the crew for the next week's worth of work was John Steinbacher. John and his wife, Linda, were pretty far along in their Spanish studies in Chihuahua. They were the next of our coworkers to be heading to a tribal work. They would be less than forty miles away from us as the crow (or airplane) flies, directly to the west, going to reach the Guarijio Indians with the Gospel!

On the nineteenth of July, however, we got some alarming news. The missionary pilot from Tucson, Arizona, Dave Wolf, was doing some familiarization flights with a new pilot for New Tribes, Charlie (I can't remember Charlie's last name and can't find it in any of my notes). As they were flying in to land on a mountaintop airstrip, which was going to be used by the Steinbachers and their partners going to the Guarijio tribe, the plane crashed on landing. Thankfully, neither of the pilots was injured. The plane, however, was badly damaged and could not be flown out. Charlie had been at the controls, and Dave had been unable to avoid the crash. Fortunately, the radio wasn't damaged, and they were able to call for help.

If that had happened in many parts of the world, it might've been possible for a large military or private cargo helicopter to carry the airplane out piece by piece. But since this happened in Mexico, no such help was readily available or affordable, and thus began a project to dismantle the airplane and carry it piece by piece down mountain trails and out to the west coast. That work ended up taking weeks.

The airplane was one that New Tribes Mission had purchased to service all of us tribal missionaries. Several of us questioned the need for New Tribes to have a pilot and airplane dedicated just to our field in Mexico. We weren't working in very many tribes and dialects at that time; in fact, only four locations. The Guarijio would be the fifth tribal location and the only one which was not accessible by road. Dave Wolf had been flying for all of us for at least three years by then. He was a very skilled pilot, having been an Air Force instructor pilot before he became a missionary. He flew for several other missionaries in other organizations also, so he was quite experienced with the mountain weather, terrain, and the politics and procedures of flying in Mexico. I had personally flown with him on three occasions and was quite impressed with his abilities on the really rough airstrip above San Rafael. We were all just extremely grateful to the Lord that both of the pilots were safe. The crash, however, effectively ended New Tribes Mission's idea to have its own aviation program in Mexico.

"Mud!"

Back at the ranch—literally, the Real ranch, that is—Butch, John, Shane, and I were laying adobes. To build an adobe house, you don't use cement-based mortar and bricks. The adobe blocks or bricks are sunbaked mud, and you simply use a thick mixture of mud to join them together in layers. Mud is the mortar. Shane and I were on one side of the house, building up a wall, and John and Butch were on the other side working as a team. The Indian helpers were working as fast as they could to keep both teams supplied with mud.

"Mud!"

The technique for making the mud was similar to what the Mexicans did in the towns and cities for small projects when making mortar for their brick buildings. We had big piles of pre-sifted dirt, which got the stones and rocks out of it, and started with a mound about two feet high and six feet in diameter. We would scoop out the center so that we could pour water into it from five-gallon buckets and would use hoes and shovels to mix it back and forth until it was the right consistency. Then it would be shoveled into a wheelbarrow, pushed to where the guys on the wall needed it, shoveled onto their scaffolding, or directly onto the top of the wall to be spread out, and the empty wheelbarrow was rushed back for another load. Meanwhile, two more guys were busy mixing the next batch of mud on the ground. When they ran out of mud, that team of two guys laying the adobes simply had to stop and wait.

"Mud!" shouted Butch in English from the other side of the house.

"Butch!" I called back to him. "They don't know what you're talking about! The word for mud in Spanish is *soquete*. You need to yell soquete to them!"

As if in response, a couple of the helpers echoed, "*Soquete, sí*" as they hurried another wheelbarrow full to us.

"So...So... What was it?" asked Butch. He repeated "so-ket-eh" a couple of times under his breath, trying to memorize the word. "That's too hard right now," he called back. "It's a whole lot easier for me to just teach them one simple word in English. Muuud!" he yelled to the helpers. John, Shane, and I just all laughed. Only Butch could get away with being such a knucklehead.

I called over to the helpers and said, "Soquete is mud in English. When my buddy shouts 'Mud,' now you know what he means."

They all laughed and repeated, "Mud! Mud!" imitating Butch's volume and intonation. They got a kick out of him and his good nature and had learned their first word in English. For the rest of the week, every time they filled the wheelbarrow up with a load of mud, they called out "Mud!" as they headed over to us to dump it off. Even I quit calling for soquete.

Butch was definitely the funniest guy amongst all of our coworkers in Mexico. If you've seen pictures of Jay Leno when he was young, he even had quite a bit of a physical resemblance to him. He had dark hair that was styled a lot like Jay Leno's and a full, somewhat rectangular jaw and face. I started calling him the Jay Leno of Mexico to our coworkers. Butch would regularly find the humor in just about any situation, even on those hard days when we were lifting twenty-pound adobes from the ground to shoulder height over and over again in the hot sun. He always found something in the situation that would make us laugh.

I shovel mud up onto the top course of adobes while Butch, on the scaffold, lays them in place and Todd Wyma keeps bringing more to us.

The rainy season was now upon us in all its glory. For my Tarahumara neighbors, it was the greatest thing in their world. Their corn crops were going to grow and do well. For us working on the house, it meant a daily interruption of about two hours.

Every morning dawned clear and beautiful with hardly any clouds in the sky. By late morning, the clouds had built up noticeably, and we had to keep an eye on the sky. Almost like clockwork, about noon or one o'clock, the rain would start. We kept long strips of plastic that were about two or three feet wide handy next to the walls. When the rain would start, we would drape the plastic over the top row of adobes and put rocks and boards to hold them down. We also had to cover up some of the tools quickly. The chain saw was always close by. Since I didn't have electricity, I did not have a Skil saw to cut all the framing for the doors and windows. That was done using a chain saw, including the notching and mortising.

The rain generally lasted for an hour and a half to two hours. During that time, we would sometimes find a place to shelter against the walls of the house with a plastic tent draped over us. It was a bit claustrophobic inside the adobe shed or sitting inside my van or Butch's pickup truck. We would catch a nap or sit around telling stories. Finally, one afternoon, we had reached an awesome milestone: we were at the top row of adobes for the first-floor walls and were ready to set the beams that held up the second floor!

Part of the advanced planning had been to get several local Tarahumara and mestizo men to cut quite a few beams for the first-floor ceiling. The beams were supposed to be six inches square and fourteen to sixteen feet long. There was also a really large ten-by-ten beam with a post that held it up in the center of the main room. All of these were hand hewn by the local men using axes. It was quite a fascinating process to watch them take a tree they had just cut down, and with it lying on rocky ground, work their way down the length of it with an ax and create a long straight side to it. Then they would roll it ninety degrees, and going from one end to the other, make another straight surface, continuing until they had a square beam. The whole time, they braced their foot against the log to keep it from moving, wearing only huarache sandals and having their toes only inches from the blade of the ax. Yes, occasionally, there was an accident, but I don't think there were any that happened while they worked on our house.

The beams had been cut and left on the ground by different fellows at different locations. Mostly, they tried to keep them close to the road where I could pick them up easily with the van, which made it so they didn't have to carry the beams anywhere. When we had pauses in the work on the walls, I had taken the van and picked up most of the beams and stacked them at the house site. However, on the afternoon when we finally got to the point we had to set all of the beams, there were still six or eight that were down by the creek where I had been picking up sand and gravel.

As I sat out the rainstorm for an hour, I kept thinking about those beams that needed to be brought up to the house site. It was killing me to sit around and wait for the weather to clear. I was sitting in the front of my truck thinking, and Butch was stretched out on the floor in the back, taking a rest. I knew the rain would be stopping in the next hour and we would be able to set those beams.

"Hey, Butch," I called back to him, "I want to go get those beams that are down by the creek, and I've been thinking about it. Let's go get them right now so that when the rain stops, we have them up here."

"What? You want to go get them in the rain?" he asked, incredulous.

"Yeah, what the heck? It's only a little rain, and it's starting to die down," I said. "Let's go!" I told the other guys what we were going to do, and they thought I was being a little too impatient also. But this was my house that we were working on, and I only had these fellows' help for a couple more days.

Butch and I drove the half-mile down to the creek where I had seen the beams, then I had to back up in the creek bed as far as I could go before I got to some big boulders. Sure enough, the creek bed was getting more washed out each day with the runoff from the rains. I stopped as close as I could to where the beams were, but the farthest ones were still about a hundred and fifty yards upstream.

"Come on, Butch," I said. "This won't take long. Help me carry them down here."

Butch did not look happy at all. "Let's just wait till the rain stops," he said.

I didn't want to be a slave driver with my friend, so while looking at the water running in the creek, I got an idea. "I'll tell you what. I think I can basically float the beams down here to the truck by myself. You stay here in the van, and when I get close, just open the back doors, and you can help me drag them in."

Butch told me I was crazy but nodded and said okay, so off I went upstream to the furthest of the beams. I rolled and wrestled it down from the bank into the water, grabbed the downstream end, and tried to float the beam as best I could. The water was knee-deep in places and flowing fast. I had to be careful not to twist an ankle with all the rocks that I was walking over but, little by little, got the first beam to the truck. Butch opened the doors, bent over from inside the van, and pulled the beam up toward the front as far as it would go. Off I went for the next one.

Of course, it got easier with each one because I was getting closer and closer to the truck. By the time I finished wrestling all of them, the rain had died down quite a bit although the creek was still running high. Butch jumped out of the van and helped me carry the last one or two. When we got back to the house site, I went and changed into dry clothes. The only other pair of shoes I had were tennis shoes, so I wore those for the rest of the day. But it was all worth it. We got all of the beams installed that afternoon!

The beams are up, but the second floor had to be made of framed lumber since quite a few adobes were made of sandy soil and broke. Have to be able to adjust!

6.6 Drunk Driver and a Close Call

After a really productive week of help from the guys, it was time for them to get back to the big city. We put in a pretty full day, had dinner, and packed up our trucks. Butch told me before we left that he was getting fairly low on gasoline. I looked at his gauge and figured he probably had just enough to get back to town. I was going to lead the way, so I told Butch that if his gas got really low, he should flash his lights at me a couple of times so I would stop. We could always siphon a few gallons of gas out of my truck into his so he could make it the rest of the way. It was a little after seven o'clock in the evening, and we started off on the two-and-a-half-hour drive to San Rafael. The next day, they would make the eight-to-ten-hour drive home to Chihuahua City. John Steinbacher would travel with me in my van, and Butch would follow us in his truck with Shane riding shotgun.

All went fine until we were about an hour from El Manzano and we came up behind a logging truck that was also heading into San Rafael. The driver had the massive blade of a bulldozer and some fifty-five-gallon drums on the back of his truck, apparently moving a roadbuilding operation back to the sawmill town. I was ahead of Butch, and we both had to settle in behind the log truck and wait for him to get to a wide spot in the road and pull over so he could let us by. He passed first one spot, then another without pulling over. This was really unusual. Those truck drivers were always quite courteous.

Finally, I flashed my high beams at him, but he went right past another spot without pulling over. We were only going perhaps ten or fifteen miles an hour, and we, in the smaller trucks, could have been going thirty or so. I was starting to get frustrated and was getting a bit irritated. I decided that at the next wide spot in the road, I would just punch it and pass him and hope that Butch followed my lead.

A couple of minutes later, we came to a fairly wide and long spot, so I floored it and went to the left. I could see that I would have no trouble getting past him when all of a sudden, he whipped to the left to block me. I couldn't believe it! I slammed on the brakes, and the big steel corner of his truck bed missed the front of my truck by six inches or less. If we would have been two feet further ahead, he would have hit me and run me off into the trees! Now I was mad—really mad.

"What was that all about?" exclaimed John.

"I have no idea," I said. Something like that had never happened to me before.

"All right, you jerk, take this!" I said to myself and turned on my high beams and off-road lights. There were two very bright off-road lights on the roof of my four-wheel-drive van, so now I gave him a little bit of my mind.

"I can't imagine who this guy is," I said to John. "With Butch low on gas, we can't afford to take an extra two hours to get into town. Butch will run out of gas long before that."

Soon we came to a fairly steep uphill incline, and the log truck slowed from fifteen mph to ten, downshifted, and then was down to perhaps five mph. Then he came to a dead stop. I'd seen many really heavily loaded trucks have to do this occasionally. Somehow, they couldn't downshift into first gear without stopping completely, maybe due to their clutches. This guy stopped with me about twenty feet behind him and Butch fifteen or twenty feet behind me. Then, instead of his truck only rolling back two or three feet as he let out the clutch and gave it the gas, he rolled back five feet, then ten feet, then fifteen feet.

"Oh my gosh," I said. "He's going to roll right into me, and he doesn't care! I sure hope Butch is watching," I said and quickly threw my gear shift into reverse and backed up.

We went backward fifteen or twenty feet before the log truck driver let out his clutch and started moving forward again.

"He would have hit me again," I said. "This guy is absolutely crazy!"

Fortunately, Butch had been watching carefully and had backed up quickly so that I didn't back into him.

We had gone at least another twenty minutes at this maddeningly slow rate of five to fifteen mph when we came up to a fairly wide section of road. The log truck slowed, then stopped right in the center of the road. The driver got out, leaving his door standing wide open. Three guys got out of the passenger side and left their door open, too, obviously on purpose. One fellow headed off to the edge of the woods to relieve himself. The driver and another guy, with Coke bottles in their hands, came sauntering back toward my truck.

Three other men who were riding on the bed of the truck climbed off, milling around in the road. As the driver came back to my door with a bottle in his hand, I started to understand. The Coke bottles weren't completely empty, which they had appeared to be at first glance. They had a couple of inches left of a clear liquid in them. These guys were all drinking *pisto*, the local mescal cactus moonshine. They were drunk, and at least the driver was in a mean mood. He walked up to my door with one of his buddies by his side. Another fellow stood in front of my truck, looking at us through the windshield with glazed eyes. I rolled down my window to see what this was all about.

"*Que pasa?*" I said to the driver. "What's up? Why won't you let us pass?"

"Ah, you Americans," he said. "Don't you know this is our road? We live here. We drive our trucks for a living here. You guys and your pickups just like to drive fast, but really, this is our road."

"We all live here," I said to him. "You know who I am." Even as I said this, I was trying to memorize what he looked like and hoped to figure out later who he was. "I've lived in San Rafael for over a year, and now I'm going to live in El Manzano. We all share the road, and you know I'm always courteous with you guys."

"Yes, but you—" he started, his speech slurred.

I interrupted him, "Look my friends and I have worked hard all day, and we just want to get to my house in San Rafael. Why don't you just let us get by? That's not a big deal, is it?"

"Ha! You just want to get by. We'll just see if you can get past me. Just try it, Gringo."

He had a mean look in his eyes. He was about forty years old, not a punk or young guy with a chip on his shoulder. He was no doubt a very experienced driver, and it was going to be next to impossible to get past him. Having delivered his challenge, he walked back to his truck. He and the others continued milling around, stretching their legs, and going to the bathroom. In just a few seconds, Butch came up to my door. "Hey, Steve, what's going on?" he said. The look on his face was as tense as the tone of his voice. "I thought those guys were coming back to beat you up. They had empty bottles in their hands. Geez!"

I told Butch what the driver had said and that they were all drunk.

"So how many of them are there?" Butch asked.

"It looks like seven to me," I said.

"Well, there are four of us," said Butch. "Those aren't bad odds."

I couldn't believe it! I almost started laughing! Butch Bennett, American missionary, living in Mexico, was ready to rumble with a truckload of Mexicans!

"Hold on there, Butch," I said, "I've gotta live out here. These guys are my neighbors. We can't be having a fight."

"I thought we were going to have no choice," he said. "When they came walking back to your truck with those bottles in their hands, I told Shane, 'Quick, look under your seat for something, anything to use as a club.' I grabbed a tire iron from behind my seat. We were ready to run up here and help you if they started swinging."

Good old Butch—and that was the old Butch coming out. He'd been a pretty rowdy guy when he was younger. Raised in New Jersey, he worked as a teenager for a smalltime mafia guy on a boardwalk, carrying and protecting payroll. He was five-foot-ten tall, three feet wide, and was one tough son of a gun at seventeen years old. A year or so after that, four or five guys had tangled with him and a buddy in a pool hall one night. Butch said the fight had been close for a few minutes, apparently, but then his adrenaline and instincts had kicked in. A vision had popped into Butch's head of him being beaten down and kicked, and he decided that was not going to happen. He and his friend broke a couple of pool cues across the other guys' legs and faces and then got out of there.

When his boss heard about it, he was real proud of him and offered him a better position. But Butch decided that wasn't the life for him and soon after moved out of that part of town. Now here in the Sierra Madre of Mexico was the New Jersey kid, ready again to defend himself and his friends. I was suddenly really glad I had a guy with some guts along. But I was the senior missionary here, and I had to handle this situation the way I thought God would want me to.

"That's cool, Butch. I'm glad you had our backs. But we've got to find a nonconfrontational way out of this. Be ready for anything. If I can make a move, and it's safe for you to follow me, do it. But you saw that so-and-so almost hit my truck twice. Don't let that happen to you. If only I get ahead, I'll drive right in front of him until you can get past him."

Then we talked about Butch's fuel level again. It was getting pretty low. We knew we might have to stop on the road and siphon some gas from my truck into his.

My last words to him again were, "Be ready for anything." Man, I wished we had walkie-talkies or CB radios or something and could talk to each other, but we didn't.

As I mentioned, John Steinbacher was riding with me. Sitting there with the engine off, we talked for a few minutes about our options, but there weren't many. It looked like it was going to take us two or three more hours to get into town. It was already now about 11:00 p.m. Then, all of a sudden, I saw our chance.

"John," I said, "look how much room there is on the passenger side of the log truck. If you were to get out, wander over to the side of the road, walk up and close the log truck's passenger door, I think I could get by. As soon as you close it, I'll start the engine and pick you up in front of the truck. Just close their door and run for twenty or thirty feet. Butch will be right behind us."

"Oh man, I don't know," said John. "They're going to get really mad. I don't think we can make it—"

"John, look," I said. "They're already drunk and ticked off and being jerks. They've almost hit my truck twice. What in the world do we have to lose? Just do it."

"I don't think so," he said. "It's better if we just get into town later—"

I couldn't believe John's attitude and had some rather unkind adjectives running through my mind for half a minute or so. Then I realized something else. *Okay, maybe I can do this myself,* I thought.

A van like mine had a very short nose and hood, so I could open my driver's door, stand in the wheel well step without getting out, and probably reach far enough forward to grab the edge of the log truck door and close it without it hitting my own truck. I'd have to mow over some small sapling pine trees that were on the right shoulder of the road, but I was now convinced it could be done.

Never mind about John, I thought. I wanted to signal Butch but was afraid of giving a heads up to the enemy. I knew that starting my engine would be an obvious enough signal. I looked in the mirror to be sure that Butch was behind the wheel of his truck and that Shane was beside him in the passenger seat and started my engine. I told John to hang on.

I raced forward with my headlights off. The less the bad guys could see and figure out the better. Only the log truck's headlights were on, and that gave me plenty of light. When I was right behind the big truck's door, I slammed on the brakes, opened my door, reached forward and, with two inches to spare, closed their passenger door. I jumped back down into my seat and floored the accelerator. Mowing down six or eight little trees, I got past them and, for a second or two, could only see dust in my rearview mirror. Then I saw Butch's headlights come on right behind me! We had both made it—how cool! We drove for a minute or so just to make sure we had a good head start, then stopped, got out, and celebrated for a minute.

It turned out that as Butch got close to the log truck, one guy had tried to jump in front of him and stop them, but he had been a second too slow, and Butch had stayed right behind me. I was impressed.

We needed some good distance on the log truck now in case we had to make a five-minute stop to siphon gas, so we took off at a pretty good clip. I told Butch again to flash his lights at me if he was starting to run out of gas.

We made it to my house with Butch's truck running on fumes. We woke up Ticker, told her what had happened, and had a snack. But we were too keyed up to go to sleep right away. Besides, I had no intention of going to sleep until I'd watched that log truck come into town and make sure those drunk guys didn't cause any trouble. The main logging road came into town barely three or four hundred yards south of our house and passed fifty yards or so in front of the house as it went toward the sawmill and the north end of town. Chances were fifty-fifty they'd drive past our house on the way to theirs.

After a few minutes, I decided we'd turn off our propane lantern, which made a hissing noise, and use the kerosene lamps while we sat around and talked. That way, we would hear the noise of their diesel truck as they came into town.

We'd gotten into San Rafael at 1:00 a.m., and at 2:20 a.m., we heard their truck. We went outside and stayed in the shadows where we could see clearly. As they got within a hundred yards of my house, they turned off their headlights and slowed down, looking for our trucks and lights in our windows. After they passed by, they turned their headlights back on and thankfully went on their way.

"Good," I said, "there will be no rumble tonight."

Visiting the Drunk Truck Driver

—⟶⟵—

About four or five months later, I came into town from El Manzano for supplies. We had moved into the new house with it only partially finished. The incident with the truck driver had been told around town, and I had learned and engraved his name in my memory in case I ever ran into him or his family members. You never knew who might have gotten an attitude about what happened that night. But on this particular trip, I came into town with someone who told me the guy had rolled his truck, while drunk, over the side of the road several days earlier. He had broken some ribs and hurt his back and was going to be laid up for at least another couple of weeks recovering. He was at his home in one of the small houses on the Ponderosa log company's property close to the sawmill. An idea came to me.

"I think we should go see him," I told my friend. He looked at me like I was crazy. "I'll just go stop in and say hello and wish him a good recovery," I said.

"But he'll think you came to mock him or looking for a fight while he's hurt," my friend said.

I realized that, yes, amongst typical unregenerate Mexicans their culture would be to go get in the face of your enemy while he is at his weakest. Then you can either humiliate him or threaten him. But I would not only do neither, I would show him that there was no ill will on my part, and I genuinely hoped he would be okay.

I went over to the sawmill, filled up with gas as I had to do anyway, and asked where the truck driver lived. I got directions, and we drove a couple of hundred yards over to a clapboard house and pulled up.

"I think I'll stay here in the truck," my friend said.

"No problem," I said and went up to the door. I asked for the driver, said I just wanted to say hello, and was walked back to a dimly lit bedroom.

"Hello," I said. "I heard you got hurt and just wanted to see how you were doing."

He just stared at me for a couple of seconds before he found his voice and said, "Oh, yeah, I'm a bit sore but am getting better."

We talked for a few minutes, and then I said, "Well, I just wanted to wish you well. As far as I'm concerned, there are no problems between us. Really. Take care and get well soon." I shook his hand and left.

Amongst the local people, a guy who had almost had his truck run off the road, then nearly had the front end of his expensive four-wheel-drive crunched on purpose—well, that guy would just as soon have pulled a club or gun or knife the next time they met. But I had shown him what a Christian was like.

The news of our visit went around the area for a few weeks, from what I later heard, and the truck driver himself was apparently the one who was the most impressed. Praise be to the Lord!

6.7 Second Floor and Roof

So many trips! Every five days or so, I would run out of materials for the next phase of the building. It was good timing to go back to San Rafael again anyway to be with Ticker and the boys, and it worked out okay since there really wasn't any place out of the weather to store the materials at the house site. One thing I had to plan pretty far in advance was getting tongue and groove flooring made for the second floor. When I went around San Rafael looking for carpenters to do that work, I was surprised to find that the only fellow who could make tongue and groove was booked for two to two and a half months!

I paid him to purchase all the one-by-six boards from the sawmill and get them to his shop. Then he had to plane them all on both sides and make the tongue and groove flooring. The timing barely worked out. The only time I had to hire a log truck to bring materials out was for the flooring and the galvanized metal roofing. I paid Mauro's son, Ernesto, to bring those items out, and it was a good-sized load.

After Butch, John, and Shane left, on my next trip, I took a full truckload of two by fours for framing the second floor. About 25 percent of all of the adobes they had made for me broke from being too sandy and couldn't be used. Not having anybody to help me for a couple of weeks was hard, but I got the second-floor walls framed. Then it was time for our annual field conference. Although I didn't want to stop the construction, it actually was a good time for a break.

The field conference that year was at a small church-related conference grounds in the hills outside of the town of Cuahtemoc.

Cuahtemoc was a little less than an hour west of Chihuahua City, so it was convenient for all the folks that lived in Chihuahua and yet allowed all of us from the mountains to be in a nice, relaxed setting away from the city.

Each of the tribal locations was scheduled to give a report on the progress of their work. On the agenda was a report from the Central Tarahumara tribe, where Ed and Debbie Capps were working as well as Marsh and Joy Milliken. Javier Ibarra, a native Mexican New Tribes missionary, was also scheduled to join their team, but I'm not sure if he ever did. In the Pima Tribe were Barry and Candy Wingo who were to be joined by Robert and Karen Stover. In the Tepehuan Tribe were Kevin and Wendy Case, who were to be joined by Gary and Liz Johnson and possibly Peter and Mary Thiessen. In the Western Tarahumara, there was just Ticker and me, so I would give the report.

On the daily calendar of events, it read "Steve Real, Roc. Tarahumara." "Roc." was the abbreviation for the community of Rocoroibo, where the Wycliffe Bible translator, Don Burgess, had lived. For the first few years, we called our dialect the Rocoroibo dialect instead of the Western dialect.

Butch Bennett came up to me on the morning in which the tribal reports were scheduled to take place and said, "So what is this all about? Steve Real, Roc. When I saw that, I thought, Oh yeah! Steve Real, Sergeant Rock! It fits! You know who Sergeant Rock is, don't you?"

Actually, I did. I knew he was a comic book character from the 1960s. His character was a blend of the outstanding soldiers who fought for the United States Army and Marines in World War II and the Korean War. I thought he was definitely cool, but maybe a little overdone, so I hadn't read a lot of his comic books. I was more into the *Fantastic Four* and a few other more fictional characters. But I got a kick out of Butch thinking of me as Sergeant Rock. In fact, for the rest of the conference week and the next couple of years, half the time he saw me, he would say "Hey, Sarge!"

After the field conference was a convenient time to head to Chihuahua City for supplies, etc. I took the opportunity to go to the doctor for an annual checkup. For the first time in over three years of being in Mexico, I had finally gotten amoeba. It was really easy getting medication over-the-counter in the pharmacies, so I purchased a box of amoeba medication but had to ask the pharmacist for the right dosage since it was not written on the box. I was quite fluent in Spanish and wrote down exactly what he told me to take. But I wasn't getting better very quickly over the next several days and lost ten or twelve pounds. I had always been on the thin side and couldn't afford to lose ten or twelve pounds.

When we got back to San Rafael and I checked our New Tribes Mission recommended medical bible, the book entitled *Where There Is No Doctor*, I found the pharmacist had told me the dosage for a child! I would inevitably trust that book dozens and dozens of times over the course of our many years in Mexico, and it always turned out to be extremely reliable.

In Chihuahua City, I also got the chance to talk to our field committee about getting someone else to come out and help me on the house. After working on the house by myself for a couple of weeks before the field conference had started, I'll admit that I felt overwhelmed with the work that still had to be done. I really couldn't see myself getting any decent help from the guys in El Manzano either. The committee members Steve Bram, Ken Gutwein, and Paul were sympathetic to the fact that I still needed a lot of help before winter came, but it felt like they were reluctant to send anyone else out since I had already gotten a lot of helpers over the last two months. Finally, though, they talked to our bookkeeper, Bill Robbins. Bill was one of our older missionaries. I would guess he was in his mid-fifties. Thankfully, he had a good deal of experience in construction, having built a couple of houses in his home state of Oregon. So they agreed to let Bill come out and help me for a week or so.

Bill's help was a huge encouragement. The week that he came out was a lot easier, too, because for a change, Ticker came out to do the cooking and cleanup for us. We were a small enough group that it worked out well with the sleeping arrangements. The Indians had cut all of the rafters, which were just skinned pine poles, and they were ready when we were. Bill and I worked well and quickly together, notching and nailing the rafters in place as well as the posts and beams for the front and back porches.

I planned for the porches to be really nice and wide. The front porch was going to have all of our winter's firewood stored there, which would be four to five cords. The back porch would be more utilitarian with the gasoline-powered wringer washing machine that we planned on getting soon as well as washtubs, a couple of clotheslines, storage for a few tools, etc. Both porches were about six feet wide and thirty feet long.

After all the rafters were up and braced, Bill and I put up the rows and rows of purlins. The corrugated galvanized metal roofing was then nailed onto the purlins. The day we got all of the roofing on was incredible! After almost three months of rainy season, which was coming to an end, we finally had the house weatherproof!

Bill brought me a special gift when he came out too. It was a pair of climbing spurs which he had brought with him from Oregon. He explained to me that they were spurs for climbing power poles, not actually made for climbing trees since they had short spikes and not the longer ones which would penetrate the bark of a tree. But they became an extremely useful tool for me for several years to come. Many times, I had to go up the sixty-foot-tall pine tree next to our driveway to install, and after a storm would tear it down, reinstall the sixty-foot-long wire antenna for our single sideband radio.

By the middle of September, Ticker and I were really encouraged about finally getting moved out to El Manzano. There was so much that needed to be done on the house still, but we really looked forward to just being in one location together as a family. For four months, I had been away from them more than I had been with them, working at least ten-hour days. Now it was time to plan for the big move!

The roof was on and the house weather proof before the cold set in and the first snow fell

6.8 Home, Sweet Home!

My mom had saved a letter that I sent her dated October 13, 1983. I found it after she passed away, and it gives a pretty good synopsis of how our life was at that time. I'll quote it here and add some explanatory notes in parentheses.

> Here I sit in the house in San Rafael as I write this. The house here is getting emptier- we now have [brought] our little Coleman camp stove, propane lamp and cooler here. Last week we took our gas stove and refrigerator, boys' beds and a desk out to El Manzano. It'll be much nicer now that we're out of the little "hut" there and living in the new house. The bathroom [there]

is Ticker's kitchen; in a corner about 5' x 7' at the foot of the stairs is our "living room/dining room" and we live in about one third of the bedroom space upstairs while we work on the rest of the house; but it's like being in a mansion after the adobe hut we've been in for four months." [Actually, I was really the one living in the "adobe hut," while Ticker and the boys lived in our two-room house back in San Rafael.]

Work on the house, almost the only thing we're involved in these days, is going slowly but surely. I was just thinking of sketching out the land for you and the house plan, since it must be hard to visualize. Perhaps I can get the Polaroid [camera] to cooperate and send a picture soon. Anyway, the layout of the land is something like this: [I did a drawing of the creek, road, new house and the adobe hut, which was about 2 ½" x 4" on the stationary].

The upstairs is wooden, stud-type construction, [and] the downstairs adobe. The floors downstairs are still dirt, the upstairs are tongue and groove pine from here in San Rafael. The roof is galvanized tin. Our 'ceiling' upstairs is still the tin roof, none of the bedroom walls are up yet, the living room is 6 inches deep in wood shavings from planing lumber by hand, the dining area is a 1 ½ foot high sand pile for when I start cementing the interior walls—but it's home!

Ticker and Eric left on the train today for Chihuahua, Dusty and I are going to get some lumber, groceries, furniture loaded into the van, etc. Ticker got a dentist appointment for tomorrow [by calling in on the radio to our office in Chihuahua City] for a molar that broke last week; then Saturday David starts a one-week break from school, so they'll be in on the train Saturday afternoon and by Saturday night we'll be all together in El Manzano! David last saw the house when we were pouring the foundation. He stayed here in San Rafael all summer as Ticker's helper. We plan on having some fun while he's out. His next break is a three-week Christmas vacation.

Dusty's getting big... He sure likes being a helper- and a rascal at times, too. This afternoon he threw the cat down the outhouse hole. I didn't know how I was going to get it out, but the hole isn't real deep and somehow the cat got out itself. I dumped pitchers of water all over it- which the cat didn't enjoy too much- but boy does it stink! I thought about all that I'd been taught at home [by you, mom] but couldn't bring myself to boil the poor thing for 10 minutes then pour Clorox on it, so I'll just have to wait and see what happens to it. Anyway, when Dusty wants to be wild and get your attention, he has rather extreme methods.

Eric is growing like a weed and is the happiest little guy. In fact, he gets so happy at meal time that he can hardly get a bite [of food] down- he grins that big "beaver grin"- four teeth on top and two on the bottom- and Ticker can't get the spoon in. After us laughing for a couple of minutes he finally calms down and can open his mouth.

He's healthier now these last several months than he's ever been. In June he was deathly sick for a while- three days solid of high (103° to 104°) temperature. [I had been in El Manzano and didn't know anything about it until I got back to San Rafael] We hope they'll both stay healthy for a while now.

So when will you get down to see us again? [They had come to see us for a few hours when we lived in Chihuahua City while we were in Spanish study, and had been going to southern Mexico on vacation almost every year for about 10 years] You can still get a pretty cheap vacation down here, especially coming out to stay with us. The views of the canyons are fantastic, the woods are all pine and oak, the birds are all pretty, the "natives" are friendly!

Yes, we had finally moved into our house, but boy, was it primitive living. Our field chairman, Paul, and the rest of the field committee thought that Ticker, the kids, and I should get moved out of San Rafael as quickly as possible. So here we were—I hand-planed lumber as quickly as I could to make our front and back doors, stapled clear plastic to the window frames in place of glass, and within just a couple of days, the house was basically weatherproof.

With apprentices Dave and Dusty, standing in 4" of wood shavings, I hand plane the wood for the doors and window shutters.

In October, the nights were getting noticeably chilly, and we knew we could have snow within a month. I brought our wood-burning heater to El Manzano with us, but I had designed the house around a central heating source—a fireplace. It would have two openings, one toward the study/guest room, and the other angled toward the main living space, which was the dining room and kitchen. The fireplace would have a firebrick-lined chamber that would extend up about four feet, then transition to stone for the main chimney and the entire face and sides would be stone. But the stone would only go up to the ceiling of the first floor. From there, there would be six stovepipes that were six inches in diameter each that would extend the rest of the way up through the roof. Three of these stovepipes would be in the boys' room and three in Ticker's and my room with a piece of sheet metal between them as a wall.

Now I hate a cold bathroom as much or more than anyone else, so I had a special plan for heating the bathroom, but I had no idea if it would work properly. The plan was to run two of the stovepipes horizontally through the adobe wall between the dining room and bathroom, only about two and a half feet above the firebox of the fireplace. From there, they would run about five feet straight up inside the bathroom, right next to the shower stall. Then just below the ceiling, they would turn ninety degrees back to go and join the other six-inch stovepipes before they went up through the bedrooms above. This was how I built it and could not wait to fire up the fireplace for the first time and test it out.

Building the fireplace—time consuming but so beautiful and worth it when finished!

I had estimated that building the entire fireplace would take me four or five days, cementing the brick and stones. It actually took me three weeks! It was a lot of work getting all those stones to fit properly with the nice faces facing into each of the two rooms.

Finally, the day came when I ran the stovepipes all the way up through the second floor and the roof. By then, I was also confident that the mortar had dried sufficiently and would not crack from the heat. I built a fire and crossed my fingers as the smoke rose up through the chimney. It took a couple of moments before I could plainly see that a portion of the hot rising smoke was indeed being sucked sideways into the pipes that ran inside the bathroom. Yes! It worked! From that day on, every time we built a fire in the fireplace, which heated the house really nicely, the bathroom was the warmest room in the entire house.

Thankfully the fireplace heated the whole house really well

As I mentioned in the letter to my mom and dad, the bathroom became our temporary kitchen. It was fairly big, about six feet wide and ten feet long. Because it was the only room that was easily closed in during the early stages of construction, it had a door that I could lock when I went back to San Rafael and one window with big wooden shutters that I had made and could lock. The big main room where the kitchen would be was wide open, and I had not yet made the cabinets, so we moved our stove and refrigerator into the bathroom, and we had a temporary plywood countertop with a couple of dish washing pans. Above that were four shelves for dishes and groceries. The walls were bare adobe for a few months.

You can imagine the challenge it was for Ticker to keep two small boys clean when we had dirt floors in the house. Therefore, it became my next priority to pour the concrete floors. Of course, that involved having many, many sacks of sand and gravel compiled by the Indians which I then trucked up to the house site. Once it was all there, along with quite a few sacks of cement from Chihuahua City, I started mixing cement. A couple of local guys helped me mix it, but I'm the only one that could do the finish troweling. That necessitated me being on my knees for most of the day, using a piece of plywood as a knee board and some old bath towels as kneepads.

Playing soccer for seven years before we got to Mexico had not exactly improved my knees, and now I really paid the price. For three nights after troweling concrete most of the day, I took more Tylenol than I had ever taken, and even then had to sleep on my back with my knees bent up, supported by pillows. I think I barely slept five hours a night. But, finally, we had concrete floors!

The finished kitchen, with our forty-something year old but faithful Servel refrigerator

In the bathroom, we also had our hot water heater, which was quite an appliance. It was a little smaller in diameter than a typical American thirty-gallon hot water heater because it didn't have a fiberglass insulation jacket built into it. It had a very clever fire box at the bottom, which had a door about six inches wide into which you could feed firewood that was cut up into very short lengths. But the hot water heater could also be fed with a kerosene drip. That entailed using the heavy gauge steel can that was attached a foot or so above and to the right side of the fire box.

This kerosene tank had a manual drip valve with steel tubing that dripped inside the firebox. The trick was to get a small fire going with wood, then adjust the drip so that the fire was just hot enough and would not blow out. It worked amazingly well. It was very clever Second or Third World technology. The bathroom was the only place we had running hot water. There was no easy or practical way to get hot water lines across the house to the kitchen, so we did what we had been doing for the last couple of years, and Ticker heated up water for dishes in a big pot on the kitchen stove. As soon as dinner was served, a big pot or two of water went on top of the propane kitchen stove for doing dishes, heating while we ate.

Late in the fall, we got a surprising and really welcome letter from some folks who supported us financially. Betty Gordon and her son, Glenn, had become our good friends while we were attending New Tribes boot camp in Ontario, Canada. We had gone to their church and gotten to be good friends with several members from their extended family. Very sadly, only the year before, Betty's husband, Harold, had died suddenly. They were hardworking pig farmers. Harold came in from the barn one evening, washed up for dinner, and sat down in his favorite recliner to rest for the last few minutes before Betty called him to eat. They called him, but he didn't respond. He had passed away quietly and peacefully, although he was way too young. I think he was only fifty-six or fifty-seven years old. Ticker and I grieved with them over their loss of such a good, godly man.

But the next news that we got from Betty and Glenn was that they wanted to come down and help us work on the house! There's no better time to get out of beautiful Ontario than in the cold of winter, so we made arrangements for picking them up and brought them out to El Manzano. Betty was a huge encouragement and help to Ticker, laughing with the kids, cooking and doing laundry by hand, while Glenn helped me finally stucco the bare interior adobe walls of the house. They were with us more than a week, and the transformation of the interior of the house was dramatic! Once again, God brought even more of His people to help us reach the Tarahumara Indians with the Gospel! All they had to do was be willing, asking with an open mind and heart, "What would You like me to do for Your kingdom, Lord?" Then they obeyed His leading, even if it meant travelling more than 3,000 miles and into a foreign country.

Chapter 7

Life in El Manzano

7.1 I Couldn't See to Drive

I really wouldn't want to be anywhere except exactly where God wants me to be. That's for darn sure. However, that doesn't mean it's going to be accompanied by a peaceful, easy feeling; in fact, it's sometimes downright painful.

It was the end of October 1983. I was sitting all by myself in my truck off to the side of the long dirt runway at Ocóbiachi. I was glad no one was around because I had tears running down my face, and there was no way I could drive at the moment. I watched the Cessna airplane as it bounced and roared down the runway with dust blowing behind it, and then it finally rose into the blue sky and banked in a turn toward Chihuahua City. In it was my eight-year-old son, David, on his way back to the boarding school in Chihuahua City after just a one week break in his first semester.

"How can this be right?" I asked myself. The emotional pain was awful. "This isn't natural. It isn't right for me to raise my son, my first son, for eight years, then have to send him off to someone else to take care of him. He's MY son. My little buddy!" The tears kept coming, and I was powerless to stop them.

"But every missionary dad, except the ones in the city, goes through this," I told myself. "Do they shed tears like this when they send their kids off? Probably not. Man, I'm being a big wuss."

It probably took fifteen minutes before I could see to drive. I dried the last tears on a napkin, thankful again that no one was watching. I drove up and out of the valley, slower this time. It would take me over an hour to get home, but I was in no hurry. This new reality was something I was going to have to accept and live with, whether I liked it or not. Dave was now in second grade and had reached the age where all the missionary kids needed to get a good education and socially acclimate themselves with other American kids.

This was the viewpoint of most mission organizations, and almost all families agreed. Some did not, choosing to homeschool their children for several years while they lived, and tried to have an effective ministry, in the Indian tribe. Some of those families were able to do a good job at both schooling and their ministry, while others were not. A gamble for all of them was whether or not their children would forever feel like fish out of water when they got back to the States or have a hard time adjusting if they entered the mission school years later than the rest of their peers. To us, it made sense to send Dave to the boarding school, so Ticker and I accepted this separation and had to keep moving forward. Still, I didn't like it, and it really hurt.

About twenty-five years later, my sons would give me one of the most unusual and coolest gifts I would ever receive: a Jimmy Buffett song with lyrics customized to match my life and experiences. There's a line in the song "He Went to Paris" that says, "And his tears were a-fallin'." When they e-mailed each other back and forth to discuss the lyrics, one of my boys said to the others, "I've never seen Dad cry." And I guess they hadn't. I was tough and goal-oriented and loved pushing ahead toward our objectives. But this separation from my son touched a chord deep in my soul. I hadn't cried in many years, but I sure as heck did that day.

Daily Life in Our New Home in El Manzano

Ticker had been doing a great job homeschooling all of the boys five days a week as part of her busy schedule. Generally, I was up first in the morning, made coffee, and tuned in to news of the United States and the world on the shortwave frequency for Armed Forces Radio. This was a service of the United States government that was beamed around the world, and we had pretty decent signal strength, even where we were up in the mountains of Mexico. If it was chilly weather or cold winter weather, as soon as I got up, I got a fire going in the fireplace and warmed the house up. Within forty-five minutes or an hour, Ticker and the boys would come downstairs, and she would start breakfast.

Dave leaves for the boarding school in Chihuahua City a couple of years later from the new airstrip in El Manzano

Breakfast sometimes consisted of eggs with tortillas and beans, and, once in a while, with our still favorite luxury, canned bacon! With such a small refrigerator and freezer, however, we had to carefully ration the fresh meat. Every two or three days, the hissing sound of the pressure cooker would fill the house. Before cooking the pinto beans, one of our staples, Ticker had to carefully sift through them and make sure there were no little stones that had made their way into the bag of beans from the fields where they were grown and the factory where they were packed. Oftentimes, there was a stone that could easily break your teeth when we were eating, so getting those out was an important step that every cook in Mexico had to do. Next, they were rinsed, then soaked and cooked. The pressure cooker made the last step go much faster.

Monday through Friday, Ticker would get the boys started on their school lessons, sitting down and going through the various subjects as needed. When they didn't need her undivided attention, she would be back in the kitchen, prepping lunch or dinner and, once a week or so, would get the laundry ready to wash. Doing the laundry involved getting enough water heated to fill up a large washtub and a separate large rinsing tub. For the first several months in El Manzano, she had to do this as she had done it our entire time in San Rafael, heating water in big pots either on the gas stove or on top of the woodburning heater. Once I had the kerosene/woodburning hot water heater installed in the bathroom, that task became much easier. Still, she had to carry buckets of hot water from the bathroom to the back porch and fill up the washtubs.

She washed the laundry like women had been doing it for hundreds of years in the United States and around the world on that ingenious invention called a "washboard." It was a wood-framed textured metal board that was a nice step up from washing your clothes on the rocks at the creek, but it was still hard manual labor and not easy on her back. It was a big step up when we were able to afford a wringer washing machine that we found in Chihuahua City on one trip. The washing machine was used, of course, and had a Briggs & Stratton engine like the ones used on lawnmowers all over the US.

The engine on our washing machine, however, was rather temperamental. Especially in the winter, it could be incredibly hard to get started. If she wasn't able to start the engine after a few pulls, I would have to stop what I was doing and go be the clever mechanic.

Sometimes that was as simple as spraying starting fluid in the carburetor or pulling the cord really hard four or five more times. Many times, it involved practically taking the carburetor apart and cleaning things before I could get it started. I was pretty good at working on my truck's engine, pretty good at working on my chain saw motor, but that little Briggs & Stratton caused me a lot of grief over the years. I almost said a few bad words to that little engine.

"Interruptions"

Ticker visits with neighbor ladies who have stopped by

It took me most of our first year in El Manzano to finish the house on the inside. So that I could get all of that work done more quickly, Ticker tried to deal with as many visitors who came by the house as possible. If it was a man who came by, she would tell me right away, of course, and I would come greet him. Oftentimes, the visitors would be women with a child or two with them since the men were busy working. Whether it was a man or a couple of women and children, the scenario played out something like this:

Ticker: Hello! How are you today?
Visitor: Good, thank you. How are you?
Ticker: Have a seat (which was almost always at our kitchen/dining room table).

Visitor(s) seats themselves, and if it's a man, says, "Is Steve here?" If it's a woman or two with their children, they have a seat, smile shyly, and say "Thank you."

Ticker: Would you like a cup of coffee?

To which they almost always say, "Yes, thank you."

Ticker starts making or serving instant coffee, sometimes with some crackers or cookies as a snack. This, of course, makes everybody happy, so there is then a little bit of small talk, but no one ever states the reason for the visit right away—ever. Unless it's a medical emergency.

Ticker or I, after a few minutes of asking how they and their family are doing, try to get around to the purpose of their visit. Oftentimes, the visitor is still a little bit shy, which to them is the way to show respect and not just be blunt. For us, too, our way of showing respect for them is to not come right out and ask what they want. That would be rather abrupt and businesslike, not neighborly. So sometimes the small talk goes on for a little while longer, even into the second cup of coffee.

Eventually, we either ask outright how we can help them or they come out and state their reason for coming to see us. Sometimes they are needing medicine for themselves or a family member, and they know that we bring medicines out from Chihuahua City and keep a small supply of things like bandages too.

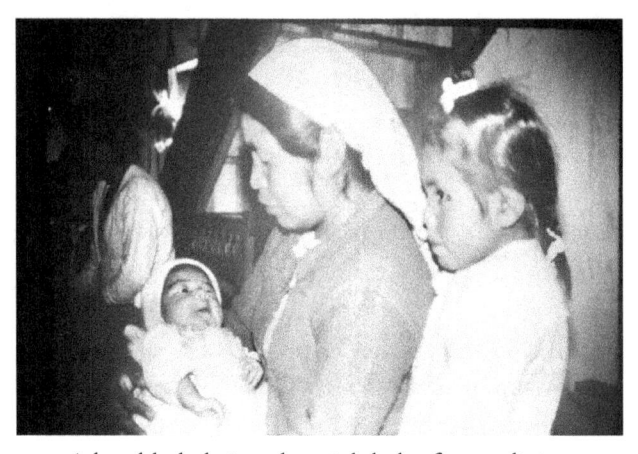

A local lady brings her sick baby for medicine

Sometimes they want to know if we are interested in buying something from them: apples, a chicken or two (which often turn out to be roosters and not chickens—haha!), and occasionally something more interesting, like parrots or baby squirrels to have as pets.

If the visitor is a man or an older teenager (all the younger teenagers are always working at their own homes since their parents have an unlimited amount of work for them there), he will oftentimes be looking for work. That could include work I might have on the property like improving one of the rock retaining walls for the yard or cutting firewood. Especially in our first year in El Manzano, we had visitors who came up with a variety of reasons, usually stating some kind of medical need for them to go to San Rafael, hoping we would give them a ride to town. After getting snookered a couple of times doing that for someone who wasn't really sick, we got wiser and I, having to be the bad guy, told them that I was just too busy.

When someone was genuinely sick, of course, either Ticker or I or both of us would check them out and try to figure out the best way to treat them or their family member. A lot of times, that would necessitate us taking a walk to the sick person's house with a medical kit and some antibiotics.

Whether it was in that first year that we were in El Manzano and simply wanted to just finish the house construction or it was in the subsequent years when I was trying to learn the Tarahumara language, an "interruption" wasn't really an interruption—it was an opportunity to build a bond with the people of the community. It didn't feel that way sometimes. I am pretty goal-oriented and wanted to make some measurable progress in whatever I was doing that day or that week. Sometimes the visitors and their slow custom of getting around to stating their purpose was annoying, I must admit. I would have to pause and let the Lord redirect my heart and attention to what was most important: the person in front of me at that moment.

Teodulo's sister Lorenza comes to visit with her two children

I did love the people that God had sent us to reach with His Gospel, so it was always with a sense of peace and purpose that I would say to the Lord in my heart, "Okay, what should I do now?" Ticker had to do the same, too, of course, and was a gracious hostess.

Our closest neighbor, old Nicolas, comes to visit

Not insignificantly, from time to time in those first years in El Manzano, Ticker was struggling with depression for at least a few days each month. That complication is something that neither one of us knew the root causes of, or how to deal with it well. But it was a reality in our lives—a really unwelcome reality. It began to encroach on our lives slowly but, like having a bad back, would remind us regularly that it was still there, and we didn't know what to do about it.

Evenings and Nights—Ah Yes!

As our day grew to a close, when I had finished my carpentry or other project for the day, Ticker had supervised the last of the boys to make sure he was bathed or showered, and we were about to sit down to dinner, I looked forward to enjoying my family for a little while. I usually managed to find a little time to play with the boys before dinner while it was still light outside. I might work with them on building a tower out of blocks on the back porch or go see where Dave thought he heard a rattlesnake rattling in the rock wall that afternoon or check out the drum set that the boys had fabricated out of pots and pans and cardboard boxes.

As the light of day would fade, it was time to light our main light of the whole house—the gas lantern that was permanently installed over the dining room table. It was a typical propane camping lantern that is used by millions of campers around the world. But to use it as our main light, I had run a quarter inch copper gas line to it from the great big tank outdoors that also provided gas for the stove and the refrigerator. It gave off a fairly loud hissing sound, but that couldn't be helped. In order to reflect light down on the table without having a big shadow cast underneath it, I had experimented with different kinds of lampshades. I finally perfected one that was simply aluminum foil glued to heavy construction paper that I had shaped into a lampshade. The opening in the center above the lantern was only about six or seven inches in diameter, so I was a little bit afraid that the heat coming off the lantern might burn the paper, but the aluminum foil and the constant flow of cool air being drawn up through the lampshade made it work. In fact, to make it a little more attractive, I also attached cotton fabric from an old bedsheet, also using contact cement, to the outside of the lampshade. In all the other rooms of the house, including the kitchen, we had to use kerosene lamps.

Then it was time for dinner, and I tried to help Ticker with whatever she wanted me to do or would let me do in the kitchen. After dinner, we always had a Bible story and devotions together. We still used those couple of Bible storybooks that we had for a couple of years by then, which were a lot more intelligible for the kids than me reading the Bible story from my old King James Bible. Afterward, we would find a little more time to play games or make forts with wood blocks and army men and take turns shooting at the other guy's army men with rubber bands to try to win a battle, then we would put the boys to bed.

Usually, I would turn on the shortwave radio again and listen to the day's news from Armed Forces Radio one more time. Ticker and I would sometimes write letters in the evening to family members or our financial supporters. If she felt the need, she would get her Spanish course books back out and brush up on Spanish so she could be more comfortable talking with visitors and using the verb tenses or vocabulary that she had partially forgotten. When I was doing Tarahumara study, if I'd had several interruptions that day or for the past couple of days and felt like I wasn't making much progress, I would often write down recent incidents and file them away in our Tarahumara culture file.

For me personally, my greatest relaxation and entertainment came from reading novels at night. I had made a bed for us with a headboard that was a couple of feet high and had a bookcase in it. The top of the bookcase was about a foot wide and was perfect for putting an oil lamp on top of to read by. The silver metal reflectors attached to the backs of lanterns that you see in antique stores that were used all through the United States and Europe from the 1600s to the early 1900s and reflected light from the back of the oil lamp, which was oftentimes mounted on a wall, definitely helped to better light up a room in a house. But they cast a shadow directly in front of the wick and burner and below the oil lamp as well, so I needed something of much better quality than that to read by.

One of my earliest "inventions" was a setup using a pair of mirrors, attached to the oil lamp, which angled the light down onto the book which I had in front of me. I had to experiment with the size of these mirrors, the angles, and the placement so that they did not cast a shadow, but I perfected it within a short period of time.

Once I was satisfied with that reading lamp setup, there is no doubt that I spent several thousand hours reading by it over the course of the years we lived out there in El Manzano. At one point, I remember counting over thirty Western novels by Louis L'Amour that I had read, besides the numerous spy and war novels by Alistair McLean and various other authors who kept me entertained for two to four hours just about every single night for years on end! Better than TV? I think so, in most ways. How I loved reading at night!

7.2 Making Friends, El Manzano Style
Playing the "Palillo"

We were barely established in El Manzano when I was invited to go with a group of my neighbors to play a game called the *Palillo* (which just means "stick") against men from the community of Ocóbiachi. Perhaps since I said I wanted to learn the Tarahumara language and culture, they decided to find out how serious I was. In every culture there always comes a point in time to see if the "new guy" can fit in or is going to just keep to himself, is a doer, or just a talker. I think that was part of their reason for inviting me to the game, but it perhaps had more to do with the fact that I had the only vehicle around that was a lot more comfortable than the back of a log truck for getting to the competition and back.

The game is played with hand-carved oak sticks that are shaped like a jai alai stick but shorter. They're about three to three and a half feet long, have a nice round hand-grip handle at the top, and a scoop at the bottom that will accommodate the ball. Just above the scoop, the shaft is carved into a flat "bat" that is eight or ten inches in length.

The ball is also carved out of oak and is in between a golf ball and a ping-pong ball in size. The idea of the game is to scoop up this ball from the ground, lift it up to a comfortable height, and then hit it with the flat portion of the stick as far as possible towards your team's goal and across the goal line.

The game is played in a dry creek bed or arroyo. The distance between goals the day we played was about two hundred yards. There were lots of small and medium diameter pine trees along both of the sloped sides of the arroyo, making for many, many "hazards," which is part of the fun, adding to the hundreds of boulders that must be run around and over as the ball is getting batted back and forth.

We started off in the middle of the course, like in a hockey game, then the scrapping and fighting for the ball began. I stayed back a ways with several others to see how this was going to go, playing defense for our side. But as I had done many hundreds of times in soccer games, as soon as the ball came near me—in front or behind—it was time to go to it and hit it toward our goal. The scrambling was vicious sometimes, with five or six guys all trying to scoop the ball away from the others, get just a little off to one side so as to have a clear shot, then bat it as far ahead as possible.

It seemed everyone was quite serious about doing well in the scrapping and batting but also got to laughing at the crazy pandemonium, the bad hits, and even our collisions with each other. It was great to see that we could all have fun, even though the competition was fierce. In my many soccer games, we never laughed like that, unless someone took a bad spill and fell on their butt, perhaps.

In one vicious tangle of seven or eight of us, one fellow thought he had the ball but had scooped up a rock. He was about four feet to one side of me. He lifted it and swung hard, hitting me in the elbow with his stick, but fortunately not enough to really hurt. I got in a few good hits on the ball, too, which elicited some cheers from my teammates.

The whole game lasted about an hour and a half. I wish I could remember which team won, but I can't. I just had too much fun and actually didn't understand anything the guys said in Tarahumara. They all spoke varying degrees of Spanish, too, but seemed to enjoy speaking their native tongue while doing this native sport of theirs.

There were several bruised shins, hands, and arms, but I think it turned out to be fun for both communities. I looked forward to playing in more games, but that sport seemed to be on the decline, much as the unique and greatly renowned long-distance races of the Tarahumara had done. At least I had the pleasure of playing in one!

When (Fishing) in Rome, Do (Fish) as the Romans Do

Teodulo, my neighbor who had shown me where the spring was that became the water source for our house, came over one afternoon.

"Hola, Esteban!" he said. "How would you like to go fishing with a few of us down at the river?"

"When are you going and what do I need to bring?" I asked him.

"Bring some good boots for hiking, lunch and water, and a big bag to bring some fish back in," he told me, obviously enthusiastic that I had agreed to go. "It will take us all day to get down there and back, so we'll leave early. I'll come by and get you about seven o'clock." I told him I thought that my son, David, would like to go and that I thought he was tough enough and a good enough hiker to make it, even though Dave was only seven or eight.

Teodulo showed up with his younger brother, Valentin, and a couple of other guys. It was to be a three-hour hike down and three and a half or four hours to get back. We went down into the El Manzano valley, then north toward the big river, the Rio Oteros. The trail was pretty easy to follow if you knew which side trails not to take. We descended about five thousand feet in elevation, and when we arrived at the river, it was a beautiful thing to see! We were pretty much out in the middle of nowhere, not having seen or passed any ranches or people along the way. We crossed to the other side of the river in a shallow area that was only about twelve inches deep and made our way upstream a couple hundred yards to the first of a few big, deep pools.

I asked Teodulo how he was going to get the fish since he hadn't said anything about bringing a fishing pole, and none of them had one. This was when I learned about a fairly common technique used in many Third World countries—they were going to use dynamite!

Kneeling down at the edge of a really big pool of water, Teodulo got out a stick of dynamite. It didn't look anything like the dynamite you see in the old Westerns, which looks like a highway flare. It actually resembled a gray sausage about ten inches long and one and one-fourth inches in diameter. It was crimped at each end with a metal clip and was kind of squishy. Into this, he pushed a blasting cap, then a piece of fuse. He cut the fuse to a length that he said would burn only about twenty seconds, and it was obviously waterproof. He walked upstream about fifty or sixty feet, told us all to get back twenty feet or so, lit the fuse, and threw the dynamite into the current so it would hopefully end up in the middle of the big pool when it exploded. The pool was perhaps thirty or forty feet across and I guessed about fifteen or twenty feet deep.

When the dynamite went off, the concussion stunned or killed most of the fish in the pool. That was bad for all the smaller fish, of course, which were the ones most easily killed, but some larger ones came to the surface too. Everybody got into the water and pulled all the fish out that they could with their hands. Some were just stunned for a few seconds and then swam away, but we got six or eight pounds of fish out of the explosion. My thoughts right away were that this was a good way to ruin the fish population in this area with all the young ones killed.

They repeated the fishing operation with two more sticks of dynamite in two other pools. Then we cleaned all the fish that we had collected, rinsing them out in the river water, and wrapped them up in some wet towels to keep them fresh for the long walk home.

But before we left the river, we had to get some food into us. We gathered up driftwood and started a campfire. With our knives, we cut long green branches from some of the bushes along the riverbank and made forked sticks for cooking the fish. They were delicious! Then, after also having some *pinole* (dried, coarsely ground, and lightly roasted corn meal mixed with sugar) for extra nourishment, we headed home. David did really well, and although he was tired, I never did have to carry him piggyback, although I was prepared for that possibility.

It was a beautiful day of hiking and getting to do my first real social activity with my Tarahumara neighbors. I didn't want to make them feel uncomfortable about my feelings about killing so many fish, so I didn't really go into detail about those thoughts of mine. After all, they had been doing this for as long as they could get ahold of dynamite and would continue doing it, I was sure.

HE WHO HAS BEGUN A GOOD WORK

Macaws, Rattlesnakes, and Bees—Oh My!

In most places in the world, people work all week and look forward to some weekend activities either relaxing at home or doing something fun and different. Oftentimes, city folks like to connect with nature, getting away from the city and technology for a while. Well, when you live in the wilderness, sometimes you want extreme wilderness as your weekend diversion. So it happened that I was able to plan a Saturday outing to try to get some baby macaws with Teodulo and his younger brother, Valentin.

The summer before, we had bought a pair of baby parrots from one of the local Indians. He had cut down a pine tree in which the parrots were nesting, so the little birds were orphaned. They turned out to be the most interesting pets we were to have. More about them later. But having those parrots made me think about the beautiful macaws that also went up into our Sierra Madre Mountains to breed in the summer months.

They made the long trip up from southern Mexico and Central America just to mate and have their chicks in the cool mountain air. Then, when the young ones were only a few weeks old, they would all fly south for the rest of the year. I had seen some of these beautiful birds from a distance and once from a couple of hundred feet above them as I hiked a mountain ridge. The colors of their feathers and wings as they were extended in flight was amazing! They were sapphire blue and bright red with yellow markings. It had occurred to me that it might be fun to have one or two of them, also, so I had mentioned that to Teodulo one day.

Teodulo was definitely becoming more of a friend as the months went by. He came by the house one day to tell me that he had some news he thought I would like.

"Esteban," he said with a smile on his face, "I know where there are some macaws that are nesting and have babies," he said. "Do you want to go out and get them?"

Dave was home from boarding school in Chihuahua City on his summer break, so he went with us. We took two other Tarahumara relatives of Teodulo's with us. I grabbed my climbing spurs and the two ropes that I used in place of a climbing harness since Teodulo told me the macaws' nest was way up high in a really big pine tree. Boy, was he right.

We also took snacks and water, of course, plus my pellet gun. There were lots of squirrels, Teodulo said, and the guys with us would eat them if they were able to kill a couple. We drove to the top of the canyon to the east of the Red Rock, left the truck there, and hiked twenty or thirty minutes down to where there were lots of big pine trees and cedars. This area had not been logged before, being in a really steep canyon.

When we got to the tree Teodulo had found, I was truly amazed. It was huge, with about a six-foot diameter trunk, about as big as they grow in those mountains.

"That's the nest up there," said Teodulo, pointing way up toward the top of the tree. "See that hollow spot on this side of the tree?" he asked. "That's where the nest is. The parents probably heard us coming so may not come back right away. But that's where the babies are."

Oh my, I thought. *That's a long climb up there, and this is the biggest tree I've ever tried to go up.* It looked to be eighty to a hundred feet tall. *Well, this should be exciting*, I thought.

Dave stayed with me as I prepared to go up the tree. All the Indian guys went off with the pellet gun to hunt.

Dave was quite content playing nearby, exploring the woods. I could see—and I was right—that getting up the lower part of this tree would be a challenge. With a huge circumference like that, I had to really whip the rope up the backside of the tree two or three feet each time I wanted to ascend another step. This involved setting my climbing spurs firmly in the bark as I leaned back into the rope which went around my lower back and around the tree. Then I'd lean forward to take my weight off the rope, whip it up the tree a couple of more feet, lean back into the rope again, step up, and firmly jam the spikes back in. I had to repeat this over and over to get up the tree, each time firmly planting the spikes in the bark.

The spikes on my climbing spurs, which had been given to me, were meant for utility poles. They were not meant for tree climbing, so the spikes were short and only went about halfway into the bark. If I didn't plant them deeply and keep my balance carefully, when I would go to take a step up, a spike could come loose, and one of my feet would slide down the tree. That meant I had to be really careful each time I stood up and leaned toward the tree to whip the rope up. I'd learned this the hard way a few times on the tree by our house that had the radio antenna strung from it. When a spur slipped, it was dangerous enough that all my weight was only on one foot, but it also made me fall forward into the tree somewhat. And if I wasn't super careful, I could slip out of the rope that went around my lower back, and in that case, the next stop would be the ground floor, literally. The tree next to our house was sixty feet tall. I knew because I had measured it once with a hundred-foot tape measure that I had. This tree that I was going to be climbing was eighty to a hundred feet tall, I was certain.

Pine trees all get little thin branches, in addition to the big ones, that just grow straight out from the trunk but never grow any bigger in diameter than one of your fingers. As the tree rapidly grows in height, these branches eventually just die, and what's left is a dried stick three to six inches long sticking straight out of the bark. It's those little nubs that caused me so much trouble that day as I was climbing that big tree. I had to flip the rope up the backside of the tree really hard to get it past those annoying nubs or break them off. The first big branch of the tree which I would have to climb onto was about twenty feet up. Unlike any of the smaller diameter trees I had climbed, by the time I got up to this first big branch, I was exhausted, soaked with perspiration. I had only been resting on the branch a half a minute when I heard Dave's voice nearby.

"Dad!" he said. The tremor in his voice made the hair on the back of my neck stand up. Dave never sounded like that.

"What is it, Dave? Are you okay?" I called down. I couldn't see where he was exactly. He was between fifty and a hundred feet away in the undergrowth.

"Dad! There's a rattlesnake! A really big one!" he said.

"Did you freeze, son?" I called back. "Don't move a muscle, not one step. Not even backward!" I had never heard him this scared of anything in the woods.

My mind was racing. I looked down to the ground. It was definitely too high to jump down or even to hang from and drop. I could easily break my ankle from that height. I would have to go down at least halfway the same way I had come up before I could drop to the ground, and that could take me five minutes. It had taken at least ten to get up to this point.

"Dave, what's the snake doing?" I called. "Is it coiled? Is it moving away from you?"

"It's moving away sort of, through the grass, but not very fast."

I decided that Teodulo could get there much faster than I could.

"Stay still, Dave. Do not move!" I called to him, then shouted, "Teodulo! There's a big snake over here by Dave! Can you help?"

Teodulo answered right away from a hundred or more yards away, then I could hear him and one or two of the other guys running immediately. They would be there in a few seconds.

After only three or four seconds, however, I got my next shock.

"Dad," Dave said, his voice a little less wavering this time, but not by much. "There's another one. It's right in front of me!"

This time, I almost did jump from the tree. I would have to quickly unbuckle my climbing spurs, use my main rope to hang from, and pray I landed well. As these thoughts shot through my mind like lightning, I called again to Dave that he needed to stand absolutely still.

He didn't even answer me this time, but that was a good sign. I knew he paid very close attention to me when I explained some of the dangers of life in the mountains. He had come upon more than one rattler on his own while hunting lizards with a slingshot or his little bow and arrow in the rock walls around our house. He was scared, but he was also well focused. This little outing had suddenly developed into the most physically threatening event since we had arrived in Mexico.

Teodulo and company were there in another ten or fifteen seconds, though it seemed like forever. I guided them over to us with my voice, then Dave was finally able to speak again, and he pointed Teodulo toward the direction in which the second closer snake had gone. I talked to Dave, calming him down, and told him to come back closer to the tree I was in. I also called to Teodulo and told him there were two snakes, to which he replied "Ha!" in disbelief.

"Teodulo, Dave is positive he saw a second one," I said, relaying and explaining quickly what Dave had been saying to me in English as he was walking back toward me. I had heard a couple of times the old wives' tale that snakes travel in pairs. Although I had seen dozens of rattlers by then, I had never seen a second one with any of them. And in all the years since, I've still never seen a second one. But that day, as He did so many times over the years, God was taking great care of Dave.

It turns out he had been walking slowly along when he saw the first snake. It was moving slowly across his path, several feet in front of him, and its length is what startled and scared him so much at first. He froze, just like I had taught him to do. Then, after calling to me, staying motionless and barely starting to relax, he looked down, and right in front of him was a second rattler, coiled and ready to strike! If Dave had taken one more step, he would have stepped right on it! That coiled snake never did rattle. It eventually uncoiled and went off through the undergrowth.

"I got it!" shouted Teodulo. "It's a big one too! Almost two meters long!"

Wow, six feet! That was the first one that they had been looking for.

"There's still a second one, Teodulo," I called to him. It took them several more minutes, but they found the second one also. It was a little shorter, about five feet long.

If either of those snakes had bitten Dave and injected very much venom in him, he could have either died or been very critical by the time I got him out of that ravine. I don't know how he could have survived for the ten hours it would have taken me to get him to Chihuahua City. God was certainly taking care of Dave that day. It was after this incident that I looked into getting antivenin and having it at our house. It turned out that purchasing, storing, and being certain of how much antivenin to inject someone with actually had its own complex set of problems.

So how did the rest of the day go? After I calmed down and realized all was under control, I continued up the pine tree. From the ground, Teodulo had pointed out to me the hollow spot about twenty-five feet down from the top of the tree where the macaws had their nest. Trees with a hollow in them obviously have a central decay problem and can have other hollows also. This tree, in fact, did have that problem, about fifteen feet below the macaw nest. As I got closer to it, I found the reason for all the bees I kept seeing flying around as I climbed up and over numerous big branches. There was a honey beehive in another hollow of the tree!

There I was, fifty or sixty feet above the ground, and I now had a decision to make. After driving this far and climbing this high, did I want to abort the mission? On the other hand, did I want to get stung multiple times way the heck up in a tree? This was crazy! Since I had left the ropes quite a ways below me and was now climbing limb to limb, I decided to judge my chances of getting past the hive without disturbing the bees. Was it possible to make myself invisible to them? *If I move slowly enough, they shouldn't feel any scraping sound against the bark of the tree and come swarming out*, I thought to myself.

After calling down to Teodulo on the ground, telling him what I had found, I decided to go for it. I went up a few more feet, then went around the backside of the tree at the level of the hive. Very slowly, I went up and passed them. It appeared they accepted me as just some unusual but nonthreatening fellow creature. In a few minutes, I was above them and finally close to the macaws.

The adult macaws had not made an appearance since I'd been in the tree. I was glad they weren't dive-bombing me or otherwise defending their nest as I got close to it. I got up to the hollow, saw the big nest tucked back inside the tree, and looked in.

Oh no, I thought. I had expected to see some little birds, sleeping or with their little mouths open, but instead saw two little down covered chicks that barely had their eyes open.

Again, it was time for a decision, and this was a really tough one. I knew next to nothing about little birds. We'd had our pair of Amazon parrots for more than a year but had gotten them as healthy young birds. Surely the Tarahumara knew how to raise them from chicks. Didn't the adult birds go out to get fruit and grains for them? Perhaps we could feed them ground-up corn and fruit preserves. I was betting we could nurse them along, so I went ahead and put them in the bag I took for that purpose, then started my laborious climb back down.

Back at home, we fed the baby macaws with an eyedropper, giving them water, a watery corn meal gruel, and some strawberry preserves. Even though we kept them warm, one succumbed to the human food within twenty-four hours. The other did better, and we were optimistic, but he only lasted about thirty-six hours longer than his sibling. I felt terrible and vowed to never take any little creatures that young away from their parents again.

We later had a pair of baby squirrels for several months, which we bought from the Indians. As they got bigger, though, they started biting us when we tried to put them back in their cage. We ended up having to turn them loose in the woods. The pair of Amazon parrots we had, however, were really great pets and gave us about two years of entertainment until we went on furlough and had to let them go. The way they learned to talk and laugh had us in stitches so many times!

7.3 Will This House Ever Be Finished?

Probably the Funniest Thing I Saw in El Manzano

Yes, finishing the house construction was a necessity before I could move on to putting myself full-time into Tarahumara language and culture study. After we had actually moved into the house, we still had some important projects to finish. Once I had the concrete floor poured, my next priority was to make the kitchen cabinets so that Ticker had the nice kitchen she deserved. For a couple of months, she had been working out of the bathroom in cramped quarters with just three or four rudimentary shelves for storing the dishes, food, etc.

I had a carpenter in San Rafael make a bunch of tongue and groove boards for me, which I was going to use to make cabinets. Plywood at that time in Mexico was outrageously expensive. I believe the reason was that most of it got exported to the US, and unfortunately for the Mexican people, it was priced like a luxury item. So one day, when Ticker had gone into Chihuahua City for some reason with both of the boys for several days, I had the house to myself and started into making the kitchen cabinets with a vengeance.

With all of them gone, I had a wide open floor area in the kitchen where I could lay out my lumber and start putting the cabinets together. I tried to never work on Sundays, saving it as a family day to visit with folks or be prepared to have them come visit us. However, that particular Sunday, I took advantage of the time and was making great progress when there was a knock on the door.

I opened it to see Jesus Sanchez, Mauro's older brother. Jesus was not quite right in the head due to some kind of head trauma that he had experienced years earlier, so the rest of the family treated him a little differently, and essentially, his brother Mauro got all the respect as the eldest. Jesus could sometimes be a little bit goofy, but this particular morning, he was beyond goofy—he was intoxicated.

As was the custom with so many folks on a Sunday, Jesus was dressed in his nicest clothes—dress pants, dress shoes, a button-down shirt, and a sport coat. He also had a one-liter Coke bottle in his hand that was about one-third full of that clear moonshine that so many of them loved called *pisto*.

"Hola, Esteban!" he said. "Do you mind if I come in?" he asked, looking back over his shoulder toward the trail coming to my house. Before I could answer him, he stepped inside and said with a slur in his voice, "Gracias! Have my brothers or nephews been here today?"

"No," I assured him, telling him no one had been there yet today. Obviously, he was rather nervous.

"Well, I came to visit with you, so that is good, but I'm wondering if you have a place I can hide this bottle." With that, he walked first to one of my windows and looked out and then into another room and looked out another window, worried that his brothers might be close behind him.

The room that was my study still had several boxes of books, etc., against the wall. I took his bottle from him and put it down on the floor against the wall hidden by the boxes. We walked back out into the dining room area, I pulled out a chair for him to sit down, and we started to visit a little bit. It wasn't going to be a very profitable conversation talking to a fellow who was drunk, so I was just making small talk with him for a few minutes when he got back up, walked into my study, and retrieved his bottle from behind the boxes. He took a swig, which he obviously enjoyed, and came back over to sit on the chair I had put there for him.

Little did I know that I was about to witness one of the most athletic feats I've ever seen in my life! As Jesus went to sit down, he misjudged the seat of the chair and barely caught the front edge of it. The chair shot backwards on the smooth concrete floor, Jesus landed hard on his butt, and the Coke bottle with the pisto in it came out of his right hand. I expected to see broken glass and liquor splattering across the floor, but in a real tribute to how tough those Coke bottles are, the bottle did not break. Instead, it hit the concrete and bounced on probably a forty-five-degree angle flying away from Jesus, who was sideways on the floor. As the bottle went about two feet up in the air, traveling away from him, drunk Jesus somehow managed to launch himself to where the bottle was about to land, and while he slid on his side on the floor, he grabbed it in midair before it could hit the concrete again!

I had watched all this in absolute amazement, ready for there to definitely be a bunch of shattered glass and alcohol on the floor when the bottle landed the second time, since it was pretty much horizontal by then. But in an amazing move for a man around fifty-five years old, Jesus snagged it out of the air, held it upright again and, in glee, declared, "Didn't spill a single drop!" The look on his face and the athletics of what he had just done was what you would expect from a Major League Baseball player who had just grabbed a line drive hit and saved the playoff game! I couldn't believe it!

* * * * *

Being in the ministry is not always about ministering the Word of God. Even when a pastor or missionary or Bible school teacher IS studying the Word of God and sharing it with others as the major focus of his or her hours in a given week are concerned, God has His way of teaching us many different kinds of lessons He wants us to learn. One of the big lessons I had to learn during the time I was building and finishing the house was patience. Another was flexibility.

The building of the house had gone pretty quickly in the first three or four months, but then it seemed to drag on forever as I worked to get it finished on the inside. It was a constant lesson in learning patience, even though I tried to spend at least ten hours every day focused on getting the carpentry and interior stucco finished. Intertwined with trying to accomplish what seemed to be pretty straightforward goals was the need to be flexible, sensitive to God's leading, and the people He would bring to our door numerous times throughout the week.

One or two members of our field committee would come out generally twice a year to see how we were doing. They wanted us to have some fellowship and be able to talk things over with them, which was great. I appreciated their visits. There was also an aspect in which it seemed like we weren't getting on with our ministry fast enough, and I felt self-conscious about that a few times. We knew that someday we would get some partners out there with us, and that would help alleviate some of the interruptions that we were experiencing with people in the community wanting a piece of our time for a variety of reasons.

HE WHO HAS BEGUN A GOOD WORK

Enter Al and Polly Clark

Al and Polly Clark with children Al Jr., Chris and Amy

In November of 1983, a new couple with New Tribes Mission arrived in Chihuahua City to start their Spanish study. Their names were Al and Polly Clark, and their children were Al Junior, Christopher, and Amy. Al Junior was thirteen years old, Chris was twelve, and Amy was four. The field committee had been very sensitive to the fact that we really needed partners, so the Clarks came out to visit us not long after their arrival. It was always exciting for someone who was starting their Spanish study to get out in the mountains and see what the tribal life and work were all about. When the Clarks came out for a visit for two or three days, we got a good feeling, seeing that they were down to earth, humble, and helpful people. They were from a small town in West Virginia and, as such, seemed that they would fit in there much better than a lot of the city folks who didn't seem to be able to make it in the tribes.

Al was seven or eight years older than me and had served in Vietnam, whereas I had barely avoided it because of my age when I graduated high school. He had also been wounded with shrapnel during a battle and had lost part of his hearing in one ear, but that was not going to discourage him from learning the Spanish language. Polly had a sweet spirit about her and was really helpful with Ticker in fixing meals and cleaning up, especially dealing with our temporary kitchen in the bathroom.

After a few days with us, they had to dive in to the year-long process of Spanish study back in Chihuahua, but Ticker and I were optimistic about the prospects of having partners again, finally, and we hoped partners that would stay!

Tarahumara Culture Study in Earnest

We had clearly defined goals laid out for us during our training in New Tribes, and I was excited to get on with those. As soon as my office was set up, I got organized with a filing system with which I would keep track of all the observations I would make regarding the Tarahumara culture. The "culture file" was an ingenious, extremely comprehensive means of recording just about every possible aspect of an indigenous culture. We were first introduced to the system in our boot camp training. There we studied the Yurok tribe of the coastal forests of northern California.

In the classroom, we learned about their hunting and fishing subsistence, learned to ask questions about the meanings of different figures on their totem poles, had to investigate their social order, including the roles of tribal leaders and the family structure. The outline was inclusive of just about anything and everything you can think of in the culture of a given people. From politics to sports, warfare to beliefs in the spirit world, it taught us to be aware of everything that happened around us when we entered their community.

We were to write down our observations from the very beginning, so as not to simply gloss over and not deeply consider our first impressions. Then as we went into more detail in learning aspects of their culture, we could see if there were gaps in our understanding. When we did discover the gaps, that gave us the incentive to either ask about those unknown parts of their culture or actually look for an opportunity to participate with the people and observe, if that was possible. Obviously, being outsiders, we would not be able to participate in certain things or would not want to participate. For example, if they went through a "spiritual cleansing" ritual, it might include praying to their pagan spirits, taking hallucinogenic drugs, or carving or painting your body. However, every single aspect of their culture needed to be understood if we were to avoid that worst of all outcomes for a missionary: syncretism.

Syncretism literally means a "meshing together" or "blending" of two distinct things. In cultures and spiritual world views it is the process in which one belief system is laid on top of or alongside of—in the sense of being equally valid with—a different belief system. When one culture has a deeply ingrained, usually centuries or millennia old, spiritual belief system, and a second belief system (for example, Christianity) comes along, people in many cultures around the world will try to combine the two systems as coequal. When they do that, they are not giving up their old belief system (which may be animistic or have a multitude of gods) but are only adding to and expanding their belief system. That is not what God wants!

When the Spanish conquistadors came to the New World, they brought Catholic priests with them. There were two goals for them in bringing those priests. One was that they hoped to "civilize" and therefore pacify any warlike behavior on the part of the native peoples; and the other, more sincerely embraced by the priests themselves, was that they could get some of the native people to actually become Christians. There was quite a range of "results achieved" from the early 1500s through the 1900s, but what was obvious almost everywhere throughout Latin America was that the indigenous people had only added the names of Jesus, Mary, Judas, and some other biblical figures to their own long list of spiritual beings. They almost never understood God's plan to redeem mankind of his sin by sending His only son to die on the cross. Instead, they have marched around stone or adobe churches, carrying straw and wooden figures clothed in a variety of humiliating or beautifully adorned costumes for hundreds of years, while having absolutely no idea who the God of the Bible is. They have just layered some completely misunderstood gods and goddesses who have names that come out of the Bible on top of their own native spiritual belief system.

We know, also, that God HAS put clues and left evidence in cultures all over the world as to who He is. It is our job as missionaries to find those clues and to utilize that evidence in the native culture when we find it. The in-depth study of their culture, which we then record in our culture file, helps us to not overlook or lose track of that information. There are oftentimes parallels to the biblical account in their own story of creation or they may acknowledge in their folk tales that their own gods realize that they are not as powerful as "the One True God." It's incredibly important to know if they have a culture that recognizes guilt, which indicates a universal sense of a conscience or one that is only sensitive to shame.

In a shame culture, one only feels a tug of their conscience when they are caught doing something evil or wrong. As Christians, we know there is such a thing as "absolute truth" and not just "relative truth." In America today, unfortunately, with the lack of parents teaching their children biblical spiritual values, we see that so many people only feel a sense of shame (relative truth) when they get caught doing something bad or hurtful to others. Accurately communicating the Gospel to people in those two belief systems requires that the missionary realizes where his audience is coming from in order to make them understand their need for God and His forgiveness. The Gospel, of course, would not be the good news unless people understand—and quite clearly—the bad news first: that we need our sin to be forgiven!

So it was that our culture study was not just an exercise in anthropology but was an absolutely invaluable and very comprehensive tool for cross-cultural communications. I don't know how it was developed within New Tribes Mission, like I understood the language learning course that Jean Dye Johnson had developed, but I considered it a world-class system. Thus it was that I began my culture file on three-by-five-inch cards, writing down specific details from everyday interactions with the people of El Manzano and the surrounding communities.

Yes, you read that correctly—three-by-five cards, although I quickly upgraded to four-by-six cards due to the fact that a vastly larger amount of information could be written on a card that size (ha ha). That was the way we had to do it in 1983, 1984, and 1985. We had no computer and no electricity, so we had handwritten notes for all of our culture and language learning. Hey, if it was good enough for Aristotle or Galileo or the Lewis and Clark expedition, it was going to have to be good enough for us. We did write most of our notes on 8.5 x 11-inch paper and kept those in a file, but those were our field notes and were too hard to organize into a concise, searchable file.

I had gotten a good start on Tarahumara culture during my hiking expeditions to the Apórabo area when I met and talked with the Tarahumara shaman/governor for a few hours. Now living in El Manzano, I was gathering new information and knowledge by the week. There was another element, however, that was causing recurring trouble in our ministry. I will call it "The Cloud."

7.4 "The Cloud"

In the years before personal computers we saved and organized reams of culture and language notes on paper file cards and in hand written notes

I said at the beginning of this account that I would be as transparent and honest as possible. Obviously, there are some aspects and incidents in recounting interpersonal relationships that cannot be shared with anyone outside of that relationship. That is out of respect for each of the parties' privacy and dignity. As I write this, I want to emphasize the utmost respect I have for Ticker and her feelings to this day.

At this point in our story, we were in the last months of 1983. Eric turned one year old on November 26. It had been quite a year for us all as a family. Within a few weeks of Eric's birth, we had (1) gone up to Chicago for a brief visit, travelling over 4,000 miles on the road; (2) come back to Mexico to find that our partners, the S's, had left us and almost resigned from New Tribes Mission but, in the end, were convinced to stay in support work in Chihuahua City; (3) the second family of potential partners, the Stivers, had decided also to leave New Tribes Mission and had returned to the States; (4) the Lord had opened the door for us to move into the Tarahumara community of El Manzano; and (5) within seven more months, we were happily living in our new home there. It had been a crazy, exciting, and very busy year.

What I haven't talked about, except right after our return to San Rafael from Chicago, was the depression that Ticker suddenly experienced in January. It was a scary experience, and it totally took us by surprise. I mostly attributed it to exhaustion from our long road trip and the hormone changes going on in her. A lot of women experience a change called "the baby blues," and in my youthful ignorance, I thought that's probably what it was. As I had related, she not only had delivered Eric by C-section but had her tubes tied while she was in surgery, and we knew that was somewhat uncharted territory as to the long-term effects it could have on a woman's hormones.

But even as we now settled into a much more normal lifestyle in El Manzano, there was a pattern of recurring depression that had us both worried. Sometimes it seemed like her bouts of depression were on something of a monthly cycle. She could sometimes be depressed and want to just sleep most of the day for two or three days per month, but some months, that would turn into a week or ten days.

I cannot honestly recount nor state today what Ticker said to me during those times. I don't know if she had a clear idea of how to express her feelings to me during those months. What I do know is that she rarely wanted to talk with me and share her inner feelings. She wanted to retreat into her own thoughts, and after taking care of just the most basic of needs of the boys on many mornings, she then wanted to be alone in the privacy and darkness of our bedroom upstairs. For the most part, I felt helpless. I just had to wait for her to be reenergized and to rejoin the boys and me.

A complicating factor, too, however, was our spiritual relationship with each other. This is awkward and somewhat embarrassing to admit here but important. Ticker rarely wanted to have a devotional time with me alone and generally did not even contribute or get involved in my devotional times with the boys. We had a brief prayer time in the morning before we started our day, then she would homeschool the boys for several hours each day, and that was her quality time with them. In the evenings, I very much looked forward to playing with them before and after dinner and then having a Bible story time after that. Before they went to bed, we always prayed one last time together. But Ticker wasn't very interested in having one-on-one time just with me, and that was really hard on my soul.

She was my life partner as my wife, and I truly loved her. She was also my only American adult missionary partner for years. She was the one I had with whom to share our progress in learning Spanish and everything about acclimating to the country of Mexico. She and I faced and discussed all the plans and decisions as we moved out to the mountains in San Rafael, then how to proceed step-by-step to find an Indian community to live in. I had worked on getting her out of the house to physically see and visit the most accessible Tarahumara communities outside of San Rafael. We prayed together and both felt definitely led by the Lord to move into El Manzano. After that, there was just a lot of planning and hard work in building the house and getting moved into it.

Now here we were, and there was something else tagging along with us which I couldn't really identify or understand. I'll just call it "The Cloud," and I did not like the shadow that it cast over our family and ministry in an unpredictable but recurring manner.

Just because I prayed that the gloom would be dispelled, that did not mean it would be. Both of us had to search for the physiological and spiritual reasons that it was there, so my prayer constantly was for understanding and wisdom from the Lord in how to be a help to her. I did my best to pick up the slack around the house and be supportive of her, ready and willing to talk, and I prayed for her relief regularly. It was a mysterious spiritual battle for me.

7.5 Culture Notes, October 1983–November 1984

Branding Indians, Witch Doctors, and Which Doctors?

Before I share some culture notes from my file regarding Tarahumara culture, I'll share something from a man who arrived in El Manzano one day on what I perceived to be a political campaign visit. His name was Guadalupe Gonzalez Gonzalez, and my understanding at the time was that he was running for the office of municipal president of Uruachic. At least that's how either he or Mauro or both presented him to me when we met.

Señor Gonzalez was about forty years old, energetic, and pleasantly outgoing. He was a little over six feet tall and solidly built. He arrived by pickup truck with one or two other men who remained quiet most of the time, and I later realized that they may have been plainclothes policemen serving as bodyguards. Three years into the future, this man was to become an important person in my life and indeed in the lives of all of us in El Manzano.

It's also very possible that Señor Gonzales had heard about the Americans who were living in El Manzano and wanted to find out if we were really missionaries as we claimed to be. On the day I first met him, as I had done with numerous other folks in the region, I explained to him that our goal in living in El Manzano was to learn the Tarahumara language and culture and to teach them about God. Everyone knew how resistant the Tarahumara had been for hundreds of years to change and to the influence of outsiders. It was with that in mind that Señor Gonzalez related the following to me:

"It's common knowledge that the Tarahumara have worked as laborers for the 'blancos' (white people, which actually meant Mexicans-those who had lighter skin than the dark skinned Tarahumara) for many years. Few people, though, realize that the bad feelings that the majority of Tarahumara have toward us is due to the almost 'enslavement' of them up until only about sixty years ago. When there were still a lot of mines being worked in this area (meaning Uruachic), there was a shortage of good help. So that one mine owner wouldn't lose his workers to another, he would therefore brand his Tarahumara laborers. This way, too, he was sure that that particular fellow was one of his workers and not someone else trying to collect wages. The hatred still smolders in some Tarahumaras because of that practice."

Obviously, I was shocked that men could be branded like cattle. I asked further about the brands and found out that the men were marked with numbers, so they essentially had an ID number branded onto their arm!

I didn't bring my complete culture file home with me from El Manzano but do still have a few of my other original notes.

Under the heading of "Worldview, Supernatural, Supernatural Beings," I have the following note from October 27, 1983:

> As told by José Reyes Cruz: "Old Nicholas Cruz was up the arroyo where the water came out of the mountain below Las Estrellas. He was getting together a load of celulosa (deadfall logs). In a small cave he suddenly saw the Santo Nino (The Holy Child—Jesus) just standing there. He told a number of people about it and quite a few went up to see if they could see it, but it appears no one else saw it."

When I asked Nicolás about it, he told me "I saw the Santo Nino just standing there inside the cave. He was "muy bonito" (very handsome). He was naked, but you could tell it was the Santo Nino by how handsome he was. He was about (he motions with his hand) 18" to 2 feet tall. He disappeared after a little while. I think he left for good... He didn't say anything, just looked at me.

* * * * *

In November 1983, Jesus Sanchez, knowing that our boys had been sick, offered to "cure" them. He told me, "They may have gotten scared. Sometimes kids get scared once they've wandered off because the earth might swallow them up. No, here around the houses, kids don't get scared, but it's dangerous in other places. There are, after all, people down under the earth and the kids are scared of them." Mauro confirmed this.

* * * * *

In May 1985, Teodulo Banda shared an experience that he and Barbara had: "What these little people try to do is steal your pulse. The pulse is a soul that you have. The little people want to rob the pulse and take it down under the earth with them. That leaves a person weak and sick."

One time, Barbara was alone at home for a few days. Teodulo had gone to be with a family whose child had died. Barbara was down in the arroyo washing laundry by herself and began to feel sad and lonely thinking of Teodulo and the child who had died. She believes that she got *asustado* (scared): that the little people snuck up on her, stole her pulse, and left her afraid.

She told old Santiago Lagarda about it, and he went to his home. He smoked a cigarette and went to bed, thinking about Barbara, getting himself in tune with the situation so that he could dream. That night, he dreamt about her experience, found out and later told her details of what she was doing when the *asustado* hit her, and apparently healed her at that time in his dream (Barbara and Teodulo don't know exactly what he did, though, or don't want to say).

* * * * *

> Every time visitors came by I had the opportunity to learn more of the Tarahumara and local mestizo culture, in addition to building relationships

In a story similar to what the shaman and governor of Apórabo had told me, both Cayetano Lagarda and Jenaro Enriquez, as well as many others, claim to have seen fires suddenly appear in arroyos near their homes. Sometimes the flames will leap eight to ten feet into the air, but there is no actual combustion of any material, and there is no mark to be seen the next day. Supposedly, there is either a gold or silver deposit, or old Spanish gold under the ground, at that location. They've never dug down to find it but came to tell me about these things hoping that I would bring a metal detector so we could go look for it there.

* * * * *

In April 1984, José Reyes Cruz, at Rocoroibo, told me: "A few weeks ago, a big aircraft of some kind passed just to the west of Rocoroibo going south. It flew fast, leaving a trail of dark smoke behind. Nobody really knows what it was, but three or four days later, people started getting the flu. Lots of people are sick now in the whole area, and that thing was the cause."

* * * * *

November 1984, Teodulo told me that some men had seen a strange shiny object that looked like a dinner plate flying over the Arroyo Del Oso. "It flew over, backed up, landed, and then started moving along the ground."

What is behind these physical observations is a mystery, of course. In the US and other Western nations, we now have absolutely hard evidence in the form of videos and photographs from military and commercial aircraft regarding UFOs. That phenomenon is no longer considered to be in the realm of crazy conspiracy theorists.

It's hard to believe that so many people were delusional in seeing the flames of fire in the arroyos and on the hillsides. Perhaps there are spiritual beings that want to play with the native people's minds in order to keep them in a state of fear and subjection. In the cases of people being "scared" and part of their soul robbed, putting them into a state of weakened health, there is no question that this is a psychological condition that makes them feel dependent on shamans and witch doctors. Thus the witch doctors maintain control over what is perhaps the most important aspect of the average person's life: their physical health.

It's interesting that as I am finally compiling my hundreds of pages of notes, letters, articles, and photographs into this memoir, the world has been in the grip of a pandemic for well over a year and a half. Between five and fifteen million people around the world have died, and in the United States where we pride ourselves on being so incredibly advanced scientifically and medically, approximately one million people have now (at the time of this writing) died! We finally know that most of the people who isolated in their homes as they were instructed to do by politicians and politically polarized "medical professionals" got sick and died unnecessarily. To have stayed active, gotten lots of fresh air, and exercised and to have taken inexpensive nutritional supplements like vitamins C, D, and other things could have saved hundreds of thousands of lives just in our country alone.

For political reasons, for many months, it was considered a "conspiracy theory" to say that the virus was produced in and escaped from the Wuhan Institute of Virology in China. Now that the former president, Donald Trump, and his administration are out of office, investigations and the mainstream media have almost conclusively decided that the origins of the COVID-19 virus did, in fact, come from that clinic in China. We also now know that there were American government research funds and very high-ranking American research virologists involved, so the origins of the virus are being covered up like perhaps nothing else in history has been. To clarify for the reader my own shock at the gravity and extent of the manipulation of this crisis, I would refer you to *The Real Anthony Fauci* by Robert F. Kennedy Jr. (Skyhorse Publishing, November 2021). Please especially note the thousands of footnotes that reveal the very exhaustive research done by the author.

One of mankind's most basic pursuits has always been how to understand, avoid, and be cured of diseases. When we read about how 'unscientific' cultures like the Tarahumara attempt to explain sickness, it's easy to call them primitive. And in the paragraphs above, you probably agreed with me when I said "perhaps there are spiritual beings that want to play with their minds in order to keep them in a state of fear and subjection" as well as when "they are in a state of weakened health…this is a psychological condition that makes them feel dependent on shamans and witch doctors. Thus the witch doctors maintain control over what is perhaps the most important aspect of the average person's life—their physical health."

So here I am, living in one of the richest countries on the face of the earth, where hundreds of billions of dollars have been spent just to treat and stop this pandemic, and we find out that the countless millions of masks that we have all worn and the hundreds of millions of doses of "vaccines" that have been administered not just in

America but around the world are basically proving to not be much more effective against COVID-19 than the annual flu shot. The virus continues to mutate and spread, and the "leading doctors and scientists" keep changing their minds and their stories and guidance about what we should do about it. I won't even go into detail on the involvement of politicians in all of this and how terribly badly they have managed this whole thing in most places in the world—that is a mind-boggling disaster.

The bottom line is a lot of people have tried hard to help in good conscience, a lot of others are corrupt and endlessly promoting the vaccines has very much to do with creating a huge income stream for them and their Big Pharma friends, and right now, we don't look a whole lot more intelligent about sickness and how to survive it than the Tarahumara were in 1983. Thankfully, a large and increasingly vocal segment of honest and brave doctors is speaking out about the efficacy of therapeutics that we already have, nutritional supplements that boost the immune system, and the mortal dangers of obesity and other comorbidities.

Only the Lord knows how to truly, effectively deal with this viral epidemic and how it will all end. But whether it would be to the Tarahumaras or to my fellow Americans, my thoughts and counsel would be that "The fear of the Lord is the beginning of wisdom (*knowledge* in some translations)" (Proverbs 1:7). While some scientists and engineers can create spaceships and exploration equipment to go to the moon, to Mars and far, far beyond, so many medical scientists and engineers obviously are not getting wisdom and knowledge from God. They have an agenda which is focused on their own profit and politicized propaganda points, not an honest evaluation of how to save lives. As a result of an entire branch of bio-engineers and medical doctors who are creating their own mRNA mechanisms to alter our immune systems, they are seriously, and perhaps irreversibly, compromising our God-designed defenses. For the first time in many decades our confidence in the medical community has been seriously damaged world-wide, leaving us to ask, "Which doctors, or witch doctors: Who can we trust?"

But enough of that. It's just that it has bothered me deeply to see such huge numbers of people die whose deaths actually were preventable. Back to the real world of the Tarahumara people.

The Spirits in the Night

It was a blessing to have Teodulo as a friend. He didn't live that far away, so it was easy to walk up the valley to his house. It was about a mile and a half by trail, and the rise in elevation was 300 or 350 feet. It took me about twenty minutes to get up to their house and twelve to fifteen minutes to get home, depending on whether I had to walk or I could jog. I had asked Teodulo if he would help me learn the Tarahumara language a little at a time, and he said yes. I didn't want to take his time away from his farming activities, but he had a small store on the side of his house, and he had to spend a fair amount of time with that anyway, so I hoped to visit with him in what was mostly his spare time in between customers.

I went up there at least two times a week for an hour or so. I would ask him for words and phrases in the Tarahumara language, and sometimes we got into discussing the Tarahumara culture also. I also tried to make myself useful to him with any random labor that I could do. One afternoon, I went up and helped butcher a hog and cut up the meat for three or four hours. I learned a lot about how they rendered the fat down and made *chicharrones*, deep-fried chunks of pork. There were a lot of afternoons where I ended up being there until it was dusk, and I knew I needed to leave and not impose on them for dinner.

Teodulo, his wife, Barbara, and a couple of other relatives that lived right around them were good conversationalists, and we sometimes ended up talking until it was dark. One evening, it was definitely too dark to walk home without a flashlight, so Teodulo lent me one of his. I returned it the next day so that he would not be without it. He probably only owned one that had good batteries in it since they were scarce. On a few occasions, the moon was bright enough that I could jog home on the trail without risking spraining my ankle on a rock or tripping. There was only one fairly dark area that went around behind a little hill for a couple of hundred yards where I really had to slow down and walk carefully. Most of the trail was in pretty open terrain, traversing his one big cornfield which was open dirt and rocky ground most of the year, and the rest of the trail was along a hillside without any tall trees on it, so I was okay by moonlight or even starlight.

Finally, I just started taking my own flashlight with me, just in case I needed it. Once we got talking about a variety of subjects, we oftentimes got carried away, and I would head home for dinner in the dark.

One afternoon, I showed up at his house and could tell both he and Barbara had something on their minds. Barbara stuck around real closely for our conversation, and it only took a couple minutes for Teodulo to come out with his question.

"Esteban," he began, "when you go home on the trails at night, do you ever see anything out there?"

I thought he meant something like coyotes, which I didn't really worry about. One evening, I had seen a fox that lived somewhere on that small hill, but it tried to stay out of sight and was pretty successful.

"No," I said. "Like what?"

"Well, like a rope or a cord that is suspended in the air," he said.

Whoa, I thought, *this is going to be an interesting conversation.*

"No, I've never seen anything like that. What would that be all about?" I asked him.

"When a brujo or bruja (male or female witchdoctor) is going to either cure or curse someone, they travel to that person's house in a dream on the end of a cord. You might run into that cord sometime or see it and wonder what it is. They say if you cut the cord that the witchdoctor will die."

I asked them if they had ever seen one. They said no, but they knew how the process worked and believed Barbara had been cured by a witch doctor once. They were quite sure he had indeed travelled to their house in that manner in a dream.

"But it's dangerous to be on a trail with that witchdoctor's cord."

"Well, I know that there are spirits out there in the world, but I also know that God protects me and my family, and I'm not worried about those spirits," I explained. I was so very tempted to tell them that I knew a lot about the spirits around us in this world and to quote 1 John 4:4, "He who is in you is greater than he who is in the world." But I was still in the period of time when I felt I needed to follow the New Tribes Mission policy as strictly as I could and not share the Gospel until I had learned the Tarahumara language. I remember biting my tongue so that I would not go any further regarding my own beliefs about the spirit world, but I think it was the Holy Spirit saying to me, "There is an open door here. These folks can understand the Gospel perfectly clearly in Spanish." It was not the last time that I would feel that way either.

Things that Make Noise in the Night

On several occasions in the first months that we had lived in our new house in El Manzano, I heard mysterious noises at night and wondered what they were. There were coyotes in the area, that was for sure, and when we had chickens and turkeys for a period of time, they had a way of either mysteriously not getting back into the roost in the evening or of disappearing at night. As much as I tried to spot one, using my big flashlight that held three D-cell batteries and was a really powerful flashlight, I never once saw a coyote. They were like ghosts. Then, one night, I heard the strangest sound.

Plink, plink went the sound that reverberated into our bedroom. It had awakened me, and I laid there, trying to figure out what it was. I heard it again and then a strange rasping sound.

"Ticker!" I said, shaking her gently. "What is that sound?"

We both listened for several more seconds, and it repeated itself a couple of times. Finally, it dawned on me. "That is the clothesline. It's attached to the porch post right below our bedroom. It sounds like someone's messing with our clothes. They're still on the clothesline, right?" I whispered to her.

"Yes, they are," she answered.

I had slipped out of bed numerous times before to check on strange noises outside. I always slept in my underwear briefs and would slip on my jeans as quietly as I could. That was especially the case on a cold winter's night. But this night, it was only mildly chilly, and I didn't want to make any unnecessary noise. I very quietly picked up the big flashlight from right next to the bed, got my hunting knife, and tiptoed down the hall and down the stairs, carefully avoiding the one stair tread that creaked.

I got to the back door. I shifted the flashlight to my left hand, the hunting knife to my right hand, and slowly put my hand on the door lock, careful not to make a sound. The clothesline was only about twelve or fifteen feet to my left. Taking a deep breath, ready for anything (almost), I jerked the door open and began to take a step forward before I flipped on the flashlight and caught whoever it was in the act.

The night outside was completely black. There was no moonlight, and any starlight was obscured by the roof over our big six-foot-wide porch. I started to step forward, but there was a large moving presence right in front of me. Instinct flashed through my brain, and I did a judo-type kick at chest height as fast and hard as I could. My foot struck something really heavy. It gave a little bit, like a three-hundred-pound punching bag might, and a strange grunt came out. But it was moving fast from my left to my right, and my kick had stopped me dead in my tracks just inside the doorway. The next thing I heard was a thumping sound going off our concrete porch and across the yard. Now I flipped on my light and saw what I had just kicked. It was a really large bull or cow, completely black, and another one in the yard had taken off, following the first one.

The realization struck me how close I had come to getting trampled by that cow or bull. If I had stepped through the doorway, it would've rammed me into the twelve-inch-wide doorjamb itself or knocked me flying onto the concrete and trampled me. That was a really close call!

I went upstairs and told Ticker what had happened, and by now, we were just relieved that it was only cows. But I was still mystified as to why they were messing with our clothes on the clothesline and what the rasping sound had been. Several days later, I told Barbara and Teodulo about what had happened and asked them why the cows would've been fooling around with our laundry. Barbara giggled with that funny laugh that she had and said, "Ah, they were licking the soap off the bottom of the clothes where it drips off when they're drying! They like that. It tastes like salt to them. That's why they were licking the inside of the laundry tub too!" She thought it was hilarious. It showed how much we did not know about cows. Apparently, country people do know that because they've had the exact same thing happen to them.

I'm really glad I never told them the part about me only being dressed in my white briefs. That would have really given them a visual to laugh over, and I never would've lived that one down.

7.6 A Strange Encounter—Adela Sanchez

Visiting at Teodulo's house gave me a chance to make friends in the community at the same time that I learned about their language and culture. I always had a plan with me of what I would like to learn that afternoon, but occasionally, the plan never got initiated because something else came up. Such was the case late one afternoon when I had been trying to get a few minutes of Teodulo's undivided attention to ask him something. But he had customers in the store and was too involved with them. I was a bit of a fifth wheel and had decided I should probably head back home when someone said, "Listen! Is that a truck coming?"

These folks had a good sense of hearing and could detect the sound of a truck engine quite a distance away. Yes, a truck was definitely coming down into El Manzano from the main logging road, and in ten or fifteen minutes, it pulled up right in front of Teodulo's house and stopped. I went outside with the others to see who it was.

It was Ernesto Sanchez's truck. It was a somewhat beat-up blue-and-white diesel log truck with a sixteen- or twenty-foot long flatbed composed of worn and weathered three-inch thick boards. On it were six or seven people who were catching a ride down into El Manzano. I could see that they had all been partying and drinking. As they noisily got down off the truck to stretch, I decided I would be heading home. But first of all, I needed to be neighborly and shake hands and say hello to whoever wanted to be friendly at the moment. I did that and headed back into the house to say goodbye to Barbara, grabbed my tote bag that had my notebook and flashlight in it, and was ready to head out the back door toward the trail to my house.

Just then, a rather heavyset lady in her fifties walked in and went to the far side of the table from where I was standing. She stretched out her hand to shake mine, so I responded in kind. She asked if I knew who she was, then told me her name was Adela Sanchez. I said, "*Mucho gusto* (The pleasure is mine)" and then tried to release her hand, but she did not let go of her grip on me. It was obvious she had been drinking, and probably a lot, so trying not to be rude, I just continued to make small talk for another few moments. Still, she didn't want to release my hand. We stood like that for at least a minute, maybe longer, and it was finally getting really annoying to me. She kept staring at me the whole time while making trivial conversation.

Finally, someone else walked into the kitchen and caused a distraction, so she let go of my hand. Yes, that was a good example of why I didn't really care to be around drunk people and their sometimes strange behavior.

It wasn't until she passed away almost two years later that I found out who she really was. She was the most powerful bruja (witchdoctor) in the area. And it wasn't until a year or two after that that I was told that when she met me, she got a crush on me and wanted to take my wife away from me! She was one of the servants of Satan who we later found out plotted and planned to ruin our ministry. But as the Lord said, the gates of hell will not prevail against His kingdom. Greater was He who was in me than he who was in the bruja Adela Sanchez! Praise him!

HE WHO HAS BEGUN A GOOD WORK

Blizzard Border Trip, December 1983

―⌇―

    Living in Mexico on tourist visas required that we go back up to the border at the end of the period that had been given when we entered. It was a hard and fast date that we put on our calendar in red letters. To overstay our visa could incur getting our truck impounded and having to pay a big financial penalty to get it back. That December, we knew our date was fast approaching, so we got everything ready for the weeklong trip out to Chihuahua City, then up to El Paso, Texas, and all the way back.

    Unfortunately, a big winter storm was coming through at the same time. Up there, at 7,200 feet elevation, the wind was wild, rocking the pine trees and the oaks every which way. It rained hard for about three days, and then the temperature started dropping into the twenties at night. I postponed leaving for a day or two, hoping the storm would let up and the roads would dry a bit. Fortunately, we had enough gas to get all the way to Creel, so we wouldn't have to stop in San Rafael at the sawmill. It was only seventy-three miles to Creel but, in this weather, would take us at least six, perhaps seven, hours.

    The morning we left, we climbed slowly but surely up the valley in four-wheel drive with snow flurries flying around us. Less than a mile up the hill, we had to stop and roll some boulders off the road. In our boots and heavy jackets and gloves, I had to have Ticker get out and help me. It seemed that they came loose more in the winter because of the freezing and thawing which happened. The two or three small trees that had fallen onto the road I was able to move myself. We got onto the main logging road going toward San Rafael and, for almost three hours, didn't see a single vehicle. Nobody wanted to be out in the storm. The logging trucks had to be fairly heavily loaded just to get traction in muddy conditions like this but then could get stuck as well. They would all wait until the rain and snow stopped.

From San Rafael toward Creel, we only saw one or two pickup trucks driving in their little local communities, and this was the roughest part of the road in those years. I was so thankful for good tires and our dependable vehicle—our 1976 Ford four-wheel-drive van. In places, water was running down the huge ruts in the road, and in others, the ground was starting to get frozen, and the snow was sticking. On the rocky areas, and there were a lot of them, the tires would spin on the freezing ice and snow until they grabbed and pulled us along.

After six hours on the road, we were now only thirty to forty-five minutes from Creel. This was also the highest section of the road at an elevation of nine thousand feet. The snow had been getting deeper by the hour and was now about a foot deep. That might have been okay in different terrain, but this was also as far as the road crews had gotten with their "improvements." We were driving along the edge of a very steep canyon. On my left, the mountainside went down at about a seventy-degree angle, and there were lots of loose rocks and boulders which the bulldozers had shoved over the edge as they made the road. There were trees here and there that had withstood the falling rocks, but still, it looked scary on that side.

Although the road had been widened compared to its old self, we soon came upon a strange sight. There were mounds of gravel about four feet high each and about thirty feet apart for as far as I could see ahead of us. Apparently, they had dumped loads of gravel from dump trucks in preparation for spreading them on the new road surface but ran out of time for some reason. To keep the gravel from sliding down over the left side of the road, they had dumped it against the right-hand uphill side. That made sense, of course, but that also barely left enough room for a full-sized truck like mine to drive past it all and right next to a drop-off.

I slowly crept up to the first mound and, keeping the driver side wheels away from the edge, had the passenger side wheels go up and over the gravel. The front end, with the weight of the engine, managed pretty well, but it felt like the lighter-weight back end was sliding toward the edge of the road. The snow was blowing sideways, so it was hard to see with my driver side mirror what was going on.

Going no more than two or three miles an hour, I went over two more mounds and had the same sensation of the back end sliding. Before I drove any further, I got out of the van and walked back to look at my tracks. Sure enough, the back end was sliding at least a foot each time, barely leaving another foot or foot and a half before it would drop over the edge of the road.

This was the most dangerous situation I'd ever been in with the family. I had a decision to make.

"Ticker," I said, "I'm not sure that either the front end or the back end of the truck might not slide off the road one of these times. If even the back end starts to go, the whole van will go off the road fast." She could see that we wouldn't have a chance of surviving if we went into that steep, deep ravine.

"I want you to take the kids and walk on ahead. I'll be right behind you. If you get cold, we'll just stop, and you can get back in and warm up." We bundled them all up in coats and hats and gloves and boots.

"One more thing," I said. "Somewhere up ahead, but I'm not sure if it's a mile or a few miles, there is a road that goes off to the left, and I think it goes to a ranch somewhere over there. If something happens to me, you need to keep walking and get to that ranch before you freeze. That's really important. Remember, even in the snow, keep looking for a road to the left. Otherwise, it's still a long ways to Creel. Probably six or eight miles."

Ticker had to carry Eric in her arms since he was just over a year old. She and Dusty looked like a modern-day version of homesteaders from the old West, walking in front of their covered wagon in a snowstorm. It turned out the stretch of road with the dumped gravel was about five hundred yards long. A couple more times, I pulled over and stopped and looked at my tracks. Yes, I was still getting within a foot or so from having the rear tire go off the edge of the road.

Once again, God took perfect care of us! There may have been some angels doing a little pushing, too, although I couldn't swear to it.

7.7 A Christmas to Remember

> Let's do something fun for the community!
> —Brainstormer Unknown

As 1983 drew to a close, Ticker and I felt grateful for all the blessings from the Lord. Notably:

- We had just returned from a visa trip to the border and had survived that blizzard over a dangerous mountain road.
- Our prayers had been answered regarding the community to move into.
- God had helped us plan and execute the building of the house.
- We were making great progress in fitting into the community and making friends.
- With Christmas coming up, we decided to not just buy a few presents for each other and the boys but to do something to open even more doors with our Tarahumara and mestizo neighbors, and that would be an opportunity to show our Christian love for them.

Although we had paid all of our workers fairly, and perhaps a little more at times than what was the standard pay, we were extremely grateful for the way numerous men and teenagers had agreed to do everything from cutting down trees for beams and rafters, to bagging up sand and gravel for making concrete, to making adobes and helping us to build the walls. We wanted to do something that was fun to show them that we appreciated their hard work and, to all the rest, just that we loved having them as our neighbors.

As missionaries, we did not have a lot of money or goods compared to most Americans, but in comparison to the people we lived amongst, we were wealthy. We had tried to show our love as Christians to them without overtly preaching the Gospel, and I think we had made a lot of progress in that respect. I think taking care of so many of their medical needs was one of the things that spoke the loudest. Anyway, to change things up, we decided to forget about hard work for a little while and throw a party!

Before we left for the border, we had announced to the community a date on which we planned to have the party, and it was going to be a Sunday between Christmas and New Year's. We told folks to invite whoever wanted to come from the El Manzano area, which basically was a thirty- to-forty-five-minute walking radius from our house. We had no idea how many people would show up, but we prepared for thirty to forty. Ticker figured out some big pasta dishes that she could make and planned on a big cake for dessert. She bought all of those ingredients plus a few modest decorations while we were in El Paso.

While we were in training with New Tribes Mission, we had worked for the mission's headquarters for a year doing a major remodel project to get the headquarters moved from Waukesha, Wisconsin, to Sanford, Florida. During that time, we attended a really nice little Baptist church in Sanford. My friend, George Marcos, in that church was a youth leader, and that role fit him so well. He was always upbeat and happy and knew how to have fun. He asked me to work with him a couple of times with the youth when they needed an extra hand, and I'm glad I did. I saw a couple of games that he did with the teenagers that I thought we could do with the folks of El Manzano. The games were designed for teenagers, so it was going to be a gamble as to whether or not everybody would join in. But we really had no other good ideas, so we decided to give it a try.

There was a great turnout for our Christmas party!

Ticker and I had bought several presents for giving to the winners in certain categories. They were wrapped up in really nice wrapping paper and bows, so no one knew what they were, but they looked exciting. The presents were on display the whole afternoon on the table, so it got folks' imaginations going.

From the advertised starting time, we waited about an hour or an hour and a half longer to see how many people were going to show up and were pleased to see a pretty decent turnout. There were about fifteen adults, perhaps ten or twelve teenagers, and ten or twelve little kids. As was always the case on a Sunday, everybody was dressed in their nicest clothes. We finally decided to start the games.

We started out with the game for the adult couples. I explained the object of the game called Bloody Marshmallows. Just translating that name into Spanish did not exactly produce a lot of enthusiasm, but that was the first and last time that afternoon I worried about anything. I then told them that the object of the game was for a husband and wife to stand about eight feet apart from each other. The wife would have a bowl in her hand with ketchup in it and five marshmallows. She would dip one marshmallow in the ketchup and then toss it in the air high enough that her husband could catch it in his mouth without using his hands. Then he had to chew it up and swallow it. The couple which had the man catch the most marshmallows out of five would be the winner. I asked for a show of hands as to who would like to play. A lot of people grinned, but not a single hand went up.

"Okay," I said, "Ticker and I will demonstrate for you how this works."

Unlike when the teenagers did it at the church event in Florida, I knew we had to protect everyone's clothes, so we took the plastic haircutting cape that Ticker used when she cut my hair and turned it around backward to cover the front of me. Ticker threw the first marshmallow and, instead of grabbing it in my mouth, it hit me in the cheek and splattered ketchup all over my face. Everybody started laughing hysterically. She threw the next marshmallow and hit me in the nose, and again, I wasn't able to grab it in my mouth. The laughing got even louder. Of the next three marshmallows, I managed to catch two in the air, chew them up, and swallow them. There's no question I made a funny face because the flavor of a marshmallow dipped in ketchup is disgusting! But I didn't want them to know that. That was part of the fun, if you can call it that, when the man found out how awful the taste was and yet had to keep trying so he and his wife could win.

The crowd was warmed up, laughing hysterically, mostly at me, and I knew we were going to have a fun afternoon. I asked for volunteers amongst the married couples who wanted to win the prize away from me by getting more than two marshmallows. The first couple that volunteered were our friends, Barbara and Teodulo. It's one thing to see somebody new in the community like Ticker and me do something crazy, but it's even more special when you watch one of your friends and neighbors trying to do something so outrageously goofy and messy.

Almost every married couple got into the game, and we even had to have a runoff between two couples that had each gotten three marshmallows. Barbara and Teodulo finally won with four! When they had won, I asked Teodulo in a loud voice how the marshmallows tasted. His reply was, "Disgusting!" and drew even more laughter. I never saw our friends and neighbors laugh more than during that game.

The next game was for the teenagers. I don't remember what I called it, but the game consisted of three cookie sheets lying on a table we had set up outside with a layer of flour about a half an inch deep in them. Underneath the flour were five coins the size of a quarter. With a timer running, the teenagers had to find the quarters under the flour using only their noses and tongues, pick up the coins with their mouths only, and drop them on the table next to them. No hands involved.

This game, too, was hilarious, and everyone watched and cheered on their friend or relative. It was funny enough watching each one get their tongue and lips completely coated with flour as they poked around through the flour, trying to find the coins. But it was super hard to pick up those coins just using their tongue and lips, and with all of us laughing so hard, once in a while the teenager in the game would burst out laughing, and a big cloud of flour would go everywhere! Once again, we watched everybody laughing with their sides splitting. It was a lot of fun.

We wanted something a lot easier for the younger kids, so we tried bobbing for apples, but the littlest kids were really hesitant because they didn't want to get their faces in water. So we let the teenagers do that game also, and we set up a "pin the tail on the donkey" game for the youngest kids. They were fine with putting on a blindfold since they did that when they broke piñatas for birthday parties.

Teodulo catches a "bloody marshmallow" in his mouth

The games and the gifts and the food were a big hit! At the end of the afternoon, everybody went home happy with what we knew would be great stories for their family members and friends in the community. There were some rather stuffy young men, including Mauro's sons, who had not come. We knew that they would be regretting that decision and hoped that they would find coming to our house and visiting be something they would want to do in the months ahead.

We thanked everyone for coming and told them that we were so glad that we were living there with them. Because of our mission philosophy, I would not explicitly share the Gospel in Spanish yet, but before they left, I told them that we were really looking forward to teaching them about God and the Bible. It had to be a bit of a generic message for now, but we prayed the Lord would create curiosity and interest in their hearts for the day when we would share the Gospel clearly with them.

7.8 Will Drs. Real and Real Please Report...

"Okay, you're going to have to make the incision right here," he said, pointing to a spot right above the lump on his side. "Don't miss and hit the appendix because that will kill me."

His partner (fortunately not me) had to do the surgery right there in the tent on the side of the riverbank. There was no time to go downstream three days to a doctor. He would have been dead by then. That's what happened when the person who had the medical expertise on the team had an emergency himself. He had to stay awake and direct his partner to perform the surgery on him!

"What did they use for anesthesia to kill the pain so he could stay awake and tell his partner what to do?"

"There was probably nothing," the instructor said.

It was a true story that happened in a Third World country where the two men were serving as missionaries. It was one of the first stories that we heard in our "field medicine" course at language and linguistics school. That phase of our training, the third and final, only lasted one semester for most students. The exception was if you "tested positive" for linguistics (had a natural linguistic ability), in which case you stayed an extra year for an intensive course in linguistics alone.

Our field medicine course was one of many classes we took during that semester. Through videos and slide presentations, we were taught how to deliver a child, suture a wound, and set broken bones. The reason all this was important was that we would most likely be far away from qualified medical help and might need to do any of those things for a tribal person, a family member, or even our own self in the country to which we were going.

Our most user-friendly guide was a book entitled *Where There Is No Doctor* by David Werner, published by the Hesperian Foundation. It was also translated into Spanish and entitled *Donde No Hay Doctor*. That translation was used widely throughout Latin America. It was

403 pages long, with additional pages that served as questionnaires, dosage charts, etc.

The other book we relied on was *Field Worker's Medical Manual*, published by the Summer Institute of Linguistics, otherwise known as Wycliffe Bible Translators. This book was 645 pages long, and the copy that I still have was printed in Mexico in 1978, so it was brand-new when we arrived in Mexico in 1980!

Both books contain numerous drawings which helped immensely for many conditions. They were, and probably still are, extremely comprehensive for the vast majority of injuries, illnesses, and diseases. The drugs have changed, of course, with us now having available at least three generations of antibiotics alone. During our time in Mexico, we would use primarily penicillin, amoxicillin, and tetracycline. Fortunately, all three of those were available over-the-counter in the pharmacies in the 1980s and beyond. Once in a while, the Mexican government would get negative publicity over a drug that wasn't manufactured properly or was widely used incorrectly and would revert to the strictest interpretation of their drug laws, which said certain medicines could not be dispensed without a prescription from a doctor. But fortunately, those incidences rarely occurred while we lived there.

The Lord Jesus Himself had immense compassion on those who suffered from physical ailments. In the gospels, He used His healing powers innumerable times to show to both unbelievers and His followers that He was indeed God in human form. It was never our intention to "play doctor" by having a supply of medicines and trying to find people we could help with their physical ailments. They came to us with a whole range of physical health and injury issues, hoping we could be of help since we had more education and access to drugs than they would ever have. Therefore, it was our intention to simply show the love of God to them in a way that was like "giving a cold drink of water."

Indeed, Ticker and I were extremely thankful that we could buy antibiotics over the counter as well as other things like parasite treatment medications, etc. Living on a missionary income, even in Mexico, would have seriously tapped us out financially at times if we had not been able to diagnose ourselves and buy medicines to treat ourselves without having to go to a doctor. We learned a lot about what was available while we lived in Chihuahua City and, of course, as we learned Spanish and got more fluent we were able to buy exactly what we needed according to the medical books that we were using and trusting. In fact, I learned not to trust the pharmacists regarding the dosages they told me to use.

The first time I needed to take an amoeba medication, the pharmacist told me a completely wrong dosage, and I ended up taking what was recommended for a child. I lost ten or fifteen pounds before I went back to our medical books and found out the correct dosage I should have been taking.

Since there was no pharmacy in San Rafael, each time we went into Chihuahua City we reevaluated what we needed to have on hand just for our own family's needs to treat respiratory infections, intestinal infections, and serious cuts or wounds. Soon after we got to El Manzano, we realized we were going to have to help some of our neighbors who were suffering with various things by using our own supply of antibiotics. We started taking significantly more out there to have on hand for treating them, and it turned out to be extremely valuable.

Most of the people we helped in El Manzano came to us with respiratory or intestinal tract infections. It was so sad to see a cute little one- or two- or three-year-old boy or girl with mucus that wouldn't stop and a fever that was making them miserable. A lot of them might have needed hospitalization or could have even died had we not treated them. It was a blessing to us to be a blessing to them. It was such a straightforward way to show God's love.

HE WHO HAS BEGUN A GOOD WORK

Ticker dispenses medicine and gives dosing instructions
to a young Tarahumara woman

Sometimes we had to deal with the results of drunkenness. A young fellow who had been working on our house as a laborer came by one Sunday morning with a big bandage on his forehead. I pulled it off and saw a nasty cut that needed five or six stitches. I asked him what happened, and he told me that he and another young guy had gotten drunk the night before and his buddy had hit him in the head with an empty five-gallon metal can. I wasn't going to do stitches on him since I didn't have sutures, and there were doctors available in San Rafael. I gave him a big dose of antibiotics, put a fresh gauze bandage on his forehead, and told him to go to one of the doctors in San Rafael.

Nicolás Sanchez Banda and his wife were in their late seventies or early eighties. Physically, they were our closest neighbors. Their house was only a few hundred yards away in a little hollow, less than halfway between our house and Teodulo and Barbara's. We seldom saw them since they didn't leave their house very much. But, one day, their son came and told me that his mom was sick and he was worried about her.

Since it was a woman who was sick, Ticker and I both went over to the house with our medical kit. Their son had described it as a respiratory infection, and it indeed was. One thing we had learned from coworkers was that the Indian people had so little access to medicine that they would oftentimes hoard it and not take it properly if you just left it with them. We gave her an antibiotic capsule and insisted she take it right then in front of us with a glass of water. We gave her another capsule to take twelve hours later and emphasized that she really needed to do it and not save it for later. We assured her that we would bring her more tomorrow as well as the fact that we would not charge her anything. We hoped that would cause her to take the medicine as directed and not "save" it.

Since she was so elderly, we didn't want to take any chances on her getting worse within a day or two, perhaps not taking the medicine as directed, so after that first visit, either Ticker or I went over every day for about a week. Thankfully, she got better.

The next year, her husband, old Nicolás, got sick too. By the time we found out about it, he was in pretty bad shape. I initially gave him a big first dose of antibiotics, and then because he was so elderly, I went twice a day to give him more. We hoped that he would have taken to heart the same message regarding how to take the antibiotics the right way, but we made quite a few trips that first week to see how he was doing and to give him more capsules. He might've had pneumonia, and it took six or eight weeks before he finally got better. Thankfully, he survived too.

Old Nicolás was the quintessential elderly Tarahumara. He always looked so dignified with his white dress shirt buttoned to the top button below his chin and his hands folded nonchalantly behind his back. At one point, I thought he might be a help to me in learning the Tarahumara language, so I went to their house to ask him if he could help me learn some things. I would ask him how to say something simple like "How do you say 'the dog?'"

He might tell me a word here or there but, more often than not, would reply with "*Quien sabe?*" the ubiquitous answer that came from so many Tarahumaras which means "Who knows?" He simply didn't want to share his language right then and there and actually probably never would. That was the old Tarahumara way, which is how they had resisted the influences of the outside world for hundreds of years and tenaciously retained their indigenous culture.

Visiting with Old Nicolas and his wife at their humble home. Thank the Lord we were able to successfully treat them both for severe respiratory illnesses.

Thank You! That Will Be One Chicken...

The rather humorous side of us doing medical work for the people was when we came up with a way they could pay us without using the very little money that they were able to earn and save. Obviously, people appreciate something more when they actually have to pay for it, so one day we came up with the idea of telling them that we would accept chickens as payment instead of money. Lots of the people had chickens, so we didn't think that was a big burden on them.

The downside was that I had to build a chicken pen, and we had to either buy chicken feed or let the chickens free-range and get them locked up before dusk. I really didn't want to buy chicken feed, so we decided on the latter. The coyotes were forever grateful for that decision since they ate far more chickens than we ever did. But that's another story.

We got the idea of "payment with a chicken" because one of the Indian ladies who had come by with sick children one day brought us a chicken in payment. Once the word got out that we were okay with that, that became the preferred payment option for them, although once in a while we bartered for apples or something similar. But the joke on us was that if there was a fifty-fifty chance of a little three-week-old bird being a hen or a rooster, how was it that we ended up with 90 percent roosters?

The sex of the bird didn't become obvious to us for another month or two when they had finally gotten bigger, and by then, it was a little too late to complain since we had lost track of who had given us what. But as I said, we didn't get any complaints from the coyotes. They knew about what time in the late afternoon/early evening we would expect the chickens to come back into the fenced-in coop on the far end of the back porch and, like the ghosts that they were, were there early.

Not Funny at All—Deadly Serious Actually

One day, at about three in the afternoon, I had a young boy, perhaps only ten years old, come knock on our door. He was a little bit shy, but he was actually quite clear about his errand.

"Señor Real," he said. "My family sent me to ask you if you can take someone to San Rafael to the doctor. He has been hurt."

"Hurt how?" I asked him.

"Nobody knows for sure. No one saw what happened. Maybe somebody came and hurt him," he said.

I had never heard of an attack on someone unless it was during one of their drunken brawls. This sounded so weird.

HE WHO HAS BEGUN A GOOD WORK

"They found him out in his field, and now they have him in the house, lying down," the boy said.

"How badly is he hurt?" I asked.

"I'm not sure, but the family asked if you could come."

We had had plenty of requests to take somebody sick to San Rafael, and it was almost never an urgent request, sometimes not even legitimate. I said, "I'll go with you and see how he is, and I'll bring some medicine with me. Where is it that he lives?"

"It's Rancho (something or other)," he said. "It's up by the Cerro Colorado (the Red Rock)."

I knew approximately where he meant, although every little cluster of houses had its own "Rancho" name. But to get to the Red Rock, I had to drive six or eight minutes south from our house as if we were going toward San Rafael, then turn back north and go up to the top of the El Manzano valley, then loop around past it further north. It would take me thirty minutes or more to get up there with the van, and I knew I was really low on gas. It would take me forty-five minutes to walk there, and I thought that would be a better choice, at least to evaluate this fella.

It was not a small problem that I was in a tight spot regarding gasoline at the moment. I knew I barely had enough to get back to San Rafael. That happened at least a couple of times per year when the logging company would run really low on gasoline, and that had been the case the last time I'd been in town. When that happened, they had to ration it in five or ten-liter allotments, so I had to be extremely careful that I had enough to get back to town.

"They told me to tell you to please bring your truck," the young boy said. "He really needs to go to a doctor."

This sounded pretty serious. I told Ticker what was going on, so I quickly got enough supplies to stay overnight in San Rafael if that was necessary. I took a sleeping bag, some food I could eat on the road, a jug of water, and a change of clothes. Then I grabbed the medical bag, and the little boy and I headed up toward the Red Rock in the van.

I asked the boy who this was that was so seriously hurt, and he told me it was Seferino. I didn't know Seferino well, but I knew who he was. He was a Tarahumara man in his late forties or early fifties, slight build, and about five feet seven. He had always looked unhappy or angry when I saw him around the community. I guessed that was a result of him being crippled. His right arm had been injured several years earlier in an accident while he was logging. A pole had snapped and hit him in the elbow, breaking something in his arm and apparently causing permanent nerve damage. He had to do everything left-handed from that point on. Then, sadly, he lost his left eye in some other kind of accident. All of this happened to him while he still had a wife and kids to support, doing hard physical labor just to plow the rough ground at his *ranchito,* and try to raise corn and beans for their sustenance. Without the Lord, he was understandably depressed, which is probably why he drank more than most people, for sure.

As I passed the Red Rock and went another quarter-mile on a barely used road, I came to Seferino's house and was unprepared for what I saw. Along a low rock wall off to the side of the road sat four or five people chatting with each other. A little ways to one side was a log that was used as a long bench. Five or six people were sitting there also. Under a tree, some standing and some sitting on the ground, were six or eight more people. Under the porch of the house were several more. There must've been fifty or more people sitting and standing around the property in little groups. They all looked up, and a few walked over to my van as I pulled up in front of the house. I wondered what in the world was going on. I'd never seen anything quite like this. And everyone seemed so somber.

The house was a typical humble half adobe and half wooden slab-board construction home. One of the closest relatives came up to me and told me, "Thank you for coming."

I said, "Let's go see how he's doing" and was led toward the back of the house to a dark bedroom. Seferino was laying there on a bed, half conscious, with blankets pulled up to his neck, someone standing at his side. I asked them to open the curtains more and to bring a light. Someone brought an oil lamp and turned it up as bright as it would go.

I asked them where he was hurt, and they turned him onto his right side. There on the left side of his neck was a blood-soaked bandage. I gently pulled it off and saw a nasty V-shaped cut about three inches long. It had obviously bled a lot since there was blood all down the shirt and onto his shoulder.

"How did this happen?" I asked. I felt like I was at a crime scene.

His relative who had taken me back there—his brother, I think—said, "Nobody knows for sure, but we think he did it to himself. He has been drinking for a couple of days. He's been *muy triste* (very depressed). He can't work anymore, you know, and I think that's why he's been so depressed. We couldn't find him this morning when he should've come in to eat breakfast, so we went looking for him and found him out in the cornfield. This is how we found him."

So this was an attempted suicide. I got out my medical bag and started cleaning out the wound. It had stopped bleeding quite a while ago but still had several pieces of grass and corn husk in it. As I cleaned it, I could see the white ends, top and bottom, of the tendons and ligaments that he had cut. The wound was over an inch wide.

"Did he have a knife with him?" I asked.

"Yes," his brother told me.

I considered what I was looking at and realized that he had taken a pocketknife in his left hand, his only good hand, and had reached around as far to the back of his neck as he could reach, then cut himself with a forward motion. But he hadn't gone far enough forward and had missed his jugular vein by only a fraction of an inch or, of course, he would've been dead within a few minutes.

I finished cleaning the wound, which wanted to start bleeding again. There's no way I could suture him, so I made and taped butterfly bandaging across the wound to keep it closed, then taped gauze over it to keep it clean.

"Are there any other wounds?" I asked.

"Yes," said his brother and pulled the blanket down further. Seferino was still fully clothed, and there was a lot of blood on his jeans from the knee down. I took the knife I had with me and cut that pantleg off just above the knee.

Whether he did this cut first or second was impossible to tell, but apparently, he had not bled out and died from the one cut, so he had done a second one. With the cut to the backside of his knee, he cut some blood vessels and more tendons but did not get deep enough to sever the big artery that he was trying for. But he had bled quite a lot from this cut, too—in fact more than from the cut on his neck.

I carefully cleaned that wound out also, then injected him with one million units of penicillin. I tucked his leg back tight again so that the wound would not open up and start bleeding and told someone in the room to not let him stretch his leg out straight. I put a tourniquet on his leg just above the knee. I knew that if this wound opened up, he could die before I could get him to a doctor.

"Okay," I said, "we're going to have to carry him out to my truck on some blankets, but first I need to make a place for him to lay down flat." I did that and came back for him. As I walked in and out of the house, I now realized that all of these people had come there to wait for him to die. It was very much like being at a wake. They figured that if he wanted to die, and he probably would have with a little more blood loss, then it was meant to be. So they were there basically just grieving for him.

Then it occurred to me that all of this had happened, and he had been discovered in the cornfield around breakfast time, seven or eight o'clock in the morning. They could have sent somebody to me within an hour or two but had waited all day for him to die. I could feel anger rising up in me.

We got Seferino into my truck, and I asked who was going to come along with us to the doctor's to help take care of him. They told me that one of his sons would go. Then I had to tell them about my dilemma.

"There has been a gas shortage in San Rafael, and I was only able to get a few liters of gas when I was there last time. I only had enough to get back to town from my house, but now I need another hour and a half's worth of gas to make sure I make it. I figure I need at least ten liters, maybe twenty. Who has some gas they can contribute?" I asked.

Of all the people standing around outside, only a couple said they had a small jug with a few liters in it. Someone else said, "Manuel Roscon and his sons always have some gas for their chain saws."

"All right, then, I will be on my way and hope that there's enough gas and I don't get stranded before I get to San Rafael."

I wrote a note to Ticker, telling her how badly hurt this guy was and that it was urgent I get him to San Rafael to one of the doctors right away. I told her that obviously I wouldn't be back home tonight since it was now going on five o'clock. I asked who could take the note to her, and they told me one of the young men could do it.

I'm sure they could see the seriousness and also the unhappiness in me as I drove away. I had not seen people be so callous up until this point in time, although as I thought about it, I guess it would qualify more as resigned apathy.

Manuel Roscon's house was right on the road as we passed the school at the top of the El Manzano valley. He had a couple of sons who still lived with him who worked on cutting logs and loading trucks, so between them, they had another ten or twelve liters of gas for the van. Most of what they got was already mixed with oil for using in the chainsaws. It took twenty or thirty minutes for the men to get their cans of gas, and perhaps they were even debating amongst themselves as to how much they wanted to contribute of their limited supply. We worked with flashlights as we poured the last several liters into my truck since it was now starting to get dark. As we poured the green tinted gas into my gas tank, I prayed it would not foul my spark plugs and cause problems with us getting all the way to San Rafael.

The trip from the Red Rock to San Rafael took us more than three hours. I had to drive slowly enough to not have Seferino get bounced around too badly in the back of the van, but I also had to make good time because of the gas situation. You learned living in terrain like that that you did not calculate your gas consumption in miles per gallon as much as you did by hours of driving time. It was almost 9:30 when we got into San Rafael, and I prayed that I could find one of the doctors at home in town and also that he would be willing to come down to his clinic at this hour of the night.

It worked out well. The lights were turned down low when I knocked on the door at the doctor's house, but I was able to get him to talk to me through the closed door. I told him how bad of shape Seferino was in. He told me that he would meet me in a few minutes down at his office. "Thank you, Lord!" I said in prayer.

It was almost thirty minutes later before he showed up, but he wasn't alone. He had taken the time to go down and wake up the other doctor in town and ask him to come and help as his assistant. That ended up being a really good decision on his part.

The doctors were also quite surprised that Seferino had not cut his jugular vein. "Good job cleaning out the wound," the doctor told me. "Now to get him stitched up. It's going to take two rows of sutures." He and the other doctor worked on that wound for about thirty minutes with one of them doing one layer of sutures and the other the next. Meanwhile, I sat in a chair nearby, getting more tired by the minute. It had been a long day.

"Now let's take a look at that leg," said one of the doctors, and they turned Seferino over onto his stomach. When they stretched his leg out straight, the big artery finally let loose, and a stream of blood shot eight feet across the room and right across my chest! I had only heard that blood could shoot that far, never thinking I would see it happen. One of the doctors immediately clamped his hand over the artery so it would stop squirting. Apparently, Seferino had nicked the artery; another one-thirty-second of an inch, and he probably would have bled to death.

For the first time all day, I got lightheaded. That was a weird sensation. I moved my chair further away against another wall while they cleaned and sutured that cut also.

The son had a family member in town where they could stay the night, so I drove him there. The relatives assured me they would watch his wounds and make sure that they didn't open back up. By now, it was too late for me to even find a room to stay in for the night, so I drove to the edge of town, pulled over on the side of the road, put my sleeping bag over me, and pushed the driver's seat all the way back and tried to get a good night's sleep.

The next morning, I was able to get gas and drive home. I thought about Seferino and how sad it was that he had become so hopeless about life. "Please, God," I prayed, "let him recover so I can share the Gospel with him. He needs You so badly." I knew that there were many more of my neighbors out there who needed the Lord just as much, and I prayed that it wouldn't be too late for any of them by the time I got to share the Gospel.

The Snake-Bitten Tarahumara

The Lord has promised to watch over us wherever we go. We know a lot of the verses: "Yea, though I walk through the valley of the shadow of death, I will fear no evil, for You are with me; Your rod and Your staff comfort me" (Psalm 23:4); "I will never leave you nor forsake you" (Joshua 1:5). Nevertheless, God does allow us to go through difficult situations, sometimes incredibly difficult and painful, so that we will lean on Him in faith and trust Him for His care. By His grace, we never personally had to go through the pain or grief of any of us being bitten by a rattlesnake and possibly dying. And the rattlesnakes were out there.

I was constantly on the lookout for them and did find an area on our property where a smaller variety called "pygmy rattlers" liked to breed. I found the first ones less than a hundred feet from where the little adobe shack was. There was a small arroyo nearby, and I think I found and killed pygmy rattlers there every year for five years, sometimes twice a year. David also liked to walk around the rock retaining walls on the property, looking for lizards, and occasionally, he would find a diamondback rattler. I made regular rounds around the property, especially within a couple of hundred feet of the house where Dusty and Eric played a lot. By God's grace, none of us got bitten the entire time we lived there. The incident in that remote canyon when I was getting the macaws and Dave almost stepped on a really big diamondback was the only time we had a really close call. Praise God!

Then, one day, Big Juliana sent word by way of a runner to us that there was a man at her house who had been bitten on the hand by a rattlesnake. After determining from the young man who had been sent to me that the victim was not in some kind of critical state, I took off on foot with our medical bag, checking to make sure that the antihistamines that we kept on hand were not out of date.

The gentleman who had been bitten was a Tarahumara man, around fifty years old, stocky, and solidly built. The day before was when he had been bitten while clearing out grass under some fruit trees. He had been wise enough to put a tourniquet around his lower forearm to keep the poison from going up his arm and toward his heart. Then, amazingly but out of necessity, today, he had hiked an hour and a half or two hours uphill from his ranch to Juliana's. The hand and forearm were now quite swollen, but there was really nothing I could do for him at this point. I told him I thought the skin was getting too purple due to lack of circulation so had him loosen the tourniquet and move it up another couple of inches. I gave him Benadryl to cut down on the allergic reaction and Tylenol for the pain.

I asked him what his plans were, and he said he would stay at Juliana's for at least one more day before he went home. I told him that was a good idea and that I would be back the next day to see how he was doing. It was about a fifty-minute walk each way from our house to Juliana's, but if he would have been looking worse the next day, possibly with infection in his hand, I would have driven him to San Rafael. Thankfully, however, his hand and skin and forearm looked a lot better the next day. He was one tough character. I told him and Juliana that if he got worse in any way to send somebody quickly to my house and I would take him to a doctor. Thankfully, he did quite well and went home a day later.

Rosa Sanchez

Two or three years later, when Al and Polly Clark had joined us, we finally faced a truly heartbreaking situation. It was a cold winter's morning and had been snowing for a couple of days. No one had been out and about visiting, so I knew it wasn't a good sign when we had a knock on our door at seven o'clock in the morning. It was a son of Mauro's who had been sent to tell us that Nacho Sanchez's wife, Rosa, had delivered her baby and was in need of medical help. He asked if we could go down there quickly.

Since it was a female situation, Ticker volunteered to go down instead of me, and she thought it would be a good idea to take Polly. I agreed, so she quickly got dressed, ran over to the Clark's house, grabbed our medical manual, medical kit, and Al drove the three of them down to the house. Nacho and his wife lived about a half a mile below us at the bottom of the El Manzano valley.

I stayed home with Dusty and Eric but did not hear any news for almost two hours, which started to concern me. Finally, another young Tarahumara came to the door with a note from Ticker: "We need you down here. Please hurry."

Obviously, I raced down the hill to Nacho's house. Rosa was lying in bed with her eyes closed and a pile of three or four blankets on top of her. Once my eyes adjusted to the dark room, by the firelight I could see their teenage daughters, two toddlers, plus a handful of neighbors and relatives. The daughters were sobbing, and everyone else looked glumly stern-faced, standing off to the sides of the room. Ticker and Polly looked really solemn. I didn't bother trying to be polite and speak Spanish. I went right into English because it looked like bad news.

"What's going on? How is she?" I asked.

"She delivered the baby about four hours ago, and it was stillborn," Ticker explained. "Then they say she got dizzy, passed out, and they couldn't revive her. That's when they sent for us. I can't get a heartbeat or pulse," Ticker said, almost about to cry. "I thought I got a faint heartbeat a little while ago, but I'm not sure I really did."

I took the stethoscope and listened. I put my face down right next to her mouth and nose, trying to detect any respirations. I couldn't sense any. I told Al where we kept the adrenaline and needles up at our house. I asked him to go get them. I still had hope that we could revive Rosa. I remembered what had happened with my old boss in Illinois several years previously.

Right before I had gone to Bible school, I had worked for a really interesting company that made Christmas and Easter displays for shopping centers. We always took a coffee break at ten o'clock in the morning for fifteen minutes. When the last guy coming in from the very back of the shop passed by our boss George's office, he saw George down on the floor and bolted into the break room. "George is collapsed in his office!" he called out. We all rushed out to see what we could do.

I had no experience in first aid, but from what I'd seen on TV and the movies, I began doing my best at chest compressions right away. The painter who had alerted us started doing mouth-to-mouth on George. Someone had already called 911, of course, so the paramedics were on their way, but it seemed like it took them forever to get there. When we checked later, it turned out it was fifteen minutes from the time we called them until the ambulance got to the shop. That whole time, I did chest compressions and then would pause for a few moments while the painter did mouth-to-mouth.

Within thirty seconds of getting there and looking down at George, one of the paramedics said to me, "Keep doing what you're doing. Here, like this," and he showed me how to do the compressions even harder. I thought I was going to break George's sternum. It took them a few more minutes to get him hooked up to a monitor while they also talked to someone at the hospital on the radio about his condition. Finally, they shocked his heart and revived him, and George lived through that heart attack.

When we found George on the floor, he was a horrible shade of purple. I didn't know someone could look like that and still be alive. When the paramedics hooked up the monitors to him, I looked over and saw that he had two heartbeats and one respiration per minute. Again, I didn't think there was a chance he was going to survive.

But I learned something that day: someone can get extremely close to dying and still make it.

With Rosa, I wasn't going to give up hope yet. I prepped a spot on her chest and gave her a shot of adrenaline. I prayed it would revive her if she was still alive.

I resumed doing heart massage, and Ticker continued with mouth-to-mouth resuscitation. I prayed the adrenaline would kick in and she would revive. After five or ten minutes, we stopped, and I listened for a heartbeat. There was nothing. She had indeed passed away.

We would never know, of course, what caused her death. It could've been that she had continued to bleed from an undelivered placenta until her blood pressure dropped too much. When I asked about her age, Nacho said she was thirty-eight years old. That was a bit too old for someone who lived the hard life these Tarahumara did to be having children, especially in light of four others that she had already.

That sad occasion was particularly hard on Ticker, Polly, and me. After successfully treating so many other people in the area, we were never going to be able to give Rosa the opportunity to accept the Lord.

Chapter 8

Life and Ministry Roll On—1984

8.1 Sweet Home, El Manzano!

The year 1984 began with a nice surprise—something changed with the schedule for the boarding school in Chihuahua City, so Dave was able to come out for a one week break at the end of February! We arranged for him to fly to the airstrip at Ocóbiachi, which was so much more convenient than me having to drive into San Rafael, take the train to Chihuahua City, turn around the next day, and come all the way back, having spent seven hours on the train and three hours on the road.

In a letter to my mom and dad, I wrote "Dusty just can't do enough with David. He moves right over next to him at meals to be as close as he can. The first day David was here, Dusty wanted to hug and kiss him every little while." Yes, Dusty was a really affectionate little guy and missed his brother just as much as Ticker and I did.

Regarding Eric, who was two years and three months old at this point, I wrote "He's like a little all-terrain vehicle. He just kind of climbs, walks, crawls over anything in sight—stacks of lumber, firewood, piles of rocks, bags of cement, etc. Ticker calls him her 'little bug,' too, because he goes around kind of humming to himself, sounding like a twenty-pound bumblebee coming toward you."

HE WHO HAS BEGUN A GOOD WORK

It was really fun to watch Dusty and Eric at this age. Anybody who has had children knows that, usually, the toys you buy them are fun for them, but they also get really creative with a lot of other things. One of my favorite photos of Dusty and Eric shows them sitting on our dirt driveway right next to the house playing the drums. The funny part is the drums consist of upside-down buckets, empty Quaker Oats cardboard canisters, really large empty metal cans, and for a bass drum, a big cardboard box. They have a variety of sticks and rulers for drumsticks. Thank goodness for photographs like that—they can make you happy and smile many years later!

Resident musicians Eric and Dusty entertain us on their drums

About this time, we were getting a big kick out of our parrots too. I had forgotten the names we gave them until I saw the caption on the back of one of my mom's photographs. At least one of our parrots we named "Shut Up." They were a regular source of entertainment. I had made a big cage for them which was mounted on the wall in our dining room. It was made out of one-inch-thick, ten-inch-wide boards and was about two and a half feet wide and four feet tall. It had some big manzanita branches in it for a roost and a chicken wire front to keep them inside.

One day, I was studying at the dining room table, and from perhaps fifty yards away, outside, I heard Dusty yell, "Mama!" Ticker was upstairs and never heard Dusty call out, but two seconds later one of the parrots called out with the same intonation, sounding exactly like Dusty, "Mama!" From a distance, I heard Dusty again call out "Mama!" And again, Ticker couldn't hear him, but the parrot again said, "Mama!" with the extra urgency in his voice.

Ticker came to the top of the stairs and said, "Yes, Dusty, what is it?" thinking he was right there. Those birds' abilities were pretty amazing and funny.

When we had company over, whether the Clarks or visitors from Chihuahua City, we normally played some kind of board game or card game at night, like Uno, and told stories. The parrots, of course, normally sat on their roost and fell asleep around sundown or a little after. But when we would be playing games and start laughing, they would wake up and start laughing along with us. Then the more we laughed at them, the more they laughed, and it turned into a hilarious free-for-all! It was pretty entertaining, but it got to where we actually had to throw a blanket over the front of their cage and try to get them to calm down so that we could get back to talking amongst ourselves. It was like having a couple of extra kids in the house.

Our Own Airstrip

Up until 1984, when we wanted or needed to use the services of the Calvary Missionary Fellowship (later named United Indian Mission) aircraft, we had to drive to Ocóbiachi, an hour and a half away, where there was the closest airstrip. I had been looking for a spot where we could make an airstrip in the community of El Manzano and there was only one possibility. That was at the top of the El Manzano valley out in front of the boarding school. There was a section of land up there that was basically bare dirt. It was a sort of yellow looking dirt, not clay, but had no topsoil so nobody had ever tried to farm that land and never would. I asked Mauro who it belonged to, and he said, "Nobody." So I asked if we could make an airstrip there, and he said that it would be fine.

One day, we got word that the Ponderosa logging company's bulldozer crew was coming to clean up some roads in El Manzano. I talked to Manuel Rascon, our local sheriff and the man who was in charge of the bulldozer crew, to see if they could create a runway for us. The terrain had a bit of a slope to it, but I knew that would be helpful since the strip would not end up being really long, and the incline would actually help the plane to land and take off. During our training and missionary conferences, I had seen a number of videos of airstrips in the Philippines and Papua New Guinea that had mountainous terrain like we did. The missionaries had ingeniously found sometimes just a mountain ridge and leveled it sufficiently to make a workable airstrip.

There were a couple of high spots that needed to be bladed down and rutted areas from years of water runoff gouging out the soil. I paced off the spot I had in mind and found out that it would have over three hundred yards of good surface, plus an extra fifty or sixty feet that could be made into a flat turnaround area. It had a nice approach from the west.

I got the go-ahead from the bulldozer crew, and I think I agreed to pay them $200 or $300. Every time we had either visitors from the field committee who wanted to fly in or we wanted to send Dave back and forth to boarding school by airplane, I had a three hour round-trip to Ocóbiachi, besides the $60 or $80 it would cost us for Dave's seat on the airplane.

I went out with the bulldozer crew, and sure enough, it didn't take them that terribly long to make the strip. I measured it when they were finished: 320 yards long! I also took a drafting compass with degree markings on it to estimate the slope. It was on about a fifteen-degree angle. I didn't think that was too bad. I believe that some of the airstrips in the Philippines were over twenty degrees. I had also paid an Indian fellow to cut a pine tree and make me a big ten-inch square beam that was ten or twelve feet long. I then anchored some big bolts in it that I could attach to a chain or cable. I knew that in the future, each time the airplane was due to come in, I would need to drag this beam behind my truck so that it would fill in the ruts in the airfield caused by rain or snow runoff. It worked really well, so I did the final grading with that beam. Now I had to let Dave Wolf, our beloved pilot from United Indian Missions, know about it so he could come and land on it without a load sometime when he was in the area. I sent him a letter with a drawing showing the slope in degrees and the length.

Dave Wolf comes in for a landing on our newly constructed El Manzano airstrip

We had to arrange for and get confirmation replies for flights by talking with our radio person in Chihuahua City on the two-way radio who then called Dave up in Tucson, Arizona. They relayed what I wanted, and I waited to hear back regarding a date. In March, they told me a specific day. I hoped the weather would be good, and it turned out that it was. It was pretty exciting the first time Dave came in and made a low pass over the airfield! He had to fly in from the north, getting a feel for the way the winds acted in the valleys that were on his approach as he came in to El Manzano. After two passes, he landed!

When he got out of the plane, we had a great visit. The airstrip, like our house, was at an elevation of about 7,200 feet. The air can be thin at that elevation, especially on a hot day, so he told us he would have to be very cautious as to how much weight he carried in passengers, cargo, and fuel when he came to El Manzano. But our airstrip was now officially open!

God's Prep School for Culture Studies

As I finished the work on the interior of the house, I tried to also transition into carefully recording as much as I could about the Tarahumara culture. Cultural experiences were coming at us regularly, of course, as I've mentioned regarding people visiting us for a variety of reasons, us doing medical work as the need arose, and being able to do some interesting social activities around the community. I reflected on the fact that although I was only twenty-eight years old at the time, and would turn twenty-nine in September, God had led me personally on a quite long and interesting road. Ticker had grown up and only lived in Des Plaines, Illinois, until she left for Bible school, but my path had been incredibly different, and I thanked God for where I was now with the Tarahumara Indians.

The Lord tells us in Romans 8:28, "We know that all things work together for good to those who love God, to those who are the called according to his purpose." Allow me to tell you a little bit about my personal preparation in God's plan. Sometimes it had felt like I had been living a gypsy life after I was seven years old, but God was preparing me with a purpose in mind.

STEVEN REAL

I was born in Phoenix, Arizona in 1955 when it was still very much a part of the old West cattle country and Phoenix was still a very small city. Several miles south in Casa Grande was where my grandfather had his cattle ranch. He owned one "section," which measured one mile by one mile. Then he leased another section when his cattle herds grew and he needed more land. At the peak of his cattle production, he had 2,500 head. I lived there until I was seven years old, my brother and I living two full years with only my grandparents, while my mom went off to Los Angeles looking for work after her divorce from my dad. Then she married my stepdad, and we moved all over the US with me attending nine schools in nine different cities before I graduated from high school. He worked for the Lockheed Aircraft company when it was very common for someone in management to be transferred to a new location when there was an advancement and promotion opportunity.

It's interesting that as a kid, from ten years old until about thirteen, I loved reading about the Apache Indians. Geronimo is well known, but Cochise was a much more intelligent and strategic chief years earlier than Geronimo. When you see the white loincloths and red headbands that the Tarahumara men wear as their traditional dress, you would think you were looking at an Apache Indian from the 1800s. The truth of the matter is they are first cousins, genetically and linguistically. When I watch the Geronimo movies from the 1980s and 1990s (I like the one with Jason Patric, Gene Hackman, Robert Duvall, and Wes Studi as Geronimo the best) and hear the spoken Apache language, I can actually recognize a lot of words that are closely related to Tarahumara. They are about as close to each other as Spanish and Portuguese.

I find it astounding that just as Ticker and I were mentally preparing to go to Indonesia when we first arrived in language school, New Tribes was newly established in Mexico and sent a representative to our language school, asking some of us linguists to consider going down there. If we had passed through the training six months or a year earlier, I don't think we would have even considered going to Mexico. Do you think God might have been involved in that?

When Ticker and I went to Bible school in Jackson, Michigan, we weren't just going to another city three hours from Chicago where we both lived. We went to a city that had the largest prison in the world at that time, the Southern Michigan State Prison, on its outskirts. Because of that, there were a lot of relatives of people in that prison living in the immediate area, we were told. The Bible school was located in a large building that had been a five-story hotel right in the center of downtown.

Just a few blocks south of the school was where the Black neighborhoods started. There was a lot of crime there, so the Bible school's policy was that we never went into that part of town when we went out, two students at a time, to share the Gospel from door-to-door. That Gospel ministry was a mandatory part of our schooling, too.

At the beginning of my second semester, the godly Black Pastor Dungy of the Berean Baptist Church, talked to the staff at the Bible school and asked that some students, men only, be allowed to go into that part of town and share the Gospel. He assured them that it would be safe during daylight hours, so the staff made that option available for us. It sounded interesting to me, so for that semester and the next, that's where I chose to go.

I learned a lot of interesting things about the Black culture and even met the daughter of a slave at one house. The lady was sitting on her front porch in a rocking chair, smoking a small cigar, and told us a bit of her life story. She was about eighty-five years old and had been born about thirty years after the Civil War. Her mother told her what it had been like to be a slave. But her mother was also a God-fearing woman, so this lady was a born-again Christian, and it was such a privilege to meet her and talk with her. Ticker and I attended the Berean Baptist Church for those last two semesters of Bible school. We loved it.

The next part of our training was in rural Ontario, Canada. We got to be really good friends with a number of the families in our church there, almost all of whom were farmers. That was an interesting cultural change for us, too, which lasted a year and a half. It was there in "Boot Camp" that we studied numerous facets of cross-cultural communications. A unique opportunity there, too, was the prison ministry. All the male students were required to go at least twice per semester, along with the designated lead student, to a minimum-security prison that was about a half hour away. It was a weekly mission with only three or four students going at a time. After I went the first time, I asked if I could go more often, and my last semester there, the staff designated me as the lead. I took two or three other students every single week for the entire semester. I was curious as to how these men ended up there and felt a calling from God to really try to reach them with the Gospel.

There were question and answer sessions, personal counseling, and short Bible studies. I became friends, in a manner of speaking, with their designated leader, a big tall stoic guy who was obviously a natural leader. At the end of the semester, before we left, we were able to organize a baseball game, us against them! The week before the game, I got really sick and couldn't go, but it became a way to have fun with them and another tool for breaking down walls and sharing the Gospel with those men. I think the annual baseball game became a tradition at the boot camp.

Before we went to language school, the third and final phase of our training, we were in Sanford, Florida, for a year. There and during our time at language school, for a total of two and a half years, we attended small Southern Baptist churches. Talk about strict! That in itself was another interesting cultural experience.

Finally, we were in language school, and I was designated as a linguist. That came with a one-year intensive linguistics training program. Close to the end of the second semester was a six-week period in which we lived full-time in the small town of Jay, Oklahoma. We twelve linguists were the only ones who went, besides three or four staff members, of course. Our spouses stayed behind at the language school in student housing, and there was only one weekend when they could come down for two days and visit us. For six days each week, for about ten hours per day, we were immersed in the Cherokee language. We also had to learn some of their culture, of course, and attended a Cherokee-speaking church on Sundays.

When you added in the backgrounds of the people who were in the new Tribes Mission training program, from Bible school all the way through language school, there was quite a variety of cultures represented. We had everybody from former hippies to pastors and their wives, insurance salesmen and engineers to folks that owned their own business in the building trades. Those who entered the training ranged from eighteen years old to their fifties, and a small handful were actually in their sixties. There were quite a few students who were missionaries' kids, and of course, we benefitted from some outstanding staff members who had been foreign missionaries in their younger years.

Thinking about how God leads us in His own way through life, it makes me want to ask you a question: Do you appreciate your own unique life experiences so far? Do you realize that God has specially designed you with a specific role in mind to be a reflection of Him in this world? He has! Think about it!

God's Army and Special Forces

It was by the grace of God that we were able to profit in our training from so many different kinds of people that God brought across our paths. Having gotten a really good start in learning and appreciating the Mexican culture, we were now focused primarily on our main mission: the Tarahumara!

On this long and winding road, we were not just beginning to be prepared for spiritual battle; it had been going on all around us for years. There had already been a lot of casualties. In God's master plan, there had also been some reassignments of personnel. I certainly can't say that so many who had left had "quit." I hoped that the vast majority of them continued to walk with the Lord and find that place where He wanted them specifically to serve. I also know that I was grateful to be at the "tip of the spear." When Ticker and I had gotten excited about serving with New Tribes Mission, I never envisioned anything other than being in a tribal location sharing the Gospel with people who probably otherwise never would have heard about God's good news.

One day, I thought about the numbers. Of all the students that went to Bible school, about half never went on to boot camp or made it to the completion of boot camp. Of those who did, about half of those never went to or made it through language school. The next challenge was getting financial support to go overseas, and about 60 percent of those folks either got discouraged and never made it to a foreign country or they found another ministry and stayed in the United States.

Of the balance that did get to a foreign country, where they had to learn the national language, many struggled so much that they opted to either go home or stay and perform one of the necessary jobs in support work: bookkeeping and accounting, becoming staff at the children's school, running a guest home for missionaries coming and going from the tribal areas, etc. It only bothered me to witness people backtracking or quitting, calling it God's will if they didn't persevere in things that were understandably hard, like language learning or adjusting to a rural lifestyle. Unfortunately, there is an underlying weakness in many Americans when they don't think that they can learn one or two more languages or that they "need" an array of twentieth and twenty-first century conveniences.

After all, Jesus chose to come to earth at a time when Israel was under the domination of a foreign power, the life expectancy was somewhere in the thirties or forties due to hardships and poverty, and he chose "poorly qualified" men like fishermen and a tax collector to be His closest followers. They, once their hearts were transformed by God's mighty power and the indwelling Holy Spirit, learned, taught, fellowshipped, and encouraged one another and then took the Gospel throughout their known world and even far beyond!

So back to the numbers. I roughly calculated that well under 8 percent, and probably closer to 5 percent, of those we had started out with in Bible school ended up as tribal missionaries. I felt so very, very privileged to be in that 5 percent.

Living out there as we were was like waking up one day and realizing that you are part of Gideon's army. Could you imagine what that would be like? You know the story, which starts in Judges chapter 6. Because of the sinfulness of Israel, the Lord allowed the Jewish nation to suffer under the Midianites for quite a few years. Once they cried out to God for help, He decided to develop a leader to get them out from under their oppression. God had to encourage Gideon one step at a time, and Gideon actually asked the Lord for signs that it was really the Most High God who was talking to him. Patiently and step-by-step, the Lord worked with Gideon because Gideon was humble and believed and trusted the Lord with each assignment He gave him.

When it was finally time to enter into battle—well, almost time—God had to make a major adjustment so that Gideon and the children of Israel would not look back later on the victory, thinking that they had done it in their own strength and by their own power. So He whittled the number of men in His army from 32,000 down to 300. And that was to go to war against 135,000 men (Judges 8:10)! Even the plan was a crazy one—fake out the enemy in the middle of the night by making them think they were surrounded by a much larger army. Then attack them with only 300 men!

What followed was not a fairy tale or walk in the park either. Gideon and his soldiers had to enter into bloody hand-to-hand combat. It was kill or be killed. He and his men were exhausted but still pursued the enemy, for only total victory would be acceptable (Judges 8:4–28.). Through hard work and deadly peril, they persisted until there was total victory. Notable, too, was that Gideon wanted no glory for himself or even his son when all was said and done. He turned down the job and prestige of becoming their national leader and said "the Lord shall rule over you" (8:23).

I have to say, it was an awesome thing to be part of God's plan and a warrior for His kingdom! Still is!

The Battle in the Mind

I'm leading an adult Bible study group right now in the church I attend, and we are getting close to the end of the book of Ephesians. I'm really impressed with how much our spiritual life hinges on learning and knowing and therefore trusting what God has done for us. As the Apostle Paul explains our redemption, the mystery of God's will for us, His grace toward us, and the "exceeding greatness of His power toward us who believe," these truths can and should result in the "renewing of the spirit of our minds" (Ephesians 4:23). Then we can "put on the new man… Be imitators of God as dear children, and walk in love as Christ also has loved us" (Ephesians 4:24, 5:1–2).

There are lots of reasons that otherwise dedicated Christians do not feel the need or urgency to reach out to nonbelievers around the world. Highly respected authors like Ernest Hemingway are frequently responsible for creating a cultural narrative that says, "Leave those beautiful cultures alone. Those people are happy with their beliefs." In his novel, *Hawaii*, Hemingway promoted this idea and deceived many millions of people around the world, including in America, that missionaries had done more harm than good to those blissful, idyllic cultures. But it's interesting that even in his own watery-eyed version of the Hawaiian culture, he noted that it was a capital offense for a Hawaiian commoner—man, woman, or child—if they should be inattentive and innocently allow their shadow to fall on the king's residence or on the king himself. They would be executed for that crime. Nope—no fear or terror there!

There is no question that in doing research for his own novel, Hemingway found out that the Hawaiian King Kamehameha I, who "united" the islands and their kings, was one of the most brutal butchers of any indigenous leader when he subjugated the other islands and several chieftains. No, Hawaii was not this beautiful, utopian tropical paradise for many, many years before the missionaries arrived.

Nor did the Tarahumara live in those rugged and beautiful Sierra Madre mountains without fear of the spirit world. But rather than let it continue that way forever, God had a plan underway to bring some Tarahumaras' hearts and souls to Himself!

8.2 Help Is Coming...

In the spring, the Clarks came out to discuss with us where to build their house. They were quite happy with a location that was about one hundred yards from our house. They decided they would have the Indians start making adobes as soon as the weather was warm enough and there was no more danger of snow. They also agreed on getting rocks accumulated for the footings for the house. They would send us money to pay workers for each of these things. Meanwhile, they would work on a floor plan for the house.

This was exciting for us, of course. We were finally going to have partners who were serious about staying!

At the end of June, it worked out for the Clarks to come out and help oversee the work going on at their house site. I had plenty to do with Tarahumara language and culture studies, and it was getting rather tedious for me to also be supervising the workers for them. It would only be a short trip, but it would be good to see them again and have their fellowship.

...If I Don't Kill Them First!

I had brought fireworks down from Missouri a year and a half earlier when we had gone up to Chicago for that short Christmas break. I'd been saving them for a special occasion, and the Fourth of July was going to happen while the Clarks were out there with us. Then we found out that Ken and Leanne Gutwein, members of the field committee, were going to come out with them. This would be a great occasion to do some celebrating! I told Barbara and Teodulo to spread the word that we were going to shoot off some rockets. I didn't want anybody to think we were shooting guns.

At the top of our driveway, where it curves around the house, was the highest, all-dirt area close to the house. I took three or four pieces of pipe and pounded them into the ground to serve as launching tubes. The rockets would be shooting south where there weren't any houses nearby. I knew Dave and Dusty would want to be part of the action, so I let them light the first few rockets, making sure they would get back quickly and it would all be safe. First, we fired a few bottle rockets, then changed to the bigger rockets.

The rockets weren't always real dependable and would sometimes shoot up thirty feet and then go off in a weird, random direction. I adjusted the tubes so that they would go more straight up in the air and that would help Ticker, the Gutweins, and the Clarks all be able to see them better too. Four or five big rockets went up really nicely, then we unknowingly got the big bad one.

Standing under the porch were Al and Polly with their daughter, Amy, Ken and Leanne, and Ticker who was holding Eric in her arms so he wouldn't run up toward the other boys and me. Remember, the porch was six feet wide and about twelve feet high where the rafters came over the wall of the house.

Finally, we lit one of the biggest of the rockets. It was designed to go about two hundred feet in the air and blow up with a big bang and a bunch of colors. However, it only went up about five feet and then turned sideways, heading straight for the front door of the house where everybody was standing on the porch. Fortunately, everybody was looking when it hit the ground right at their feet, and they started to duck and run. It ricocheted off the wall of the house, went up and hit the bottom side of the tin roof, ricocheted back to the ground again, right where everyone was running in every direction, then shot off toward the hill where our water tank was and exploded about a hundred feet away!

I was watching in horror and fear, thinking someone was going to get hit and seriously burned. But they did all turn their backs, covered their faces, and started running. But when the rocket hit the ground at their feet, they also started jumping up and down like in one of those old Westerns where someone was shooting bullets at their feet to make them dance. Once the rocket streaked away from them and exploded, I breathe a big sigh of relief. Then the humor of watching them jump and dance overwhelmed me, and I started laughing. Watching from sixty feet away, it was incredibly funny! However, I'm not so sure they thought so, so that was unfortunately the end of the night's fireworks display.

During the summer months, all of our normal daily routines continued: studying language and culture, treating medical conditions when they arose, etc. It was so good to have Dave home from school for the summer, and we did a lot of visiting around the community. Since I got out with the people a lot more than Ticker did, we tried to make a habit at least every two weeks of taking a walk together somewhere around the area on a Sunday to visit our neighbors.

The Cloud Takes No Break

Unfortunately, the Cloud—Ticker's depression—would also creep in regularly. Sometimes it lasted two or three days, sometimes for a whole week. It was hard for her to deal with it, of course, but it was also really confusing to me. Despite my attempts to try to figure out what to do about it, nothing seemed to work. She still didn't want to share her thoughts and feelings with me and told me basically to just leave her alone and let her rest and be by herself.

I know, we men are always trying to fix things or find a solution. I couldn't exactly be like a female companion to her, which I hoped Polly would be within a few months. I think that taking walks and getting exercise was helpful to a certain degree. I thought that visiting more in the Tarahumaras' homes would help her branch out, feel more a part of the community, and realize how valuable she was there. Yet, it was hard to tell what helped and what was just another day in the life.

* * * * *

It's three in the afternoon on another beautiful summer day. I'm at my desk in my office when Dave comes in to tell me that two ladies are here to see Ticker. I pass through the kitchen/dining room to the back door just as they arrive.

"*Kwira!*" I say to them in the Tarahumara greeting for hello. "Come on inside," I say as I usher them into the dining room. They take a seat at the table. I ask them how they are today, and they ask me the same.

"We've come to see Dorotea," they tell me, using Ticker's name in Spanish. "How is she today?"

"Well, she's not feeling too well today. She's in bed right now, resting," I tell them.

One of them is seated closer to the bottom of the stairs than I am, and knowing that our bedrooms are upstairs, she boldly stands up and starts to go up the stairs. This is really unusual behavior for these folks who are usually much more reserved.

I stand up immediately and move toward the stairs, where now the second lady is only two steps behind her companion. "I really don't think she's ready to have visitors today," I insist as I follow them. "Let me go see if she's awake," I say as I try to get them to stop.

"Well, that's why we came to see her," says the first lady. "We heard she wasn't feeling well, and we have some herbs that we want her to try. They're very good for giving you energy and making you feel better," she says.

There isn't any way to pass them on the steps going upstairs, but I get them to pause at the top landing in the hallway. "Please, let me go see how she is first. I'll be right back." Perhaps the tone of my voice made them wait there.

Ticker was awake enough to hear our conversation. She comes to the bedroom door, looking sleepy and disheveled. The ladies tell her that they heard she wasn't feeling well and brought her something, an herb to make into a tea.

Ticker tells them to come into the bedroom and sit down, which is the first time that had ever happened. I go back downstairs to resume my studies, but of course, I'm really curious as to how this might turn out.

Thirty minutes later, the two ladies come back downstairs with Ticker, who escorts them to the door, and in a friendly conversation, thanks them for coming. She assures them she'll make the tea and see how it works. Not looking very energetic, she goes back upstairs and back into the bedroom.

I study for another couple of hours, keeping an ear out for the boys who are all playing outside. Knowing that we'll be taking showers soon, I go into the bathroom and light the hot water heater, carefully waiting thirty seconds or more to fine-tune the kerosene drip into the burner chamber before I leave. Just about the time I'm thinking it's time to get ready for dinner, Ticker comes back downstairs. She just looks tired and exhausted but says she's going to start fixing dinner and asks if I could get the boys to come inside and take their showers.

I call the boys over, and they decide who is going to go first, second, and third into the shower. I go into the kitchen to ask Ticker how she's feeling but just get a mumbled response.

"Did you enjoy your visit with the ladies?" I ask.

"Not really, what do you think? I just wanted to rest, but it was nice of them to think about visiting me."

Yep, same old thing, I think. *What will ever bring her out of this funk?*

I go up to the little hill next to our house, where I can see 360 degrees. To the east, I see the El Manzano valley, far to the north the mountains drop away toward the Rio Oteros canyon. To the South, I can see Barbara and Teodulo's house and the other homes of San Miguel. This has become my favorite place to sit and pray, sheltered by just a few pine and oak trees and with a rock that I have positioned into my place to sit. I quiet my mind for a few moments, reflecting on how the day has gone.

"Lord," I pray, "please help Ticker get her energy back right now as she's up again and in the kitchen, working. Please help her to feel encouraged. Only You know what's going on, God. I never know the right things to say to encourage her. Does she need a doctor? How are we going to find one for her? Please give us an answer.

"Lord, you said that if a son asks for bread, would his father give him a serpent? I'm not asking anything for myself, Lord. If I was, I could understand You not giving me an answer. But I'm praying for healing for Ticker. Our family needs her. The boys need her. I need her. It's tearing me up seeing this depression come back time and time again. Please, God, bring someone along and give us some answers and help her."

I have no idea how many times I prayed that prayer, often in that very same spot. But it was a lot.

House Construction, Take 2

I was so relieved each time the Clarks would come out, and Al would take the time to work with and direct his own workers. Yes, his Spanish studies were essential. He and Polly would not be allowed to join us until they both finished all seventy lessons. But I had spent many hours hiring workers for him and directing them as they accumulated all the building materials for his house. I had definitely had my fill of building houses for a while with the long drawn-out project of our own.

In November, Al came out with three of our field committee members to not only visit with us but also to help with the construction of their house. The committee members only stayed a few days, but it was a nice boost for the Clarks. It was finally time to give their house project a big push with the potential for winter weather and snow getting closer by the day. In three weeks, they had all the adobes laid for the walls and got the roof on!

8.3 Mom Comes to Visit or "You Can't Make This Stuff Up!"

We had been in correspondence with my mom about coming down to visit us for a few months now. Finally, she and Dad had worked out the details for her trip. She would arrive in Chihuahua City by plane on October 29, and we would go pick her up and bring her out to El Manzano. With that in mind, Ticker, Dusty, Eric, and I drove into the city. We were only allowed a short visit with Dave at the boarding school, and I remember feeling slighted, as if he was going to get too distracted and not readjust easily after we left. Oh well. The school had their policies for unscheduled family visits, and we had to abide by them. We hurriedly moved on to getting all the supplies and groceries we needed for the trip back to El Manzano.

Mom said, "Steven, you know I have to have my cigarettes. And, no, there isn't any other brand that I can smoke. I've tried. They have to be Kents. Filtered 100s."

I replied, "But, Mom, if they ran out of them at the grocery store, which is the biggest store around, how do you expect me to find any here? This is Mexico, not the States."

Mom said, "Please, don't you have some friends to ask to see if they might be available anywhere else?"

I asked our coworkers who managed the guesthouse where we were staying. Laughing, Peter said, "All I can think of is that the liquor stores might have them."

In Mexico, they did apparently have liquor stores that were full of lots of brands, and yes, it might be that they brought in American brands that were not normally found in the big grocery stores. I was up against a deadline, too, since it was now six o'clock at night, and we were leaving for the mountains by seven in the morning.

There was a commercial area in Chihuahua City, away from downtown, that had a lot of liquor stores. It was also the home of the red-light district. "Great!" I said to myself. "Now I'm going to go cruising around the red-light district, having to go into who knows how many liquor stores to find my mom cigarettes? I sure hope nobody from our old church here in town sees me! What a great Christian testimony that would be!"

As I drove down there, I was conscious of the fact that my truck did not exactly blend in with the other vehicles either. It wasn't a four-wheel-drive pickup truck like thousands of others. It was a big white four-wheel-drive van. There was probably not another one like it within five hundred or a thousand miles.

I drove slowly down the busy two-lane street in the old commercial district. I saw bars and restaurants and liquor stores on both sides of the street. I spotted the biggest liquor store I had seen so far and had to go around the block to find a parking spot big enough for my van. I got out, locked the truck, and had to walk almost a block to the store. I was coming up behind two women who were sauntering down the sidewalk. I normally walk pretty quietly, a habit I got into as a kid reading about how Indians walk so as to be able to stay quiet when they are hunting. As I got to within only a couple of steps behind the women, I thought I heard rather normal, even deep men's voices. Then I noticed one of the women's arms as I tried to figure out how to go around them on the sidewalk. That looked like a pretty hairy wrist below those long sleeves.

As I finally got to a spot wide enough to pass them on their right, they saw me out of their peripheral vision. Immediately, their voices changed into women's voices. *Oh my gosh!* I thought. *That was a couple of transvestites! What in the world am I doing down here?*

Mom had been very specific. She needed at least two and a half cartons of Kent cigarettes to last her the next two and a half weeks. Why oh why had she not brought more cigarettes for herself from home?

I passed men in festive mariachi suits who were looking for work, sometimes in groups of four or five. There were women—at least I think they were women—in super tight short skirts on every block, working their "trade." I had to go into five or six stores to find enough of her cigarettes. Only two or three of them even had her brand. After an hour and a half of driving around the liquor store and red-light district, finally with enough cigarettes in hand, I headed back to the guesthouse. That had been a pretty grueling experience for someone who had no desire to smoke or drink for the last twelve or thirteen years.

Our van was loaded with supplies that we had bought in Chihuahua City. I left the city early to head for the mountains, but we got some coworkers to drive Ticker, Dusty, Eric, and my mom to the train station. They would take the train as far as San Rafael, which saved them from getting beaten up on that last grueling two-

HE WHO HAS BEGUN A GOOD WORK

and-a-half-hour stretch right before San Rafael. I got into town a little while before the train, topped off on gasoline at the sawmill, and picked them all up at the train station. We only had one stop left to make before we got on the road to El Manzano.

With everyone snugly tucked into their places on the bench seat of the van, and all of our supplies stacked and secured behind them, I pulled up to one of my favorite little grocery stores. I said, "This is our last stop. Sit tight, and I'll be right back" and jumped out of the van. I think I heard Mom starting to say something to me as I closed my door, but I knew Ticker would answer whatever question it was.

You need to understand what the little stores out there in the mountains were like to appreciate this part of the story. They were very much like we used to see in the Western TV shows and movies. You walked up to a wooden counter, where one or two of the proprietors would ask you what you wanted, and then they would go up and down a few aisles behind them and pick out your merchandise and bring it up to you. There were only a few items hanging on the wall or on displays where you first walked into the store. If you wanted five kilos of beans, for example, you told the clerk that and either handed them your bag or paid for a paper bag or gunnysack. They would go down an aisle, bring a sack, and measure out your five kilos of beans, and leave them there on the counter for you. If you wanted a box of crackers, they would go down another aisle and bring it up to you, and so on.

The only thing I needed, since we had bought everything else in Chihuahua, was two "flats" of eggs. Each flat held eighteen eggs, and they would put another cardboard flat on top for a lid and tie the whole thing together securely with twine. There were two ladies inside the store being waited on when I walked in, so I patiently stood off to one side in the little six-foot-wide, ten-foot-long space until they were finished being served.

I had only been there perhaps three minutes when the door opened, and my mom walked in. I was pretty surprised to see her, but before I could ask her what she was doing, she looked at me and said, "*No tiene usted huevos?*" She had meant to ask, "Do you have your eggs?" but had asked me, in Spanish slang, "Don't you have any balls?"

You can imagine my shock. But it wasn't just mine; the two ladies who were being waited on had just finished paying for their groceries. They looked at each other, looked at the floor, and hurried out, pushing past my mom. But the more memorable reaction was from the proprietor. I had been coming to this store for a few years so knew her quite well. She did her very best to not burst out laughing. I saw the smile flash onto her face, then saw her jam her lips together, turn on her heel, and go back down the aisle behind her so she wouldn't lose it right in front of me.

I spun around and looked at Mom. "Mom! Didn't I ask you to stay in the van? Do you have any idea what you just said to me?" I said to her in English.

Sputtering, Mom said, "No. W-What did I say?"

"You just asked me if I have any balls. Didn't you see how those two women rushed out? Oh my gosh! I can't imagine what they're talking about right now."

The lady who owned the store waited at least a half a minute before she came back up another aisle. She had her composure pretty much under control, but I could still see the amusement on her face. I have no idea what I said to her at that point except, "I need two flats of eggs, please. Yes, that is my mom visiting from the States." I'll bet she had a good story to tell everybody for the next few weeks.

The day after Mom arrived in El Manzano was November 1st. Here in the States, we call it All Saints Day, but in Mexico, it is the Day of the Dead. There are lots of rituals associated with it, so we took Mom down to the cemetery to see what was going on. Some people were kneeling next to their relatives' graves, others came with family members for a little while, just did the sign of the cross, and left. We very discreetly took a couple of pictures but had to be very careful about the people's sensitivity to that. It was also an opportunity to introduce Mom to some of the folks who lived nearby.

We made a couple of short trips around the El Manzano communities in the van since it wasn't an option for Mom to walk very far on those trails. The Mexican boarding school for the Tarahumara kids who lived in the outlying areas was pretty close to the cemetery, so we walked over there. The kids must've been taking a short walk while they were on some kind of a break, so Mom said she wanted a picture with them. She was really enjoying meeting the people already. I have a great picture of her with a schoolteacher and twelve young Tarahumara kids standing with her.

Mom was born and raised Catholic—very Catholic. We had some interesting conversations with her regarding our goal of sharing the Gospel with these people. She was very opposed, of course, to us "changing their religion." It was good to take the opportunity once again to share the Gospel with her, explaining that it's not our religion that gets us to heaven but faith in the Lord Jesus for His death on the cross paying for our souls.

One morning, Mom told me that she was getting low on cigarettes. We still had about four or five more days before she was scheduled to leave, so I only had a day or two in which to find her enough cigarettes for another two or three days. I told her this was going to be next to impossible, finding cigarettes way out here. Besides, I told her, there are only two brands of cigarettes that the Indians out here can buy: one is like the old unfiltered Camel cigarettes, and the other is filtered, but there's only one particular Mexican brand.

Since there were a couple of guys working on things at Al's house, I walked over and had a talk with them.

"Esteban! So now you've started smoking cigarettes? What happened?" they laughed. Everybody knew I did not smoke or drink, so they were not going to pass up this opportunity to give me a ribbing. They told me they only had a couple of cigarettes with them, which they oftentimes would light up during their lunch break or at the end of the day.

"Could you ask around when you get home and see if anybody you know has some?" I asked. "I need two or three packs of the filtered ones if you can find them, please. I'll pay you double what they cost."

"Oh, so you only like the filtered ones, huh? Yeah, they're the best!"

I wasn't going to hear the end of this for a while.

The next day, they managed to rustle up one and a half packs for me. Then I went up to Teodulo's store, and fortunately, he had one pack left. I told him I was desperate, and he started laughing so hard he almost cried. I did manage to get barely enough to satisfy Mom for the remainder of her trip.

Mom and Dad had been going to Mexico and Belize on vacation for years. She loved to use her Spanish whenever she could, and there was always a funny story or two about something she had said when they came home. It had been a little over two weeks since she had embarrassed me in the store in San Rafael. We were now in the van, driving up out of our valley toward San Rafael again, and Mom was going to get one more chance to practice her Spanish.

The custom out where we lived was that anytime a vehicle, log truck, or pickup truck was heading down the road and someone needed a ride, the courteous driver would pull over and let them jump in. It was not uncommon to see one or two men or even a family with women and kids seated on top of a loaded log truck, hanging on as it rumbled for hours toward the sawmill in San Rafael.

As we climbed out of the El Manzano valley and got close to the main logging road, I could see a stocky man with graying hair running on a little side trail to try to catch us before we passed him. He just barely made it, getting to the shoulder of the road thirty feet in front of us. It was one of our neighbors, Agustino. Mom, Dusty, and Eric were sitting on the bench seat, and we didn't have much else in the van, so I told the boys to go in the back and make room for Agustino as I slowed down. Then I had just enough time to tell Mom I was picking up a neighbor to give him a ride, so she should slide over behind me on the bench seat.

Agustino climbed in, a little bit out of breath, so I gave him a moment to get settled down and introduced him to mom. They each said, "Mucho gusto (My pleasure)," in response. When I last turned around, I remember the look on Mom's face. She was blinking like a nervous teenager at an eighth-grade dance. It seemed like she was trying to come up with something else to say but couldn't quite figure out what it might be. We got underway again, and I talked with Agustíno over my shoulder for a minute or so. Then all was quiet for

HE WHO HAS BEGUN A GOOD WORK

about two or three minutes. You know when you have that feeling that it is too quiet? Yeah, I was getting that feeling.

Agustino was a real nice, generally quiet gentleman. He was also actually good-looking with blue-gray eyes, which was quite unusual for a mestizo out in our area. He obviously had European or American blood, probably from a gold or silver miner who had lived out here and found himself a girlfriend. He had salt and pepper hair and was probably fairly close to Mom's age. Now Mom wasn't one to lapse into silence for very long, and a few minutes later, she had decided what she wanted to say.

She meant to comment on how rough the road was to Agustino, but instead of the word for road, *camino*, she decided to say "the trip," *viaje*. However, turning in her seat and facing Agustino, with her eyelashes fluttering a bit nervously, instead of saying, "What do you think of this trip (*viaje*)?," she said, "What do you think of this old lady (*vieja*)?"

Oh my gosh! Ticker and I were flabbergasted, of course. I looked in the mirror at Agustino, then over my shoulder, as Ticker blurted out, "Viaje! Viaje!" I've rarely seen anyone so shocked with their mouth literally hanging open, but that was Agustino at that moment.

Mom, of course, was asking what Ticker meant and was trying to interpret Agustino's reaction. First, I let Ticker explain to Agustino what Mom had meant to say in Spanish so she could take care of that misunderstanding. I started explaining to Mom in English what she had just said—"How do you like this little old lady?" I turned my rearview mirror so I could look at her, and it was classic how embarrassed she was. Poor mom! For the next few minutes, I kept hearing her say under her breath, "Oh my gosh, oh my gosh" and "Hmph. Oh my." There wasn't a window right next to her in the van for her to turn and look out of, so she just had to look straight ahead and at the floor for a while.

I started up a little conversation with Agustino again to change the subject. Although I had to carefully negotiate the rocks and ruts in the road, I would turn and look at him every minute or so over my shoulder. I bet it took five minutes before the red left his face.

Yes, my mom was a piece of work!

Chapter 9

The First Believers

9.1 The Gospel Brings Light!

At the end of July, God—in His sovereignty—dramatically changed our ministry as He opened a door for us completely out of the blue. Barbara's younger sister, Trini (short for Trinidad), was at our house for a few hours one day helping Ticker. We were hiring her for one or two half-days per week to help Ticker with laundry, cleaning, and cooking. It really was a big help to Ticker too. Trini was only seventeen years old and didn't know much about the world outside of El Manzano and San Rafael. She and Trini talked about a lot of things, and one afternoon Trini was really curious about why we had come there. To most outsiders, it seemed that we were just living amongst the people from day-to-day, not doing anything that they didn't do, except plant corn and raise animals for our sustenance. Trini asked Ticker to explain to her this "message from God" that we wanted to share in the Tarahumara language someday in the future.

Ticker felt that God had opened a door of opportunity and walked right through it. I wasn't in the room when all of that happened, but Ticker was quite good in Spanish by then and shared the Gospel clearly and completely with her. It was late afternoon, and

Trini usually went home about four o'clock so she could help up at her house with making dinner there.

I remember walking into our dining room and seeing Trini with the biggest smile on her face and light in her eyes that I've seen from anyone. Ticker turned to me and said, "Trini just accepted the Lord!"

I was astounded. I hardly knew what to say for a moment. As I've mentioned before, New Tribes Mission wanted us to wait until we were quite fluent in the Indian language before we shared the Gospel for a number of very good reasons. I also had no idea up to this point that Ticker might share the Gospel in Spanish with anyone. She hadn't told me that Trini was curious or anything of the sort.

But looking in her face, with the most obvious joy of a new Christian, I was thrilled! "Oh my gosh!" I said. "That's wonderful! Tell me about it."

So Ticker told me how she and Trini had gotten into the conversation about why we were there in El Manzano. Trini said, "Well, you can tell me in Spanish. I don't even speak Tarahumara, so that's not going to do me any good to wait." Obviously, she had a point, so Ticker shared the Gospel with her, starting with our need for salvation and the fact that good works would never get us to heaven, then telling her all about Jesus dying on the cross to pay for our sins.

Trini went home a few minutes later. Ticker and I talked for a while as she finished making dinner. Then, an hour later, Trini was back with Barbara and Teodulo! They never went out visiting on a weekday that I remembered. And to come right at dinnertime?

They were pretty animated. They wanted to know all about the Gospel since Trini was so excited about it. So we had them sit down, Ticker served all of us coffee, and I shared the Gospel from beginning to end. Being nominal Catholics, they were certainly quite clear on the fact that we are all sinners and in need of God. But they had no concept of the fact that God had sent His Son here to the earth to die on the cross as payment for our sins. Ticker and I shared those facts and read several verses from the Bible with them. Then we explained that what God wants us to do is put our faith in what He did for us and accept Him into our hearts.

When we asked Barbara and Teodulo if they wanted to do that right then, they both said yes. We now, all of a sudden, had three new Christians sitting in front of us!

It would be an understatement to say that there was now a seismic shift in what our ministry would be like going forward. We explained to all of them that when we accept the Lord into our hearts, the Holy Spirit is given to us by God to live in us, to teach us and guide us. We knew that we would now need to teach them from the Scriptures about the Christian life and becoming disciples of the Lord.

Ticker and Trini

Ticker and me with Barbara and Teodulo

I don't remember what day of the week that was, but we agreed on them coming back over to our house at least twice a week to have Bible studies with us. Within a week or two, we were meeting on Sundays and one weeknight. Since it seemed to be best for them to come after they could finish their day's work in their fields and at their homes, they would have an early dinner at home, then come to our house for Bible study. By the second or third meeting, they asked if they could bring family members, and we told them, "Of course!"

Every time after that, they brought someone from their family, and usually, it was three or four others. Teodulo brought his mother, Doña Petra, the very next time as well as his younger brother, Valentin. We spent time talking about how God had created the world, then gave the law to Moses. Then we taught them from the Scriptures about the life of Christ. They had no idea He had done so many miracles to prove that He was God in the flesh. Then, when we read about how He had been betrayed by Judas, arrested, humiliated, and crucified, they were deeply shocked. We could see the Holy Spirit working in their minds and hearts each time we got together as the truths of the Bible became clear to them. They were truly humbled and appreciative of the unspeakable gift of God's own Son.

9.2 Team Teaching

Around the end of November, we were having some issues with Al and Polly. They had just moved into their home, and we were working on our relationships with each other as team members. Ticker and I had now been in Mexico for almost four and a half years and in the mountains for three years. Al and Polly were still struggling a bit with Spanish, and that always makes someone feel at a huge disadvantage. Al was only about seven years older than me, but it sometimes felt like he was a bit condescending. That is why New Tribes Mission had us go through the experiences we did in boot camp so that we could sort through issues like this, have the mind of Christ, and develop a good working relationship.

Ticker and I were obviously quite excited about Barbara and Teodulo and Trini accepting the Lord and told the Clarks about it right away. I'm sure they had the same initial reaction that I had: "Wait a minute, isn't this jumping the gun?"

But when God is at work, who are we to say, "Naw, I don't think so"? I told the Clarks that we would be having a Bible study in the next day or two, continuing to teach the new believers about the Christian life. We invited the Clarks to come over to our house, but on that first Sunday, they never showed up. Then for the next Bible study, they didn't either, so I talked with Al and asked him why they weren't coming.

His reasons were rather vague but mostly revolved around him not feeling like he could contribute. I told him, "But, Al, we're partners. We'll figure this thing out a little at a time. I think you should come anyway."

By the time we were two weeks or more into having Bible studies and the Clarks still were not coming, Teodulo just came right out and asked me why they weren't there. I told him that Al felt like his Spanish wasn't good enough yet.

"That's not true," Teodulo said. "We talk to him all the time about other things. Tell him to just come."

So that's what I did. "Al, even Teodulo is wondering why you don't come to the Bible studies. It's starting to look like we don't get along with each other, and you know that's not good. Please just come and participate in any way you can. Your Spanish will get better by the week, you'll see," I told him. So the next time we had a Bible study, they showed up, and it made everyone happier!

Within a week or two, I told Al what I planned on covering in the next Bible study. I asked him to do whatever studying he felt he needed to do and look up whatever Spanish words he didn't know to help him explain the Scriptures. He came prepared with notes, and he did really well. Hey, it was a struggle for me half the time to read and explain scriptural truths in Spanish. We hadn't even been able to attend a Spanish-speaking church in almost three years ourselves.

When you're learning a new language, there is a transition point that you come to where you can finally think in that language, rather than just translate each word and sentence in your mind before you speak it. If we don't put ourselves into situations where we have to learn to speak a lot, we will never make that transition and be fluent. Having our Bible studies was forcing me, Ticker, Al, and Polly to memorize and then be able to speak naturally using an ever-growing vocabulary of spiritual terminology in Spanish. Praise the Lord that this was the case because in four or five more months, Ticker and I would be leaving for our one-year furlough in the States.

Bible study at our house with Al, center, leading the discussion

Having those Bible studies helped us in a lot of ways that we didn't expect. Our relationship with the Clarks grew closer as we learned to appreciate each other in new ways. Both Al and I were using our spiritual gifts as the Lord meant us to do, and it refocused our attention on the spiritual condition of all the unsaved people around us as well as the saved. It also helped me to get back into the Word of God in a deeper way. Even though we were much encouraged with the Clarks joining us as our partners, there was a spiritual disconnect between Ticker and me that was not getting any better with time. We rarely had devotions together, and I had no idea why she didn't want to open up and talk with me more. Unfortunately, I let that bring me down psychologically, and it sapped my spiritual strength away. It should not have affected me that way, and the responsibility was really and truly on me to maintain a close and vital relationship with the Lord Himself. Having the privilege and responsibility of teaching new believers definitely revitalized my desire to get into God's Word. Our Bible studies encouraged me more and more each week! I could feel the "living water" of God replenishing my soul.

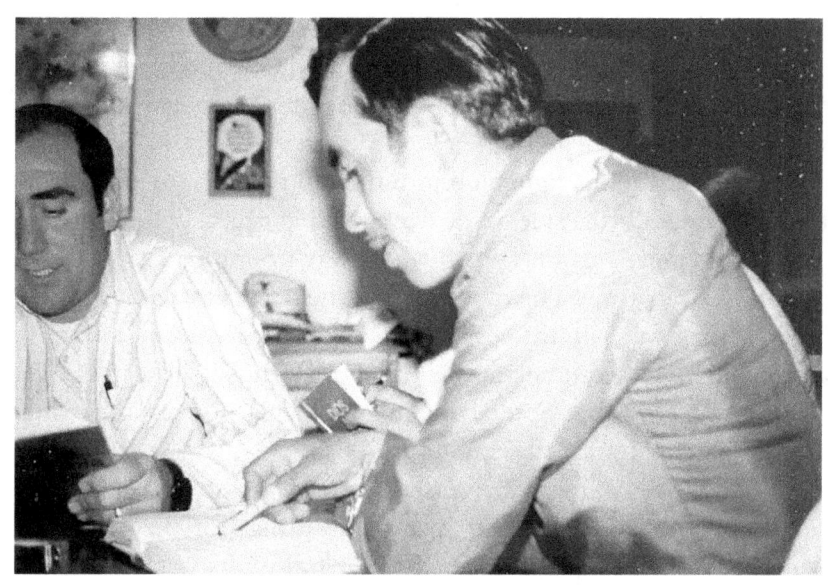

Teodulo, during a Bible study, closely following, reading the scriptures and growing daily in his faith in the Lord

9.3 Spiritual Warfare, Drug Warfare

Just to the west of us, in the Guarijio tribe, the Steinbachers were beginning to make good progress in getting established. John and Linda and their three children had only been out there a year or so by now, but they were doing well in many regards. They had gotten their house built relatively quickly and had come up with a way to get supplies and transportation by air. Since there were no year-round roads for them to use, they were getting supplied entirely by airplane. Obviously, they couldn't take big loads of people and groceries in a small plane in a single flight, like we could in a single truckload, but they were figuring it out a step at a time and doing well. When an airplane could schedule a flight, either they or their neighbors would take several burros from their community down in the canyons up to an airstrip that was on a mesa. It was a trip that took a couple of hours each way, much less convenient than what we had to deal with, but their ministry was off to a good start. John was making some decent progress on learning the Guarijio language. But there was another group that was also making "progress" that was a very real threat to them.

A drug cartel had gone up into the mountains near them from the Gulf of California side to the west with big plans. They wanted to grow drugs in an area that was further away from the reach and eyes of the Mexican army. The first year that the traffickers came into the Steinbachers' valley in the spring, they had offered a lot of money to any Indians who would plant their crop of marijuana instead of their traditional corn crop. Several Indians took them up on their offer and were richly rewarded with money.

The next year, the traffickers were not nearly so nice. They told the Indians that they "would" plant their drugs for them or there would be dire consequences. By then, the traffickers were also taking guns out to the Indians, sometimes in payment for those who wanted to have guns as well as money, but they were also forced to "guard and protect" their crops against anyone who may show up—a rather vague, futile, and deadly idea should the Mexican army suddenly show up.

The Steinbachers had been seriously rattled one day when visiting some neighbors by trail. As they came around a bend on foot, a young Guarijio man who had fallen asleep while "watching" his field suddenly jerked himself awake and pointed a rifle at them before he realized who they were.

One morning, during our standard radio call, when we checked in with our office in Chihuahua City, John told us that he needed an airplane as soon as possible to do a medical evacuation. He only said that it was a young man who had been injured and needed to be taken to a hospital. Our coworker on the radio said that he would talk to John again in an hour once he had called for an airplane and knew when it could arrive at their airstrip. It all worked out fine, and the young man was evacuated.

We didn't know until weeks later what had actually happened. The night before the radio call, several young Guarijio men had been drinking. One of them was John's language helper. The young men started arguing about a girl, then one of them got angry at John's helper, pulled out a pistol, and aimed it at his face. His helper put his hand up to push the gun away, and the other fellow pulled the trigger and shot one of his fingers off.

We knew enough to never, ever say anything about the details of incidents like that over the radio. In fact, although drugs were being grown in various areas throughout the mountains, this was the only location where we worked as a mission where it got really dangerous for our coworkers. The Steinbachers had to prayerfully consider what the future of their ministry might look like on pretty much a month-to-month basis as that particular drug cartel took over the region.

On February 7, 8, and 9, 1985, a horrible incident took place south of us in central Mexico. A US Drug Enforcement Agency (DEA) agent named "Kiki" Camarena was kidnapped off the street near his office by members of one of the drug cartels. For three days, they tortured him to get information about DEA operations and who in Mexico knew about them. They suspected that elected governmental officials, state police, federal police, or military personnel were cooperating with our DEA. A huge shipment of marijuana had been seized and burned, a setback which cost one of the cartels millions of dollars. On the third day, he finally died from the torture.

I heard some of the news about Kiki's disappearance on Armed Forces radio about the time that it happened. There was quite a widespread search for him, since it was unheard of for an American law enforcement agent to disappear and/or be killed in Mexico. They were supposed to be off-limits to the cartels and crooked cops. Months later, while we were on furlough, a made-for-TV documentary revealed a lot of the details about his torture and death. As horrible as that was to watch, in 2020, there was an Amazon documentary done that shed a lot more light on the whole situation. It is entitled *The Last Narc*.

In four episodes, several investigators, as well as some of the crooked Mexican police who were working for the cartel, go into great detail on Kiki's torture and death as well as revealing how bad the trafficking and corruption was. With hundreds of millions of American dollars to be made, Mexican politicians from the level of president on down and police and military from the generals on down were deeply involved in the drug trafficking.

We were focused on our ministry, of course, and had no idea how bad the corruption was at the time. I suppose that's a really good thing. We live in a very corrupt world, even in America. It's incredibly important that we keep our minds focused on the Lord and our hearts sensitive to what He wants us to do on a daily basis. On the one hand, "The fool has said in his heart, 'There is no God.' They are corrupt, they have done abominable works" (Psalm 14: 1); and on the other hand, "The Lord is my shepherd… Yea, though I walk through the valley of the shadow of death, I will fear no evil, for You are with me. Your rod and Your staff they comfort me" (Psalm 23:1, 4). There are so many times in our lives that we walk past or through the middle of the most ungodly people who are part of the "valley of the shadow of death" and don't even know it.

Notwithstanding the epic battle going on behind the scenes with the politics and the dramatic destruction of morality in Mexico, we were having our own spiritual struggles in El Manzano. Al and Polly were both witnessing the periods of depression that Ticker was still experiencing on a regular basis. Having Polly as a new partner did not seem to help out in any measurable way as far as someone Ticker could confide in. We still thought in the back of our minds that there was a fair possibility that her depression was caused by a hormone imbalance. I know Al and Polly had shared their concerns with the field committee. It was now only a matter of a few months before we would be up in Chicago for our one-year furlough and could look for some professional help.

9.4 Spiritual Hopelessness

On April 29, 1985, Al and I went to the funeral of a woman named Adela Sanchez. She had passed away the night before, probably from liver failure or excess alcohol consumption, even though she was only in her early fifties. She was also the most powerful witch doctor anywhere in the area.

I won't go into the details from my culture notes as to how elaborate all of the rituals were that the people went through. Suffice it to say that with all the superfluous decorations and preparation, you would think that a well-loved and respected person had just passed away. At the average funeral, I had never seen more than twenty-five or thirty people. I would estimate there were eighty or more at her funeral. Big Juliana had just told us a few months earlier that she tried to have nothing to do with Adela and her family "because they all drink so much and are mean." Yet, there at the wake and the funeral, there was no one who did more than Juliana.

Right after Adela was buried, we saw a couple of fires going right outside the cemetery. Two or three different people brought green cedar branches over and threw them on one particular fire, creating a lot of smoke. Then those who were standing by the fire walked over and moved both arms and both feet around in the smoke, then got smoke on the front and back of themselves. Next someone else would go over and do the same thing. I saw a mother who took both of her little children over and did likewise.

I asked Teodulo and Nacho what they were doing, and they both told me the same thing: they were covering themselves in smoke so that Adela's spirit could not see them. The Tarahumara believe that the person's spirit can remain in the area for hours or up to a few weeks. During that time, it may want to take vengeance on someone who did not show them enough respect, even at the funeral, or had slighted them in some way during their lifetime. So rather than it being an indication of respect for the deceased, because they had been a highly regarded person in the community, they had come to the funeral out of a sense of fear.

The contrasts between the Tarahumaras without the Lord and a Christian were so apparent. For a Christian, "to be absent from the body is to be present with the Lord." For the Tarahumara, there is no promise of where they will end up in the afterlife, and none of the possibilities looked promising. For a Christian, we know that we battle "the principalities and powers of this world," but "greater is He who is in [us] than he who is in the world"! For a Tarahumara, every man, woman, and child is in danger at any time of being made sick or even being killed by an evil spirit who is deceased or by a witch doctor who is still alive.

No, Ernest Hemingway and the non-Christian men and women who write effusive stories about the "beautiful native cultures" don't go into those realities at all. To do so would take the magic out and their book and movie sales would never materialize. There are indeed honorable, notable, and fascinating things about many cultures of the world, but outside of saving faith in the one true God, their spiritual world and destinies are not some of them.

9.5 "Redeemed...to God...out of Every Tribe and Tongue and People and Nation" (Revelation 5:9)

One of the many Bible studies with several of Barbara and Teodulo's family members and neighbors in attendance

A few days later, as the Bible study was about to begin at our house, I was looking around the room, and then Ticker took some pictures for us to have as memories. They would also be great to show to folks back home in a couple of months. After all, "a picture is worth a thousand words."

In one photograph, I'm seated in the middle of one of the long sides of our dining room table. To my right is Teodulo, wearing a really nice blue and white Western shirt. He is about an inch taller than me, six years older, and is clean-cut and shaven. He is square-jawed and physically fit, like most Tarahumara men. In the two years we've lived here, I've gotten to know him better than anyone else in the community. He's a carpenter and has always impressed me as honest as well as intelligent. He's always inquisitive as well as responsible, which is why I ended up becoming good friends with him. Now we are brothers in the Lord!

To his right is his wife, Barbara. She is three years younger than Teodulo and is mestizo but with no Tarahumara blood. She has a more rotund figure, like most Mexican women. Barbara is always pleasant, and when she gets a kick out of something, she laughs like a teenager. I've only seen her yell or get impatient when their dogs sneak into the house, looking for scraps of food and get underfoot. Other than that, she is a nice, honest, and a hardworking woman.

On the other side of the table is Doña Petra, Teodulo's mom. I would guess she's about sixty years old, five feet three or so, has gray hair, and a wiry build. She is a widow. Teodulo's dad died several years ago. She is always immaculately dressed, wears a headscarf, and looks as if she never works, although she surely does. She is rather reserved, but when she speaks or asks questions, she does so very intelligently.

Seated back a little ways is Valentin, Teodulo's younger brother. He is tall and thin, probably a little thinner than I am. He wears his hair long and a little bit shaggy. He laughs easily and often and can sometimes be quite the goofball. But during the Bible studies, he is a great listener and thinker and asks good questions. Valentin is single and in his early twenties.

Javier is seated next to him, wearing a brown and white checkered Western shirt. He is a little more stocky, wears his hair on the long side, and has big chop sideburns. He's pretty quiet and is a fellow who does laborer's work. He is around twenty-eight years old and is China's husband.

Trini is round like her sister Barbara. She's only seventeen years old with rosy cheeks. Like Barbara, she also has a sweet and cheerful personality. She's pretty talkative a lot of the time, but like all of the women, she stays pretty quiet during the Bible studies and listens attentively.

On the corner of the table is China. She is tall and slim with long black hair that reaches almost to her waist. She is a no-nonsense type of person and oftentimes is pretty outspoken. I've always noticed her to be a good hardworking mom to their two or three children.

Al is seated at the end of the table with his notes in front of him. He is about my height, five feet nine, but about sixty pounds heavier than me. He has a little bit of gray hair appearing at his temples. Al will be leading our study tonight. He has a warm smile and makes everybody feel at ease.

Ticker sits back from the table a little ways to allow everyone else to be closer to the overhead light. We purchased several paperback Bibles in Spanish, and six or seven people have them open in front of them. These folks are lucky if they've had an education at the local school that got them to the equivalent of a sixth- or seventh- or eighth-grade education. All of them can read a little bit, but some are much better than others, like Teodulo and Barbara.

Tonight they have brought a couple of other women whom I don't know. They, too, sit quietly and listen, crowded together at the table.

Last but not least are the young kids. We have a bench that's about four feet long, pushed against the stairs. One of Teodulo's little nieces, Suzena, who is the cutest little five-year-old, is sitting there. Next to her is her ten-year-old brother, Ramon. He has longish straggly hair like his Uncle Valentin. Oftentimes, Dusty and Eric will be sitting off to the side with these kids, and they stay pretty well behaved all evening, which is amazing.

Our study runs at least an hour and a half, sometimes a little longer by the time we finish with questions. It's amazing and encouraging to see these people who were raised so far away from any chance to hear the Gospel being so curious about the Lord. Here we are, a small group of fifteen or so people, representing various ethnicities—European, mestizo, and indigenous Mexican peoples. Just as the Lord said through the Apostle John in the book of the Revelation, we have been "redeemed out of every tribe, tongue, people and nation"! What a miracle, what a joy!

9.6 Off to the USA

In a letter to my mom and dad, I had written "The mission board wants us to take a one-year furlough, but I think we will only take six months instead." That pretty much sums up how I felt about leaving. There were too many good things happening, and I did not want to be gone away from the ministry for that long. I'm sure Ticker felt differently, but I don't have any of her thoughts recorded about that time.

I sure do praise the Lord that Al and Polly were such solid people. After a few months of really getting into teaching the believers, his Spanish was much improved. They were going to be in good hands with Al teaching them. We also taught the Clarks everything we could about our experiences in doing medical work. We buttoned up the house and left El Manzano on our way to Chihuahua City on May 15, 1985.

Our annual field conference went from May 27 through June 1. It was always a good time to catch up on news with all of our coworkers. We rarely sent letters to each other, so hearing their field reports was great. It was also our chance to find out how the students in Spanish study were doing and who's team some of them might be joining in the coming months. The attrition rate continued in almost every tribal location and support job, but the new missionaries in Spanish language study were not always hanging in there too well either. We ourselves continued to "pray to the Lord of the harvest that He would send forth laborers into the fields, for they are ripe for harvest."

By June 2, we were in Globe, Arizona, with my grandparents. The next day was Ticker's birthday, and Grandma had made a birthday cake for her! I really enjoyed those visits we had with my grandparents whom I hadn't seen in so many years. My mom had kept us separated from them for twenty-eight years, which was a travesty. Even though they had done a favor for her which could never be repaid by keeping my brother and me on their ranch and raising us as their own for two years, her desire to keep us separated from them was a strange thing. She thought it might affect our devotion to our stepdad, which actually never would have happened. I loved talking with my grandpa and wish I would have asked him hundreds more questions about his life while he was still around. Isn't that how it so often is in families? You don't know what you've got until it's gone.

Fortunately, Ticker saved the calendars we made notes on for the entire year of our furlough! No, my hopes of getting back to El Manzano in six months were not meant to be. We didn't go north to Chicago right away—far from it. We were taking a route west then north to visit family and financial supporters for the next several weeks before we would get to Chicago.

I spoke at churches in Tucson, Arizona, then Oxnard, California. We visited relatives in Palm Springs and Los Angeles, then drove north to Monterey, California, where we started camping. We had to be really conservative with our finances, so we camped as often as possible. We drove through the redwoods in Northern California and up to Mount Hood in Oregon. We visited Ticker's brother Jack in Oregon and saw him present a case in court in his role as a public prosecutor. We stayed up till six o'clock in the morning, catching up on news, and had long conversations with Jack and his wife about the Scriptures and the Lord!

From there, we went to North Dakota, camping and swimming. On July 8, we arrived at the home of our good friends, Gary and Laurie Barrett, who had been in our original college and career-age Bible study group years earlier. Gary was pastoring a church in Minnesota, and we had a fantastic visit. On the sixteenth of July, we finally arrived in our hometown of Des Plaines, Illinois. From there, we shot up to Durham, Ontario, Canada, for a few days of their annual field conference. We were able to share news of the work in Mexico. We took a side trip on the way back to the Chicago area to go see my mom and dad in St. Louis, Missouri. Finally, on Saturday, August 3, we were back in Des Plaines to stay. Whew! This furlough was busy already!

Family portrait, 1986

Chapter 10

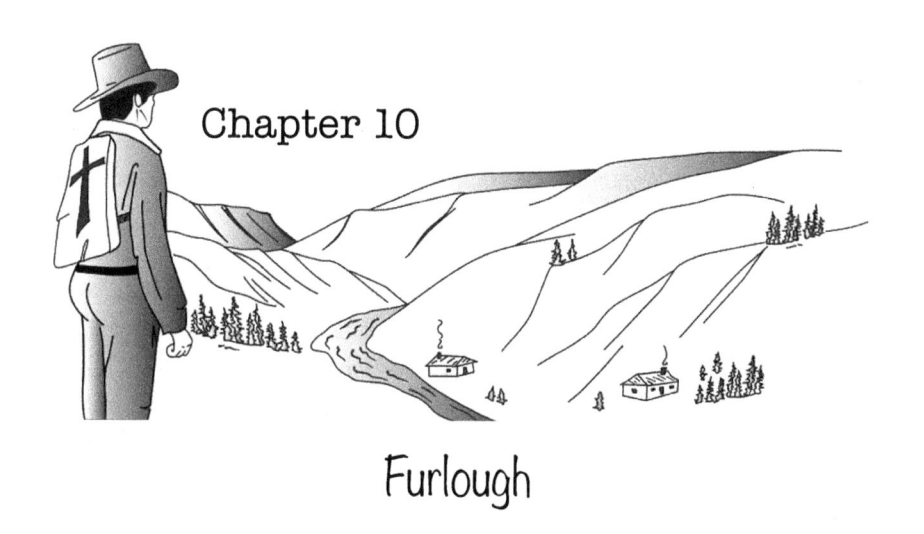

Furlough

Stranger in a Strange Land

Culture shock can be described as the psychological and emotional effects of being separated from a person's native culture. This is different than what people would commonly consider to be culture shock, which would be to have a psychological reaction to a new and unfamiliar culture. Although the latter is indeed a psychological phenomenon, think about the reasons that people moving to a foreign country try their hardest to live and work amongst people of their own language and culture: they crave what is familiar to them. We want, first and foremost, to speak and listen in our native language. Then we want to be able to eat the food that we've been used to, have the kinds of housing and clothing that we are used to, trust in the kind of social order and law and order, etc., that are familiar to us.

When we willingly move to a new part of the country or to a foreign country, we know without a doubt that there will be new kinds of food, customs, etc., and we are psychologically prepared for that. Most of the time we are flexible and learn new ways little by little. As missionaries going to a foreign country, we were quite well-prepared for the changes that we would encounter or at least the realization that there would be changes in many areas of life.

Nevertheless, the first time I personally experienced culture shock was when we returned to the United States for our one-year furlough.

Does that seem absurd to you? It surprised me. Upon arriving back in Des Plaines, Illinois, the suburb of Chicago where Ticker was born and raised and where our home church was located, I quickly began to feel like a fish out of water. It wasn't the language—Ticker, the boys, and I and all of our coworkers spoke English for the entire five years we'd been in Mexico. But it was what we found people talking about in Chicago that was so very different. They were much more interested in material things than we had been for the last five years. In fact, the urgency and necessity to spend so much of every day commuting back and forth to work and earning a living at a profession, which would pay the best possible wage, despite the stress it might cause in our friends' and relatives' lives, was without a doubt the major focus of life in Chicago.

Everybody knows that "time is money," right? This priority was at the top of everyone's list, it seemed, and the importance of family relationships, personal communications, and spiritual truths and principles were all significantly less important. In fact, their much-diminished relative importance was shocking to me.

It seemed that wherever we went, whether a family gathering or a church service, the concept of taking time to enjoy personal relationships and communicate well—and half of communication is listening—was not an important priority. It seemed that everything had to be on a schedule too. For example, once the church service was over, there was a fairly limited amount of time allotted for visiting with friends or the pastor before it was time to get home, get some lunch, and turn on the TV. Surely there was a good baseball or football game going on, right? And if you were actually going home with some of those friends or family members, to have some lunch, and then turn on the TV for "the game," don't count on anyone being interested in a good conversation about spiritual things. At least not for more than three or four minutes.

I can't speak for Ticker and my kids, but I know I had some serious mental readjustment to do moving back to a culture where so many things moved so fast, even on the weekends, and so much of life revolved around money and material things. To be sure, this was largely due to us having spiritual things and people as our priorities because of our ministry. But the Indians and mestizos actually probably had a better reason for using every minute they could to work hard and earn more money than the wealthy Americans had whom I was now living amongst.

Week after week, and actually for many months, I looked at this life in America and felt like I was living on Mars. Hmm, I can only imagine (actually, no I cannot) how God must feel looking at us human beings, scurrying around, busy with our little existences, having so many shallow priorities in our lives.

It wasn't a bad life, don't get me wrong. It was just really different. Our church, Des Plaines Bible Church, let us move into a large brick house that was right behind the church for a reasonable amount of rent. Since our total monthly missionary income would barely even pay the rent, however, I very soon had to find work. I went back to being self-employed, doing carpentry and painting primarily. People in our church were very supportive in that respect, giving me work doing all kinds of odd jobs.

Being back in the States, living in the most prosperous country on earth at a very prosperous time in history, was indeed something to be thankful for. After all, I was a healthy young adult, with three wonderful boys and a wife who loved the Lord. Still, I wished that this was only a short break in our ministry. Were these really dedicated Christians I was around? Or just very nice moral people who liked the same church we went to? What if I became more like these people than like the missionary I had been only a month or two ago? I wasn't sure that would make God very happy, and it wasn't making me very happy. I began to look at things a little more objectively and realized that I must, daily, choose the culture I would belong to. This would be a conscious choice for my family.

God was central to us. Our country was a source of pride, but our family would now become my most closely guarded pride and joy. We would glean the best from all we had seen, from everywhere we had been, and I would not let anything or anybody or any corrupt materialistic influence change us or split us apart, so help me God. And He did help me; and He did help all of us. It was not easy, but in stages, I got over the culture shock of being back in America.

Medical Help for Us, Ministering Still in Chicago

As our top priority, we knew we had to try to find some help for Ticker's depression. That involved opening up to our pastor as much as we could at that time about her struggles. But his abilities and interest in helping us were quite minimal. Unfortunately, he was not the "people person" that our really awesome previous pastor, Craig Massey, had been. Ticker did, however, open up with several old friends of ours and was soon starting to work through the issues that were causing her depression.

A few months after we were home, she was having counseling sessions. Again, however, she was not willing to share with me the details of what was going on most of the time, so I was left pretty much in the dark and oftentimes felt like I was part of the problem. That was definitely not very encouraging.

After several months at home, I was asked to be involved in teaching an adult Sunday school class in our church. I chose to teach a class based on a Christian book I was reading entitled *Money, Sex and Power*. It tackled some American culture issues that definitely needed to be looked at with a Christian perspective. I don't think I did a great job teaching the class, but I think I did a good job, and the class was very well attended. Perhaps some of that was due to the S-word in the title, something which I don't think had ever been actually advertised as a Sunday school subject in a very conservative church like ours.

There were other really important things we were able to do regarding our ministry as we settled in. The first was to improve the slide presentation we used when speaking to churches, Sunday school classes, and all kinds of other groups. We had lots of new photographs and slides of our work, so we compiled those and enlisted the help of a friend in our church who was a radio and TV producer in the area. Darrell was an amazing help, and I wished I could've been a much bigger help and encouragement to him in return. It wasn't apparent until we had met to work on the presentation four or five times over the course of six or eight weeks, but Darrell's marriage was on the rocks.

After a while, I could see the real pain and helplessness in him. I'm extremely unhappy to say that I don't think I was much help in talking with him about his situation. That fact has bothered me over the years. I was, after all, in a similar state of confusion in husband-wife relations, although not as badly as he was. But Darrell was very good professionally, and we ended up with a really great quality slide presentation that had an excellent soundtrack and narration.

Da Bears!

I had always been a big football fan, and the Chicago Bears were on a roll in 1985. It was a great year to be home! They had an almost perfect season, only losing one game to the Miami Dolphins. This was also the year when someone had an incredible inspiration—a football team doing their rendition of a music video! Who would have thunk? "The Super Bowl Shuffle" came out, and it was a huge hit. The song played multiple times every day on the local radio stations, and the video was played over and over on the sports news. All of Ticker's family loved "Da Bears" also, so we watched every single game together.

That 1985 season and 1986 Super Bowl were ones for the record books. The super-talented but rebel quarterback, Jim McMahon, became a celebrity across the league. "Refrigerator" Perry, a huge but nimble lineman, was also a star player. With the great coaching of Mike Ditka, "the Refrigerator" was even able to score a surprise touchdown as an offense player! Running back Walter Payton was at the peak of his career and was a marvel to watch. An annual trophy to honor football players who made an outstanding impact on their communities was named for him just a few years later after his untimely death. Big, tall defensive end Richard Dent and middle linebacker Mike Singletary were part of the best defense that ever lined up. That lineup included Gary Fencik, one of the toughest and nicest guys to play the game.

In what turned out to be a super fun opportunity, Ticker took Dusty and Eric down to our local bank for a meet and greet photo session with Gary Fencik. They had a great time, something they could never imagine getting to do, especially as missionary kids in Mexico. The icing on the cake was when our local newspaper, the *Des Plaines Journal*, came out with its next edition. There on the cover was Dusty, missing a couple of front teeth because he was six years old, with the biggest smile on his face and light in his eyes, looking up at Fencik as he got to meet him, and Fencik signed his autograph!

I even got into the Bears fever in a unique way. A little kids' toy company called Tyco Toys made a big plastic toy box that was in the shape of a football. It was almost three feet long and the height of a coffee table. I bought two of them and painted them in blue and orange, the Bears' colors. Then I made a birch plywood tabletop for one and had an oval glass top made for the other one. On a gamble, I took them to a sporting paraphernalia and collectibles store at Woodfield Mall, at the time the largest shopping mall in the world, and they bought them from me! Not NFL licensed? Oh well.

Busy, Busy, Busy

Our monthly calendars from that year are filled with so many activities we got involved with. Ticker went to a ladies' Bible study on Tuesday mornings, and the boys were involved with children's church groups called "Sparks" and "Awana." There were couples that were around our age who invited us over for dinner numerous times, and that fellowship was really encouraging. They wanted to hear about our work in Mexico, and those folks were the exceptions to so many others who didn't seem to be interested in spiritual things. It seemed that after a while, the speaking engagements in which we presented our work multiplied. I'm sure the improved slide presentation was a big factor in that.

In April 1986, I was asked to speak at every Wednesday night service at our church. I wouldn't call it being on a treadmill exactly, but when I look back on those calendars, we were really pretty darn busy!

What I don't have in my notes from that time were things that had to do with most of the doctor's appointments and counseling appointments for Ticker. She had been experiencing chest pains on and off for a year by then, which were eventually attributed to stress. With one doctor, she tracked her menstrual cycle since we still strongly suspected hormone issues due to her tubes being tied after Eric's birth three and a half years earlier.

There is also, however, a separate personal calendar that Ticker kept starting in June 1986, a full year after we had left Mexico to start our furlough. I don't know who the counselor or doctor might have been who had her start that, unfortunately, but two months' worth of that calendar ended up with our file of "Memories from Furlough." It is very revealing, showing daily values for the severity of five different conditions: withdrawal, depression, irritability, highs (emotionally), and lethargy. She also added notes regarding stress levels from "none" to "high" to "extreme." She was not doing really well. She was struggling, but again, I was not permitted to be aware of that. I never saw it until years later.

What I do remember clearly was that whoever she was getting counseling from in the spring of 1986 was on the right track. I could sense her anxiety issues diminishing, and her bouts of depression were not so dark. I asked her how she felt about going back to Mexico in the next couple of months, and I could see she really wanted to follow the Lord's leading. I certainly didn't want her to feel any pressure since we were in a location where she could find some help, and that would not be the case when we got back to Mexico. Still, the reality was that we would have to make plans for either our return to Mexico or to extend our furlough. Our housing situation was a factor, too, since the church was going to need that house that we were staying in for another family coming soon.

In May, Ticker said she felt ready to go back to Mexico. She said she knew that's where the Lord wanted us to be, and she felt stronger with the time that we had been in Chicago. I was relieved and happier than I had been in a while since she was still reluctant to share her feelings with me month after month.

New Wheels! Computer? Electricity?

"Hey, Steve," our friend, Ken, said to me when I picked up the phone. "I think you guys need to take a new truck back to Mexico with you. That van is not going to hold up for another five years down there."

"Well, I've been working and saving toward our expenses to go back down there, but there isn't money in the budget for a new truck, that's for sure," I told him.

"I want to meet with that fellow in your church you said has a loan business who helped you with the loan on your van, and I'll bet we can work something out," he said. I gave him Don's name and phone number, and Ken said he would get back to me once they had spoken.

A week later, Ken called me and said that we were going to meet at Woodfield Ford. We did, and the most appropriate vehicle on the lot was a brand-new 1986 Ford F-350 crew cab four-wheel drive pickup truck. It was a big, beautiful vehicle but had not sold for six months now, and the dealership wanted to make a deal with us.

Ken and I talked about how much I could get for selling my van, how much he and Carol could put in, and he knew how much Don was willing to contribute. In the end, we still came up about $800 short of the dealership's lowest price offer to us. On the afternoon that I went back there and told them that, I watched the manager "wrestle with God." He paced back and forth in the office cubicles area with the salesman that we had been dealing with, not looking very happy, for ten or fifteen minutes. But in the end, the salesman came out and said we had a deal! God had kept that truck on the lot for us for quite a few months!

Thank you, Ken. Thank you, Don. And most of all, thank you, God!

Two other developments happened pretty much in the last two weeks before we left. A fellow in our church who was a computer whiz, at a time when personal computers were very new, insisted that I take a computer back with us to Mexico. I had talked about what I did in producing an English- Spanish-Tarahumara dictionary with our language learning lessons, as well as the linguistics that I would have to do shortly. This relatively new member of our church was shocked that I was doing all of this on paper and four-by-six inches card files.

"I have no idea how to use a computer!" I told him. "Besides, I told you we don't have electricity out there and probably never will."

"There is some word processing software called Shareware (anybody remember that?), and I will give you some discs so that you can learn how to use it," he told me. "So I guess you'll just need to buy a generator! Maybe somebody in the church will help you with that before you leave," he said.

Then this really great fellow, whose name I cannot remember, besides the computer and software, gave us a printer to take with us! With advice from someone who knew, a week later, I bought a generator, something I never thought I would have done. Electricity? In El Manzano? No way! Big changes were coming to our lives when we returned to Mexico.

Chapter 11

Back Home in El Manzano

11.1 On the Road Home Again!

On June 14th, we left Des Plaines, en route to Mexico. We stopped and saw my folks in St. Louis for a couple of days and then kept driving south to Camdenton, Missouri, where our language and linguistics institute is located. Every missionary at some point during their furlough is required to go to what was called the refresher course, an annual event. This was to bring us all up to date on a whole variety of mission policies, guidelines, and information.

Refresher Course and a Serious Reality Check!

This particular refresher course was of immense importance. On October 4, 1984, nine months before we had left for furlough, four of our New Tribes Mission coworkers had been captured by leftist guerrillas in Colombia. One of the men, Paul Dye, was a man I admired immensely. He was the son of Cecil Dye, one of the first five New Tribes missionaries who had been martyred by the Ayore Indians in the neighboring country of Bolivia forty-one years earlier.

He was a senior pilot and had been one of the speakers at the missionary conference in Wisconsin that I attended the summer before I enrolled in the New Tribes Bible Institute.

Paul was about to go on his one-year furlough at the time and was giving his replacement pilot a final familiarization flight to a remote jungle location. The missionaries there were sick with malaria, so when Paul and Steve Estelle circled the field to land, they attributed it to their illness that the missionaries had not put out the customary "everything is okay" marker on the ground. They were also flying into a thunderstorm that was bearing down on the airstrip with big black clouds, lightning and strong winds, so they expedited their landing. As Paul congratulated Steve for a good landing in the worst possible conditions, five armed guerrillas came out of the jungle and surrounded the airplane!

The book *God at the Controls* (Copyright 1986 by New Tribes Mission and later republished as *When Things Seem Impossible* in 2017), written by his aunt, Jean Dye Johnson, chronicles their captivity experience and Paul's unbelievably miraculous escape. With the prayers of literally hundreds of thousands of people around the world, the negotiations between the New Tribes Mission leadership, Colombian government officials, and the FARC guerrillas, the other three missionaries were released on November 7, 1984. The book is something every Christian should read. The details of Paul's night escape will amaze you!

For many years in the 1960s on there had been growing threats from communist guerrilla groups all over the world against missionaries. The accusations, as they were directed at us in Mexico also, were that we were either CIA operatives or gave information to the CIA. Nothing could have been further from the truth. Helping the CIA was light years from our mission and would have destroyed the opportunities we had worked so hard to bring to fruition. The kidnapping of Paul and his three fellow workers was the first direct physical assault on New Tribes missionaries but was not going to be the last.

In his book, *12 Strong*, Doug Stanton quotes Special Forces Major General Geoffrey Lambert, a former Army Ranger, asking his men a very blunt question, "How will you die?" He wanted his men to think of all the ways the enemy could annihilate them so that they would plan on how to avoid it.

The mission leadership told us that everyone in a tribal location was to come up with what they called a "contingency plan." That would essentially be an escape plan should the need arise due to insurgent or dangerous criminal activity in the area where we were living. A couple of months later, back in El Manzano, I gave a lot of thought to this and came up with a plan for ourselves. I decided that our best chance of escape would be to completely avoid the road leading back to San Rafael and the trail leading to Uruachic. The distance going west toward the Gulf of California coast would be excessive for our family to walk. So I decided that our best route would be to go east, toward Creel.

I thought there would be the least possibility of us being detected if we used whatever trails we could find going to the bottom of the Oteros River canyon, especially if we traveled mostly by the light of early morning and late evening dusk, hiding during the day, and then used carefully shielded flashlights to travel in the dark. Once we got to the ridge on the east side of the river, the terrain would not be nearly as rugged, or so I hoped. I estimated it would take us two and a half to three days to reach Creel, and we could carry a reasonable amount of food and water for a hike that would take that long. I really doubted that anyone would look for us going in that direction.

I had a couple of packs prepared for us with waterproof matches, a topographical map, a compass, and other camping supplies. If we were to get news of an imminent threat, whether day or night, it would only have taken us about ten minutes to put water, dried food, a few jackets, knives, and flashlights in the packs, and we could be on our way. I also knew that Al and Polly were going to have to evacuate by road since they were not used to walking and hiking like our family was. That was simply a matter of facing reality, so I prayed that if the need arose, there would be enough advanced notice for them to leave their way and for us to leave ours.

This preparation for a worst case scenario was not urged upon us by our executive committee leadership lightly or without serious prayer on their part. In the years to come, there would be numerous examples of how real the threats to our lives were and to our like-minded fellow evangelical missionaries.

In 1993, three New Tribes missionaries in Panama were kidnapped by the FARC, the same leftist/communist guerilla organization that had captured Paul Dye and the others in 1984. They were moved through the jungles to Columbia where they were eventually killed.

In 1994, two other New Tribes missionaries were taken from the school for missionaries' children in Colombia and killed.

In 2001, Gracia and Martin Burnham were kidnapped at a resort in the Philippines where they were staying for a one-night trip to celebrate their eighteenth wedding anniversary. After fifteen years of service as a pilot for their fellow missionaries, Martin and his wife treated themselves to an extremely rare day of celebration. When the Muslim extremist Abu Sayyaf guerillas swept them up in the middle of the night along with sixteen other nationals and foreigners, they were trying to raise money by demanding ransoms as well as promoting their Muslim "holy war" against any and all nonbelievers.

The Philippine military, due to constitutional issues, would not allow US Special Forces to participate in rescuing the Burnhams or the others. On the seventeenth rescue attempt by the Philippine military, Gracia was shot through the thigh and survived, but Martin was shot three times in the chest and was killed. Gracia's book of their captivity and rescue, *In the Presence of Mine Enemies*, by Tyndale Press, is a very moving account.

Rather than being alarmed into fear, we need to realize that there is no better and, indeed, no safer place to be than in the middle of God's will. There have been far more American soldiers killed, for example, in car accidents in the last few years than in the war against terrorism in Afghanistan and the other areas of conflict. We must face the possibility of giving our lives in the Lord's service because even Jesus told us to—as well as being willing to give up family ties should our families back home not agree that God has called us to serve Him rather than pursuing wealth and physical things. If the truth were to be revealed to us and someday in heaven I think it will be, we would see how many millions of times we were spared and protected from physical harm because God has a plan for us and will keep the evil powers at bay for our sakes.

Once in a while, we will see that a servant of God will have to pay the ultimate price, and we will again be reminded that it's a very conscious and willful decision on our parts to choose (or continue to choose) to follow the Lord. Those losses of life have always resulted, however, in an outpouring of prayers and comfort for the ones left behind, deeper resolve in the ones who remain to continue God's work, and inspiration for new candidates for the Lord's work. Such was the case when five of the first handful of New Tribes missionaries were lost and later found to have been killed by the Ayore Indians in Bolivia in 1943. At that time, God was beginning a worldwide outreach by His people to the unreached tribes of the world with the Gospel. New Tribes turned into an organization that has now sent out many thousands of missionaries for eighty years, sharing God's Word with millions of lost souls!

Jean Dye Johnson, the newly married wife of one of those first martyrs, Bob Dye, wrote an amazing book about the experience, *God Planted Five Seeds* (published by Harper and Row, 1966). One of the most inspirational aspects of that story is how Jean processed her own personal loss and grief. It was a spiritually healthy and godly process, something not often seen in our modern "warm and comfortable prosperity gospel" influenced Christian churches. Jean went on, of course, to become the linguistic and language-learning course architect for New Tribes Mission for the next fifty-plus years and was one of the most solid, wonderful, intelligent women I ever knew.

Jesus put it this way:

> **If anyone desires to come after me, let him deny himself and take up his cross and follow me. For whoever desires to save his life will lose it, but whoever loses his life for my sake will find it... For the Son of Man will come in the glory of his Father with his angels,**

HE WHO HAS BEGUN A GOOD WORK

and then he will reward each according to his works. (Matthew 16:24–27)

In making our evacuation plans, we did not fear death. We planned to care for ourselves and our families and live to share the Gospel another day! Our physical lives would be, and still are, in the caring hands of our mighty God.

Almost There...

We arrived in Chihuahua City in August, just a few days before our annual Mexican field conference. We finished filling the truck up with groceries and other supplies before heading to the outskirts of Cuauhtemoc where the field conference would take place. It was a really good time of catching up on news from all the tribal locations as well as the support folks in Chihuahua City. Al and Polly had good news regarding the believers out in El Manzano. They said they would catch us up on all the news once we got out there in a few days. During the days of the conference, however, they needed to have discussions with the teachers and dorm parents of the boarding school. Their sons, Al Jr. and Chris, would be going to the school within just a few days. It was always a really difficult step to leave your children there after they'd been home all summer, trusting them to the care of other people for the next school year. We knew this so painfully well ourselves since we were leaving Dave there in the city too.

There's No Place Like Home!

I didn't even mind the rough roads this time for the ten-hour trip from the conference grounds to El Manzano. We were heading home! The weather was clear and beautiful, the forest and mountains and the blue sky so welcoming. When we got to Barbara and Teodulo's house, which was right on the road before the El Manzano valley, we had to stop and say hello, of course! With lots of embraces and laughter and greetings, we were welcomed back home like long-lost family members. They were in awe of our shiny new pickup truck. Finally, we climbed back into it for the final five or six minute drive to our house. Home sweet home!

We stop for a photo with our beautiful new F350 crew cab pickup as we get near to El Manzano and our friends!

We all cleared out the dust and a few cobwebs and got settled back in quickly. A couple of days later Al and Polly arrived and we got caught up on all the good news regarding how the believers had been coming faithfully to the twice weekly Bible studies all year long. Al had started having some of the studies at Teodulo's house. That made it more convenient for their family members who lived up there, and this way, younger children were able to sit in, too, and didn't have to walk home after dark in the evenings. That was a great idea and contributed to several more people being able to learn from the Bible stories and hear the Gospel.

HE WHO HAS BEGUN A GOOD WORK

New Realities in El Manzano
Financial Support

A couple of weeks later, Ticker and I sent out a letter that we had been pressed upon to write to our friends and financial supporters back home. First, we thanked them for their support, and then we wrote "It has been brought to our attention that when there are folks like you who are very genuinely concerned, we actually go beyond the realm of trusting completely in the Lord and perhaps are guilty of not trusting the Lord for what are very real needs." We went on to give them the figures of our income from 1984, the last full year before we went on furlough. After expenses for schooling for the boys, supplies used in our ministry, the 10 percent administration cost which the field deducted, etc., we had a net personal income of $7,668. After paying self-employed Social Security tax, our net personal income was $6,802. That was for the entire year.

We continued, "Our mission recommends a minimum of $1,200 per month or $14,400 per year of personal support for our size family. [That gave us about 47 percent of what the mission recommended for minimum support, and 22 percent of the maximum amount.] Although the Mexican peso continues to devalue against the dollar, prices continue to skyrocket too. For example, the value of the dollar has risen 3300% since we arrived here in Mexico in 1980 but the price of gasoline has risen 5200%, postage 4000%, meat is about 20% more expensive than in El Paso and we now have to drive three hours one way for groceries, mail, etc. rather than just a few blocks.

"What we have been especially encouraged to share with you, by concerned friends back home, are some of the areas of life that we neglect because they have been financially out of the question. These include some areas of better healthcare, taking a good, relaxing one week break each year, and of particular concern to us due to the current political and economic situations here in Mexico, there is a need for our partners and us to help the community in areas of socioeconomic development."

We stated that we would like to put the following dollar amounts on getting additional income: $75 per month for health needs, $150 per month additional personal support, and $50 per month for community help projects.

I'm glad that several friends back in the States encouraged us to write that letter. It's not an easy thing to financially "live by faith," but it is necessary. It was very hard for us to ask for money, but it did result in an increase in our financial support.

Ticker's Hormone Treatments

Another new reality for us was that Ticker was now taking liquid hormone supplements. A doctor and clinic in Chicago had prescribed this, and we had taken a two-month supply with us, which had to stay refrigerated when we had come back. The next thing we arranged for was for more to be sent out by airplane with Dave Wolf. That required it being sent to Tucson and staying refrigerated the whole time. We would plan to have it brought to us about every two months. That, of course, became an extra expense, too, but we saw it as a way to continue her therapy and were optimistic.

11.2 Mauro's Big Threat

I remember a day or two after the Clarks got back, standing in Al's yard, enjoying the gorgeous weather, and talking about our community of El Manzano. Al told me that during the past year, Mauro had gone up to cross the US border—illegally, of course—to try to get work and had gotten caught by the border patrol three times and sent back to Mexico. It had cost him a lot of money, and he was broke and angry.

"Oh yeah, Steve," Al said. "I told Mauro you would be back here this week. He said he wants us to go down to his house and meet with him. He said we're going to have to start paying him rent."

"What!" I said. "He can't do that! We have an agreement with the ejido for this land. He knows that. What a snake! So he finally got around to figuring out how to get some money out of us," I said. "I always knew that somewhere in the back of his mind he had a plan of some kind. He just had to let us get established here before he could move on with it."

"Well, he wants us to have a meeting with him as soon as possible," said Al.

"That's fine, but I plan on visiting our friends and neighbors first," I said. "We've been gone a long time, and I think that's much more important right now. He can wait a few days. That way, you and I can talk about what we're going to say to him too," I said.

Over the next several days, I got around to visiting with Barbara and Teodulo, Trini and Valentin, as well as the other believers, friends, and neighbors all around the area. Finally, Mauro sent his youngest son up and called for Al and me to go down to his house and meet with him. I told him we would be there the next morning at nine o'clock.

Al and I talked things over. Since I had negotiated the agreement with the ejjido, I would do most of the talking. But I told Al that he also needed to speak up and show Mauro that he was not a soft target. Al chuckled that coy Southern laugh that he had and said "All right. Sounds good to me!"

We went down to Mauro's house in the morning, and the air of confrontation was palpable. His two or three older boys were there that day, and I noted how much they had grown in the year that we'd been gone. However, they did not look friendly as we stood outside Mauro's house. I'm sure they had heard from their dad all about how he was now going to get some money from these Americans. We shook hands all around, but the looks in their eyes were rather ominous.

As was the custom here, we were served coffee, and then in a very few minutes, Mauro began with what he had planned to say.

His oldest son, Ernesto, was now engaged, and Mauro had always planned that his son would live on the land that we were now on. He was going to need to farm land of his own, and it was unfortunate that he could not live up there on the only available land. He said we would need to start paying rent for the land, and then he could help his son get started somewhere else.

"We are going to have to start clearing some land that has trees on it right now," Mauro said. "That's going to take time and money. You will need to start paying rent right away."

"No, Mauro," I replied. "We have an agreement for the land we are on directly with the ejido. You yourself offered that land to us, and someday everything that we built there will be returned to the ejido."

His tone and language became more aggressive. Al chimed in, "Steve and I are of the same mind on this. If we need to, we'll take the issue back before the entire ejido."

"I am the authority here," said Mauro. "I am the governor, and the land in this community is under my jurisdiction."

"Well, then, we will bring this issue before the entire ejido," I said. "That's where it will be decided."

I looked at him and his boys and his wife staring at us with those hard looks in their eyes.

"I don't believe there's anything else to talk about right now," I said. "We'll be seeing you." Al and I turned around and walked back up the road to our houses.

11.3 The Ejido Meeting and Psalm 35

Plead my cause, oh Lord, with those who strive with me; fight against those who fight against me. (Psalm 35:1)

I composed a letter to the president of the ejido and drove it to Bachámuchi, forty minutes away, where the ejido meetings took place. I explained our situation with Mauro and asked that this issue be resolved along with whatever other business had to take place at the next meeting. I had asked around and found that the next meeting would be in about a month, in October.

I wrote a letter to Paul, our field chairman, and told him about what had happened. I said that he may be interested in coming out to attend the meeting, since it had to do with our official status with the authorities, namely the ejido itself. I had not been made aware that anything significant had happened in the year that we were away on the national landscape. But a year is a long time, and there could've been changes in sentiment that I didn't know about. In Chihuahua City, however, the mission had come under intense scrutiny from the state government because of our school for missionaries' children. A new dormitory and school program for all of the missionary kids had to be opened in El Paso, Texas, to reduce our footprint in Chihuahua City.

Meanwhile, I had a full plate and got back into my Tarahumara language study, reestablished old relationships, and was immediately swamped again with work.

Paul came out by train to San Rafael the day before the ejido meeting, and I picked him up at the station. We talked about several aspects of the tribal work while we drove home as well as that evening at our house. But Paul seemed to have a lot of thoughts going through his mind; he seemed a bit too quiet and polite.

The next morning, before we got in my truck to head out to Bachámuchi, he said to me, "Steve, I'm not sure what it could be, but you must've done something to offend Mauro. I don't think you'd be in this situation otherwise."

"Paul, I've explained everything to you, and it's really not complicated. Mauro's greed has finally surfaced. We always thought that something like this was in the back of his mind when he invited us to live out here. Good grief, I wasn't even back here long enough to do or say something dumb when he made his demands. And he had already told Al what he wanted before we even got back from furlough."

"Well, Steve," he replied, "I understand it from your point of view, but this puts New Tribes Mission in a tight spot. We'll do what we have to do to salvage the work, but if there's any liability involved here, I'm afraid you'll sort of be on your own. If you need to make amends—"

I felt like I had been slapped, and then a chill went through me. So when things were going well, I was a good missionary, but when I hit the first snag and really needed help, the moral and spiritual support from my field leader—I was "on my own?" So I was probably the one in the wrong? This was unbelievable!

> **Say to my soul, "I am your salvation." Let those be put to shame and brought to dishonor who seek my life. (Psalm 35:3–4)**

Like a number of other times, especially during the last several years as we pioneered the work amongst the Western dialect of the Tarahumara, I felt like I was on my own. But I could not dwell for too long on what had just hit me broadside. In an hour or two, I would be standing before 150 or more voting members of the ejido with the last five years' worth of my blood, sweat, and tears—literally—on the line. I could get knocked off-balance by doubt and fear or refocus on why I was even here in the first place.

I chose to refocus on how and why God had led and guided us up to this point in time. I was His servant, and this was His battle. I would simply do my part, with or without the support of a human coworker. My responsibility and accountability was always to the Lord Himself, so this day would be a huge test of God's plans for us and my faith in Him. Different day and battle—yet the same. I asked the Lord to calm my spirit.

> **Let the angel of the Lord chase them…let the angel of the Lord pursue them… My soul shall be joyful in the Lord; it shall rejoice in His salvation. (Psalm 35:5–9)**

We drove up to the big gymnasium-like meeting building, and I introduced Paul to the few people from outside of El Manzano whom I knew. I actually did not even know them very well, and the president, who was from Rocoroibo, I only knew from attending the meetings. Back inside the assembly hall, I introduced Paul to a few more of our El Manzano neighbors, and finally, the meeting got underway.

There were over 150 people inside and just outside of the building. Most of the ones inside were leaning against the walls or standing around in small groups, chatting with friends and family members. Paul and I stood perhaps fifteen or twenty feet in front of the Council, down on the main floor, listening politely and waiting for my case to come up.

The usual agenda items were rather boring to most of the folks, so at least two-thirds of them paid little attention. If and when an agenda item came up regarding roadwork in a certain community or a dispute regarding a piece of land or a cow, perhaps twenty people would come up close to the raised stage where the Council sat so they could hear and be heard as they gave testimony. Sometimes there would be a vote by a show of hands and sometimes not.

Finally, the ejido president announced that "the issue of Mauro Sanchez claiming ownership of the plot of land where the Americans are living" was next. "Would the two parties come up to the front, please?"

I was gestured up onto the stage and went in front of the group with a copy of our agreement with the ejido in my hand. I was asked to present my case first.

> **Behold, I send you out as sheep in the midst of wolves. Therefore, be wise as serpents and harmless as doves. But beware of men, for they will deliver you up to councils and scourge you in their synagogues. You will be brought before governors and kings for my sake, as a testimony to them and to the Gentiles. But when they deliver you up do not**

> **worry about how or what you should speak. For it will be given to you in that hour what you should speak- for it is not you who speak, but the Spirit of your Father who speaks in you. (Matthew 10:16–20)**

There was no PA system, so in as loud a voice as possible, I related to the assembly once again the reasons we had come to live in El Manzano. I stated that we were focusing on learning the Tarahumara language and that we were endeavoring to help the community in a number of ways. Someday, I said, we would also translate God's Scriptures into the Tarahumara language.

"We were invited to El Manzano by Mauro Sanchez, to live on the land where we now have our house. It had been abandoned land where no one had lived for more than five years. We came to this assembly of the ejido four years ago and asked permission to build a house there and to have one other family join us as partners someday. I did this at a meeting in which Señor Sanchez was in attendance. I have here the signed and dated agreement between us and the ejido.

"Now," I said, "Señor Sanchez wants to charge my partner and me rent for the land, and I don't think this is right. He has also said that if we won't pay him rent that he will take the land and houses away from us. I would like the ejido to please again confirm and recognize that our permission to live there is between us and the ejido."

> **Lord, how long will you look on? Rescue me from their destructions, my precious life from the lions. I will give you thanks in the great assembly. I will praise you among many people. (Psalm 35:17–18)**

As I had walked up on the stage, I could hear the conversations around the big building quickly quieting down. Inside and out, people stopped what they were doing and began gathering closer and closer to the stage in order to hear what was being said. The small crowd in front of the stage where Paul and I had stood for over an hour grew from thirty or forty people to about two hundred. In the three or four minutes in which I spoke, everyone inside the building had come to the front, leaving no one at the back of the room or against the side walls, chatting like before. As I finished talking, there was complete silence. I stood there, looking out at the crowd, almost in disbelief.

I looked over at the Council President and said, "That is all I have to say, sir."

He nodded, and I walked back down to the main floor and stood with Paul. He, too, was in amazement at how everyone was now pressing up to the stage and paying attention. The president called on Mauro and Ignacio Sanchez. They walked up the steps and stood on the stage, facing the assembly.

Mauro started off, "I had only intended to lend the Americans that land for a couple of years." There were several snickers and comments made from the floor.

"Really?" someone said.

"Now I need it as a place for my oldest son to live," Mauro said.

Nacho (Ignacio), Mauro's brother, then spoke up. "I had farmed that land years before and said it should remain in the family." There were more sneers and comments from the floor. He and Mauro only said a couple of more sentences and then said they were finished.

> **Let them not rejoice over me who are wrongfully my enemies… They do not speak peace, but they devise deceitful matters against the quiet ones in the land. They also opened their mouth wide against me. (Psalm 35:19–20)**

The president then asked for comments from the floor. Teodulo spoke up, "Why would the Americans build houses if they were only going to have the land lent to them for a couple of years? Ignacio, you moved off that land because the soil is so poor it won't even produce corn. You tried for three or four years, then left it." There was a low rumbling of approval by those standing around us.

After a few more minutes for comments, the president called for a vote. He reminded everyone that only registered *ejidatarios* could vote. He would now ask for a show of hands.

This is where I got nervous. I knew that for the past several weeks, Mauro would have been calling in favors, counting on family members to back him and doing his best politicking. A lot of money was at stake for him.

> **This you have seen, oh Lord. Do not keep silence. Oh Lord, do not be far from me. Stir up yourself and awake to my vindication, to my cause, my God and my Lord. Vindicate me, O Lord my God, according to your righteousness, and let them not rejoice over me… Let them not say, "We have swallowed him up." (Psalm 35:22–25)**

The president said, "All who believe the land should be returned to the Sanchez family, raise your hand."

Mauro and Nacho, still standing on the stage, off to one side, raised their hands. I looked to the left, then to the right, then behind us. There was not another raised hand!

"Those in favor of letting the Americans live there under their agreement with the ejido, raise your hands."

All around the building, scores of hands went up, well over a hundred, and then the murmurs of "Andele!" (Yeah!) began, and then cheers started. I looked at Paul next to me. His eyes were opened wide in amazement, and he was speechless. He just kept looking left, then right, then behind us again and again. Finally, he reached out his hand and gave me a big, firm handshake. His expression had gone from anxiety to shocked amazement to joyous relief.

In the next few moments, I had friends and neighbors from El Manzano coming over and slapping me on the back, shaking my hand in congratulations. I felt like I had won some kind of big election, and I guess in a way, I had. No, definitely <u>God</u> had!

> **Let them shout for joy and be glad, who favored my righteous cause, and let them say continually, "Let the Lord be magnified, who has pleasure in the prosperity of His servant." (Psalm 35:27)**

I glanced over at the corner of the stage where Mauro and his brother stood, stunned. They began an obstinate, offensive exchange with the president, who finally gave them a sound reprimand in front of everyone present. As dozens of folks patted me on the back and shook hands enthusiastically, Mauro and Nacho finally formed up with four or five family members and headed out of the hall.

> **Let them be ashamed and brought to mutual confusion...Let them be clothed with shame and dishonor. (Psalm 35:26)**

I felt like I never wanted the celebration to end. The whole building was filled with loud chatter and laughing. I wished we could have headed off to a big restaurant for a proper celebration, but there was nothing like that less than four hours away. Apparently, that was the last item of business on the agenda, so the ejido building emptied out.

It was a glorious day! Paul went back to Chihuahua City—happy, of course. He kept saying he'd never seen anything quite like that. He sort of tried to make up for his lack of confidence in me and in my earlier evaluation of the situation with Mauro. I said, in some diplomatic way, that, yes, we out in the tribe really do need the trust of the folks who aren't in our situation, especially when the chips are down.

> **My tongue shall speak of your righteousness and of your praise all the day long. (Psalm 35:28)**

It was just as much of a learning situation for Paul, I think, as it was for me. I know it was tough for our leadership to deal with the stress on them due to the Mexican government's investigations and pressure to move the kids' school, etc. for the previous two years. Paul was a godly man, so I prayed that that situation showed him that God had <u>His</u> victory that day. God indeed had His angels there where He had begun His work, and the gates of hell were not going to prevail against it!

NOTE: I wrote the entire text of this incident above and then one day found a couple of verses from Psalm 35 that I thought applied. I was only going to highlight those two verses, but then I read the entire psalm. It fit so perfectly from beginning to end with that whole ejido meeting that I simply had to start inserting the appropriate verses here and there where they applied, until I had used almost the entire psalm. It is amazing how God's Word so often reflects an exact incident in our lives! That's why He gave us His Word! How can we not rejoice in Him and in His written revelation to us every day of our lives?

11.4 The Trip to Uruachic

> **Let all those rejoice who put their trust in you. Let them ever shout for joy, because you defend them. Let those also who love your name be joyful in you. For you, oh Lord will bless the righteous; With favor you will surround him as with a shield. (Psalm 5:11–12)**

I dropped Paul off at the train station, and he headed back to Chihuahua City. There was still an incredible joy in my heart because of how the ejido meeting had gone. The only disappointment was that Al hadn't been there. He and Polly had gone off to either Chihuahua City or El Paso on business. They were really relieved when I shared with them how the meeting had gone, though. Teodulo, of course, also shared with Al the details of the meeting. It was obvious to him, too, that it had been a victory for the Lord. Our Bible studies were continuing every week. The believers were doing really well. As before, Al and I rotated in teaching, and sometimes we would ask Teodulo to read and comment on certain Scriptures. There was consistent personal growth in the believers and also in the numbers of people who would come to just listen in on the Bible studies. There was nothing that thrilled me more than seeing those dear Tarahumara brothers and sisters of ours grow in grace and knowledge!

A couple of weeks after the ejido meeting, Mauro sent a note up to my house with his youngest son, Martin. It turned out that by way of a messenger, Mauro had received hand-carried invitations from the municipal president for several of us in the community to travel over to Uruachic. The president was planning special events for the Mexican Independence Day, the *Veinte de Noviembre* or Twentieth of November. That date celebrates the beginning of the Mexican Revolution of 1910, like our Fourth of July, to end the last dictatorship and eventually establish a democratic republic in Mexico.

In his invitation to me, the municipal president, Guadalupe Gonzalez Gonzalez, stated that he would like me to be his personal guest in his home. It would be an understatement to say that I was surprised and honored. He remembered me from his visit to El Manzano a year and a half or two years earlier when he was running for the office of municipal president. The invitation stated *if* I could come so it wasn't strictly binding or absolutely expected.

I talked it over with Ticker and with Al and Polly. Since the president knew me personally, not Al yet, he did not feel like taking time for the long trip by road to go to Uruachic. Indeed, it would be a ten- to twelve-hour trip, going all the way to Creel, then north of San Juanito turning west, continuing for a few more hours on dirt and gravel roads. Uruachic lay at the bottom of a deep canyon, an historical town that sprang up hundreds of years earlier due to several very rich gold and silver mines in the area.

I was very much interested in going over there for the celebration, especially in light of the personal invitation. After the realization that New Tribes was a bit under the microscope with the Mexican government, I knew it would be a really good idea to have friends in government. Perhaps in the interest of also showing Mauro I harbored no ill feelings toward him, despite the resounding rebuttal he had received at the ejido meeting, I went down to his house to talk about this invitation. I had already talked to Teodulo about going, but he wasn't interested.

Mauro was a bit surprised to see me but greeted me nicely enough.

"Are you going over there for the celebration?" I asked. "How long does it take to walk over there?"

"Well, several of us are going to go over on horseback," he said. "Are you thinking about walking over there? It's a long way, you know."

"Yes, I think I would prefer to walk instead of driving all the way around. It's a long drive, and I've heard that it takes about, what, eight hours to walk over?"

In typical, somewhat exaggerated tough Tarahumara fashion, he said, "Some people can make it in six and a half or seven hours."

I had heard from Teodulo and a couple of others that it would take eight hours, maybe even eight and a half at the most. I had pretty much decided that walking over there was what I wanted to do. I liked being in good shape, and it would be more along the lines of what a local person would do to walk it.

"Do you know anyone who's going to walk over?" I asked. "I would need someone to show me the trail. I've only been as far as the river before." That had been when a bunch of us had gone fishing down there with Teodulo and company almost three years earlier.

"Martin, my son here, will be going on foot, and you could go with him." This was interesting. I had the distinct feeling that Mauro wanted to turn back the clock so that we were not going to have any bad blood between us. That was a good thing and made me feel right about my decision to go down and have this talk with him.

"When would he be leaving?" I asked.

Mauro said that he would leave about eight o'clock in the morning on the nineteenth. That way, we should get in by four o'clock or so. That sounded good to me. I had my guide!

Looking north from El Manzano toward the Rio Oteros, which I would cross going to Uruachic.

You eat where they eat. You sleep where they sleep, and think like they think. This was the essence of the Special Forces training and experience (Doug Stanton, *12 Strong*, p. 348).

This was not going to be a short walk, so I really wanted to travel light. I thought about taking hiking boots but, in the end, decided that I could probably make do with my bull-neck leather cowboy boots. They were fairly new, so they looked really nice when you wiped the dust off them. I had worn them walking around the El Manzano area on Sundays when we visited folks, and I wanted to have something nicer than work shoes or hiking boots to wear when I got there. I was really impressed with how tough they were, even though they were cowboy boots with a Western heel.

I definitely did not want to take some kind of an American-looking backpack, even though I had one with a frame. That would look really touristy, exactly the image I did not want to project. In the end, I decided on taking a nylon net bag like everyone used for bringing groceries home from the store. I would take a few snacks, a change of clothes, razor and soap, a canteen, and a folding knife. The only other thing I would need, especially if the plan fell through for me to stay at Señor Gonzalez's house, would be a lightweight blanket. I found a single bed-sized nylon blanket, rolled it up tight, and made a strap out of rope so I could carry it over my shoulder. It didn't take up much room at all and was lightweight. Rather than a blue denim jacket, which would not be the least bit "dressy," I had a fairly new nylon vest that would be comfortable on a chilly evening.

Uruachic is at an elevation of about 1,800 feet, so it was going to be pretty warm over there. Our weather in El Manzano had been really nice. During the days, it was in the seventies and, at night, was only going down into the upper forties. We were having a nice temperate fall.

Martin, fourteen years old but already very responsible, and I left El Manzano closer to nine o'clock that next morning. Apparently, he had not yet finished his chores around the house when I got there. His mother had to get some food for him as well as for the men that were going to go over there a couple of hours after we left. The trail headed almost straight north for several miles, dropping down from the high plateaus and mountains where we lived. It was a well-traveled trail and was easy to follow the huarache sandal, boot prints, and hoofprint tracks of animals. At about 5,000 feet elevation, the switchbacks started and went back and forth as we descended steeply to the Rio Oteros, which was at about 2,500 feet elevation.

Perhaps 1,000 feet above the river, it was getting quite warm, and we were thirsty. We caught up to several slower travelers, and about the same time, we came to the only good spring on that whole section of trail. The spring was dug into the mountain, right next to the trail. There was a basin that was about four feet above the path itself, just a hole about the size of a large cooking pot. This was the place for people to drink from. About three feet away and closer to the ground was another basin for the horses, mules, and burrows to drink from. Looking at this water source, you hoped that the animals were always supervised and that the people dipping out of the "people spring" didn't have any illness you could catch. I dipped water out by tilting my canteen on its side. Martin had a tin cup with him and used that. The water was a bit salty tasting, nothing like the sweet mountain spring water we had in El Manzano. After a five-minute rest, we took off again.

At the river, we looked for a shallow place to cross. I took off my boots and socks, rolled up my pant legs, and waded across gingerly, stepping on the big round river rocks in water that was just about knee-deep. Once on the other side we drank again, from the river water this time, then Martin said we were going to go look for something to eat. Without questioning him about what he meant, because I didn't realize he hadn't brought much food from home, we started going through the tall brush and grass on the far side of the river and then turned slightly upstream.

It had been about an hour and a half since we had left the spring and three and a half hours or more since we left El Manzano. We were hungry. We climbed a bank about twenty feet high, and Martin was scanning ahead of us, left and right. I wondered what he was looking for.

For years, I had been drying apples and making beef jerky, so I had some of each of those with me for my food. I shared some of that with Martin, realizing now that he had only brought an apple and a couple of tortillas from home for food. Then he finally spotted what he was looking for. Ahead of us and only a couple hundred yards away was a goat herder with twenty or so goats. Martin's eyes lit up, and he said, "Let's go! Let's get some milk if we can."

We came up to the goat herder who was only about twelve years old, and Martin greeted him with the Tarahumara "Kwira!" It seemed that this younger boy was either a relative or a friend of a relative. Martin soon had this guy talked into letting us get some milk from one of his goats. He milked one of the females and first gave Martin, then me, a full cup of warm, frothy, creamy milk.

One other food item I had brought with me was *pinole*. It was homemade, hand ground and lightly toasted cornmeal with a small amount of sugar mixed into it. The men who worked out in the hills doing logging or maintaining the roads often took it for lunch or a snack. It was really nourishing and had good carbohydrates for energy. They would usually mix it with water, but right at that moment, I knew it was going to be really, really good mixed with milk! And it was. I would have to say it was one of the best-tasting and most refreshing snacks I've ever had.

I had been down to the Rio Oteros once before, but I had not been across to the other side. I knew from the topographical map I had at home that we were going to now turn mostly west while still going a bit to the north. We'd be going through hill country, up and down a range of hills to an elevation of about 4,500 feet before we dropped down into Uruachic. Reading quite a few Western novels, as well as having hiked a few times when I was younger in unknown territory, I knew enough to keep an eye on which compass direction I was basically heading in and for how long I went in a certain direction.

As we came down the long winding trail from El Manzano to the river, I had also glanced to both sides of the trail and occasionally looked back behind us at the mountains to get an idea of what they looked like from below. It's vital to see what a hillside or canyon or rock formation is going to look like when you're facing it from the opposite direction on your way back.

In his novel, *The Skyliners*, Louis L'Amour put it this way:

> A man riding Western country just naturally looks at it all. I mean, he studies his back trail and onto the horizon on every side. Years later he would be able to describe every mile of it- As if it had been yesterday.
>
> First place, they just naturally had to be that way. There were no signposts, no buildings, no corrals, or anything but creeks, occasional buttes, sometimes a bluff or a bank… As there wasn't much to see you came to remember what there was.

I had no idea at the time how much I would rely on those observations a couple of days from now.

Martin and I thanked the young goat herder for the milk, and we were on our way again. As we now headed due west along the north bank of the river, I kept looking for where the trail had come down the mountain. That was where I would need to cross on my way back in a couple of days. Then we were once again on a pretty well-traveled trail; there were also numerous smaller trails that branched off to the north every so often. Those were the trails that the goat herders used, bringing their animals through the hills to find water and grass to graze on. When a herd went through, it obliterated all of the tracks left by the people who were wearing huarache sandals or boots.

The hills in this area looked very much the same too. They were rather nondescript with just a bit of scrub brush, low oak trees, and dry grass for several miles. I tried to commit to memory the prominent rock formations that were a couple of thousand feet higher toward the north as well as on my left-hand side, across the river to the south.

It was a relief when the sun got lower and the air started to get a little cooler. Martin and I had both rationed our water carefully, and it was a good thing we did since we never came across another spring. Finally, we started seeing some small ranches here and there, and I knew we must be getting closer to Uruachic. At about 5:00 or 5:30, which was just before dusk at that time of year, we crested a hill, and there before us was the old mining town at last.

We spotted one or two men from El Manzano who had left earlier than us and found out that the festivities for the evening were getting underway at a community center. As we made our way in that direction down the dusty dirt streets and wooden boardwalks of the town, I asked around about hotel rooms. I was told that all the rooms were almost certainly taken because of the holiday visitors. Martin was vague about where he was going to stay, only saying that he had to find some relatives before he would know. His father and at least two uncles were there somewhere, he said.

I knew that the adults always found a way to stay with someone at their house, hotel, or place of business. But the teenagers and young men, especially if they were not from influential families or didn't have much money, would very likely end up camping on the edge of town or in someone's backyard. I didn't want to get stuck doing that and was confident that the president would help me out.

The building that we had been directed to was two-stories tall, wooden framed, and large. I dusted off my shirt and jeans—I had worn some nice tan denim pants that I felt would hide the dust—wiped the dust off my boots, climbed the stairs to the second floor, and went into the fiesta. There was a big main room that was probably used for weddings or other fancy events and served as the town's convention center. To the sides of the big room were hallways that went to the kitchen and some smaller rooms. There were some long tables with lots of food set out in chafing dishes. Boy was I thankful—I was starving.

The main dishes consisted of a variety of beef and chicken with beans, tortillas, and salsas. Those who were eating were being very polite and taking small portions. I quickly set my bag and blanket down under a table, went to the line, got a small amount of everything, then made my way off to one side to eat. At first, I spotted absolutely no one I knew. Martin had left me before I went up the stairs, saying he was going to look for some of the others from El Manzano. Since he was young, a Tarahumara, and rather shy, I now understood why he hadn't come upstairs with me.

In the main hall were all the businessmen and political leaders of Uruachic and the surrounding ranches, looking fine with their wives beautifully dressed. I was now wishing I brought more changes of clothes. But I would need the two fresh shirts I brought for the next two days, so I just admired the elite in their nice clean clothes and wandered around, hoping to find someone I might know.

As I strolled from one side of the room to the other, I met and made small talk with a dozen or so people. Several of the men had already begun drinking. I found some of them entertaining but others just to be boring partiers. Eventually, after about an hour, I think, I found one or two fellows from El Manzano. It was great to visit with someone I knew, of course. Finally, someone took me over to meet the president. I had seen him visiting with different people around the room for the last hour but had not recognized him from his visit to El Manzano two or so years earlier.

He was about forty or forty-five years of age, solidly built, and very pleasant. My neighbor from El Manzano didn't take me right up to meet him face-to-face. That would've been rather presumptuous. Instead, he waited to see who amongst the president's friends seemed approachable, then introduced me to him, adding that I was the American from El Manzano across the river who had come at the president's invitation. He told me that the president's nickname was El Bocho, then my friend from El Manzano turned and melted back into the crowd.

My new acquaintance introduced me to the president. "Señor Real, this is our presidente, Señor Guadalupe Gonzalez Gonzalez."

"Mucho gusto, Señor Presidente!" I replied.

"Señor Real, I am so glad you could make it!" he exclaimed. "How was your trip?" He was all smiles, shaking my hand like we were old friends.

"A bit long but quite pleasant," I assured him. "That's the most walking I've done in quite a while."

He looked astounded. "You walked?" he said. "You actually walked all the way here from El Manzano? That's incredible! Why didn't you drive?"

"Actually, it would've taken longer to drive," I explained. "It's quite a drive, having to go back to Creel, then San Juanito, then all the way down here. And, actually, believe it or not, I really like to walk. It keeps me in good shape. I do so much desk work as it is that I need the exercise. And the weather is perfect right now," I said.

He was truly amazed. As he introduced me to people for the next two days, he told many of them over and over again that I had actually walked over from El Manzano. Some said, "Oh, you mean you came on horseback?"

"No," he would interject. "He came over on foot with one of the young men from El Manzano as his guide. Incredible, no?"

Señor Gonzalez insisted that we call each other by our first names, and so we did for the rest of the weekend. He had many people to greet, some of them dignitaries from Chihuahua City to talk with and attend to, so he excused himself after a few minutes, telling me he would be back shortly.

"You are my guest and will be staying in my house," he said. "I have a lot of people to talk to. I'm sure you understand. But I'll be back, and we'll go over to my house later. You stay here, enjoy the party, and get some food. Have you eaten?" he asked.

I told him I had, but that I would have a little more, so as he went off to greet more people, I went to the food tables one more time. I finally got my fill, which was very gratifying after that hike.

It was a little awkward talking with many of the people, but that's how it often was when they asked what I did for a profession and I told them I was a missionary. I would quickly add that I was a linguist, too, and was studying the Tarahumara language and culture. Some people appreciated that, and some did not. It was sad to realize how many people thought the Indians were subhuman and that I was wasting my time on them. But I also looked for opportunities to talk to the ranchers about their horses and cattle or businessmen about the economy and how their particular business was doing. I avoided talk of politics, of course, but told them about the United States a little bit and of my family when they asked.

The band was playing by then, and there was some dancing and drinking. As the evening wore on, some of those in the hall got a bit intoxicated but were all pretty good-natured. When I had to go downstairs and outside later to go to the bathroom, I saw the difference between the people upstairs and those outside. While many outside were just standing around in small groups, talking, others were drinking a lot, getting noisy and rowdy. Several were falling down drunk, and their friends eventually helped them stagger off to wherever they were staying for the night. A few sounded like they were going to get into fistfights, but I don't think any did, at least not on any of my two or three trips outside.

I found a few neighbors from El Manzano whom I talked with for a while. But unlike back in El Manzano, they now understood that I was with the people "upstairs" and was a "guest of the presidente." After only a few words of greetings with me, they would turn back to their peers and carry on with their own conversations. Yes, there were definitely two or three social levels there, and for the time being, I was in the top strata.

It was getting rather late, about eleven o'clock or eleven thirty, when Guadalupe, or "Lupe" as he insisted that I call him, finally came back to the social hall. The last of the food had been cleared away by then and perhaps half of the crowd had gone home. Now he could formally wrap up the evening, which he did with a last round of handshakes and slaps on the back and *abrazos*, the hug you give to friends. He motioned for me to join him. I went over to where I had left my bag and blanket and retrieved them, and we went off together up the street.

"First, we're going to my house and get you settled in," he said. "Then we'll meet with some more friends, and I want you to meet my mother. We'll have *posole* at her house tomorrow night. Does that sound okay? Are you tired? Would you rather go to bed?" *Posole* was a soup with big corn kernels and tripe—pig intestines.

I assured him I was fine and would very much enjoy meeting his friends and mother. Thankfully, I was young—thirty-one at the time—and had recuperated quickly from the hike by sitting for a couple of hours at the fiesta.

At Guadalupe's house, I was given a nice comfortable guest room. We then went downstairs into a very comfortable living room with heavy, dark furniture that had nice, comfortable cushions. In a few short minutes, three or four of his friends arrived. One of them was the previous municipal president. We talked about a lot of things, and I learned a fair bit about old Tarahumara history. About 150 years ago, the Tarahumaras had been hired—or were forced—to work in the mines or on building roads and trails for the mule trains. The men were actually branded on their arms to prove their identities for the sake of collecting pay or paying off their debts to their employers!

After the last of the guests made their way home at about one o'clock in the morning, Guadalupe and I went to meet his mother. It was a short visit, thankfully, and when we got back to his house, I finally got to take a shower and go to bed clean.

After a great breakfast the next morning, we headed off to Guadalupe's office. He had told me earlier that morning that he'd summoned Mauro to be there at 11:00 a.m. We walked from his home to his office with two big, quiet, and well-dressed men. Most of the time, they walked behind us, and I wondered who they were. When we got to his office, he quietly asked one of them to stay outside and the other one to come inside with us. By the way they followed orders and composed themselves, I finally realized that they were his bodyguards, probably state police.

Guadalupe sat down behind his desk and motioned me into a chair close by. His bodyguard stood behind me, against the wall next to the door.

Earlier that morning at breakfast, he had said, "I understand that there's been some difficulty between you and Mauro." He asked me what it was all about, and I told him simply that Mauro was trying to charge us rent for our house and property.

"But you have a written agreement with the ejido, don't you?" he asked.

"Yes," I told him, "and the matter was resolved at the last ejido meeting."

"Well, we'll have a short talk about that," he said.

When Mauro showed up with his brother and a couple of others, the president asked them to remain outside. Just Mauro was instructed to come in and sit down. The bodyguard resumed his position next to the door, with the other one right outside.

"Tell me what this is, Mauro, that I hear is going on in El Manzano. Is it true that you want the Americans to pay you rent for the land they're living on?"

Mauro was nervous and started squirming in his chair. He looked at the floor, hemmed and hawed a bit, then answered in the affirmative.

"And what is your understanding of the arrangement you had when you built your house there, Esteban?" he asked me.

"I have written permission from the ejido for the free use of the land until we finish our work there. There is no time limit, but when we leave, the ejido is to get the property back," I answered.

Guadalupe looked at both of us, then turned slightly in his chair to face more directly at Mauro. Up until this point, he had been very judicially balanced in his tone of voice and choice of words. Now his demeanor changed quite noticeably.

"Mauro, I've been asking a lot of questions of my people here and of those who know El Manzano quite well. You may be a long way from here in one sense, but I care very much about what goes on over there, and I don't want any trouble for the Americans."

"Isn't it true," he continued, "that your mother was very sick last year? To the point of dying? Didn't these Americans go and treat her with medicine and get her well?"

He paused momentarily, expecting an answer. Mauro shifted his weight in his chair and, trying not to look too nervous, answered with a barely audible, "Yes. True."

Guadalupe continued. "In fact, Mauro, I understand that these generous people have done a lot of good for many of your family members and your neighbors. As someone who is supposed to care for your people, I'm surprised that you are not more appreciative of them. Instead, you're practically trying to run them off. I'm amazed at this and am embarrassed at the lack of hospitality and kindness on your part. These people are guests in our country and deserve to be treated far better than this."

The president picked up a file from the corner of his desk and opened it. He started reading about the fact that we had not only treated Mauro's mother who had been seriously ill but also his uncle. Then he read from another page, describing how we had helped people who were injured get to San Rafael to a doctor for medical treatment. From the third page, he read that we regularly transported people to ejido meetings, even though there was no business on the agenda that pertained to us and that we regularly gave rides to people to go into San Rafael for a variety of purposes. He read notes from two more pages, for a total of five, naming people who we had helped treat with medicines and in other ways over the course of the previous three years. He was making it obvious that he had a very active interest in things that happened in El Manzano, although we were so far away from Uruachic. Putting the file back down on his desk and looking up at Mauro, he said, "Do these sound like people who we should be treating poorly?"

Again, Mauro shifted his weight and appeared to want to say something, but the president cut him off and said, "Let me make something very clear to you, Mauro. Other things have also come to my attention. There is the matter of a cow that was not sold to you but which you have taken possession of. I realize money was owed to you, but again, even though this was a family member—your aunt, I believe—you have chosen to be more concerned with taking something from someone else to enrich yourself than with doing the right thing and with serving your community."

Mauro now wanted to interject and defend himself from this onslaught. "Well, Señor Presidente, there are issues with the brand on the cow and—" he began.

But Guadalupe cut him off. "The details of that incident are quite well-known to me, and here at the municipal level, we will let you know what we will decide. My constable is still looking into that. But what we are talking about here, today, is a separate issue. What I want to impress on you is that in the case of you trying to take advantage of the Americans, you need to know how I feel.

"Your actions," he continued, "are completely out of line. You need to immediately desist from bothering them and leave them to their work. Everything they are doing is for the betterment of the indigenous community. Again, it bothers me deeply to have to have this conversation with you."

He paused for a moment, then looked briefly at his bodyguard. It was then that I noticed that the man was taking notes of the meeting. He was apparently a cross between a personal assistant and a cop. In pausing to look at him, Guadalupe was making it plain that something very official was going on here.

"In fact, Mauro, I want to be very clear. If I so much as hear of any more instances in which you hinder or create trouble for these Americans, there are other issues besides that of the cow which will not go well for you. Are you very clear on this?"

I was embarrassed for Mauro, in a way. He was a middle-aged man, about twenty or twenty-five years older than me, and the

HE WHO HAS BEGUN A GOOD WORK

Indian governor of El Manzano. The way he had just been put in line was more like what a father would have to do with an obstinate teenager. But I was also incredibly thankful that this had just happened. Mauro was the initiator of the trouble, was a corrupt, money-hungry man, and had thought for a while that he would get the upper hand against me. I was really impressed with Guadalupe and how he had taken interest, and then decisive action, in this situation between Mauro and me. His judicial intervention was very timely and I hoped would end Mauro's ambitions immediately. I could not believe my great fortune and the powerful ally who had miraculously appeared on my behalf.

"We have a great afternoon ahead of us. Now let's get on with the day. I trust I will not hear anything more of this issue between you," Guadalupe said. Then he stood, and we all did likewise. When his assistant and Mauro had left the room, I thanked Guadalupe for his interest and help.

"It's no problem, Esteban," he said. "You're doing good things for the people over there, and I want you to know we appreciate that. The government can't do all we need to do for all the people, so we appreciate you folks. I think that will be the end of the trouble with Mauro. Let me know if he tries anything else. I'll be keeping an ear out to see how things are going, you can be sure."

With that, he said, "Okay! Let's go out now and enjoy the parade!" We walked a block to the plaza where the parade for the big holiday was about to start. Hundreds of people were gathering on the sides of the streets of the old town, many standing on the second- and third-floor balconies of homes to watch. Down in the street, the parade organizers lined everyone up in some kind of order.

I stayed close to Lupe. Then, just as we got ready to start, he said to me, "Steve, I want you right here in the very front of the parade with me. In fact, I'd like it, if you don't mind, if you would carry the flag."

You can probably imagine my surprise! My mind was racing regarding what I should do. Had he corralled me into doing something that wasn't really appropriate? After what he had just said to Mauro less than a half an hour earlier about us being guests in the country and people that should be respected for the humanitarian work we were doing, I knew I couldn't refuse. To refuse, I decided, would be an insult to him. How was it that I, the only American there, would be carrying the Mexican national flag on Mexico's Independence Day? Perhaps it was a real-world test of my nonpolitical affiliation and a demonstration to both him and his friends of my love of Mexico. I immediately thought, *When in Rome, do as the Romans.* So I took the flag in my hands and walked with him in the very front of the procession.

The parade was long, taking about an hour and a half, and it was a very warm day. I was glad when it was over and we could stop and get some water and then a cold Coke. I don't remember what we did for lunch, but then we were off to the big event of the day—actually of the whole weekend—the rodeo!

And a good rodeo it was. There was calf and cow roping, stunt riding, then the highlight—the bull-riding. The riding of the toughest bull was the grand finale. I'll never forget that animal—a big, gray Charolaise that was almost as wide as he was tall. I wondered how anyone could even stay on his back at all, and not many did. But there weren't too many riders willing to take on that beast, so the announcer continued to put out the challenge to any potential, daring would-be riders to come forward. There would be good prize money but also fame and glory just for making the attempt at the ride.

It sounded appealing. I had this feeling like I did when I almost raced motocross several years before in Chihuahua City. The thrill of giving it a shot would have been really exciting. When the rodeo was getting ready to start, I had left Lupe and his group to look for some of my friends from El Manzano. I was sitting with them in the stands now at the end of the rodeo. They were tempting me with the announcer's offer, saying I should try it, seeing in my eyes the sparkle of interest. But in the end, I pictured in my mind that huge thousand-pound beast stepping on my arm or leg or body after I fell off of him, so I didn't take up the challenge. Neither did anyone else from El Manzano.

The rodeo ended, and I found Lupe again, and we went to his house for a shower and dinner. That evening, even more friends were at his house, and the visiting continued through the evening. Everyone was enjoying wine, tequila, and fine brandy. The interesting variety of people at his home included a couple of politician friends from Chihuahua City and an actress of some renown. She was Elisa Eims, sixty years old or so, and was retired from the movie industry but had apparently been very well known in her day. She was at that time active in doing humanitarian work for the Tarahumaras. It was fascinating for me to listen to their conversations, and occasionally we talked about my life in the United States prior to moving to Mexico. After dessert, we left to visit two or three friends of his in their homes.

His friends were all getting tired from drinking, and I had to hand it to Lupe for not drinking too much himself. At one o'clock in the morning, he said, "Let's go to my mom's house. She's expecting us." It was an invitation I could not refuse, of course, but I was not looking forward to having posole.

Posole is a late-night and holiday delicacy. It consists of a thin broth with lots of tender kernels of corn and pig intestines instead of meat. I didn't care for the idea of eating any animal's intestines, especially a pig's. In the mountains of Mexico, pigs eat the most disgusting things. I will just leave it at that.

It turned out the *tripa*—intestines—were really tough, too, harder to chew than overcooked calamari. I hoped the displeasure didn't show on my face as I forced it down. As I chewed the rubbery tripa, I forced my mind to think of the soft, delicious corn that was still in the bowl. It was an interesting experience, lasting until almost 3:00 a.m., when Lupe was finally content that his social life for that day was a wrap. Quite contented, we headed back to his house and got a good night's sleep.

One had to pay attention to what the terrain looked like from different directions, memorizing it for the return trip

The next morning, by about nine o'clock, I got up to another really good breakfast, then had to say my goodbyes and make my way through town to find my friends from El Manzano. I sure didn't want to get left behind when they got on the trail to go home. There were only a few little grocery stores and hotels in town, and I felt that somewhere I would find them either out in front of or inside one of them. I finally found a couple of fellows out of the eight or ten men and older teenagers from El Manzano. But I was a bit surprised when they told me that none of them were going to go back to El Manzano that day. They had been invited to go to a big fiesta at someone's ranch outside of town and were going to go there for the afternoon and stay overnight. I knew what that meant—lots of drinking. That was not something I planned on being around.

I was determined to go home that day, and by the time I found out for sure that no one was going back to El Manzano that I could travel with, it was noon. Now I was going to be in a bind because of the time. I bought a couple of oranges and some crackers for a snack and headed out of town. I knew it would take me until probably eight o'clock at night to get home and hoped that I could stay on the right trail, asking directions if I needed to. So off I went alone.

Since it was November, I knew it would be dark by 7:00 p.m., dusk at six, so I was really motivated to make good time. I did, too, not losing the trail at all until I got to the river. Then two main trails could be seen going up the far side. I had to make an educated guess, and about a half hour up the mountain, I came across a mestizo fellow resting on the side of the trail, having a cigarette. Thankfully, I was indeed on the right trail, but now I had another problem.

I had been watching the sky, and the weather was changing rapidly. The wind was picking up considerably, carrying more and more clouds which at first were white but became more gray by the hour. The thought had occurred to me that I didn't have a flashlight with me since I'd never intended to travel at night. If I got stuck on the trail before I got home, I was also going to want matches to start a fire, and I hadn't taken any with me. I asked the mestizo fellow if I could buy some matches from him. He was quite reluctant, but I offered him about five times what they were worth. He sold me a little box that had maybe eight matches in it. I was grateful for that and thanked him and quickly got back on my way.

During the next hour or two, the sky got darker gray and solid with really nasty, fast-moving clouds. The temperature was dropping far faster than was to be expected for the rise in elevation. I was walking as fast as I possibly could, but by four o'clock, I knew I was in trouble. It started raining lightly off and on, nothing too bad. But the solid black overcast made the sky go dark at least an hour earlier than I had expected. I was having a harder and harder time seeing the trail, and I started looking for cover. Finally, I came across a massive angled rock with an area large enough to lay down underneath it and stay dry. I built a little fire from twigs and pine needles under the overhang, but it was so dark I couldn't get out and find any firewood now. What I did find was damp from the drizzle, and I couldn't get it to stay lit.

Soon, I'd used the last of my matches. It was time to try to get some sleep. I really, really hoped that I wasn't sharing my shelter with a rattlesnake or some black widow spiders. I unrolled my thin little blanket. Worrying wouldn't help me sleep, so I thought about my warm bed and family at home and finally dropped off and slept.

I woke up at 4:00 a.m. It was pitch black, the wind was blowing, and rain was coming down hard, but my spot was still dry. It was so chilly now that I couldn't sleep. I tossed and turned for another two hours until the sky had just barely enough light for me to see the trail. I rolled the blanket up, retied it with the two short pieces of rope that I had made into a sling, and got back on the trail. Or so I thought.

Trails in the mountains are an interesting thing. If you know exactly where you want to go and are familiar with the trail, you can virtually "see" it in the dark. That's how I operated on a couple of trails near our house, no matter what the weather, season, or time of day or night. An unfamiliar trail was still fairly easy to navigate in dry weather, given the number and types of tracks—both animals and people. But any trail in a rainstorm became a whole different thing.

In most places, the trail was an approximately twelve-inch-wide flat path that ran along the side of the mountain. In other places, it became a twelve-inch-wide, twelve-inch-deep drainage ditch, catching the pouring rain that came coursing down the side of the mountain, channeling the water until it overflowed and then made its own way down into the canyon below. As I walked along those flooding sections, I had to get up on the high edge of the trail to avoid sloshing along in racing water that was almost as high as the top of my boots. Then in still other places, the trail simply disappeared where there was an escarpment—sections of the mountain where there was no soil, just bare rock.

On the way to Uruachic, I had been able to see the scuff marks of people's tracks, of the horses and mules that were shod with metal horseshoes, as well as those of unshod burros. Now, in this rainstorm, the sections of bare rock had only a shiny half-inch-thick sheet of water washing over them. There were no more tracks, there was no more trail. I had to try to find the trail again on the other side of each of these escarpments, and they were numerous.

Several times, I lost the trail for only a few moments, and then once or twice for a minute or two. I started thinking about how far

I was from home. I would guess I had spent the night at an elevation of about 4,500 or 5,000 feet. Our house was at 7,200 feet, so I estimated that I had one and a half to two hours of hiking ahead of me when I started that morning. And that would've been true in dry weather, when I would have easily been able to follow the trail.

It was one thing to follow a trail in dry weather, but quite another in rain and snow with the mountains obstructed by clouds

I was wearing a long-sleeved shirt and a nylon vest. I had not taken a jacket on purpose. The weather had been gorgeous, actually quite warm at the river and in Uruachic at the low elevations. Now I wished I just had at least a plastic poncho or a big trash bag to use as a makeshift one. But I had neither. It was probably fifty degrees when I started walking that morning, but both the rise in the altitude and the changes in the storm were combining to push the temperature lower—much lower. Within an hour of starting, I was soaked to the skin. Now, two hours later, I was starting to get hypothermic.

Twice I lost the trail in the washout conditions. The first time, it seemed the trail just took a short dip, but when I kept descending for four hundred or five hundred more yards, I realized it was a trail to someone's ranch in a side canyon. The visibility was terrible. I was literally surrounded by blowing clouds. I couldn't see more than fifty or sixty yards in any direction, and the rain was steady. I backtracked, picked up what I hoped was the main trail, and kept ascending. This was good—I was back on track.

About forty-five minutes later, I came out on a ridge. I figured I should have been coming to El Manzano by now, and the first house I would see at the bottom of the valley would be Mauro's. From there, it was only five or six minutes to our house. Instead, I came upon a little ranch that I was only vaguely familiar with. It took me a long moment, looking at it from this direction, to realize where I was. I was too high up and just to the west of the Red Rock! The main trail I wanted would have been heading generally south and a little east. This one had curved around almost due east and risen 400 or 500 feet above the El Manzano valley. With the lack of visibility, I couldn't even tell the direction I was heading, and I certainly couldn't see any of the ridges through the clouds, some of which were only a quarter of a mile away.

I was really unhappy with myself. How could I have gotten so far off the main trail? No, it was understandable. I was hiking up in the clouds. I just had to backtrack again. It wasn't the end of the world. At least I knew where I was now. It would be okay in a few minutes. I told myself this over and over.

I also started praying fervently. "Please, Lord, help me stay on the trail. I can't keep wasting this much time. I'm getting really cold!"

I had to hike at least twenty minutes back down to find the main trail again. Ugh! Forty minutes of wasted time. The trip was no longer a simple physical exercise. It had become a psychological challenge too. Me versus the weather, the passing of time helping mother nature—not me.

The temperature now was close to freezing, and the rain had given way to snow flurries. I had tried to keep my blanket dry in case I needed it again, and now I needed it. I tried to untie the two short loops of rope holding it in a roll, but my fingers were too numb. I fished in my pocket and got out my pocket knife. I managed to get the blade out and locked, cut off the two pieces of rope, and draped the wet blanket over my shoulders. That felt better right away. But my fingers were too cold, and I couldn't depress the blade lock to close the knife back up, so I just dropped it as it was back in my bag and kept walking.

Being back on the main trail, I got optimistic again. The direction and incline felt right. After about a half hour, there was a minute when the clouds got blown away, and I saw that I was, in fact, on the edge of the canyon that led up to El Manzano. Now it was snowing steadily, and by the time I got to El Manzano, there were two inches of snow on the ground. I passed Mauro's house. About 200 yards past it was the back trail up to our house. It was pretty steep and only one-third of the distance compared to staying on the road and going up by way of our old "driveway."

I only considered it for a moment. If I fell on that shortcut, I could get hurt, and I didn't know if I could get back up. My hands had been numb for hours. My feet were numb. My mind was almost numb. But I knew the road was a safe bet, so I went up it, one step at a time, across the creek and up to our house.

Ticker couldn't believe it when I walked in. She had been really worried. I had told her I'd be back the night before, and I always managed to do what I told her I would do. I said I was freezing cold and could she please make me a cup of hot chocolate. She had one ready for me in just a couple of minutes. Meanwhile, I took off the wet blanket and just put a warm dry one over my wet shoulders. I stood in front of the fireplace which was burning nicely. She handed me the mug of hot chocolate, but I couldn't grip the handle. She had to give me sips for four or five minutes until I could get my frozen fingers to work again and hold the cup. She started telling me about her night and morning.

The night before, as the storm came through, the wind had started blowing hard. She could see the trees around the house swaying wildly before it got dark. Then, sometime in the night, with the wind howling, there was a loud boom! She got the boys up out of bed and moved all three of them downstairs, fearing something bad was going to happen with the roof. She felt that the big support beams on the first floor would give them the best protection. She took the old bench seat from our van, which served as a couch in my study, for their bed. They would camp out there. The storm, however, kept her awake at least half of the night.

At eight o'clock in the morning, she had gotten on the radio for the daily call-in to the Chihuahua City office. She said that the reception was really poor but that when it was her turn to talk, she was able to communicate that I hadn't made it back on schedule the day before. Peter Theissen in Chihuahua assured her that everything would be okay, but at least she had made her report. She signed off, realizing there was nothing else she could do about the situation for the time being.

I looked at the clock and realized that my hike that morning, which should have taken me one and a half to two hours, had taken me four and a half hours! I told Ticker how, once I knew I was getting close to the El Manzano valley, I had just put one foot in front of the other. Praise the Lord! Now I was home!

I gave her the short version of the weekend events while I warmed up by the fire. Then I knew I had to look around the house and property. I changed into dry clothes as soon as I could use my fingers again. I put on dry boots—ah, what a luxury!—and went outside. Already my tracks in the snow were covered over. There were almost four inches of snow on the ground, and before the day was over, there would be six inches of beautiful fluffy new snow on our ranchito.

The first thing I found outside was that our two-way radio antenna had torn loose from the sixty-foot-tall pine tree that it was attached to and was lying on the ground, covered in snow. It was absolutely amazing that Ticker had even been able to communicate with Chihuahua that morning. I found a pole and got the end of the antenna re-rigged so it would work for the next morning's radio check-in. Then I decided I had better get to work on the pine tree that was in our backyard.

Ticker's description of how that tree had been bending and bowing in the wind the night before had me worried. It definitely had the potential to come crashing down on the house, especially if the wind shifted and came a little more out of the south than normal. I'd seen enough storms since we lived out there to know that lots of things were possible. About an hour after getting home, with hot chocolate and some good strong, black coffee in me, I got out the chain saw, got out my climbing spurs, put on a work jacket and gloves, and proceeded to trim that pine tree. I cut about half the branches off it so it wouldn't catch so much wind and perhaps blow over. After an hour or so, I was satisfied. Now, if the storm picked up again, that was one serious threat I wouldn't have to worry about.

Next, I went up into the attic to inspect the house itself. Ticker had described a loud thud or boom and then the sound of the tin roof flapping like it wanted to come off. What I found startled the heck out of me.

The southwest corner of the house, which had the most direct exposure to these storms that blew in from the Gulf of California, had taken the brunt of the wind. Several of the rafters had been lifted up from the top of the wall and slammed back down. About two inches of the six-inch long spikes that held the rafters down were now sticking up with the heads just underneath the metal roofing. It was impossible to nail them back down without removing the tin roof first, so I wired each rafter to the top of the wall with some super-heavy gauge wire that I had. Then I knew I needed to add weight to the wall itself. It was a three-foot high, two-by-four stud-framed wall that sat on top of the adobe walls of the first floor.

I still had a few dozen of the broken adobe bricks that had been intended for building the second floor but which had too much sand and not enough clay in them. Now they were going to serve me well. I carried them upstairs and placed them on edge in between the studs. I then nailed boards up to hold them in place and, in this way, added several hundred pounds of dead weight to keep the roof from blowing off.

We had no visitors that day, which was normally the case when there was a storm like that. No one wanted to go outside on the cold, snowy, slippery trails. It wasn't until a few days later that I found out how the others from El Manzano had fared on their return trip. They had all been miserably cold, and those on horseback had actually been the coldest. They had all been unprepared for the cold weather, too, so I didn't feel like an amateur after all. They, however, had not lost the trail numerous times like I had. We were all nice and warm now, so we ended up having a good time swapping stories about the whole thing!

11.5 The Miracle Child

Barbara and Teodulo were such an amazing example of sincere Christians who grew in the Lord consistently. They were indeed "the good fertile ground" that the Lord Himself spoke about in the parable of the sower and the seed. Their faith in Him grew by the week and through the months and into the second year. But there was one thing they really wanted God to grant to them—they did not have a child of their own. That is a really big thing for most people in Mexico. They want children to whom they can pass on the fruits of their hard work, their homes, and ranches when they get older. They had talked to us about that a few times, their desire to have children.

Ticker had shared with Barbara the story of Abraham and Sarah, and that Sarah had a child in her old age. I remember Barbara being in amazement of that story, and perhaps, like Sarah, laughing about it. Did Barbara laugh because it seemed so impossible? God had promised a child to Sarah, but Barbara had no such promise. So we made it a point of prayer to ask God to give them a child if He so pleased. As women will do, Ticker and Barbara prayed about it a lot more often than we men were even aware of.

Then, one day in the spring of 1986, while we were still in Chicago on furlough, Barbara realized that she had become pregnant! When we found out, we were thrilled for her. That December, Barbara delivered a healthy baby boy. After fifteen years of marriage and two years of praying for a child, God gave them the desire of their hearts!

There's a sad reality, however, in places like the mountains of Mexico where there isn't good health care, which is the high infant mortality rate. Because of it, parents often don't name their children until they reach several months or even a year of age. If the infant or young child should die, they don't want to remember it by the name they had given it. So in addition to praising the Lord for their young son, we also asked the Lord to help him to grow up and be strong and healthy. They named him Hugo, but Barbara would forever after refer to him as "our miracle." Hugo did, in fact, stay healthy and grow into a fine young man. He is a huge blessing to his parents to this day.

11.6 "Those who will believe on You..."

Speaking to his Father, Jesus said, "As you sent me into the world, I also have sent them into the world... I do not pray for these alone, but also for those who will believe in me through their word... That they also may be one in us, that the world may believe that you sent me." (John 17:18–21)

Bible study at Al's house

It's January 25, 1987, and though it's cold and windy, it beats the blizzardy weather we hear they're having up north in the States. As we walk the last steep fifty yards to Teodulo's house, I have a chance for a silent prayer: "Please, God, use the Bible study to really bring understanding to each one who will be here. And help many of them to come tonight. They need You so very much." The door opens, light spilling out, and we enter, exchanging greetings and shaking hands all the way around.

HE WHO HAS BEGUN A GOOD WORK

Ladies from our Bible studies, with Ticker in the back

In our chronological teaching of the Bible, we're just finishing the life of Christ. How my heart has been deeply stirred as my partner and I teach on Christ's last days, then hours, of life; of His condemnation by cruel mouths and death by cruel hands. The stinging seriousness of sin has again been etched on my own mind. *Lord, has it been so with these people too?* I wonder.

These faces—is that conviction of sin I see in Valentin's eyes? The study is over now. Teodulo, a believer, says that his nephew, Ramon, is perhaps ready to accept Christ. Sobs begin to break loose from the ten-year-old boy in the corner. He and I go into the next room where we can talk. How that young boy's heart has been touched by the wonderful prospect of going to heaven, yet cut to the core realizing he's a sinner and won't be allowed to go. Before we emerge from the next room, though, Ramon has had his entry guaranteed by forgiveness through Christ. Right away, he meekly tells us something else on his mind: that his mother and dad might accept Christ too.

I look again at Valentin—there is no doubt that God's been working in that man's heart. For a couple of years, we've shared the Gospel with him. For months, he's been listening more attentively, and for weeks now, there's been a real seriousness on his face, in his actions.

"Valentin," my partner says, "are you ready to accept Christ tonight?"

That serious brown face hesitates only a moment, then moves as to all our amazement, he nods 'Yes.' Although we begin to share with him several key verses pertaining to salvation and asking those important questions to make no mistake about his understanding, we realize he knows full well that he's making a soul-saving decision to accept Jesus Christ.

A week later, we watch a similar scenario unfold as little Ramon's father, Javier, accepts the Lord. Javier's wife is still unwilling; but little Ramon doesn't sit back in the corner and weep at the close of the Bible studies now.

He just has a whole lot to be happy about.

(I sent the above to our mission's headquarters, and it was published in the September 1987 issue of *Brown Gold* magazine.)

Left to right—Javier, Valentin, myself, Cristobal, Teodulo and Javier's little boy

HE WHO HAS BEGUN A GOOD WORK

Daily Life, Daily Ministry
Fall 1986–March 1987

The following is something that I wrote in February 1987, and it pretty accurately described our lives at the time:

> For several minutes, the sun slices through the pine trees on the ridge before it can make its way over the top and throw its warmth down on our house. A new day is underway in El Manzano.
>
> In the study, Ticker and David read together through his fourth-grade materials and find out that white light is made up of a gorgeous spectrum of different colored lights which, when blended, are somehow made transparent.
>
> In the backyard, a contest has begun anew, though no one has come to watch. This arm-wrestling match is of incredible importance. The two sides face off. At a small table, my Tarahumara language notes stare back at me unflinchingly. I've firmly seated myself across from them in a lawn chair, and we're once again engaged in a battle to see who has greater endurance. This language has been around for thousands of years; my strength to master it had better come from One much stronger than myself.
>
> Dusty and Eric laugh in delight as they've just found the greatest oak tree (that's *rojá* in Tarahumara) in which to build a tree house (that would be *cuchi galila*).
>
> Around the hill and down the road come Lorenza and her children. She brings us a stack of fresh corn tortillas, and in her quiet way, Ticker knows she wants to talk. When Lorenza is gone,

Ticker tells me that she came to say that she really wants to accept Christ as Savior but feels her husband would prefer they make the decision together. When he returns next month from the town where he's working, they will both come to our house to have us explain the Gospel in detail. It's incredible—what an unusual, genuine desire for marital unity!

The incessant hiss of the pressure cooker finally dies down, and Ticker calls us for lunch: a bowl of beans with grated cheese and Mexican picante sauce on top and a tall glass of the sweetest mountain spring water (our water!) I think I've ever tasted.

It's off to Teodulo's house for a couple of hours of *beniá rarámuri ra'ichali*—that means "speaking the Tarahumara language" for you gringos.

The rumble of the boys' Hot Cycle wheels as they fly down the rocky dirt road greets me on my return home.

While filing language material on the computer, the engine of the gasoline wringer washer chugs to a stop for the fourth time in fifteen minutes. "What could be wrong with that thing, anyway?" I mutter as I head outside to start it again.

"C-at, cat. M-at, mat. H-at, hat," says Dusty as he follows along with the cassette tape and Ticker's finger in his reading book.

"Mommy, there's a lady here who wants medicine for her baby."

"Boys, bring in wood for the fireplace."

"Steve, I'll be driving up to the Bible study at 6:30," calls my partner, Al.

"Oops, get a fire started right away in the hot water heater so I can get a shower.

"Mommy, Eric flipped over on his Hot Cycle and cut his head!"

"Steve, the oil lamps are empty."

"Mommy, Anita is here and wants to buy a kilo of sugar."

Reply from the other room: "There's sugar up at the store!"

For the twentieth time, "*Cho orá morámué chiba wécá* (What do you do with so many goats)?"

"Daddy, two men are here to see you."

Finally, at the Bible study, "Tonight we are studying Mark chapter 16."

To myself: *Isn't it great to see Petra and China come again tonight as well as Teodulo, Barbara, Valentin, Lorenza, Trini, Eriberto, Ramon, and Javier?*

The clearest moon throws a silver light through the clouds as we walk home, leaving the flashlight off and enjoying the night sky. It's been another full day *Oh, Lord, this is the toughest way of life I could ever love.* With one last look at the lightly lit pine slopes, we head indoors to a cup of coffee, a good book, and hopefully a restful night's sleep.

Thus shall you be filled at my table, says the Lord God. And I will set my glory among the heathen, and all the heathen will see... my hand that I have laid upon them. (Ezekiel 39:20–21)

STEVEN REAL

Acts Chapter? More Thoughts from February 1987

Of the book of the Acts of the Apostles, it has been said that the title could have been "The Acts of the Holy Spirit." It is here that the work of the indwelling Holy Spirit is begun, and soon, His ministry is fanning the sparks of a few believers into the flames of churches all over the Middle East, southern Europe, and north Africa.

The story of God's work continues still. Not too many years ago and from different parts of the United States, several "sent ones" embarked for the bypassed, inaccessible regions of Mexico where hundreds of thousands of tribal people live, still unexposed to God's salvation plan. A few established their base of operations; the others were enabled to penetrate the mountains and canyons to take Christ's offer of eternal life to the people there. But just as God guided Peter, Philip, and the other early Christians to places such as Gaza and Joppa, these modern missionaries were just as assuredly being led too. The "Acts of the Holy Spirit" is still being written today.

Acts chapter 10 begins, "There was a certain man in Caesarea called Cornelius, a centurion of the band called the Italian band, (and although unsaved) a devout man and one that feared God."

Our twentieth century chapter might open this way: "There was a certain man in El Manzano called Teodulo, a leader of the Tarahumara people, (and although untaught from the Bible) a devout man and one who was ready to fear God."

It was to this man, his wife, and community that a couple of those missionaries were led. The very ones who just a few years before had been quite lost themselves now sat with these Tarahumara and mestizo people telling them the most exciting story they were ever to hear. Into the crack of open minds fell the golden seed of the Gospel. The glimmer of God's words revealed how wonderful He really was. The honesty with which He detailed their hopeless plight as sinners washed away those false hopes which didn't seem to comfort anyway; like warm, soft earth, their hearts closed over the seed that they now knew held real life. Genuine understanding faith had replaced the hopeful, but helpless, seeking of their hearts. It was a real live twentieth-century miracle! Just as Cornelius, Teodulo and his relatives have now "received the Holy Spirit just as we have" (Acts 10:47).

Several more of Teodulo's extended family came to accept the Lord in the next few years. Suzena, right, was one of the first children to accept Christ while we were there.

The Lord Keeps Building His Church

In a two-week time period in January and February of 1987, four more of our Tarahumara neighbors came to know the Lord. God was building His church amongst the Tarahumara! Al and I realized the need to teach the younger believers the fundamentals of the faith separately from those who'd been saved for over two years by now, so we divided the responsibilities between us. We were now having a total of three Bible studies each week. All of these believers were joyful in the Lord and growing together, encouraging each other just as we Christians are meant to do.

At the same time, the Clarks were getting more concerned about Ticker's depression. It was valuable to have their objective point of view. Polly was a helpful, sensitive Christian woman and had tried in many ways to talk with Ticker and be a source of encouragement. She wasn't making any progress, however, so she and Al shared their thoughts with our field committee. In February, our field chairman, Paul, made a trip out to talk with Ticker and me. He had been in consultation with the other members of the committee, and after a lot of prayer, they felt that we needed to find some medical care for Ticker in the States. It was true, the liquid hormone therapy that she had been taking for five months by this time was not helping her. She had once again become just as depressed as she was two years previously before we had gone on furlough.

Our coworkers, Larry and Karen Loper, had been dealing with issues that they believed were hormone related with their younger daughter who was in her late teens. Through some financial supporters, they had found out about a gynecologist in Chattanooga, Tennessee, and had moved there temporarily to try to get help for her. This gynecologist was doing extensive research through the University of Tennessee on female hormone therapies and had published the results of some of his work. It seemed really promising, and the Lopers had shared this news with us and the field committee. They were optimistic that this could be a source of help for Ticker.

The decision was already made for us. We would pack up our things and go on a medical furlough, not anticipating to return until Ticker was very definitely better.

Chapter 12

Medical Furlough

Chattanooga, Tennessee

I tried to imagine what I would do in Chattanooga, Tennessee. It didn't seem to me that the Lord was telling us to leave our ministry in El Manzano, so I packed up my backlog of materials in the Tarahumara language, field notes to continue working on the grammar and English-Spanish-Tarahumara dictionary and Bible study terminology that I wanted to expand upon for teaching in Spanish. I would make use of the time for personal study regarding discipleship and cross-cultural church planting principles. This could be a good time by staying focused on all of those things while not having to do the time-consuming work involved in simply living in the tribal area. The Wycliffe Bible translators, as well as other very successful groups of missionaries, had been doing this sometimes remote-type ministry for decades. I prayed that I would be able to stay disciplined and motivated and make good progress while we were away from El Manzano.

God blessed us in so many ways as we arrived in a city where we knew no one except Larry and Karen Loper. We lived with them for a couple of weeks in the house where they were housesitting but immediately started looking for something available that we could afford.

The Lord answered our prayers through a local church member who allowed us to rent a house on a month-to-month basis.

We had called ahead from El Paso to schedule an appointment with the gynecologist. From Chattanooga, it was a two-hour drive to his office. He did an initial evaluation with Ticker and started her on a certain regimen of progesterone and estrogen, designing different dosages for different times during the month.

After two months, he modified the dosages since there didn't seem to be any change in Ticker's system or depression. He had told us at the beginning this would be an approximately six months process to fine-tune a tailored regimen of hormone supplements. At the end of five months, however, he had already made some drastic changes, but absolutely nothing was changing with Ticker's moods and depression. At our last appointment with him, he looked at the extensive daily logs Ticker had filled out every day for five months and said, "I'll be honest with you. I don't think I can be of help to you with these treatments. I think the best course of action for you would be to go to your home area in Chicago and find a doctor up there."

We walked out to the truck and sat down. Ticker was both discouraged and angry. She let her anger rage for a minute or two, and then we both sat there somewhat in shock and disbelief. "Okay, God. What do we do next?" was our prayer. We were both discouraged that this had not turned out to be the right therapy for her, but we had to keep moving on. We drove back to the house in Chattanooga, planning in our minds how to get settled in Des Plaines, Illinois, once again.

We had really been blessed in Chattanooga during those five months. A warm and friendly church had welcomed us, and we enjoyed and appreciated so much their fellowship and the pastor's teaching. For the first time in our lives, we lived in a neighborhood with that warm Southern hospitality that most people only get to read about or see in movies. It seemed that almost any evening, right after folks had gotten home from work and had eaten their dinner—er, supper—they would sit out on their front porches and

HE WHO HAS BEGUN A GOOD WORK

talk, visiting with neighbors from next door or across the street, perhaps taking a stroll around the block in the peaceful evening air.

We got all three of the boys enrolled on baseball teams and had so many good days and evenings going to their practices and games. Eric played T-ball, which I never even knew existed until then. Dusty was on a team that did slow pitch, and I never saw a kid swing a bat as fast and hard as he did. The humorous problem was he oftentimes closed his eyes when the ball was halfway to the home plate, so he missed a lot of pitches. But when he connected, his hits were some of the best of any kid on the team! Dave was on a really good team and played quite well. It was his first time in organized sports, and it was a great beginning with supportive coaches and an all-American culture of work ethics. With good memories yet with heavy hearts, we packed our things again and headed north. "Oh Lord, You alone are our hope. Now what?"

In Chicago (Des Plaines, Actually)

I didn't keep much of a written record of our time in Chicago during that medical furlough. I had to work full-time to support us financially. Our supporters continued with most of their monthly giving, but it was perhaps half of what we needed to live on there. One good thing about the timing was that we were able to get up to Chicago in time to get the boys enrolled in school. We weren't happy about the fact that they would be in the public schools since that world was much less godly than the way we had been raising them. Therefore, we enrolled them in Immanuel Lutheran school for the 1987–1988 school year. We hoped that this would be a good decision. Ticker had more than enough on her plate after having home schooled all of them, including Dave, for the past year.

STEVEN REAL

Counseling and Spiritual Warfare

The gynecologist in Tennessee had told us rather bluntly that he believed Ticker's depression issues were not due to a hormone deficiency but rather were psychological. The word *psychological*, of course, can encompass a lot of things. In the life of a Christian, this is especially true due to the fact that we have a battle going on in our minds between our old human nature and our new spiritual nature. The influences of the world around us are driven in innumerable ways by what different writers of the Scriptures call "principalities and powers," "rulers of the darkness of this age," "spiritual hosts of wickedness," "the fiery darts of the wicked one," etc.

The Apostle Peter is quite clear that there is an actual being, Satan/ "the devil," who is our adversary. When Peter walked with the Lord, Jesus explained Satan's existence and nature numerous times. Right before Jesus went to the cross, in fact, He told Peter that "Satan has asked for you, that he may sift you like wheat. But I have prayed for you, that your faith should not fail; and when you have returned to Me strengthen your brethren" (Luke 22:32). Imagine what it would be like to be sifted like wheat: shaken vigorously until the husk is removed, perhaps like what happened to Job when he was stricken with horrible trials and physical sores all over his body.

Satan's methodology is to fight any servant of the Lord in order to discourage them so that they will no longer be effective. Whatever the means he might use, Satan's ultimate goal is to make any Christian that he possibly can (1) question God's goodness and ultimate power in this universe and (2) stop glorifying God by our words and actions and become powerless. This is a rather simplistic and short synopsis, and it is not my purpose here to do justice to the subject of spiritual warfare involving Satan and his hosts of wickedness. However, what the Lord makes abundantly clear to us throughout the Scriptures is that the battle for hearts and souls involves our minds; and our minds are sometimes more fragile than we have any idea.

The Apostle Paul tells us to "be transformed by the renewing of your mind" (Romans 12:2), "be renewed in the spirit of your mind" (Ephesians 4:23), not to be "shaken in mind or troubled" (2 Thess. 2:2), and to rely on this amazing truth: "God has not given us a spirit of fear, but of power and of love and of a sound mind" (2 Timothy 1:7).

After the great disappointment of hearing that gynecologist's words that he could not do anything medically, that Ticker's problem was "psychological," I knew that I needed to start trying to learn something about that whole realm of science. Within a couple of days of us arriving back in Des Plaines and moving into Ticker's parents' house temporarily, I went to the local library and checked out four or five books on psychology. I took them out to a local park and spread them out on a table. One or two of them were big and thick, but all of them contained something I needed to try to understand, so with a bottle of water and four hours of free time, I started reading.

What I gleaned over the next week was that psychology—the study of the human mind—was probably the most misunderstood science in all of the natural realm. In fact, one of the books that I chose had to do with the progression of psychological theories for the past hundred years or so. It was quite revealing in that only a few psychologists drove 95 percent of the theories and focus of studies for the entire genre. Not all, but most of their foremost theories were disproven or mocked or abandoned within a couple of decades by their peers. The minds and lives of those "leaders" were sometimes discussed in these volumes that I read and demonstrated to be twisted or immoral in nature, which explained many of the abject failures of their "therapies." Reading about the field of psychology was like having a vantage point from hundreds of feet above a massive maze in a cornfield where blind people were calling out clues to other blind people on how to find their way out.

After a month's foray into trying to expand my understanding of what could be going on with Ticker's depression, I knew I had to go back to the only absolutely dependable source of science that I could think of: God Himself.

STEVEN REAL

The Answer to Our Prayers!

I'm pretty sure it was during our one-year furlough in 1985 through 1986 that we had watched a video series on husband-and-wife relationships by Dr. James Dobson, founder of Focus on the Family Ministries. At one point in that series, he said essentially the following: "Let me be clear about something. Although my life and ministry revolve around counseling, I am very aware of the fact that I cannot be the counselor to my own wife. She would need a third-party person to do that."

Ticker had given me all the signals over the past few years that said the same thing—she did not want to confide in me or look to me for wisdom on how to handle her depression, so I had backed off. I didn't have that "place of prayer" on the little hill next to our house in El Manzano anymore, but I certainly did get back to the business of praying to God that He would bring someone into our lives who could help her be healed and become well.

I believe it was one of the ladies in our church in Des Plaines who directed Ticker to a pastor who apparently was a really good counselor. His name was Howard Westlund of the West Chicago Bible Church in West Chicago, Illinois, a suburb thirty-five or forty minutes south of us. Ticker went down there for sessions with him about every other week for several months. I could see that she was making good progress just by her demeanor and the fact that she wasn't having to spend days and days in bed in depression. I would ask her how the session went, and her response was generally, "Good." No details would follow, so I learned to not ask any more questions and trust the Lord for the results. Month after month, things seemed to get better, so we had to address the inevitable question: Were we ready to go back to Mexico? We had now been back in the States on this medical furlough for a year and three months.

Ticker and I had a good long sit-down conversation. She really seemed to be like her old self from a few years back—joyful, relaxed in the sense of not feeling regular stress, and was happy to plan the next step in our lives.

"I really do feel ready to go back to Mexico," she said. "I think after furlough, I was optimistic, but I feel so much better this time. I don't know if I'm ready to go back out to the tribe, but I do believe God wants us in Mexico."

"Are you really sure?" I asked. "I really, really want to be sure that you're okay," I said.

She smiled and said, "I'm ready."

I felt encouraged, but I knew not to ask too many questions. I was only able to visit with Pastor Westlund once or twice and found him to be a kind and insightful man. I knew that our field leadership wanted to have definitive feedback from someone who was a third party regarding whether or not we were ready to go back to our ministry in Mexico. I asked Pastor Westlund to write a letter to Marsh Milliken who was serving as acting field chairman while Paul was on furlough. The following is the majority of that letter:

August 3, 1988

> Dorothy... Came to me with a record of her struggle both in Mexico and in this time here in her home area. Very early in my counseling with her we dealt with her intense anger toward Steve and the cause of it. I pointed out to her that this anger was part of her plan to control not only their life and relationship but also to control her own life rather than experience the control of the Holy Spirit.
>
> In these weeks, she has come/begun to understand and experience the Exchanged Life as taught by Maj. W. Ian Thomas and to discover the practical control of the Holy Spirit and the fruit of the Spirit in daily practice.
>
> I believe that Dorothy has come a long way. She is able to put behind her many of the

thoughts that have crippled her in the past. She is also learning to live by the principle of thanksgiving that allows God to use the hard experiences of life as the building blocks of Christian character.

I have spent some time with Steve and helped him to see more clearly what his role is and where the strength for his life has its source. I have not spent as much time with him as I would like to have.

The Reals should be useful servants with New Tribes. Weakness out of past problems can lead to repeat of all problems but I believe that they go well armed with instruction, experience and purpose. Further, should they have a future problem, I would expect that they would call me. My prayer is that over time they will be a help to others who face troubles like theirs.

Please feel free to contact me with any questions that you have. I have been the senior pastor of the West Chicago Bible Church for nineteen years. Fourteen of those years I was also the Pastoral Consultant of the Evangelical Child and Family Agency of Wheaton, Illinois. I am a member of the board of TEAM.

In the name of Him who taught us to love,
Howard Westlund

Pastor Westlund sent this letter to us, which was a copy of his letter to Marsh, so we would know he had, in fact, written to Marsh. However, it was returned to the pastor and finally got re-routed to us sometime in September with a personal note to Ticker on the back. I didn't even see it until many years later when I discovered it amongst some miscellaneous letters from our last year in Mexico. Obviously I was quite shocked with the description of Ticker's "intense anger toward Steve" as well as the rest of that paragraph regarding "to control her own life rather than experience the control of the Holy Spirit." So this was what had been going on for the past seven years rather than "the baby blues" after Eric was born, a hormone deficiency, and other factors that we could have dealt with between us!

As we all know, as Christians, our humble and healthy relationship with the Lord on a daily, even hourly or moment-by-moment basis, is absolutely fundamental to us being healthy and happy people. That doesn't mean that we never have struggles, of course. But it does mean that we get through the struggles and busyness and craziness and misunderstandings, etc. of life only by staying connected to Him. This has to be the foundation for life, just as Jesus said that He Himself is the solid rock on which we build our house. That was not meant to be a cute little picture cliché; it was meant to be a description of how we build our lives, one brick and room at a time. He is the Vine, and we are the branches. Without the nourishing sap of His strength, we will dry up and die. How had Ticker let her "intense anger" squeeze out the life-giving love and nourishment of the Holy Spirit for all those years?

But I still had not seen this letter in August when we headed back to Mexico again.

I will simply include here part of what we wrote in the June/July 1988 newsletter to our supporters:

> The process of understanding and dealing with one particular spiritual dilemma began for Ticker while we were on furlough 2 ½ years ago. Our Bible school education and missionary training have helped us immeasurably to know and follow the Lord, yet we, like you, have not experienced the annihilation of our old natures. For quite some time one hidden and tenacious area of that old nature has continued to plague Ticker's heart, defying our attempts at even identifying the true root problem. We can see God's gracious hand in bringing us back to the Chicago area in the tremendous help we found in a pas-

tor here who is especially gifted in counseling. He has helped us both to trust Christ as our very fountain of spiritual life daily. Ticker and I have found an incredible weight lifted from us. God has truly been transforming our outlook, relieving us of the oppressions of self-doubt and condemnation.

We had been corresponding with our field committee members in Mexico, and it was their opinion that we needed to spend a year of time in a ministry in Chihuahua City for them to be confident that we were ready to resume our life and ministry in the tribe. They wanted to see for themselves that Ticker was free of the depression that had been so debilitating. It was a wise and very reasonable decision, in my opinion. My heart's desire was to return to the ministry in El Manzano, but I knew that in the long run, God's will was all that really mattered. He was continuing to do great things in our lives as well as in El Manzano. I needed to be open to His guidance, one step at a time.

With renewed optimism and the healing power of the godly counseling of Pastor Westlund, we once again said goodbye to family and friends, loaded up our truck, and headed south to Mexico.

Chapter 13

Ministry in Chihuahua
(August 1988–August 1989)

13.1 Back to Chihuahua—August 1988

What I saw was my wife who was very happy and upbeat. She wrote a really positive and cheerful letter to her family on October 3, describing our trip back to Mexico where we did a couple of fun things along the way, found a really nice house to rent in Chihuahua City (this was never an easy thing to do), and of how the boys were enjoying not only school with their old friends but also having a blast playing with the neighborhood kids and getting in all kinds of fun "boy" situations. She described briefly my new job of teaching students the Spanish language and of how she was teaching a kindergarten class with one of her coworker moms.

Then she wrote:

> We're so glad to be here and we feel so at home. I'm glad that we are in Chihuahua City for now, but we all hope and pray that we can return to the mountains in a couple of years. By the way, we visited out in El Manzano for three

days. We had a wonderful time. We stayed with our Indian friends, as our house was taken over by critters. We hope to get out there again soon. We miss it so much. I love you all!

Ticker

Our field committee wanted us to be close by, right in Chihuahua City, where they could see for themselves that Ticker was much improved before they would let us go back to El Manzano to our tribal ministry. They also had a need for someone to do two things: (1) teach Spanish, Mexican culture and a tribal orientation course to the four families who were newly arrived in Chihuahua; and (2) revamp the seventy-lesson situational Spanish language learning course that we had been using for years. The Spanish language course had been created using South American Spanish, and there were a lot of vocabulary and idiom differences in Mexican Spanish, all of which had to be changed and added each year with each new missionary or missionary couple that came to the field. In addition, there were twelve families who were in various latter stages of their training or in working on getting their financial support in the States who would be arriving in Mexico in the next two years, so the revamping of the Spanish course needed to be done sooner rather than later.

"Da Bears" of Chihuahua

As Ticker wrote in her letter to her family, things started off really well for us in Chihuahua City. Dave, now twelve years old, had wanted to get into playing football, and the opportunity presented itself with a Mexican Pop Warner team. The name of the team he ended up on? Los Osos—The Bears! How crazy was that? His coach wasn't in any way physically similar to Mike Ditka, the legendary Chicago Bears coach. He was only about five feet tall, but he was a fireball, very much like a young version of Mike Ditka, I would imagine. I went to every one of Dave's games, and he was one tough player. They didn't have enough good players for both offense and defense, so some of the better players had to play both. Dave was one of those.

There was one particular game where his coach had him line up against a kid that was eight or nine inches taller than Dave and probably forty pounds heavier. Dave was playing offensive line, and this other kid was supposed to rush his quarterback. The coach told Dave, "Hit him hard, right above the knees! Don't let him back you up. You'll see—he'll be afraid of you after a while!"

Dave turned and looked at me, and in confirmation, I called back, "Yes! Do it!" I pointed to that spot right above the knees where his coach had told him to hit the kid to show I agreed. Dave had been getting tired out, but he got a second wind. Sure enough, within fifteen minutes, that big kid was getting worn down. For the whole second half, Dave controlled him!

I have an article from the Chihuahua newspaper dated November 28, 1988, with a great picture of Dave's entire team. The headline is "Bears Devour the Vikings 80–0 and Continue as Champions of the American Football Kids League." The article goes on:

> Dominating by a 'scandalous' final score of 80- 0 over the Vikings… The powerful team "the Bears" got their sixth victory in a row in the regular season…in the Kids Intermediate League. The team is decisively led by the experienced and enthusiastic coach Daniel "Muñeca (The Doll)" Garcia who accomplished an extraordinary victory which demonstrated their perfectly balanced team, not demonstrating a single flaw in their execution.

It's pretty funny to look at the team picture where Coach Garcia, on the far left, is standing up and is an inch or two shorter than some of his players who are all ages eleven to thirteen! I know it was the most fun that Dave had in a long time, and I enjoyed it quite a lot too.

> **Who can understand his errors? Cleanse me from secret faults. Keep back your servant also from presumptuous sins. Let them not have dominion over me... Let the words of my mouth, and the meditation of my heart be acceptable in your sight, O Lord, my strength and my redeemer. (Psalm 19:12—14)**

With the above verses and others like them in our minds, Ticker and I got into our new lives and ministries in Chihuahua City. I had a variety of new missionaries to teach each week, splitting the responsibilities with some of our other experienced missionaries. To do the revamping of the Spanish language course which had been developed in Bolivia thirty years earlier, I needed the help of my two Mexican coworkers—Ruben Cañes Reyes and Javier Ibarra. I started with lesson number one and identified dialogues and vocabulary that needed to be changed. When we were happy with the changes, Javier, who had excellent diction and very clear pronunciation, did the audio recordings for the revised lessons. We did this for all seventy lessons.

It was actually a bit of an honor for me to be in charge of this project. I enjoyed the opportunity to become even more fluent in Spanish. I got back into reading newspapers and books, growing more knowledgeable in terminology regarding food, politics, the arts, international affairs, mechanical issues, crime, construction, agriculture, religions of the world, etc. It was a very gratifying learning experience.

You Can Take the Missionary Out of the Tribe, But...

The teaching job I had was important, but my heart was still very much out in the mountains with the tribal people. After a few months of being settled into my responsibilities in Chihuahua, I was just waiting for the chance to help out one of the tribal teams. The opportunity came up to do a room addition on Barry and Candy Wingo's house in the Pima tribe. They were going to need to have a lot of lumber carried from a sawmill several miles away to their house in a small community called Maycova. I had our nice tough F-350 crew cab four-wheel drive truck, so I volunteered, and the field committee gave me a week off to help them. We got the majority of the work done that week but, a few weeks later, needed to go back and finish some things.

For this trip, we decided to take Dale Taylor's pickup truck. Dale had just recently bought himself a used Ford F-150 super cab, the kind with the cramped bench seat behind the two nice front seats in the cab. We decided that Barry should get the passenger seat up front since he was about six feet two and would've been incredibly cramped in the back seat. Peter Thiessen was the fourth guy who was going to go with us, so he and I would sit in the rear jump seats.

I had plenty of experience in driving much worse mountain roads than we would be on going to this town of Maycova, and I felt the need to look over Dale's new truck a little bit before we left. Two days before the trip, I went over to his house to check it out. I walked all around it and checked out the tires. They had a fairly decent tread on them, but still, I squatted down to see how heavy-duty they were. On the sidewall is an industry standard rating, and the only really appropriate light truck tires for the kinds of roads and work we did are Load Range D or E. I could not believe it when I saw that two of them were Load Range B! I didn't even know they made fifteen-inch tires that were that light weight in their construction. The other two were Load Range C, the typical passenger car rating, which might be barely passable, but I wouldn't count on it for carrying much weight in the bed and for holding up on bumpy, and sometimes rocky, roads.

"Hey, Dale," I said, "I'm a little concerned about your tires. They are really lightweight as far as their load rating. I'm not sure they'll hold up on the road we'll be on. Those load range B tires look like something someone took off a car just so they could sell the truck."

"Well, the spare is in really good shape," he said. I checked it, and it was also a load range C.

"Do you have a tire repair kit with you?" I asked.

"Yes," he said, and I could tell he was getting a little annoyed with me regarding the tires. "And it's a fairly new one. I'm sure we'll be okay."

"I would really encourage you to get a second spare to take with us. I have some serious doubts about these tires, and it can't hurt since we're not carrying much of anything else in the back. Our tools don't take up that much room," I said.

On the morning we left, I was really happy to see there was a second spare tire in the back of the truck. I had grabbed my electric air pump from my truck, which operated off a cigarette lighter jack. The trip out was not too eventful. The road, after three hours of pavement, was a pretty good wide gravel road. It was actually the longest stretch of good gravel road I'd seen so far in Mexico. In places, we had to slow down to fifteen or twenty miles an hour where water runoff had created grooves in the road, and occasionally, there were a few rocks the size of tennis balls, but that was nothing.

We were almost an hour from Barry's house when we got a flat tire, which we changed easily enough. It was a ten- or twelve-hour trip from Chihuahua City, so we got in in the evening just as it was becoming dusk. When we got out of the truck, I walked around and looked at the tires again. One was half flat. We had barely made it into town.

Over the next few days that we were there, Dale hauled a couple of loads of lumber from the sawmill a few miles away and got two more flats. We repaired those flats also, but his tire repair kit consisted of one little tube of glue and three or four plugs. We had now used all the glue fixing those tires.

The day before we left town to head home, I said we really needed to look for some more glue. There was only one small store in town that sold groceries, so we went in and asked if they had any glue. The proprietor pulled a one-quart can of contact cement down from the shelf and said that he sold the glue "by the job."

"How much do you need?" he asked. I guess he would sell a couple of tablespoons at a time. Wow, just when I thought I had seen everything!

"We'll take the rest of the can," I told him. "How much?"

He didn't want to sell the rest of the can, so I said to my companions in English, "If he wants $20 US for that half can, it will be worth it." They looked at me real funny but didn't argue, and the fellow ended up selling it to us.

We were barely on the outskirts of town as we started back to Chihuahua when I saw part of an inner tube laying on the shoulder of the road.

"Stop!" I called out to Dale.

"What's up?" he called back to me as he slowed down and stopped.

"There's a piece of a truck tire inner tube right back there on the shoulder. Back up, and let's get it because I think we're going to need it," I said. We were driving on two tires with plugs in them and had two more tires in the back that had been repaired and were full of air, but were questionable.

Thankfully, now the guys were not quite so quick to think I was being nutty. Barry got out of the truck and got the piece of inner tube, which was about a foot and a half long and ten inches wide. Thankfully it was in good shape, not rotted by the sun or anything. He threw it in the back of the truck, and off we went again. God takes care of us in some of the craziest ways. Some truck driver lost that piece of inner tube out of the back of his truck. It fell on the shoulder on my side of the road, and I happened to spot it and immediately knew it was going to "save our bacon."

Within fifteen minutes, Dale could feel a tire going flat and slowed down. When he stopped, he got out on his side to walk around the truck, and Barry got out on the other side. "Yep," said Barry, "it's the rear tire on this side."

By now, everyone knew where the tools were, so we got right to work. Someone pulled out the lug nut wrench and started to loosen the lug nuts. Someone else got out the jack and started to jack the truck up, and someone else got out the spare tire that looked like it was in the best shape.

When we were all back in the truck, Dale paused for a minute. "We still have one good spare. Let's hope we get all the way home with it." He was trying to be upbeat, but I had a bad feeling. We weren't even thirty or forty minutes further down the road when I could see Dale looking out his side mirror, trying to see the rear tire on his side. He could feel another tire going flat. Barry followed his lead, rolled down his window, and looked at both tires on his side.

"Looks like the front one over here this time," he said.

Now we had two flat spares. While everybody worked once again with the tools and the jack, I said, "I'm going to pick the tire that looks like it's in the best shape and patch the hole in it. Maybe we haven't been letting the glue dry long enough before we put air in the tire and the weight of the truck back on it."

So I cut some strips from the innertube that we had picked up off the road that were about the same size as what came in the tire repair kit. I plugged the new hole in the tire but we didn't put air in it right away this time, just putting it in the back of the truck.

I didn't have a paper and pen handy, but I had noticed how much dust was on the hood of the truck. "I'm going to start a tally up here, guys," I said. "I have a feeling this is going to be a long trip, and it'll be interesting to see how many flats we end up having." I hoped that being a little lighthearted about it would take away some of the sting of the reality that this was going to be a long day.

Then something else occurred to me as we were rolling down the road a few minutes later. "I think we should start making bets on which tire will be the next to go flat!" I said. I don't think Dale thought that was very funny, but I urged the guys, and we all started making bets anyway. "Whoever gets the most right, the rest of us buy him a nice dinner once we get to Chihuahua City!"

I don't think it was even an hour later that we realized another tire was going flat. Peter and I, in the backseat, would crane our necks to look in the side view mirrors and try to see if it was a rear tire on our side of the truck. Then one of us or the guys in the front would call out "Right rear!" or "Left front!" and Dale would slow

HE WHO HAS BEGUN A GOOD WORK

down quickly so we didn't ruin the tire completely. Before we even came to a stop, the guy who called the flat tire correctly would tell us his score, we would all figure out who was ahead, then get to work changing that tire and patching the other tires that were in the back. Since we only needed three of us to do those three things, then the guy who had guessed correctly didn't have to do any work that time. One time, Dale said, "I think it's the left front."

Barry said, "No, it's the right rear."

When the truck stopped and we got out, we found that they were both right! I put two more hashmarks in the dust on the hood.

The tallies on the hood were adding up, the day turned into evening, and we weren't even halfway home. It was December, and it was getting really cold at night. Thankfully, there wasn't any snow. Still, starting at about eight o'clock that night, each time we would have a flat tire, we did the same routine regarding the tools and jack and patching, but we added one more job: the fourth guy would look for firewood along the side of the road and start building a fire on the shoulder so that we could stay warm. I was the only coffee-holic and had my thermos of coffee with me, which I started sipping in the late afternoon once it had gotten chilly. With the cold night coming on and the campfire to stay warm, I started heating up a half a cup of coffee at a time from my thermos. There were more ways than one to deal with this craziness! Might as well make the most of it.

It was pretty late, about 10:30 or 11:00 p.m., when we were stopped repairing another flat, had a fire going, and were waiting another twenty minutes or so for the glue to dry in the plug when we saw headlights coming down the road toward us. We had hardly seen any other vehicles most of the day and none after it had turned dark. A nice, fancy, lifted four-wheel-drive pickup truck with a lot of chrome on it pulled up in front of us, and the driver didn't turn his lights off when he stopped.

I had a weird feeling about this, so I said to the guys that were standing closest to me, "This doesn't feel quite right. Be careful what you say, and keep an eye on these guys and on our stuff that's in the back of the truck."

The Mexicans got out of their truck and started milling around both sides of our truck. "Don't speak English either," I said quietly. "These guys are young enough they could've worked up in the States, and they'll understand us." There were four of them, all in their mid-twenties to mid-thirties, and they had been drinking.

All of us noticed that they were really nicely dressed with fancy Western boots, nice Western shirts, and cowboy hats. These were no country ranchers heading home after a long trip to town for supplies. My first thought was, *I wouldn't be surprised if these guys are involved in drug trafficking. They seem to have a lot of money for somebody living way out here.*

The driver was obviously the head honcho of this little group. He was Mr. Personality, asking all of us lots of questions and being jovial. But I could see in his eyes something rather cunning. After a minute, he made eye contact with his three buddies, and they all fanned out around our truck, two of them going to the back end where the tailgate was down.

They checked us out pretty well for fifteen or twenty minutes, looking through the windows into the back of Dale's truck, doing everything short of opening the doors of the cab and looking inside. We let Barry do most of the talking since he was going to be living out in their "neighborhood," and he explained that we were all missionaries from Chihuahua City, except him, and he would be living in Maycova. Thankfully, the tension sort of toned down after a little while. They decided they wanted to get back on their way, we didn't get robbed, and of course, we were really relieved when they left.

Eventually, we reached the paved highway, and what a relief that was! We had no more flats the rest of the way and arrived at Chihuahua City at 5:00 a.m., twenty hours after leaving on what should have been a ten-hour trip. Not counting four or five tires that didn't hold air after patching them, and not counting anything before we started on the trip home, what was the total count on the hood of flat tires? An even ten!

Who got the free dinner? We were so tired we just wanted to go home to our own beds, so we pretty much decided in the fog of fatigue, 'Who cares?'

And why did I include this story in an account of a ministry in Mexico? Because so much of ministry is filled with days of "nonspiritual" stuff—or so we think. Our "ministry" that week was to be as helpers to our coworker Barry for a room addition onto his house, and our trip home should have been mundane. Instead, we got to put into practice the character development that God had been perfecting in each of us for years. As we all pitched in to take off the flat tire and get a patched one back on the truck, our teamwork developed even further. Egos and complaining, if there even were any on display before (which I don't think there were), evaporated quickly as we worked like a pit crew at a car race but a lot more slowly, of course, and with patience.

We joked and accepted our new lot in life as tire changers instead of ordained ministers of the gospel. We got dirty and dusty and cleaned up over and over as our ten-hour trip home turned into a "who knows how long this will take" trip. I know I personally thanked the Lord for having such a good group of guys to work with, truly patient Christian friends who powered through with no clashes or ugly attitudes. You don't get that every day even with full-time Christian workers.

I bet that in heaven, we'll look back on a lot of things that happened on earth and wonder why we sweated the small stuff. I know I'm already looking back and thanking the Lord for such good coworkers as Barry, Dale, and Peter. Who knew Load Range B and C tires could cement friendships and develop character?

13.2 Community Development and Politics

With time, and a lot of hours invested, I finally got the situational Spanish course completely modernized with Mexican Spanish. The classes with my students went pretty well, too, but there was still a disappointing attrition rate. The field committee, myself and my coworkers all wondered if the fact that we were living physically so close to the United States was a big reason why such a high percentage of people decided to go home. Would there have been this many people quitting if they had gone to Indonesia or New Guinea or Brazil and had to buy really expensive plane tickets to get home? I think not. Those people might have tried harder to learn the national language, and even the tribal language, for another six months or more before deciding to throw in the towel. So even though we regularly had new single missionaries or couples arriving, we never took anything for granted and continued to "pray to the Lord of the harvest that He would send forth laborers into His harvest."

The fact that the total number of people on our New Tribes team in Mexico, and in particular in Chihuahua City, had grown significantly from about 1984 or 1985 had caught the attention of certain people around the city. There were always going to be those who were anti-American or who were just anti-foreigner. The large number of dorm parents and kids in the missionary boarding school was the first thing that caught the attention of some people in their particular neighborhood. Our field committee, and Paul as chairman, had to explain our presence to certain individuals in the city and state governments. Just as had been the case with me and the municipal president of Uruachic, we found that it was vitally important that we demonstrate ways in which we were a practical help to every community where we lived, but especially each tribal community.

Faced with that necessity, the field committee had designated one or two couples or individuals to be completely focused on community development. Gene and Martha Purcell served in that capacity for a while, but a lot of their efforts were concentrated out in Baborigame with the Tepehuan tribe. That was a really big help for Wendy and Kevin Case who then became more freed for language learning, Bible teaching, and eventually Bible translation.

My heart was still very much with our Tarahumara friends and neighbors in El Manzano. A really big issue in my mind while we had lived there, and even for the Clarks after we were gone, was the need for a medical professional who could treat the people. We had treated numerous people for a variety of ailments and injuries, and, thank the Lord, had never seen any of them have an allergic reaction to anything we had given them. As a precaution in case that should ever happen, we had taken injectable adrenaline with us and always kept some on hand. The only time we had used it was when we tried to revive Rosa when she died right after childbirth. Ticker and I knew that having a medical clinic in El Manzano would be a really big help to the Clarks as well as to all the people of the community. But how to do it?

While ministering in Chihuahua City, Gene Purcell told me about an aid group that was bringing Mennonite blankets down from the States by the hundreds for distribution in various areas because of the harsh winter weather. The blankets were beautiful, as well as thick and warm. I asked the representative of the Pentecostal Christian group that was bringing them down, a fellow named Christopher Petroff, how I could get some for our people out in El Manzano. I was told I would have to talk with a fellow named Black Buffalo, was given his contact number, and established a rapport with this man. I was able to go to a warehouse and get almost half of a pickup truck load for Al to take out when he came to Chihuahua the next time. Then a plan started to develop in my mind.

From things I had read about successful projects around the world, people could sometimes be motivated to do something for their community by receiving something else in return. I knew that I couldn't just ask ten or twenty or thirty Tarahumara and mestizo neighbors in El Manzano to voluntarily make adobes, cut pine trees for beams and rafters, and build a clinic building in their spare time. But what if they were paid with blankets, picks, and shovels that they could then keep, and maybe even corn or beans? There were sometimes ways of getting items like that from the Mexican government which had been designated for rural areas. The key to a lot of this was to make friends in the government as well as in other organizations that were charitable in nature.

Our field committee was understandably quite leery of getting on the radar of the Mexican government, so whatever we came up with would have to be low-key and tactfully done. From our experience in El Manzano with the municipal president and the ejido, I felt strongly that we could be a positive influence in any of the tribal locations if we approached this correctly. Just as Jesus said to His disciples when He sent them out on one occasion:

> **Behold, I send you out as sheep in the midst of wolves. Therefore, be wise as serpents and harmless as doves. But beware of men… You will be brought before governors and kings for My sake, as a testimony to them and to the Gentiles. But when they deliver you up, do not worry about how or what you should speak. For it will be given to you in that hour what you should speak. (Matthew 10:16–19)**

We had already had that experience in El Manzano before the municipal president and the ejido, so I felt rather like young David had felt when he had to slay a lion and then a bear in his role as a shepherd over his father's sheep. That had been a time of testing and training for him, and perhaps that had already been a similar kind of training for me.

The Clinic in El Manzano

I did not take it lightly at all to think about making a foray into the possibility of getting a clinic built and staffed by a Mexican doctor. I prayed that if the Lord was in these thoughts of mine that He would help me along a step at a time. If He was not, I prayed that He would give me a definite sign to back off. I shared my thoughts briefly with Paul and perhaps some of the other staff members about getting a medical doctor from the government program out to El Manzano. They certainly didn't want to get involved with any of that since they had plenty of other things on their agendas. That was understandable. But I did have time in my schedule to begin pursuing this idea.

There had been a clinic in Rocoroibo for several years with a "resident doctor" who was at least there eight or nine months out of every year. Why couldn't we have one in El Manzano? I asked friends and neighbors and any other contacts I could find about how the system worked for doctors having to perform their "social service." I found that upon graduation from medical school, every new doctor had to serve one to two years, earning a rather minimal wage, somewhere in the country in order to provide low-cost medical care for the local population. The doctors were able to choose where to do their service based on their grades. Those with the best grades could choose their home city or town or someplace else where they were interested in living. Those with the lower grades were assigned to a community. Not a very promising proposition for our friends in El Manzano but a huge step up from what the Clarks were able to provide.

I found out about a friendly doctor, Dr. Hugo Irigoyen, who was the director of the Clinica Las Americas. He graciously agreed to let me visit him and go over my idea. It was he who filled me in on all of the details noted above. I asked him if it would be a help to us if we had a clinic and residence for a doctor built and waiting for him and then sought to get approval from the branch of the government that assigned the doctors to their social service. He assured me that it would, so I thanked him for his time and joyously headed out to make some concrete plans.

I arranged a meeting with Paul and told him about my plan for getting the clinic built. He admitted that it was a good idea but was a bit doubtful that we could pull it off. I told him I would give him progress reports on a regular basis. From what I was told by Black Buffalo, who was able to bring large truckloads of things across the border, we would need to get a letter of recommendation from a local government official affirming and declaring our plans for distribution of those goods. I read to Paul the notes that I had taken in talking to him, and Paul agreed to draft a letter of request for recognition as an organization doing social work in the state of Chihuahua. This was a big first step!

At that point, I could see the way the Lord had "worked all things for good" which, at the time, had seemed like a challenge from Satan: the threat by Mauro that resulted in Paul and me going to that pivotal ejido meeting. I think Paul saw and could put confidence in my track record of working alongside different government entities and personalities. I think he believed that I would not be a "pushy American," so he backed our new effort.

It took me many hours over several weeks to find out who to meet with in the Chihuahua government and how our documents needed to be drafted. Eventually, I was able to secure the proper letters of authorization, and I then picked up an entire pickup truck load of clothes, blankets, and tools to take to El Manzano. In the spring of 1989, I took the first of three or four loads out and left it with the Clarks. Ticker and I brainstormed, and then got Al's thoughts, on what would be an acceptable exchange rate for labor for all the various items that we had to offer. I wrote up the rate on a sheet of paper and made a few copies so that we would not forget and would be fair with every single transaction.

So many hours of work making adobes would net the worker five items of used clothing; so many hours of digging the foundation for a shovel; so many hours of cutting beams and rafters for a blanket, etc. Once the goods were there, the local men started getting all the materials made and piled up, covering the stacks of adobes by making a temporary shed. Once they saw the Mennonite blankets, one of those became the most coveted prize! We "priced" each blanket appropriately and never had a complaint or a lack of workers.

Having come up with a solid plan in the spring, I had then written a letter to our home church in Des Plaines. I asked if they would be interested in putting together a group of six or seven people to come down and help us build the clinic. The response was awesome! Five young adults in their mid-twenties to early thirties, including one young lady and a really energetic children's church leader who was in his fifties, Cliff, planned their trip for June.

Several volunteers from our church in Des Plaines,
IL came down to help us build the clinic

We, the Clarks, and both of our home churches contributed the money to purchase the cement and metal roofing, and by June, we had all the materials on hand that we would need. The team from our church drove down to Chihuahua City in a van and then got on the train to San Rafael where we picked them up. We were all crammed into our F-350 crew cab: Ticker and myself, Dusty and Eric, and one or two others up front, then the rest of the younger people had to sit in the back on the bench seats that I had made for just that purpose with all their duffel bags, suitcases, and sleeping bags. We had planned ahead for all of the groceries, which were at the house in El Manzano, but we had not been able to stockpile gasoline. I always had two twenty-liter plastic jugs with me for carrying gas, but the sawmill in San Rafael was running low and would not fill them for me this time.

Right before we turned off the main logging road to go down into the El Manzano valley was a small group of houses called Cerro Prieto. A log truck driver friend of mine lived there, Emilio Cruz, so I left the two jugs and some money with him and asked him to get them filled for me the next time he went into San Rafael. I told him I would be back in seven or eight days and would need the gas to get back to San Rafael with my visitors.

Building the clinic in El Manzano was quite an
achievement in community development coordination
between our missionaries and the local people.

We had scheduled the construction for no later than the middle of June so that we could get the roof on before the rainy season started, which pretty dependably arrived the last week of June or first of July every single year. The construction went perfectly. Everybody who came was a really good worker. Doug and another fellow were good carpenters, but I told them, "This is going to be a lot different than what you're used to. Our only power tool here is a chain saw. We are going to be doing Mexican mountain-style carpentry." We had five or six local fellows who helped us every day by mixing mud for mortar for the adobe walls, carrying the adobes, and then eventually, all the beams and rafters. The weather was perfect, thank the Lord!

Cliff was a big hit with all the local people. He was a real character, joking around and practicing as many words as he could in Spanish and Tarahumara. He kept us laughing every day. It was such an encouraging time for me personally to be back out there in El Manzano, getting something really solid and impactful done. The Clarks were not there to help us out with all of this, being gone once again on a border trip or vacation, I'm not sure which. Some of the crew slept at their house each night and some in our house. Ticker did a lot of cooking of meals each day, which was extremely helpful.

We got all the walls up, the roof on, door and window jambs in place, leaving only the interior stucco and interior doors to do later. On the last day, we took pictures with all of the local people that helped us, had a short wrestling match between Cliff and one of the younger Tarahumara guys that once again left us laughing, and said goodbye to all of our El Manzano friends and neighbors.

13.3 Out of Gas

We left after breakfast, needing to get to San Rafael for our crew to catch the train by 1:00 or 2:00 p.m. We had burned a lot of gasoline going back and forth from our house to where the clinic was being built, which was right by the boarding school and airstrip at the top of the El Manzano valley, so I was glad I had left the gasoline jugs and money with Emilio Cruz. He was a dependable fellow. Twenty minutes after leaving our house, I pulled up in front of his. His log truck wasn't there, but smoke was swirling out of the stovepipe, meaning his wife was home.

"I'm so sorry, Esteban," she said. I was looking at my two big gas jugs sitting there on their back porch, empty. "I think he tried to get your gas, but they still don't have any in San Rafael."

We were in trouble. A lot of trouble. I probably only had enough gas for twenty minutes of driving, and it was still two hours to San Rafael.

"Is there anybody here who knows where there might be some gas?" I asked.

She called one of the young men over from a house nearby. He told me there was a winch truck that was working just a few miles away, pulling logs up out of the canyon where they had been cut.

"I think it's either the next road on the left or the one after that," he said, pointing down the road toward San Rafael. "You'll be able to hear it running when you get close by."

I went over to my truck and told everybody the predicament we were in. I said that I would take whoever wanted to go with me, and the rest could stay there and wait until we got back. I wasn't sure how long we would be gone, so they would be more comfortable not bouncing around in the back of the truck. Three of the guys stayed with me, and everybody else stayed at Emilio's house.

We drove about two miles down the road until we came to an old logging road on the left. I stopped and got out and walked down it only a short distance. I could tell that no vehicle had driven over it for some time. We got back in the truck and went several more miles. I was looking at the gas gauge every minute, it seemed, and I was getting worried. We came to another old, unused road, and I was sure that it, too, hadn't been used in quite a while.

"Okay, we are only going to drive to the top of that next ridge, and we're going to listen to see if we can hear that winch running somewhere. That's our only hope right now," I said.

We drove to the next ridge, got out of the truck, and listened carefully for several minutes. There was no sound but the gentle wind in the pine trees. We were in a jam.

When we got back in the truck, the needle on the gas gauge was on "Empty." I had been driving as conservatively as I could, and now I just hoped we could get back to Emilio's house. I gently accelerated the truck down the hill and then let off the gas so it would not kick into passing gear going up the other side. I did this on two more hills, then on the uphill of the third one, with us still a couple of miles from Emilio's, the engine coughed and sputtered, then quit. I put the gear shift in Neutral and coasted back to the bottom of the hill. Everybody was looking at me. *Now what?* I thought quietly.

After a few moments, I said, "I have an idea of how we can at least get back to Ticker and our friends."

A few years earlier, I had read the biography of Nate Saint, a missionary pilot who went to Ecuador in 1955 to support missionaries down there that were attempting to reach tribal people deep in the jungles. The movie *End of the Spear* does an excellent job of telling the story of him and four fellow missionaries who contacted, and then were martyred by, the Huaorani—or Auca—Indians.

In his biography, *Jungle Pilot*, was a story that I remembered. Nate was living somewhere in Latin America—I'm not sure if it was

Ecuador or not—when he saw an interesting incident and learned an invaluable lesson. He was walking through this remote mountain town one day when a big delivery truck came down the road toward him. The hood was off, and a young boy was sitting on the side of the engine compartment, on top of the fender, dribbling gasoline down into the open carburetor. The truck pulled over to make a delivery at a business, and Nate went over to find out what this strange situation was all about. He found out that the fuel pump on the truck had gone out, so the man who operated it came up with a clever solution. He took off the hood, removed the air cleaner, and told his son to carefully dribble gasoline into the carburetor from a quart bottle.

When the dad wanted to accelerate or had to deal with a steep hill, he would indicate through the windshield for the boy to dribble the gasoline faster. Too much, and it would choke; too little, and it would just cough and sputter. Pretty soon, they had it figured out. The dad told Nate that it was going to be a week or more before the new fuel pump could be sent out to the town, and in the meantime, he had to keep earning a living, thus his ingenious solution.

Gasoline with dirt or water contamination is common all through Latin America, even in the aviation gas. Nate had been concerned about that very thing for some time. A clogged fuel line while flying over the jungle would mean a crash landing into the trees and almost certain death. He had been trying to figure out a way to rig up a backup fuel system, and the incident with the truck gave him an idea. He came up with a fuel bladder that he attached to the ceiling inside the airplane with a fuel line that ran down the corner of the cockpit windshield and into the top of the carburetor. With a small manual valve within reach, if his fuel from the main tank got clogged, he could use the emergency fuel and head for the closest place to land safely. He ended up using this on at least a couple of occasions, saving him and his airplane from crashing. He passed the word on to fellow pilots, and it became a prototype for a backup fuel tank that would end up saving quite a few lives in the years to come.

Thankfully, I had all of my wheels firmly on the ground, so I wouldn't crash, but my mind went to the fact that I still had some fuel in the very bottom of my gas tank. I was able to disconnect my fuel line underneath the tank, fill a couple of empty Coke bottles that we had in the back of the truck with gas, and reconnect the line.

I told the guys what my plan was and asked for a volunteer to sit on the side of the engine compartment with the hood open. Doug was the smallest guy, so he worked out perfectly.

I couldn't take the hood completely off, of course, so I had to lift it up all the way, which was high enough that I could see the road through the gap between the top of my engine and the bottom of the hood. With the passenger-side window rolled all the way down, I was going to call out instructions to the guy in the passenger seat, who would have to yell to Doug over the top of the engine noise. We replicated the scene that Nate Saint had witnessed: air cleaner off, gasoline being dribbled by a fellow with his thumb over the end of the Coke bottle full of gasoline, practicing quickly ourselves, however, because we didn't have much gas to spare.

We got the truck running, and when I could feel the engine bogging, I would call out for more gasoline. We got to the top of the hill, went down the other side, up another hill, around some bends in the road and, after a couple of miles, got to Emilio's!

I got the truck pulled over next to his house and told everybody what the score was. They were going to have to sleep there for the night, and I was going to hitch a ride to San Rafael on the next vehicle that came by with my gas jugs. I didn't know how long it would be before I got back—that night, which wasn't very likely, or the next day.

We hated to impose on these nice people, but Ticker, Dusty, and Eric and everybody else, except Doug, was going to stay there until I got back with gasoline. We took sleeping bags for Doug and me and a little bit of food that we had for snacks on the road and waited for a ride. Fortunately, the next vehicle that came by was a pickup truck, not a loaded log truck. Sitting on top of a loaded log truck for seven or eight hours would have been miserable. This pickup truck would have us in San Rafael in two hours.

When we got to town, it was early afternoon. At the sawmill, they told us that they were still rationing gas, limiting people to five or ten liters. The next tanker car had still not arrived by train. When

I told them of my predicament, however, they let me fill up both of the gas jugs. A really great development, too, was that the fellows who had given us the ride into town worked for the logging company and were going back out the next morning. Again, that was a blessing to not have to "take the slow boat," a lumbering log truck, which would've taken probably four or five hours to get back to our people.

So in the end, we got the gasoline back out to my truck and were on our way again, delayed by thirty hours, but at least we were on our way and we all had one more interesting story to tell.

Thank you, Nate Saint, for showing me how to get my truck back to my family and friends!

Chapter 14

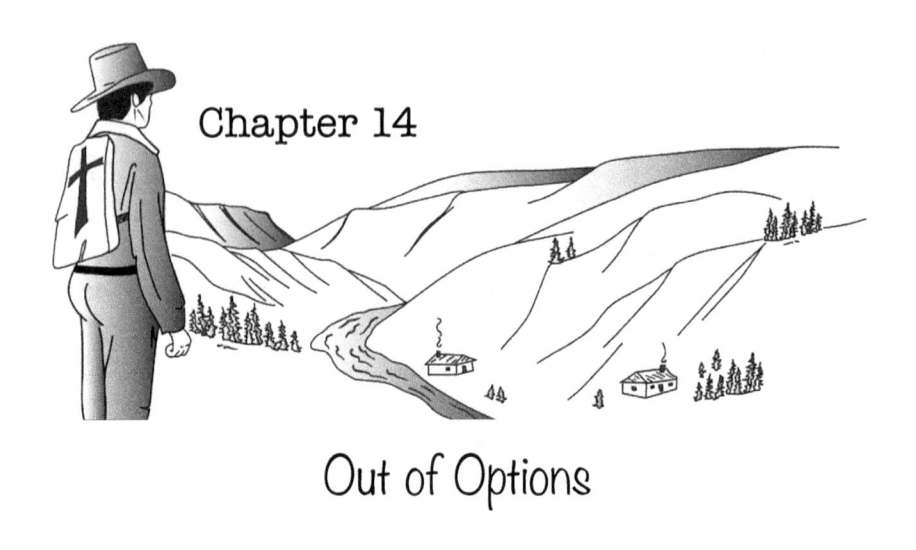

Out of Options

14.1 Counseling, Quote, Unquote

Sometime in November or December of 1988, Ticker was getting exhausted at the end of each school day pretty frequently, and the "school day" for her was teaching kindergarten with a coworker from usually nine o'clock in the morning until one o'clock or one thirty in the afternoon. She enjoyed what she was doing, but for some reason, even those few hours of work were wearing her down.

In the spring of 1989, when we were making plans for building the clinic in El Manzano and my main ministry was teaching Spanish to our new missionaries, Ticker began having conversations with one of our coworkers, a single woman. I will let her remain anonymous and just call her Joan.

Joan was a few years older than we were and had never married. She had a partner, another single woman who was a few years younger than her, and the two of them were waiting for guidance from the Lord and the field committee as to which tribe they would end up going into as partners for one of the married couples. Joan had apparently dealt with some difficult situations in her own life and had some experience with counseling and/or therapy. Once Ticker started sharing some things with Joan about her depression,

Joan decided to help her to dig deep and find out what the root sources of her problems were.

The intention was to help Ticker "process" her depression, which she and her sister had begun to believe was due to childhood abuse or trauma of some kind. Ticker and her younger sister had talked about this off and on for a few years, never being able to put their finger on exactly what the trauma clearly was or who in their family was to blame. In fact, Ticker had told both of her younger sisters that they should go to the same pastor in Chicago, Pastor Westlund, who had been such an amazing help to Ticker at the end of our medical furlough. Now, seven or eight months after we had returned to Mexico, Ticker and her sister were corresponding regularly, trying to clarify old memories and identify the wounds.

One evening, when I came home from teaching Spanish at the office, Ticker told me that she was going to go over to Joan's house to talk to her, woman to woman. She said that she had a lot of confidence that this was going to bring out some things that were deeply troubling her so that she could deal with them once and for all. She was quite sure that this was the right route to go. I told her, "All right, I'll watch the boys, and I'll see you in a few hours."

She was gone probably three hours that night and came back looking physically exhausted.

"Are you okay?" I asked. "You don't look so great. What's going on?"

"I've been crying," she said. "It's part of the process, but I don't really want to talk about it. Did you put the boys to bed?"

Several days later, basically the same scenario unfolded. Another day, I came home, and Joan had been there for a few hours, and she and Ticker seemed to have struck up a good friendship. I could talk about anything in the entire world except for asking Ticker about her depression, what she was thinking, or what she and Joan were talking about. Neither one of them wanted to discuss those things, even in a thumbnail sketch. I was beginning to get real unhappy about the secrecy and the cold shoulders.

After a couple of months of these kinds of visits, Ticker left one evening right after dinnertime and didn't get home until after one in the morning. I was really, really worried about her. I had called Joan's house at about ten o'clock to see if Ticker had left yet, and Joan told me, "No, she's still here and will be heading home in a little while probably." Three hours later, she came in exhausted, had obviously been crying, and went straight to bed. Now I was getting really concerned but also unhappy about this "counseling relationship." There was just too much that didn't feel right about it. That was my gut feeling.

As was always the case, our life was a kaleidoscope of issues and activities. At our Mexican church in Chihuahua, I was asked to speak from time to time, which was a good experience for me in teaching the Scriptures again. I had been away from that for so long, it seemed, since the years during which we had so many Bible studies with the believers in El Manzano. My primary responsibilities of teaching Spanish to the new missionaries were going pretty well, but it was disappointing sometimes to see the lack of work ethic in some of the people in the Spanish program. Dave and Dusty were doing well in their studies, and Ticker was homeschooling Eric very much like she had homeschooled Dave and Dusty for years.

I don't remember us having the boys involved in any sports in 1989. We lived on the far north end of Chihuahua City, and I had to drive down to the office every day since there was no one to carpool with. On days when I didn't have classes to teach, Ticker would use the truck and go shopping, so she wasn't homebound all the time.

Ticker's friendship with Joan had started in the spring, but the time they spent together really became quite a regular thing right before and right after we built the clinic in El Manzano. When we came back from the mountains in July, they were getting together at least twice a week, sometimes three times. That is when things took a definitive turn for the worse.

My Reality Shock

One afternoon, I came home from teaching and went upstairs to the bedroom to change clothes. Glancing around the room, I noticed a book standing open on Ticker's nightstand. Something about it looked strange, so I walked over to it. It was a journal that she kept, which I had never looked at out of respect for her privacy. It was normally lying either there or somewhere else around the house. But this particular afternoon, it was lying open, and the pages in it had been slashed numerous times with a knife, shredding eight or ten pages deep below where it was opened. I was horrifically shocked.

I asked Ticker to come upstairs, so as to be away from the boys, and tell me what was going on. She was obviously feeling some violent aggression and had taken it out on her journal. Once again, however, she didn't want to talk about it. She just said that she was processing some thoughts that she had from her childhood. Next to the journal was a letter from her sister. I asked her what was in the letter and whether that's what had caused her to get so angry. She said yes, that was part of it. But mostly, she was feeling anger toward her father and brothers.

She then told me that she and her younger sister were trying to put pieces together from their childhood, and although everything was quite vague and blurry in their recollections, somehow they felt that their father and some of their brothers were part of the reason that they both had repressed memories and very upsetting emotions.

A danger signal that had recently been glowing yellow in the back of my mind as Ticker got more involved in conversations with Joan went to full, flashing red. It was obvious to me that we needed to get some serious professional counseling for Ticker. Her depression had given way to aggressive anger and more suicidal thoughts. Her state of mind was going the wrong way fast. It was my role as her husband and the head of our family to get help for her, and soon.

"We can't carry on like this any longer, Ticker," I told her. "I think we need to go back to Chicago, and I think this time it might be for good. What do you think?"

"I think you're right. I need to sort out all of these thoughts and feelings going through me. I can't do it here. I just can't."

At this point, I came to grips with the stark reality that Ticker's conversations and "counseling" sessions with Joan had precipitated this breakdown. What was going on in Ticker's mind was a complete 180-degree turn from the successful, godly counsel that she had gotten with Pastor Westlund in Chicago. The "secret sisterhood" that Joan and Ticker had developed was a disaster for Ticker and our family. For far too long I had been told, "Just be patient, we'll work it out" and "Sorry, we can't talk about any details. Just be supportive." Well, I had been supportive for years, and there had been good, godly healing through Pastor Westlund and one or two others who were not just Spirit-filled men but who also had years of counseling experience and worked with respect for the God-ordained framework of the family and our marriage. For the first time in our lives, I told Ticker I would not allow this outside person, this intervention by Joan, to continue.

"Yes, we need to get some godly counseling, and we're not going to be getting it here. It's time we started looking into some help back in the States," I said.

Ticker, through correspondence with a few different people, had found out about some Christian counselling organizations and practices. One well-respected one was in Colorado, and we made a phone call, then sent a letter to them, asking for more information within a day or two. While I asked her to give me feedback where she thought we should go, I had to organize my thoughts so that I could have a meeting with our field leadership.

The process of leaving to go back to the States could not be dragged out. Within a week or two, we drove back out to El Manzano to go through the house and get the last few personal items that we wanted to take. There were only a few things left in the house that we cared about. We put them in a couple of boxes and put them in the back of the truck. I looked around at the beautiful house I had built with loving care through so many hours for so many months. I had wanted it to be a house that had all the comforts of home for Ticker—something better than a rough, pioneer-type house. I turned and locked the door for the last time.

We got in the truck and drove away, not just from a house but from a dream, from a goal that thankfully had been partially fulfilled. What was left inside I hoped would be of good use to the next family who would take our place as partners with the Clarks.

We had a short visit with Barbara, Teodulo, Trini, and a couple of others who were there at their house. We all knew that this was likely to be goodbye forever. As we gave hugs all around, I looked at each one of them and realized that I was hugging a brother or sister in the Lord now, where just a few years before, there had been a priceless but lost Tarahumara or mestizo neighbor who had never heard the Gospel and who was destined for an eternity separated from God. They were the reason God had sent us; they were the reason we had come; they were the reason we had stayed through so many hard months and years.

And yes, they were worth it all. Every bit of it.

14.2 My Father in New Mexico

Amongst the other things happening in our lives during those last several months in Chihuahua were two visits from my father. When I say "my father," I mean my actual biological father who my mom had divorced when I was five years old. After my mom remarried my stepdad, my brother and I always called him "Dad." That's how we looked at him—he was a good, kind man who, never having been married, took on a woman that he fell in love with and two boys that he had never seen until he and my mom drove up at nine o'clock one night and carried us away from my grandparents' ranch where we had been living for the past two years. That initial shock aside, he turned out to be a good father.

Then, I believe it was at Christmas 1987, my brother Bryan and I both received a Christmas card from our birth dad, Roy. My grandparents had given him our mailing addresses. Roy had been down some bad roads for many years of his life due to drinking and chasing women, then over a period of a few years, he had apparently made some profound, permanent changes to his life. Bryan and I talked about what kind of response we wanted to have toward him, but both of us felt really strange since he had not reached out to us in the last twenty-eight years. We both ignored his Christmas cards and went on with our lives.

Over a year later, Ticker and the boys and I were passing through Globe, Arizona, for a visit with my grandparents on our way back to Mexico. After being at their house for a couple of hours, my grandmother came over to me and said she had gotten a phone call from Roy. She said that right that minute he was driving to Globe from San Diego and wanted to meet us, but he would understand if I didn't want to, and he would turn around and go back. He was going to call again in a few minutes and talk to my grandmother and see how I felt.

After all the miracles and transformations I had seen in people's lives, especially for God to rescue me who had been a self-willed and somewhat angry teenager at seventeen years old, I certainly knew that Roy could have changed. All my mom had ever said to me about him was bitter and hateful. Her anger toward him and hate had not diminished at all over the years. I didn't have to overanalyze this. From the time I had received the Christmas card from him, I felt that he had changed and wanted to get to know his kids.

I told Grandma, "Yes, tell him to come. I would like to see him."

Less than an hour later, he arrived at Grandma and Grandpa's house. He got out of his car and walked over to greet me. He was six feet tall and in good physical shape for a man of fifty-five years of age. He had a bit of gray in his thinning dark brown hair, and with his blue eyes, he looked a bit more like a taller version of my brother than me. I, however, was his oldest child. His demeanor was friendly and easygoing. We shook hands and talked outside. The boys were playing close by, and I called them over to meet him, then Ticker came out, and I introduced her. I called him Roy from the start, and that seemed to be okay for all of us.

HE WHO HAS BEGUN A GOOD WORK

Me with my grandparents and my father, Roy

After visiting for an hour or more, he told me that he was trying to make amends for the lost years of his life in which he had a drinking problem and had alienated everyone that was important to him—my mom, Bryan, and me; his second wife and her two children; and the third wife that he had no children with who had left him years ago. He acknowledged that he had been callous and negligent for years, dealing with his own personal problems, but after being clean and sober, he had recently spent several months living at a Buddhist retreat in the southeast US.

He asked us about our lives, and we told him what we were doing and that we were now living five hours south of El Paso in Chihuahua City. At the end of our two-hour visit, he asked if we would consider letting him come and visit us down in Chihuahua. I told him that yes, that would be good. I'm a pretty good judge of character after a few minutes with most men (not always so much with women) and was certain he had experienced a profound change in his life. It would be good to get to know him and know more about that change.

In Chihuahua City we had a telephone, just like people in the modern world are supposed to have—a big change from living in El Manzano. Whether it was by phone calls or letters, we arranged for a time when he could come down to Chihuahua and visit us for a couple of days. It was pretty amazing to catch up with him after all those years. I was especially thankful that he had a penitent heart regarding the way he treated my mom when they were married.

He was really friendly and positive with my boys and Ticker, and the boys really got to love him more as an uncle figure than as an actual grandfather. He came down and visited a second time with us in Chihuahua City before we left, and he was very empathetic regarding Ticker and her depression. So it was that when we were wrapping up all of the loose ends that we needed to in Chihuahua City that I called him and told him that we were going to be going up to Chicago, probably leaving Mexico for good.

At the time of his first visit to see us in Chihuahua, he had been living just north of San Diego, selling real estate, which was his forté in business. The visit had gone so well, and he was ready to break ties with the less-than-ethical broker he was working for that he decided to look for work a lot closer to El Paso, Texas, so that he could come see us more easily and perhaps more often. I was amazed, to say the least, that we were so important to him. We had indeed become the only family that he really had. His relationship with his mom and dad was not that great due to a lot of issues in their past.

Within a couple of days of us telling him we were going to be leaving for Chicago around the first week of August, he called us again. He wanted to do something special for us. He was selling time-shares at a ski resort in New Mexico called Angel Fire. He said it was a beautiful, mountainous resort, and he wanted to give us one whole week staying at a condo there as a vacation- "Before," as he put it, "you head back to the rat race up in Chicago." He said that he felt it was something that especially Ticker needed, which was really sensitive and kind of him to do.

Once we had finalized the actual day on which we would be leaving, I called him back, and he blocked out the week for us. It was the first truly kind thing that anyone had done for us in quite a while. I told him how much we appreciated what he was doing. Of course, Ticker and I were in a whirlwind of activity at the time in Chihuahua—selling furniture, giving away other things, closing our utilities accounts, and cleaning the house to turn it back over to our landlord, etc.

Our visit in Angel Fire was restful too. It was a beautiful place, situated at over 9,000 feet elevation. One evening, coming back from a short drive around the area, an owl swooped down and perched on a light post just ahead of us at a rural intersection. I slowed down and turned off the headlights, rolled to a stop, and all of us just watched him for three or four minutes before he flew away. It was a serene moment, perhaps so enjoyable because it reminded us of El Manzano and nature and the life we had surely left behind forever.

It was especially memorable, I think, as a gift from God in its tranquility. I think the boys and I actually enjoyed the time at Angel Fire more than Ticker did, but I know she appreciated it, and it did her good. I had no idea that this trip marked the beginning of what would become a three-year period of hurt, loss, and heartbreak for all of us.

14.3 A Lesson From the Book of Job

If you are a Bible believing Christian, then you know that Satan is real. Jesus told us that numerous times in the Gospels, and from the oldest book of the Bible-- Job-- to the last-- The Revelation-- we learn what a powerful adversary he is. In league with his fallen spirits, "the principalities and powers of this world", they are constantly fighting God's purposes and agendas of reconciliation and peace for mankind. They are not all-powerful of course, but they are effective in winning many battles- not the war, but many battles. If you read your Bible, watch the news and look around closely at your church or any Christian organization, you will realize it happens. It is called "spiritual warfare", and it is real.

Like in military warfare, the objective is to take as many of the enemy's soldiers out of the fight as possible. Satan's goal does not revolve around who is right-- rather, it has to do with who is left.

Like in physical wars, soldiers of the Lord can be and are wounded regularly. Some are mortally wounded, while others recover. Of those who recover, some return to the fight. In our many years of ministry we had seen both. Our role and participation in the awesome building of God's Church among the Tarahumara people had seen many wonderful victories, and He was not finished by any means in that "good work" which He had begun. I do believe, however, that Satan was reveling in the fact that he had taken us physically out of Mexico. But he wasn't finished in his goal to crush our family and our faith in God.

Allow me to share with you that part of this story, too. We <u>will</u> get back to the "good work" God was continuing with the Tarahumara and mestizo believers of El Manzano and beyond.

I had no idea that we as a family were about to suffer painful losses in those most vital of areas of life: family and Christian fellowship. As they came, however, I was often reminded of the confusion of Job as he suffered multiple losses while wondering where God was and why He was allowing those things to happen to him. I was also acutely conscious of the essential lesson for us from that book of Scripture: God was NOT the designer of such loss and pain, and He would eventually be glorified by Job's-- and by my-- correct response to that pain. I must not blame and get angry at Him! He would heal and restore in His perfect time and way (*right?*). I will admit, however, the pain was all too real as it happened.

14.4 One Loss...

After expressing our heartfelt thanks to Roy, we got on the highway heading toward Chicago. I calculated how many more nights we would be on the road before we got to St. Louis, where we would visit with my folks. From there, it was just about five more hours north to get to Chicago.

With a handful of change, I went to a pay phone and called my mom and dad. Mom answered the phone.

"Hi, Mom," I said, "we're on the highway now driving up from Mexico. We should be in St. Louis the day after tomorrow, so I wanted to let you know."

With a strange flat tone in her voice, Mom said, "No, Steven. You don't need to bother stopping. We know where you have been. Visiting Roy."

Obviously, I was stunned. I didn't know what to say for a few seconds. How could she have found out?

"Yes, Mom," I told her, "we did go see Roy. He's a changed man, and he wanted to get in touch with us last year—"

"Don't you tell me he's a changed man!" Mom said into the phone, her voice seething with anger. "That man is evil! Do you know what he did to me? I can never forgive him for that," she raged.

"Well, Mom, don't you want to hear what I have to say—" I tried to interject.

"NO! I don't want to hear what you have to say! I called your office down in Chihuahua, and they said you had gone to see your father for a few days before you went up to Chicago. I told them your father lives here in St. Louis. The woman on the phone said that, no, your father was in New Mexico and that you were going there to see him first, then go up to Chicago. You have betrayed your father and me and hurt us very, very deeply. We don't want to see you. You just keep right on going on your way up to Chicago. Goodbye!" she said and hung up.

I was absolutely shocked. This was bad. So someone in Chihuahua City, who I later found out was our old partner in the tribe who had quit, had answered the phone and spilled the beans. It wasn't her fault, of course. But this was a painful development. I went back to the truck and told Ticker what had happened. In a way, it simplified things for us since Ticker had never gotten along well with my mom anyway.

Although I tried to patch things up with my mom, whenever I called in the future, if my dad answered, he would just hang up the phone. It was a painful experience from that point on for the next three years. No, it wasn't just painful. Sometimes it was horribly hurtful. Anytime we did talk for more than just a few minutes, she would say hurtful things about both me and Ticker, sometimes being especially critical of Ticker. She had no idea what was going on with our relationship, and I was never able to tell her or my dad that.

A couple of months later, I opened a letter that had come from my mom. In it, she said, "I guess your father and I made a mistake when he adopted you. Your brother has remained faithful to us, choosing not to have anything to do with Roy. But you have been disloyal and unfaithful, so I am returning your adoption papers to you."

At a time when I needed family the most, I could certainly not look to my parents for any comfort or advice. My career had certainly ended, and my life with Ticker was anything but certain. It was becoming a cold and lonely time.

14.5 After Another...

When we arrived in Des Plaines, we stayed in Ticker's parents' house for about two weeks, then by the grace of God, we found a house to rent in a really beautiful, quiet neighborhood called The Villas. God was taking such good care of us in the midst of the storm. We had struck out pursuing one or two leads for good counselors, and Ticker did not want to go back to Pastor Westlund. She now believed that she had a very specific kind of problem and therefore needed to seek a different type of therapy completely.

Out of respect for Ticker, I won't go into some of those details here. I disagreed with her self-evaluation and told her so. I had now been through seven years of trying to understand the issues involved from a somewhat objective point of view. Although I didn't know a lot, I had certainly seen what did work and what definitely did not. The contrast between Pastor Westlund's counseling and the worldly "therapy/ counseling" of "Joan" for several months were like night and day.

Ticker had her mind made up, however, and found out about a program that was apparently run by a Christian organization called The Minirth-Meyer Clinic. They had their foundational roots in the Dallas Theological Seminary, which we knew to be a reputable Christian organization. Both our current and previous pastors at the Des Plaines Bible Church were graduates from there. I trusted that it would be a good program with astute and godly Christian counselors who would soon pursue a comprehensive diagnosis for Ticker.

In the Chicago area, they ran their program in a local hospital that was about thirty minutes away from where we were living. Within less than a week of moving into our new house, with the boys in school, Ticker and I drove to the hospital for her initial diagnosis. After an hour or so of a private interview with Ticker (once again, I was not included), a couple of staff members met for a consultation. Their consensus was that Ticker's treatment could not be done as an outpatient. She would need to be admitted, and we would need to be told that the fee for thirty days of inpatient therapy and care would be $20,000–$25,000. After sitting down with both of us in a small conference room, and us confirming that we did not have medical insurance, we were told that they would not be able to start therapy and treatment for her.

Obviously, this was a huge shock for us. We went home and called our pastor and told him what they had said. He told us he would work on the situation for us. Over the next few days, he met with the chairman of the church board and made calls to our mission headquarters in Florida. He got commitments from the church board to pay $5,000 and from New Tribes headquarters to pay another $5,000. He then called the Minirth-Meyer clinic and informed them of this arrangement. I called the clinic and said that I would sign a financial responsibility agreement and would make monthly installment payments for whatever the balance would be. They then agreed to admit Ticker for inpatient treatment.

During the check-in process on September 1st, Ticker was glum and her mood dark. The two staff members that I talked with seemed professional enough. I asked what the next couple of days held and was told that her counselor or caseworker would contact me and we would have a family conference before the end of the week. That sounded encouraging. I felt there was a strong possibility that in a few days they might come to believe she needed to be treated for something which we had just been hearing and reading about-- bipolar disorder. I explicitly told her caseworker before I left that there were other issues going on long before she ever came to feel like her problem was that which she now believed it to be. I asked that they please look deeper than that. After the painful debacle of her "counseling" with Joan in Mexico, I was finally attempting to be more frank and give my perspective, limited as it was.

There were no cell phones in those days. I had to rely on communications through our home phone and, if I missed a call, the answering machine. For two or three days, I had no phone calls from the hospital. Finally, on the fourth day, before I left for work in the morning, I called the hospital and asked to talk with her caseworker.

"We're still doing evaluations, Mr. Real," he said. "You know that she has had suicidal thoughts for a while now, don't you? She said you did. We don't necessarily suggest divorce in situations like this, but we do think that a time of separation might be best for you—"

His voice faded away in my brain for a few moments. Wait—he just said "divorce" and "separation" in the same sentence! *Best for you? "He's bringing these up as possibilities for us? If he is having the same kind of conversation with Ticker, I wouldn't be surprised if she grasps for one or both of those ideas as a solution to our problems.*

I thought we had found a solid Christian counseling organization to help us out, and now I was hearing words and suggestions that seemed so far from godly.

After six or eight days, I still had not gotten a phone call regarding a family meeting with the case worker or counselor, so I was getting concerned about this organization. I called our pastor, then was able to go over to the church and have a talk with him.

"Steve, I have to tell you something. Ticker has requested that no information be released to you. The hospital is only to give me updates on her condition. It's a matter of patient confidentiality and is a process that happens in instances like this. I don't know why she doesn't want you to have any information, so you'll have to talk to me, and I will call the hospital and can try to talk to Ticker and get back to you."

Once again, I felt like I had been punched in the gut. It was bad enough that over the years Ticker didn't want to talk to me about her thoughts and feelings. Then her "counseling sessions" with Joan in Chihuahua had gone to an entirely different place with me being told to "be patient" and "trust us, she's working through this." Now, even though I was her husband and responsible for many thousands of dollars' worth of bills coming up, I was absolutely to be kept in the dark.

I told the pastor that her caseworker had promised that we would have a family conference within just a matter of days, and it had now been about ten days. The boys were also beginning to wonder what was going on with their mother. We were approaching a weekend, and I asked if we could at least go down to the hospital so the boys could visit with her for an hour or so.

"I'll put in the request for you," said Pastor. "I'm sorry, Steve. I'm sure this must be really difficult for you."

You have no idea, I thought. I left and went home, completely at the mercy of these people who now had my wife in a secure facility and my pastor was legally obligated to give me only the barest of information.

I got a call later from the pastor that we could have a visitation session with Ticker that Sunday. The boys and I went down to see her—the boys with optimistic enthusiasm, me with a strange sense of foreboding. We were led in through a short hallway to a patio area that opened up to a small open air courtyard. Ticker was sitting in a chair, waiting for us. She didn't look very good but greeted the boys a little bit enthusiastically. She pretty much kept her eyes averted from mine.

Again, I won't go into specifics out of respect for Ticker's privacy, but her demeanor and our conversation shocked me to the core. Things had gone from bad to worse.

Our visit lasted less than an hour, and Ticker simply said that she was ready to go back inside. We only had one other visit with her a week or so later, which went about the same. A couple of days later, I was asked to come in and make another progress payment on her bill. I had never been informed of how much the daily charges would be, since they had been very vague about knowing what kind of therapy she would be receiving and how many doctors or other personnel would be involved. I told the finance office that they would have to send a bill to me, and I would submit it to our insurance. I didn't bother telling them that we were part of a mission organization that had a cooperative fund for medical expenses and it was going to be a rather unusual application process for me to try to get reimbursed.

After Ticker had been in the hospital for three weeks, I got a phone call saying that I should come down and talk with the psychiatrist who was in charge of her program. She was going to be released in the next couple of days.

"Mr. Real, I think we have gotten as far as we can with your wife at this point in time. It also appears that your finances have been maxed out. It's not a help to you or to her that we keep her here any longer, so we're planning on discharging her in the next couple of days," she said.

"Doctor, may I ask what your role has been in her treatment? You are the first person I've met with face-to-face since she checked in here. I was promised that we would have a family conference each week, and that has never happened. I've only talked with her caseworker on the phone. He has always been vague about when he would schedule a conference, and it has never happened."

"I am her psychiatrist and am the director of the program here at the hospital for the Minirth-Meyer Clinic. The others on staff are counselors or therapists, depending on what treatment is indicated. As you know, your wife checked in, telling us that she believed she had a specific type of problem. We believed that it was unhealthy for her to meet with you. That's why there weren't any family conferences and why you were not included in us determining her diagnosis, etc."

"Doctor, we've been married for fourteen years and, for the last nine years, have been missionaries in Mexico. We thought that we were coming here for the best possible therapy for her, and I told whoever checked her in that I did not believe that her current self-diagnosis was the real issue. I said that we had explored hormone therapy for her, and it had not been effective. I don't understand how you can keep her diagnosis from me, her husband, who has loved her and brought her here to you."

"I can understand that a lot of this doesn't make sense to you," she said to me, "but that is how we have to operate in this field of psychiatry and therapy. There are laws regarding confidentiality that we can't violate."

"Even though I'm her husband? And I'm paying the bills. It's not like I'm some third-party."

"That's how it works," she said. "Here's what I can tell you at this point in time. I believe that she has a bipolar disorder that is going to take time to further diagnose. You have exhausted your resources at this time, so we are recommending that you get her admitted to a state facility. Before you react to that, I can assure you that they are much more professionally run than they used to be. It may take a few weeks, and it may take a few months, but they will get to the bottom of what is causing her depression and suicidal thoughts."

Oh my gosh, I thought. *This is going even further downhill. How can this have gotten so crazy?*

"Your wife will have another therapy session or two tomorrow, and by the next day, we will have processed her paperwork, and you can pick her up and take her to the Elgin State Hospital. I think you will find that to be your best course of action. Someone will call you and tell you what time of the morning to pick her up."

I went away shocked, once again. The reputation of the state hospital was abysmal. Sure, we had been gone from the area for quite a few years, but stories still circulated in the news and amongst families who had relatives admitted or "treated" there, and they were always bad. "Dear God," I prayed, "please give me wisdom and the endurance to get through this. Why do we have to go down this horrible road?"

The following morning I checked her out of that hospital and drove her to the other one. She checked herself in, then hours later called me to pick her up from there. Yes, the state hospital was still a nightmare.

Ticker wanted to stay at our house, at least for the time being, so we took bedding so she could sleep on the couch in the living room. Right away she started calling her mom and her sister to see if she could stay with one of them. After talking it over with them, she soon moved out of the house. Did this mean that she wanted to be separated? "Yes," she told me.

"Don't worry, Ticker," I told her. "We'll get through this somehow," I said to reassure her. Or was I trying to reassure myself?

Over the next several months, she would end up living two or three weeks with one person, then several weeks with someone else. One woman from church talked to her husband, and they let Ticker move into their house for about a month and a half. I rarely knew where she was staying at any given time unless someone called me to tell me, and occasionally, Ticker would tell me so that if anything came up regarding the boys that she needed to know I would know where to call. The separation had indeed started.

Sometime during that first year, Ticker was diagnosed with bipolar disorder, sometimes called manic depression. A couple of months after she moved out of the house, she was given medications, lithium and Prozac, which seemed to be a big help. One of my first priorities was to find a good used car for her to have, which I did, and she was able to get a part-time job. She wanted to be able to pay her own way, buying groceries, etc., for the people she was staying with. But after two or three weeks, she would feel better and stop taking her medications and would once again crash.

This pattern repeated itself a few times. She continued to live in different places with different people and, once or twice, moved back in to the house and slept on the couch for a week or two. I know the boys enjoyed seeing her, and she enjoyed seeing them, but after a little while she was off to someone else's house.

More than a year and a half after she had checked into that first hospital, I got a message on my pager that I was now relying on to keep me in touch with people, especially the two different schools that the boys were in. It was one of the large area hospitals contacting me with a message to call back right away. I got to a phone and talked to a receptionist who said that Ticker would like to have a conference with me. I should come down to the hospital and ask for a certain person in the counseling department.

When I got there, the young lady that I was supposed to ask for greeted me. I would guess she was in her mid-twenties, probably just two or three years out of college. She told me that she was Ticker's counselor and that Ticker wanted to have a meeting with me. I sat down in a small conference room, and the young woman went out and came back with Ticker. Ticker came in wearing a hospital gown and looked really haggard. The young lady sat down at the table across from me with a pleasant smile on her face as Ticker sat down a few feet away.

I let Ticker start the conversation. "Steve," she said, "you have been telling me for almost two years now that we will find a doctor or a treatment and things will be better and 'you'll be home again soon.' I want you to know that I will not be coming home. Not ever. It's over. I don't want you to keep waiting for me. I'm not coming back home, and that's just how it is. You need to accept it."

I was absolutely shocked. I was silent for several seconds, not knowing what to say. I looked across the table at the young woman counselor or therapist or whatever she was. She had been smiling and optimistic thirty seconds earlier, and now she looked like someone had slapped her too.

I found my voice finally and just said, "All right Ticker. I will try to accept it."

The young lady stood up, and I'm sure the look on my face and what I had just said drove home the fact that this was the end of a relationship. She looked really unhappy as she sheepishly escorted Ticker out the door and back to whatever room she was staying in.

I don't remember where I was working at the time, but I went back to work and finished up my day. I picked up the boys after school and brought them home. They had their snacks and then went to play or visit their friends. Maybe I had them start on their homework, I don't know. We had dinner as usual, but I didn't tell them about my visit with their mom. Not yet.

All day long, I had been trying to process what Ticker had said, and how bad she looked, even after almost two years of trying to find help for herself. Yes, it was over between us. The hurt was now fully settling in on top of me.

In the midst of the confusion and pain, I wondered where God was. I also realized I had no one I could pick up the phone to call. Not my pastor. Certainly not Mom or Dad. It was the deepest pit I had ever been in, and I couldn't even see God anywhere around.

An hour or two after the boys were in bed and asleep, the tears started. I don't know when I had last cried in sorrow, but it had been a long time. Now I couldn't stop the tears. I didn't know that a human being could produce that many tears. One hour turned into two hours which turned into three hours. I would sob for thirty minutes straight, pause for ten minutes, trying to get my mind to calm down. I said to myself, "No, Ticker and I are not supposed to be one of those statistics of people who get divorced. God, why is this happening?" Then the tears would start again and then again and then again. I finally fell asleep sometime in the middle of the night, exhausted.

The crazy thing, too, is that perhaps the next night, perhaps a week later, it would happen again. I had been holding out hope for so long, and it was so very hard to accept that Ticker wanted out of our marriage. I contacted a divorce lawyer and had first told Ticker, and then told the lawyer, I would agree to a divorce if I were to get sole custody of the boys. Ticker had agreed right away. The lawyer was quite surprised as was the judge when we got into court. I was granted sole custody of my boys, and for that I was incredibly grateful to God.

14.6 ...After Another...

I was wondering when the bad chain of events would stop, but it didn't. My mom and dad had disowned me via first a phone call and then two months later by my mom sending my adoption papers back to me, telling me that they had "made a mistake" when my stepdad adopted me when I was ten years old. Ticker's hospitalization and inpatient "therapy" for almost a month through Minirth-Meyer had been a disaster. Then, six months later, I got a phone call from Roy telling me that my grandfather was going into the hospital for stomach surgery. He thought I would want to know so that I could pray for him.

The next morning, I got a phone call from him again. "Steve, I'm sorry to tell you that your grandpa didn't make it through surgery. His lungs weren't strong enough, which was our big concern. I know how close you had gotten to him, so I thought I would tell you as soon as possible."

Regardless of how my mom and dad treated me because I had seen Roy, my Grandpa Sikes had always been one of the best male figures in my life. In fact, he was the first real father figure for me. My mom and Roy had a rough marriage from the time I was only about three years old, and unfortunately, I remember a couple of their fights. My grandpa, however, had been a strong, stable, and kind man consistently. In fact, he had been such a loving and stable influence for my brother and me that when my mom, who had to divorce and flee from Roy, my grandpa's only son, he and my grandma agreed to let my brother, Bryan, and me live with them until she could get on her feet emotionally and financially and return to get us back. That process for her turned into two long years.

From the time I was five years old until seven, I had some of the greatest memories of my life living on my grandparents' ranch in Casa Grande, south of Phoenix, Arizona. I was grandpa's first grandchild and became his little pal. I found him to be wonderfully patient and kind. I also knew him to be tough as nails when the work was hard or he had to deal with a hired hand who was a slacker.

Besides his amazing work ethic, I remember the way he would have family devotions, Catholic style. He and Grandma would get their Bibles out, Grandpa would read a passage, and Grandma would follow along. My brother and I would sit and listen quietly. Then Grandma and Grandpa would say the rosary, so we heard the Lord's prayer many times while we were growing up. They took us to mass at the Catholic Church fairly often and enrolled us in catechism classes when I was either six or seven years old.

Those classes seemed to me to be very mysterious for a while, but then there was the day where I found myself totally fascinated by Jesus and God the Father. I distinctly remember feeling that there was a connection between us and realized later that through my grandparents, and the Catholic Church, God had opened up to me a consciousness about Himself.

After so many years of keeping us apart because of some misguided "protection" for my stepdad from my real dad, at my grandma's request, my mom had finally sent Bryan's and my addresses to my grandparents. That was how we finally reconnected with them after twenty-five years of silence. We only had the chance to visit with them four or five times while living in Mexico before we had come back to Chicago for the last time. I had thoroughly enjoyed talking with both of them, learning how my grandpa had been a cook for the highway crew during the construction of Route 66 (or US Highway 60—I'm afraid I am not positive regarding which highway it was that my dad, Roy, told me about).

Grandpa had the best restaurant in about a two-hundred-mile stretch of the planned route for the highway, so the advance planning crew asked him if he would cook for the road crew for about a seventy-five-mile stretch during its construction. He hired extra people to keep running his restaurant located in the prestigious old Dominion Hotel in Globe, Arizona, and set up a mobile kitchen that fed almost a hundred construction workers daily. The work on the mountainous Salt River Valley stretch of the highway was dangerous and tedious, so it took longer than most of the other stretches. Every few weeks he would have to move the kitchen further "down the road," literally. When his contract was almost up with that section of the highway, the planning crew went further ahead but could not find anybody who could do as good a job as my grandpa had, so they hired him to cook for the next section too!

He had been saving his money to buy a ranch since he had been a cowboy in his twenties, and a job back then had fallen into his lap to be a cook for the crew of cowboys he had been working with. As the ranch cook, he earned twice the wages of the average cowboy! With more profits from the restaurant in Globe and then by cooking for the highway crews, he finally had enough money to buy his ranch. Grandpa purchased an entire section, one square mile, and then he leased a second section.

At the peak of his operation, he had 2,500 head of cattle. He also had the foresight and ingenuity to drill for water on land that he leased from the federal government. During years of drought he actually had enough extra water to sell to other ranchers. He grew cotton as a cash crop, grew alfalfa for his own cattle, and came up with a custom cattle feed that gave the best flavor to his beef and resulted in him winning the blue ribbon prize for the best beef in the entire Phoenix area for several years. It was obvious to me that God rewarded him well for his hard work and his godly spirit. I was going to miss him immensely.

14.7 ...After Another.

Roy checked in with us by phone every couple of months or so to see how Ticker was doing. He felt badly that things had turned out so poorly for us. One day, he called and said that he had an idea for a business that he thought had great potential. He wondered if I would be able to go out to Los Angeles and help him build a warehouse building. He knew I was into construction and was hoping I could find a way to help him out. What he didn't realize was how busy I was being a single parent to three boys.

He said he would send me some literature on what his business plan was. I still have the brochures. At the time, it sounded like a pretty monumental process because it was! What he envisioned was a computerized warehouse, possibly using robots in the near future to do some of the work, which would be a centralized shipping point for a whole variety of products. It was exactly what Amazon was destined to become, but he had the idea fifteen years or more before they actually became operational!

Roy had been in numerous business ventures, involving millions of dollars, that eventually failed because of the partners he had teamed up with. In the numerous conversations that we had, he told me that the failures always came from him choosing poorly when it came to a business partner. One project that he spent several years on, which he was especially proud of at the time, was the purchase of a large tract of land in Costa Rica and dividing it up into five-acre coffee farms. His idea from the 1980s was basically what we've come to hear about in the last several years as "locally sourced co-ops." Once all the farms had been developed and were being sold, his partner, who was a Costa Rican lawyer, forged paperwork and stole Roy's entire half of the enterprise from him. He said that the best ventures that he got into he basically did on his own, importing emeralds, blankets, and handmade sweaters from Peru and Ecuador.

In that first year after we came back from Mexico, it seemed that we talked a little less frequently. It certainly wasn't that I didn't want to talk to him because we always had a good conversation. He made some money selling real estate in the North County San Diego area but didn't like the business and the broker he was working for, so he was getting ready to embark on a new venture. To divide up the workload, he once again got himself a business partner. I wasn't too clear on what this new business was going to involve or if it was another approach to the warehouse and distribution idea. I didn't hear from him for several months, and then one morning, I got a call from my grandmother in Arizona.

"Steve, I have some bad news for you," she said. "Roy took his life yesterday. It seems he was really despondent over a business that went bankrupt. I have phone numbers for the woman he was dating not long ago as well as a longtime friend of his out there in California. I think it would be good for you to talk to both of them. Someone needs to go out there and take care of his affairs. I can also give you the number of the detective at the San Diego Police Department who called me."

Shock. What? No, no, no, not another loss. Oh God, what is going on here? Roy must have been feeling so helpless. What happened?

In addition to the police contact, Grandma also gave me the phone numbers for Roy's other two children, my stepbrother and stepsister who lived in Colorado. I talked to them as well as my brother to see if anyone wanted to go out there with me, wrap up his affairs, and get his personal belongings. No one wanted to. In fact, my half-brother was the most unpleasant of everyone about the whole idea. It seemed that he had a similar attitude as his mom toward Roy, which was not very nice.

To make a long story short, after only being back from Mexico for a year and a half and reintegrating into the working world of the United States, I had to deal with closure in one of the most unpleasant and heartbreaking things a person might be asked to do in this life. Meeting with Roy's friend was very enlightening; meeting with his ex-girlfriend went well, too, and she was really gracious and had arranged for the cremation of his body and for his ashes to be scattered out at sea off the coast of San Diego. Once she knew that I would be on my way shortly, she said that she and her boat captain friend would wait for me so we could all perform the ceremony with the ashes together. We did so on a beautiful, sunny day.

We sailed just outside of San Diego Bay where I dropped his cremated remains overboard. They turned iridescent in the aqua water and seemed to have a beyond-natural light of their own as they drifted down, down, down. That was the last earthly view I got of a man who had tried and failed in so many endeavors in life but who, in the end, had endeared himself to his oldest son and his three grandsons.

I met with the San Diego police detective who had determined that it was indeed and in fact a suicide. Then I was authorized to pick up his personal effects, which were not that many but which did include a briefcase with his business papers in it. I still had two other things to do with the information I got from those papers.

The first was to make a visit to his bank and find out from the vice president of the branch why they had allowed the financial scam called "kiting" to take place. It turned out that Roy's business partner with whom he had a joint checking account had basically stolen all of the money that Roy had put in the account and was using it to cover for a separate failing business of his own. The bank vice president knew what was happening, and he knew that it was 100 percent the partner's fault and scam because of the way the transactions were handled by the partner. When I asked him if he had talked to the partner and how the bank planned on handling it, his reply to me was, "Yes, we knew what the partner was doing was illegal, but rather than threaten prosecution, it was my responsibility just to get the bank's money back."

"So you didn't try to get the money back into my dad's business account. You just wanted your bank not to suffer any loss?" I asked.

"That's right," he said, squirming in his chair and averting his eyes from me.

"And now my dad is dead because of it," I said to him, and I left.

Those who desire to be rich fall into temptation and a snare, and into many foolish and harmful lusts which drown men in destruction and perdition. For the love of money is a root of all kinds of evil. (1 Timothy 6:9–10)

Yes, welcome back to the land of the Golden Rule where those who have the gold make the rules, I thought. Just like when I had come home on furlough, I was experiencing another wave of culture shock. After living a life for the last eighteen years in which truth and integrity mattered, I was now in a land with very corrupted morals. So this was the America that I now lived in?

My next and last stop was to see Roy's business partner. I met with him late in the afternoon at his office. He was about Roy's age, fifty-five or so, and a bit heavyset. I didn't get a good vibe about him right off the bat. Like the vice president at the bank, he had a hard time sitting still and looking me in the eye. After a couple of minutes, he asked me if I had my dad's business documents. I said that yes, I did. He asked if he could have them. I said no, he could not. That made him really uncomfortable.

I'm pretty sure there was something in there that he wanted to recover, or just cover up. I wish I could've thought of something ominous to say before I left, but I couldn't. I just had to leave, hoping he felt a vague threat of some kind of prosecution or retribution hanging over his head. He was a scumbag, to be sure. However, I wasn't savvy enough in the ways of the world to try to figure out if there was any way to get him to pay for what he had done. I had to leave that in God's hands, as I'm sure it was supposed to be, and I flew home the next day.

14.8 A Lesson about Suicide

It's really important at this point in the story for me to say something about suicide and how it so tragically touched my life. Roy, my father, had grown understandably despondent after suffering a pretty significant financial setback at about fifty-seven years of age. It was getting harder for him to earn a living with each passing year, and he had had more than his share of unethical business partners. When he had finally tapped what he considered to be his last source for a loan to get him through another month or two and that had failed, he made his decision. Sitting in bed in the motel where he was living, he smoked one last joint and ended his life with a gunshot.

I really wish I could have known how despondent he was. Sure, I was extremely busy with my own life as a single dad, but I still feel badly that I was not more sensitive to what was going on in his life. I wish he would have called me and we could've talked. But we didn't, and he didn't feel that he had family or friends close enough to make a difference so he lost all hope and ended it all. The completely unforeseeable event in the future was that, within less than two years, I would be living forty minutes south of him in San Diego. We could've visited a lot. By then, I could have helped him build his warehouse and his business. He could've watched my boys grow up, and they could have known him as a grandfather. He had no idea how things could have dramatically turned around for the better within less than two years.

I know there are varying reasons for, and depths of, depression and despair. Some seem to just go on and on with no relief in sight. That's what my dad had experienced, but things would've turned around dramatically in less than two years if he would have—if he could have—waited on and trusted in God. That is the most important lesson that I got out of that whole heartbreaking experience. I hope I never forget that, even in my old age. And I hope you, the reader, will take it to heart as a real-life example of how close at hand the Lord always is.

No matter who we are or where we are in life, God cares. It is only by trusting Him to get us through even the darkest of times that we can have a full and satisfying life on this earth. But trusting Him means we also have to reach out to Him, to accept and grasp His outstretched hand. He has given us His counsel in His Word, the Scriptures, and by opening those pages, we open our hearts and eyes to the help He is patiently and eagerly offering. If we choose not to look to Him, then we are turning away from the life preserver He put right there for us to grab. It's a life preserver designed with amazing love and wisdom.

> **Although I walk through the valley of the shadow of death... you are with me. (Psalm 23:4)**

> **Oh Lord my God, I cried out to you, and you healed me... Weeping may endure for a night, but joy comes in the morning. (Psalm 30:2, 5)**

> **Peace I leave with you, my peace I give to you; not as the world gives do I give to you. Let not your heart be troubled, neither let it be afraid. (Jesus' words in the Gospel of John 14:27)**

Chapter 15

Life After New Tribes

15.1 Blessings and Being a Single Dad

As I said in my account of our trip out of Mexico and back to Chicago for the last time in 1989, I had no idea that three years of grief were just starting. The losses of our ministry, our house in El Manzano, the relationship with my mom and dad, Ticker's downward spiral which resulted in our separation and divorce, the death of my grandfather, and the death of my biological father, Roy, all happened in less than three years. Nothing before or since has been that painful in my life, but it would not be fair to not mention all the good things that happened as well. God had not abandoned us and, in fact, was taking care of all of us in His own ways.

Thankfully, "He who ha[d] begun a good work" in me, in Ticker and in our Tarahumara brothers and sisters was not finished with us.

It seemed like each week or each month brought some bad but also some good. It was deeply disappointing to me that the pastor of our church, as well as the elders, did not put more effort into talking with me or trying to be a help to me. If there was ever a time in my life that I needed moral support, it was then, in the pain and confusion of my marriage falling apart. After all, I was actually an ordained minister, just like the pastor of our church, and you would think that we would have had a "fellowship of the ministry" in common. I'm also sure that it was hard for people in our church to reconnect with me under circumstances that they didn't understand either.

It looked like I had failed as a "successful" leader of my own family. So perhaps they just didn't know how to relate and perhaps they didn't know how to encourage. Now that I can look back on how painful those years were for me and how little fellowship I was offered by some of the people I had known for ten years or more, it has certainly sharpened my sensitivity to others. It has absolutely made me want to be an encouragement to others, even if I don't understand all the tangle of details in their personal lives.

That's, in part, what trials are supposed to do, too, aren't they? Bring out the true depths of love that the Holy Spirit has planted in our souls? Jesus said it best (of course) when He said in John 13:35, "By this all will know that you are My disciples, if you have love for one another."

There were three or four men in the church who did try to remain encouraging, even though none of us knew what was going on in Ticker's mind and heart. One was Jeff Beck, who invited me to attend the weekly men's breakfast Bible study that met on Wednesday mornings at some ridiculously dark hour, like 6:00 a.m. He also invited me to his birthday party and some other event during that first year I was back. And there was Paul Sherman, another fellow who attended the Bible study, who had been fascinated by our work in Mexico and who continued to be an encouragement to me after we got back.

I remember one day during those first painful and confusing weeks when Paul said to me, "Steve, God has another ministry for you now. It's raising those three boys of yours." Those words of Paul were both encouragingly kind and spot on.

I had truly not minded leaving our home and ministry in Mexico when compared to the importance of finding help for Ticker and dedicating myself to my family, no matter where we lived. God helped me keep that in the very forefront of my mind day after day, week after week, and month after month. The first huge step in that process was when we got a perfect place to live in Des Plaines, a house that Ticker's dad actually found for us. It was only two blocks from the elementary school which both Dusty and Eric would end up attending and about six blocks from Dave's high school, Maine West. It was a really peaceful, interesting neighborhood with massive elm trees that created a canopy over the streets and had gravel easements on each side of the streets instead of concrete curbs, giving it a really unique country feel. God knew we needed that "country feel!" He is so gracious!

There was a family in our church who was pretty well-to-do financially. They had three children, the oldest of whom was about fifteen at the time. One night, about an hour after dinner, there was a loud knocking on our back door. I thought it was the next-door neighbor, of course, but when I turned on the porch light and opened the door, there were six big bags of groceries out there for us! I recognized a couple of the kids as they ran away toward the street, and then the whole family jumped in their car and drove away, wanting to be an anonymous blessing to us. That was extraordinarily thoughtful of them. God kept reminding us that He was caring for us in a variety of ways.

Other people in the church wanted to know right away if I was interested in doing work for them in order to give me some income. In previous years, I had done carpentry and painting for several members of our church, so almost from the beginning I had enough work and enough income to meet all of our needs. That in itself was a huge blessing from the Lord. He always knows what we need, even before we do.

I had a fair bit of experience in the building trades going back to my earliest years in school with New Tribes Mission. Now that my missionary career was apparently over, I considered a couple of options: (1) going to work for a company doing construction or (2) looking for a job doing Spanish translation or even getting into a career using my linguistics training. I looked at the pay rates in those fields and found that, starting new at my age, I would probably barely be able to support our family in either profession. If I were to be a contractor, rather than the worker, I would make at least 30 percent more and could hopefully get ahead financially. I was thirty-five years old when we returned from Mexico and was already ten or fifteen years behind many other men my age who wanted to be a contractor. With the work that people from our church offered me as well as work that I got by advertising, I decided to start in the profession that I would happily end up working in for the next thirty years—being a general contractor.

Despite the challenges of being a single dad, and there were a lot of them, my greatest joys, without a doubt, were attending probably a hundred or more of my sons' baseball and football games during those next three years and beyond. Dave really wanted to play football and was starting high school as a freshman the fall that we arrived. I had told him, "Dave, you have a small build like me. You did really, really well playing football in Chihuahua on that team last year. But you are going to find now that there are lots of big guys your age. You will shoot up in height, probably like I did somewhere around the end of your junior year. I wanted to play football, too, but had to be realistic—I would've ended up with broken bones or worse playing with kids that much taller and heavier than me. That's why I played soccer, and I ended up loving it."

"But, Dad," Dave pleaded, "there's no other sport I even want to try. You have to let me play."

"I'll tell you what, Dave," I said. "I'll let you play until I feel like it's dangerous for you. The worst thing that can happen, worse than a broken arm, is if you get a concussion or a neck injury. I'll let you play, but if you get hurt, that's it. You'll have to find a different sport that you like. I won't risk having you get a serious or permanent injury. Okay?"

Dave agreed and started off on the freshman football team. But within six weeks, he and another kid had a helmet-to-helmet collision during a game. The other kid got up and walked off the field, but Dave was down and stayed down. I was freaked out with worry but had to let the coaches handle it, and after a couple of minutes, Dave was able to get up and slowly walk to the sidelines. "Okay," I said to myself. "That's it. I'm not going to allow my son to be paralyzed or have multiple concussions. No sport is worth that."

We had that conversation that evening, and although Dave wasn't exactly happy, I think the injury scared him, and he didn't fight me on it. Later that season, he actually transitioned to gymnastics! He was quite good at it and ended up liking it a lot.

Dusty and Eric loved baseball, and I went to almost every one of their games. As most parents know, the kids have a blast playing these sports. The only downside of the games was the hyper-competitive, sometimes jerks of parents that were in the stands. But the boys all did really well playing team sports.

Our Friday nights were special for the boys and me. We would go to Blockbuster video and maybe another local video rental store and rent a couple of movies, then go across the street and get a Little Caesar's pizza. Friday was our movie and pizza night, and I loved it.

I thoroughly enjoyed my time with the boys, but I had been drifting away from the Lord, little by little. I was numb, emotionally and spiritually, from the years of disconnect between myself and Ticker. In the spiritual realm, I let my devotional life become a low priority. I started just depending on going to church to meet my spiritual needs, but that did not nearly take care of my soul by itself. The messages at my home church seemed to be rather dry and lifeless. After a year and a half, I decided to check out a really large church, which I guess even at that time was referred to as a megachurch.

It was Willow Creek Community Church. The music and worship part of the service was fresh and dynamic, and the teaching was excellent. The boys enjoyed the groups that they were in too. The only problem was that the church was forty minutes from where we lived in Des Plaines, so there was almost no opportunity to socialize with anyone there. I did try, however, by joining a midweek singles Bible study group that met at the church. There were kids' programs at the same time on those evenings, so it gave the boys a little more time to get to know some kids their age. So it was that we passed another year in Des Plaines.

15.2 Processing the Losses, Facing the Future

Perhaps it's partly that I'm a man and am supposed to "hold it all together." Perhaps it's just that I'm a vulnerable human being, although the Lord does live in me. The reality is that I was trying to process the losses as they came, and I was doing fine part of the time but not so well part of the time. The really huge loss, of course, was that Ticker had not gotten over the depression. Experiencing her withdrawal from our marriage and family life was like trying to hold on to a rope tied to a house that was sliding over a cliff. I didn't want to let go, but I had to. Ticker had made her decision, and God had essentially said, "You have to face reality and let her go."

The other reality of having to let go of our ministry to the Tarahumara, especially of our teaching and discipleship of the believers in El Manzano, was rather like suddenly looking into a mirror and seeing a sixty-year-old person looking back at you, then looking down at the pink slip in your hands that says, "Thank you for your years of work here at our company, but your services are no longer needed, effective immediately." I knew God was not that uncaring, but I did not see anyone around who I could go to for help, so I struggled. I wasn't even thirty-seven years old but had to figure out what my next "career" and purpose in life would be.

I recently finished reading a book written by a Christian woman who went to Yemen with her husband to work for a nongovernmental aid organization. Their desire was to share the Gospel in that very conservative Muslim country. Interestingly, they also had three boys, and their oldest son's name was David. At the end of nine years in Yemen (like our nine years in Mexico), after numerous miracles and breakthroughs in which several Yemenis came to accept the Lord, suddenly, political pressures due to religious intolerance forced them to leave the country. Amiira, the lady writing their story, says this of their transition:

> "We felt something was about to change. There was tension in the air, a tension we couldn't ignore.
>
> When we first left Germany [to live in Yemen], we thought it would be forever. We knew that God had called us, and that was all we needed to know.
>
> [N]ow change was being forced upon us and our plans were unraveling. We had to look at what the future had in store for us. Only then would we survive. That meant turning our backs on everything familiar. It was a challenge for each of us to embrace this involuntary change, but we would learn and grow in the process.
>
> Had I been holding on to something and not willing to let go? Had that kept me from seeing the new things God had in store for us? Or had God changed his mind? I was confused and had many questions.
>
> We wanted to bring the "good work" we had begun here to a successful conclusion… The work we had lived for and sometimes fought for should not fall apart.
>
> I read something during those months that really spoke to me: "Often we can't see the many doors opening in front of us because we are so focused on the single door that is closing behind us. We are so set on the negative that we don't see the blessings."

Amiira goes on to say that during their last days in the country:

> "Locals came and asked us for a Bible study. Another person wanted to be baptized. It seemed that what we had planted and watered over the years was finally blossoming! Chris (her husband) worked with the locals, training them to take over the teaching responsibilities. He showed them how to live the Christian life and explained to them how they could be set free from all their chains of traditional thinking.
>
> The time was ripe to place the work in the hands of the locals. We were grateful that potential leaders were available… We had to trust that God had a hope and future for all of our Yemeni friends, and our family as well.
>
> It gave us great joy and satisfaction to see the first Yemeni Christian fellowship established on the Arabian Peninsula… Our friends would never be alone because God had promised to build his church and watch over it.
>
> Our children…just couldn't understand why we had to leave our beloved homeland and all our friends behind. It was painful and distressing for each of us… We were leaving everything behind and had no idea what awaited us!
>
> On the way to the airport, I couldn't hold back the tears any longer. Our hearts were breaking and we were filled with grief. But Chris and I had to remain strong for the sake of the children."
>
> (Amiira Ann, *Sunrise in the Valley of Death* (YWAM, 2019), pp. 265–268)

Once again, like in the early years in San Rafael and El Manzano, I wished I had a partner to share all of this with and help me process it. But I didn't have an earthly partner. I did, of course, have the

Lord. But I was struggling to understand the big picture and how to handle it. In the face of Ticker's condition and in consideration of our financial supporters, I wrote a letter of resignation to the New Tribes Mission Executive Committee. On February 28, 1990, our resignation was officially acknowledged in a gracious letter from Mel Wyma at headquarters. So ended our sixteen years of schooling and service with New Tribes Mission.

It would take me years to look back and realize how it was God's timing for us to leave and let the Christian believers in El Manzano—as well as Al and Polly—develop into the strong members of the body of Christ that they were meant to be. Right then, my most important responsibilities revolved around being the best dad I could be for my boys. They were also struggling to fit into their new world of schools and making friends in our suburb of Chicago. It wasn't an easy transition for them, and I constantly had to keep tabs on corrupting moral issues, a couple of questionable "friends," and some social struggles they had in school. Together, we were doing better a month at a time, and I thanked God for my wonderful boys a thousand times.

15.3 The Middle Years

God's work in the hearts and minds and souls of numerous Tarahumara believers was continuing, week after week, and month after month. The Clarks ministered faithfully, went on their one year furlough, then returned as some new team members finished their Spanish studies and joined them in El Manzano. I, however, lost all touch with them as I gradually re-focused all my energies on my own life: being the best single dad I could be to my three sons and expanding my skill set as a general contractor.

In 1993 I re-married and moved to San Diego, California, choosing a woman I thought I could have a very compatible relationship with and a successful blended family. However, I put a higher value on our humanity than I did on my spiritual life, which had basically gone onto life support. I had only myself to blame for that. Our marriage lasted ten years, finally succumbing to the spiritual chasm that I allowed. Tragically, twelve years after our divorce Diane died in a head-on car accident in San Diego.

By God's grace, and true to His nature, as is stated in Romans 8:28, "...all things work together for good to those who love God, to those who are called according to His purpose." I did love God, and He loved my sons. He led two of them to the women who would become their loving wives in San Diego. I was able to realize a dream I had since childhood and learned to fly an airplane. I was assistant chairman of an airshow in San Diego for one year, then chairman for the next seven years. My remodeling business grew year over year, with three Christian designers sending me a vast amount of business and the best clientele I could have asked for.

Gradually I turned my heart away from my own goals and back to God in repentance. Attending a small local Christian fellowship re-invigorated my spiritual life. I could sense a new chapter in life approaching and I wanted to hear God's voice and do things His way again! I had indeed been beaten down by the adversities of life- the world, the flesh and the Devil. I had to face my sinful weaknesses and ask God to forgive and restore me. He healed the spiritual battle scars- but not until I finally let Him by reading His Word daily and seeking out Christian fellowship, flawed though it may be.

By His grace, the restoration process was soon to allow me to re-connect with those beloved believers in El Manzano, several faithful servants of God who had carried on His work, and get to know some of the new missionaries to the Tarahumara people. The realities of the Lord being my Shepherd re-emerged, as if from a mist. As the Psalmist David said, "You are with me. Your rod (of correction) and staff (of help), they comfort me" (Psalm 23:4). He was indeed restoring my soul. He was leading me in the paths of righteousness for His sake. Once again, my cup was running over!

Chapter 16

This is About <u>Him</u>

16.1 "He Who Has Begun a Good Work in You Will Continue It Until the Day of Jesus Christ" Philippians 1:6

Writing this book has been on my heart for years. When I had barely begun the first draft of the manuscript, I was curious as to how I would figure out a title for it. I wasn't worried about it, but was curious from time to time as I wrote the story out, and really wanted it to be an appropriate title. I think it came to me one day as I was writing, and it was truly like a whisper, but it struck a chord in my mind right away.

My personal perspective in this story started just as I've written it for you--with the night I consciously accepted the Lord Jesus Christ as my personal Savior. Previously there had been the godly influences of my grandparents reading the Bible with my brother and me present when we lived on the ranch with them as young kids--plus, God had used Catholic catechism classes to make me wonder about Him when I was only six or seven years old. That's what I know about the earliest beginnings of <u>my</u> involvement with the Gospel getting to the Tarahumara Indian people of northern Mexico. But when did it really begin? Eons ago, that's when.

Getting that Good News out there involved a LOT of work, too, and a plan. But I'm not referring to all the details contained in this memoir I've written so far. I'm thinking about the plan that God made to provide a way for the incredibly valuable souls of Tarahumara men, women and children to be able to hear about Him, choose to accept His love, love Him back and spend all of eternity in His presence. He first designed them just like He designed you and me, to be like Him ("after His image") in so many ways: intelligent, capable of genuine God-like love and amazing insights, able to create and appreciate and imagine things His other created beings could never begin to do. Then He came up with the plan to show His incredible, selfless love by having His own Son pay the ultimate price on the cross of Calvary to draw us to Himself. He opened a way for us to be truly spiritually "born again." Even the most savvy human beings or evil spiritual beings didn't think God would go <u>that</u> far! But He did, and executed His plan and is still executing it in real time today. It's beyond belief almost, an ingenious plan slowly being unveiled to all of creation, blossoming like fields of millions of gorgeous wildflowers that have sprung up on mountains of rocks or sand or ice and snow, places where they shouldn't even be able to survive.

The counter-intuitive reality of His self-sacrificing redemption plan? It crosses—indeed, ignores—every boundary of race, skin color, economic status or political persuasion. It's been heralded for so many years, and is today being repeated, in thousands of places around the world. In jungles, and in cities. On the plains of Africa, and in the sordid backstreets of American and European and Chinese cities. In crowded ghettos in India and hot, sandy towns in Iraq and Iran, the Gospel message is being told and those who recognize and want to accept the love of the God of the universe are doing so. They are telling others, and the chorus of their thanks and excitement keeps spreading. The more cruel and hurtful the evil ones make the world, the sweeter the music is to those like you and me, who can't get enough of it!

"He who has begun a good work…" First of all, the understated simplicity of the phrase struck me. The Apostle Paul was writing, of course, to the believers of a church in Greece that God had used him to start, and it was a solid church from the very beginning. "A good work," huh? Such an understatement! Is English that limited, or has God just chosen to beguile us with the word "good?" A nice, long book could be written about the terms God couples in the Bible with the word "good." The Gospel is the "Good News." Jesus is "the good Shepherd." God created the heavens and the earth and various creatures, etc. and then "saw that it was good" (Genesis chapter 1). Really? No, it was <u>incredible</u>! Finally, in Genesis 1:31, God does say that upon finishing His creation, "He saw everything that He had made and indeed it was very good." Or, as we should note, it was 'absolutely beyond fantastic!' Likewise, the spiritual new birth of the Philippian believers, the establishment of their church and the way they supported Paul and the gospel ministry as it spread throughout Asia, Greece and all of Europe was far beyond "a good work." No human language can accurately describe that supernatural miracle in the making!

What about the "He" of "He who has begun a good work?" Is it God the Father, the Planner? Is it Jesus, God the Son, our Redeemer and future Judge, who died and rose again and is the Author and Finisher of our salvation? Is it the Holy Spirit, who Jesus promised would come to perform a myriad of spiritual works after He, Jesus, ascended to heaven? The answers are yes, yes, and yes. The Trinity had planned and created and prophesied and carried out, and was still working a miraculous orchestration of events in the lives of those Philippian believers.

This story about taking the Gospel to the Tarahumara people is very much like that. In fact, as I recently re-read the account of Paul's missionary journey where he traveled to eastern Greece, his second missionary journey, I came upon a fact that I had not thought about for a while: Paul and Silas, with Luke as their companion, were actually "turned aside" by the Lord from going to Asia, and when they tried to go to their next choice of destinations—Bythinia—the Holy Spirit again did not permit them to go according to their own plans. Instead, God re-directed them to a new region where He had <u>His</u> plans for them: Macedonia. There they proceeded to "Philippi, which is the foremost city of that part of Macedonia" (Acts 16:6–12).

It was there that Lydia would come to know the Lord, along with her household, as well as the Philippian jailer and his household, and a whole exciting chapter of the early church would be written. Similarly, Ticker and I were re-directed from Indonesia to Mexico, then specifically to the community of El Manzano. "Ideally," we should have gone to a more monolingual area near where we settled, and waited longer to share the gospel in the Tarahumara language, not in Spanish. But God—yes, indeed. But God! He led Ticker to explain the gospel to Trini that fateful day in Spanish. He began His good work in one after another after another of our neighbors, knowing ahead of time who was open to His message and would accept Him. Today, Teodulo and many from his household and the surrounding ranches are a vibrant, spiritual community, brothers and sisters of ours in the awesome family and kingdom of God!

Paul's account of that one "good work" in Philippi was two thousand years ago. This account about the Tarahumara church is much more recent, of course. Same God. Same "good (actually, incredible!) works." Now let me update you on several people I've introduced you to already, and tell just a bit about others who came along and are part of this ongoing story.

16.2 God's Work Grows

1989-2016 The New Tribes Ministry to the Western Tarahumara Indian People

God wasn't finished in El Manzano…not by a long shot! When we left El Manzano in 1988, and then finally left Mexico in 1989, Al and Polly faithfully carried on the ministry with the believers. A year later they went on furlough. Teodulo had become a solid believer and became the leader of the church there. He continued meeting with the other Christians and the church grew and matured. When the Clarks came back from furlough some new missionaries were completing their Spanish studies in Chihuahua City. One couple was

Ted and Sharon Wingo. Ted was the younger brother of Barry, who was still ministering in the Pima tribe, whose house I had worked on doing the room addition when we had those ten flat tires on our way back to Chihuahua. Ted was a linguist and ended up taking my place on the team. Unbelievably, he, Sharon and their children moved into the barely expanded adobe shack that was on our property!

Another family with three children, the Roberts, lived in our house in El Manzano for almost two years. After a couple of years in El Manzano, the Wingos and the Roberts decided they needed to move to a community where there were a lot more Tarahumara speakers, so made the move to Rocoroibo. Ted became good friends with Don Burgess who had lived there for many years and Don was a huge help to him in the field of linguistics. Don had already translated quite a bit of the New Testament and several books of the Old Testament. Ted went on to translate ten New Testament books himself into the Western dialect of Tarahumara. They served for over twenty years in Rocoroibo.

Ted and Sharon Wingo

During those many years of mastering the very difficult Tarahumara language, they formed bonds with quite a few folks in that area. They held meetings with a small group of believers for a few years who hopefully are growing in their faith and being lights in a culture where drinking and drug use have become so pervasive. In his testimony, numerous times Teodulo shared how drinking had been a waste of his time and money, making life more of a struggle, not more enjoyable. He lost all desire for alcohol after he embraced his love for the Lord. It's my hope that Teodulo himself will continue to be an inspiration to those believers struggling to make the Lord first in their lives.

Dave Wolf and Company

Dave, the pilot who flew for so many of us with New Tribes and other missions, continues to do so to this day! He also trains new pilots and flies in ministries in Alaska in the summer months. His fellow pilots with United Indian Mission occasionally fly into Rocoroibo, too, visiting with and encouraging Tarahumara believers and friends of the Burgesses, Wingos and Robertses.

Remember the New Tribes pilot, Paul Dye, who inspired me to join the mission when I was eighteen years old? He continues to serve the Lord to this day in his church and a prison ministry in Arizona.

The Clinic

Although not a person, it's worth mentioning that the clinic building we constructed is still serving its intended purpose, too. With the help of so many loving Menonites who made beautiful, warm patchwork quilts for the needy folks in Mexico, with the other donated materials and the work of the dedicated and fun group from our church in Des Plaines, Illinois who helped us put up the building, the effort was worth it. Al followed up with the Mexican government officials and they sent out a doctor and nurses who took the medical work load off of the Clarks. The government eventually built a separate clinic building of its own close by, and the doctor or nurses rotate in their medical services, still living in the building we built.

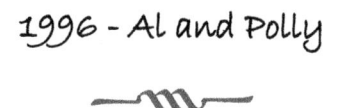

1996 - Al and Polly

Al and Polly stayed in El Manzano for a few more years after we left, teaching and discipling the believers. Although Al and I didn't talk about that, it must've been hard for him and Polly to be alone once the other two families moved to Rocoroibo. When their daughter Amy was in high school they moved to Chihuahua City and engaged in a variety of ministries there. Once she graduated, they resigned from New Tribes and moved back to South Carolina. That tenacious old partner of mine, who at one point felt he "didn't have anything to offer" at the Bible studies in our house with the new believers, went on to become completely fluent in Spanish! In fact, when he got back to South Carolina looking for what God would have him to do in the ministry there, the pastor of his home church asked him to start a Spanish ministry. There was a sizable Hispanic community in the area, and Al was exactly the man for the job.

1997 - Ticker and Dan

As the years passed, I had very little idea of what was going on in Ticker's life, what was working for her regarding the treatment of her depression and what was not. I hope that she can tell her story someday about that long and winding road to healing and stability. Millions of Christians, both men and women, battle with depression every day. The church needs trained, sensitive lay people and professionals to patiently help those who are suffering and confused.

Where are the men and women who care more about being wise, effective, discerning counselors than about being able to charge enormous amounts of money for their services? I only know of a very few godly counselors who selflessly give themselves to the Lord and His most needy saints as a <u>ministry</u> of love rather than as a profession. And yes, it is a ministry of love, utilizing some of the spiritual gifts of discernment, compassion, admonition and encouragement.

Part of Ticker's story is that she eventually got accurately diagnosed with bipolar disorder and was prescribed medication that was appropriate for her. Like a lot of people who get started on a certain medication that they need, sometimes once they feel better they decide they don't need it anymore and stop taking it. That apparently happened to Ticker several times before she made taking it consistently a habit in her life and was able to become stable and well. Sometime in the early to mid-1990s she met a very understanding and kind man. Dan worked for the Cook County, Illinois, government as a counselor to the homeless. They found in each other a loving companion and were married in April, 1997.

2008 - Electricity and Cell Phones

In 2008, the Mexican government finally got electric lines run all the way to El Manzano and beyond. With electricity came cell phone towers and cell phones. Teodulo and Barbara got their first cell phone not long after that. That opened an opportunity for them to stay in touch with the Clarks on a regular basis.

HE WHO HAS BEGUN A GOOD WORK

2009 - Dave Re-visits El Manzano

In 2009, I was living in San Diego and my son Dave and his wife, Jen, were in Norfolk, Virginia, where Dave was stationed in the Navy. Dave had a burning desire to go back to El Manzano and visit. He wanted to see everything there as an adult, and how it actually compared with his childhood memories. He really wanted me to plan a trip with him. I told him that I felt it was far too dangerous with the drug cartels operating with impunity. From what I was reading and hearing, a major source of income for the cartels had become kidnapping for ransom. Dave was adamant – he was going to go with me or without me. With that in mind, I was compelled to tell him what I thought was vital in planning the trip. I talked to him about not taking anything that could identify him as a member of the US military: not boots (which I had remembered from the ex-DEA agent who had visited us in San Rafael), not a pocket knife, not a belt buckle, absolutely nothing with a US military insignia on it. I also told him that he should tell absolutely no one that Jen was a doctor. That would make her an especially high profile target for kidnapping and ransom.

I also told Dave that I wanted him to buy or borrow a satellite phone so that I could talk with him twice a day and find out where he was and how he was doing. With that in mind, I went back into the maps of the area which I had kept. I was really happy when I found what I was looking for—I had two copies of a very detailed topographical map of the entire region from San Rafael to El Manzano, including all the dirt roads and trails. I mailed one to Dave and told him that each day when we talked he could tell me where he was by identifying the closest community. If anything were to happen to them and they had to abandon their vehicle and try to get away on foot, he could tell me really accurately exactly where they were. We had code words that we would use each time we talked to indicate whether or not he was under duress—in other words, had a gun pointed at him or had actually been kidnapped.

In my mind, the risk of something bad happening to them was significant enough that I came up with a rescue plan in case they were kidnapped. I would never have forgiven myself if, after considering the dangers, I had not come up with a plan and they disappeared. Dave gave me the names and phone numbers of four individuals who had been highly trained, and two of whom were actual trainers, in military special operations. If I needed them, I was prepared to pay a very significant amount of money per day to have those men quickly go down to Mexico, meet me, and help me find Dave and Jen. My other sons, Dusty and Eric, were not on deployment with the military at that time so they were also vital parts of Plan A as well as a backup plan. There were a couple of other people as well who I talked to who were willing to play vital roles if need be. What Dave and Jen were planning to do, essentially being tourists going into an area where a drug cartel was growing and transporting millions of dollars of marijuana and heroin, could have turned into a life-and-death situation very quickly.

God is <u>always</u> ultimately in control of any situation, which I had to remind myself of many times, even as I made plans for a search and rescue. Dave and Jen each worked with their bosses on the dates that worked out for both of them to make the trip, and it turned out that Easter week was their first and perhaps only opportunity for quite a while. When David told me that, I had to thank and praise the Lord! There are two times of the year when millions of Mexicans from all over the country and abroad travel to see their relatives: Christmas and Easter. With the protective graces of the Lord, Dave and Jen would hopefully just blend in with all those other people who were on the road and visiting family.

Dave was able to borrow a satellite phone to use on the trip, and we didn't speak twice each day but we did speak once every single day. After a few days of travel they finally got out to El Manzano. They had a great surprise arrival at Teodulo and Barbara's house. Teodulo was just then working on the rock foundations for the church building he was constructing. Dave was able to help him do some physical labor for a couple of days, and Jen worked with Barbara fixing meals and learning her first words and phrases in Spanish. They went down and looked over our property and house, which by then had been vacant for several years.

Dave and Jenn

The highlight of their trip however, was getting to visit with Barbara and Teodulo and meet a good number of the believers. The church that Teodulo was building was going to be named "Cristo Viene" "Christ Is Coming." Dave brought back the good news to me that there were somewhere close to fifty believers in the El Manzano area! He also happened to run into a lady that I had apparently shared the gospel with and led to the Lord in a town east of San Rafael called Areponapuchi. He said there were quite a few believers in that area, too. We never know how God will give the increase when we plant and water the seed of the Gospel! It did my heart good to hear such good news after all those years away from that ministry.

2012 - Go West, Young Man!

In 2011 and 2012 I was growing increasingly unhappy from being surrounded by the Southern California "It's all about me" culture. I considered strongly moving back to Arizona where people generally have a good head on their shoulders and there is still a strong Western cowboy "God bless America" culture. I traveled around the state a few times, visiting with my grandma before she finally passed away, looking for a small town or rural community to move to. Then one day, my son Dave said that he and his wife Jen wanted to move to Hawaii, to the Big Island, where they could do year-round farming.

"Why didn't you tell me you were interested in Hawaii?" I asked Dave. "You know I love it over there!" By then I had gone to Hawaii fourteen times on vacation over the course of twenty years. I had even thought about trying to go into business on Maui for half or a third of each year and also keep my business going in San Diego. The logistics had just seemed to be too much, with all the extra tools and an additional truck that would have been necessary. However, now Hawaii suddenly seemed like a much better idea than Arizona.

I remembered that famous newspaper man of the 1800s, Horace Greeley, who had said "Go West, young man!" Well, from Chicago I had gone to San Diego, where if you go any further west you'll get your boots wet, but then one day realized that I could go even further west and still be in the United States!

On September 12, 2012 I moved to the Big Island of Hawaii, where Dave and Jen had arrived just three weeks earlier. We all rented a big plantation manager's house together for nine months, then I was drawn to a unique and awesome rural community of seven thousand people called North Kohala, which is on the northwest corner of the island. With God's help in overcoming ridiculous state bureaucratic hassles, I then got my general contractor's license and was finally able to begin making a decent living. God opened doors for me through some interesting contacts, and my business has gone well ever since.

Dave and Jen found a big, rugged undeveloped 150-acre property an hour and a half away and built a house there on the slopes of the huge mountain of Mauna Kea. With tons of hard work and innovation Dave built a unique business around working with exotic hardwoods. Jenn, an MD, was insightful enough to leave two or three medical practices and get into doing telemedicine a year or two before the Covid-19 pandemic hit in early 2020. That job has been a great fit for her ever since.

2014- Dusty and His Family

Dusty was on his last and most dangerous deployment to Afghanistan while in the Marine Corps when we invited his wife Rachel and the kids to come visit us in Hawaii. They fell in love with the Big Island, and as soon as Dusty got back from deployment he came to visit, too. Dusty loved his job in the Marine Corps, and was just about to reenlist for another three years, but Dave and Jen, Rachel and I and even their kids prevailed upon him to reconsider. He decided to end his career in the Marines after nine years, and in 2014 they moved to Hawaii. For seven years they lived on the Hamakua Coast, not too far from Dave and Jen, and loved their adventure here. Then Dusty and his family fell in love with Alaska in June, 2021 when they went there on vacation. Dusty decided to pursue another dream he had been thinking about for many years and become a police officer. Walking closely with God, he feels that his purpose in life is to be a help to those in need. He was recently hired by the Kenai Police Department and moved to Alaska in December, 2021. As I write this he has now graduated from the four-month long Alaska State Troopers Academy. As Dusty put it, "We're ready for the next adventure!" Rachell Gavin and Mckayla all agree!

A late note: My daughter-in-law, Rachel, recently wrote a book in which she is amazingly transparent about her growth in the Lord. Going back to her childhood, she addresses a variety of struggles she has had to deal with and how she found and enlisted God's help in them. For her bravery and insights as a wife, mother, nurse and diabetic I am so proud of her. Her book is entitled *Joyful Chaos and Little Miracles* by Rachel Real, published by Christian Faith Publishing in 2022.

Dusty and Rachel, Gavin and Mckayla in Alaska

2014- Enter Cynthia

Twenty minutes from my house in Hawaii, at a really unique outdoor music and restaurant venue called The Blue Dragon, I met a beautiful, blue-eyed woman named Cynthia. She tells the story about how, in one of our first conversations, I told her I am a born-again Christian and had been a missionary in Mexico. Her first thought was, "Really God? I asked you to bring me a good, godly man. You actually brought me a missionary?" After dating for three or four months I felt that she was my soulmate—but I did not want to fool myself again. So after five years of dating and a lot of prayers as we grew closer spiritually, we got married on November 1, 2019!

Our wedding ceremony was at our favorite beach with just family and a few close friends. As I write this two and a half years later we were finally able to go on our honeymoon. The pandemic threw a big monkey wrench into our original plans, so we'd been waiting on the Lord for the right time. Everything worked out fantastically and we enjoyed Montana, Wyoming, Florida and Chicago for an awesome vacation and honeymoon! We even went to see the old New Tribes Mission headquarters building in Sanford, Florida that I had worked on for an entire year during our training in 1976–77. Vacated by the mission just a couple of years ago, it's now destined to become a restored historical site!

Cynthia and I were married on our favorite beach on Hawaii Island

2018- First Hand News from My Old Partner!

It wasn't until 2018 that I finally got back in touch with Al Clark after way too many years of losing track of him. When I finally got a phone number for him from somebody in New Tribes and called him, it was so amazing to hear that old familiar voice again! We talked for about an hour that first time, catching up on so many things that had happened over the years, especially regarding El Manzano, Teodulo, Barbara and the believers out there. A particularly great piece of news was that Teodulo's mom, Doña Petra, had accepted the Lord not long after we left. Teodulo then showed Al a deep pool in the creek where they could perform baptisms, and a number of believers were then baptized. Seeing the photos of Teodulo's and Petra's baptisms was priceless. We had a couple of more conversations after that, and

Al filled me in on so many things he had learned from his regular conversations with Teodulo by cell phone.

Teodulo was extremely careful to never talk about the drug trafficking and cartels out there. But Al had seen enough before he left, and the Wingos had seen even more over where they lived before they left for good, that Al was able to put together the pieces of what was going on. The details that became widely known by everyone out there, some of them even published in the Mexican media, were shocking to me, and saddened both of us.

Several years previously, a son of an influential Tarahumara man in the community became enamored with all the wealth to be made, and with the prestige and power flaunted by the drug cartel that was working the area, and invited them to come and operate in El Manzano. It was in fact one of the largest and most brutal of the cartels, run by one of the most powerful drug lords in the world. From news reports I knew their leader had been arrested by the Mexican government, then had escaped from prison not once but twice. Even while he was in prison, like so many gang leaders around the world, he was able to continue to run his cartel, earning billions of dollars while he brutally pushed back against rivals and maintained control of his empire. But then the United States government reached an agreement with Mexico to have him extradited to the U.S. Once he was moved to a U.S. federal prison, his communications with and control over his cartel effectively ceased.

His organization had been in sole control of the drugs being grown in El Manzano and the surrounding region for several years, then there had come the sudden pause. A competing cartel moved in and took over for a year or two, pressuring the locals to grow for them and they reaped the profits. Finally, the reorganized original cartel came back to reassert its control. Their local enforcers went to El Manzano, called for a gathering, and confronted the local men over why they had changed allegiances. By this time, it appeared that some of the local people were tired of the pressure exerted on them and having to deal with the conflicting groups. Several just wanted to go back to their traditional ways of life: raising their children in peace, growing corn and raising their pigs, chickens and a few cows.

Al didn't go into detail with me regarding who all the individuals were, but one fellow who had been a good friend to both of us was Cayetano. He had been a regular visitor at my house, curious about various realms of science, astronomy and even the gospel preachers that he heard on the late-night AM radio programs that he could pick up. We had some very interesting, intellectually stimulating conversations for years. In fact, it was Cayetano who made me realize how incredibly observant tribal people living in the rugged mountains like we did can be. When our troops went into Afghanistan against the Taliban, I began to understand what incredibly astute adversaries they would be up against. Some of those tribal mountain people can focus and spot a bird or a squirrel moving on a mountainside from half a mile away! Cayetano was one of those people. One day, standing on my back porch, he helped me spot a stationary satellite in the bright blue daytime sky above El Manzano. It was amazing.

I don't even know what Cayetano's role in the community or with the various groups was when the cartel upheaval occurred, but he did go to the meeting called by the cartel enforcers. He had to be about sixty-five years old by then, which was just a few years ago. Apparently he was speaking for a number of the people there who wanted to get out of the drug business.

"So you want to get out, huh?" said one of the enforcers.

"Yes," said Cayetano.

"Ok, you're out," said the enforcer. He pulled out a pistol and shot Cayetano point blank in the chest, killing him in front of the group of local residents.

"Does anybody else want out?" he asked.

Al didn't tell me if it happened right then or shortly thereafter, but a gun battle ensued and sixteen men were killed, some of whom I knew well. The army was called out to restore order and some of the lower level local men were swept up and sent to prison for a year or so to send a message to the community to cool down. Because of a combination of things-- the Ponderosa logging company cutting back on operations, the fear and pressure from the cartel to grow illegal drugs as well as the violence itself-- many of the people in the El

Manzano area moved away to San Rafael, to some of the even bigger towns, and to Chihuahua City to find work and a new way of life.

    I wish more Americans could understand the horrible, deadly consequences of the illegal drugs they consume every day in our country. Most of them wouldn't care, of course, and willfully want to stay ignorant. But there is a huge human toll in the illegal drug trades. The brutal, heartless leaders become incredibly rich. The organizers, traffickers and other members of their armies sell their souls to them in exchange for fancy expensive trucks and clothes. The temporary but tangible feeling of power that comes with carrying and using their automatic weapons becomes the energy and purpose of their lives. Then, if and when a life gets snuffed out in a gun battle or ambush, another poor, aimless, impressionable soul steps forward to take their place as he too seeks macho glory and a purpose in life. Meanwhile, not only do their mothers, fathers, brothers and sisters grieve their loss and wasted lives, but so will the family members of their rival armies' "soldiers" who will also fight and die. All this transpires so that millions of partying or addicted Americans can snort, shoot up or smoke their illegal drugs.

2022 From Boys to Men to Warriors

Eric—US Navy Chief Petty Officer and Deep Sea Diver

HE WHO HAS BEGUN A GOOD WORK

David, Dustin and Eric all grew up to be fine men and outstanding citizens. They also all became warriors for our nation. Dave had been in the U.S. Navy for five years when 9/11 happened. He went on to become a Navy deep-sea diver and finished his sixteen year career with several years as a Navy intelligence officer. Eric was the next one to join. Two days after 9/11 he made his decision after considering community college or joining one of the branches of the military. He followed his brother Dave's advise, qualified as a Navy deep-sea diver, and was rewarded with one of his earliest assignments being a member of SEAL Delivery Team 2 on the East Coast. With twenty years of service so far he recently reenlisted for another three years and continues to train Navy divers and SEALS for SEAL delivery teams.

Dustin worked for me for a while in San Diego even as he was going to college full-time, and of all the employees I ever had I can honestly and without question say that he was the best. His intelligence, great attitude and work ethic enabled him to learn a variety of skills in my remodeling business. After a couple of years of working for me, he went to work for an electrical contractor and completely ran several of their jobs. Just a few years later, seeing the war on terror rage on as it kept America's enemies at bay, he couldn't watch from the sidelines any longer and joined the Marines. He served for nine years, with his last deployment being to a small forward operating base in Afghanistan in an extremely dangerous and deadly part of the country.

I am honored to be able to say that all of my sons have served with distinction. Their service has been recognized by the exemplary service commendations they have received from their commanding officers for a variety of reasons. Eric had the exceptional honor to be chosen as "Sailor of the Year" a few years ago out of over two hundred fifty divers and sailors at his command at Pearl Harbor, Hawaii. It was also amazing to have had all three of them living here in the Hawaiian Islands, with Dave and Dusty only an hour away and Eric forty-five minutes away by airplane on Oahu.

Teodulo Barbara

Barbara and Teodulo

—∽∽—

    I now have regular conversations with Teodulo and his family through the miracle of cell phones. Like all of us, they are getting older, but by the grace of God they are relatively healthy. Teodulo is now seventy-three years old, Barbara is sixty-six and their son Hugo is thirty-six, I believe. The church that Teodulo leads, "Christ is Coming," has services twice a week, with anywhere from twelve to twenty-five people attending. Just like any church anywhere, some of the believers have drifted away and need prayer, and so every Wednesday evening the faithful have a prayer meeting, also. Teodulo is also nurturing the next generation of believers who contribute to the worship and teaching every week. In one especially great conversation recently I asked him if he still played the guitar, which he had occasionally done when we lived there. He said that yes, as a matter of fact, he and a younger fellow in the church had written a Christian song that he was especially proud of, so he played it for me over the phone. Hearing that original song of his put a big smile on my face. Were there angels listening who were also tapping their toes along with the beat and the words of praise? I could almost bet there were!

Just a few months ago, as I wrote a particularly painful part of this story, I was feeling down. I stopped writing and had to just sit out on my porch and get past that sad portion of the reality of what had happened. Only a few minutes later my cell phone rang. It was Teodulo! He and I talked for over an hour and a half, and when we finally said our goodbyes and hung up I just burst out in a joyful "Thank you so much, God!" to the Lord. How did He do that for me?? Because He is all-knowing and loves me. And Teodulo! And you! Only God could encourage me like that, continuing to do that work that He began so many years ago.

Don Burgess, A Marathon Running Servant of God

There is no one that I have known longer in the service of the Lord to the Tarahumara Indian people than Don Burgess. In fact, there are very few I have known who have served the Savior for so long, period. The Tarahumara, for many decades, have been known to be incredible long distance runners, having a race that they do in competition with neighboring communities that will go on for twenty-four hours! The same runners compete for their community, stopping to rest like in a relay race, but then get back into it and carry on for twenty-four continuous hours, all on the rugged trails of the Sierra Madre mountains.

Don is like one of those runners. He has continued going and going and going. I still have what I think was my first letter from Don, dated 1982. I also now have emails from him, one dated October 11, 2020 in which he said, "We are getting rather old and this (the Gospel of John translation in the Bocoyna-Creel dialect) might be our last book." Don was 81 years old then. Now, after many more hundreds of hours, another pace maker for his heart (the third), and probably a few thousand more miles of travel by pickup truck back and forth between Mexico, Texas and Arizona, Don has completed even more translation of books of the Bible and Bible story materials in <u>three different dialects</u> of the Tarahumara language! All of this from a man-- and helped by his loving and supportive wife, Marie- - who is soft-spoken and humble. I have no doubt that there is a whole chapter in God's book entitled "Acts of the Holy Spirit, Twentieth and Twenty-First Centuries" (which we may get to read in Heaven) that has been written about Don. And it's still not finished!

Don's going to blush when he reads this, but I don't care! It's been a great blessing to know you, my friend.

Note: I emailed portions of my manuscript for this book, including the paragraphs above, to Don for fact-checking purposes in early 2022. I'm not sure if he blushed then, but he did tell me that he was blessed to know that I, his old friend (from "now Hawaii, of all places"), Teodulo, and a few others were currently making a renewed effort to get his translated scriptures out to several remote Tarahumara areas.

In May he suffered a stroke, and then was promoted to heaven on June 8, 2022 while at home with his loving and extremely dedicated wife of almost forty years. Their legacy of service, and that of their five children, is too long to go into here. In addition to what their son Bryan has done as a missionary pilot in Africa and in North America for over thirty years, their work in furthering the gospel of Jesus Christ would be a great section in a sequel to this book.

Don and Marie Burgess

A Tribute to Al Clark

Al Clark passed away on July 12, 2019. His wonderful wife Polly felt the loss the deepest, there is no doubt, but also had the blessing of hundreds of loving Christians who poured out praise for him. Their Hispanic church in South Carolina was his final, crowning achievement on this earth. When I asked him a year or two before when he expected to retire, he said, "Steve, I don't know what else I can do but what I'm doing." In his faithful way, he preached and encouraged others to the very end.

Their sons live not too far from Polly, and his daughter Amy married a godly and loving Mexican man, Oscar, in 2017. He has been key to their continuing ministry to the Spanish speaking community.

When I was thinking of Al a few days ago, a Christian song from years ago, based on a psalm, popped into my head and says it all: "Not to the strong is the battle, not to the swift is the race; but to the <u>true</u> and the <u>faithful</u> victory is promised through grace!"

Looking forward to seeing you again in heaven, my friend!

16.3 "He Will Complete It Until The Day Of Jesus Christ" (Philippians 1:6)

As for me, I'm happy to say that walking with the Lord each and every day brings me the greatest joys in life. I've been able to do a lot of fascinating, fun, interesting, adventurous and hard things in my sixty-seven years so far here on earth. By the grace of God, shortly after moving here to Hawaii, I found a rock solid Christian fellowship, Kohala Baptist Church, that Cynthia and I attend. We have a wonderful, God-fearing, humble and wise pastor-- Stephen Hedlund. Cynthia and I are growing in our friendships with some of the best Christian folks a person could ask for. In our "small group" Bible studies on Friday nights we meet for food and fellowship, a Bible study and prayer time that usually lasts two hours or more, and so we help disciple each other!

Nowadays my dear wife and I are members of God's team who have the supporting roles that I needed and appreciated so much when I was out there on the front lines. We are praying for spiritual victories in small, daily struggles and big, decisive battles in the lives of the missionaries and the people they are working with in various parts of the world. We are sending Spanish Bibles and helping to get Tarahumara language gospel materials to our brothers and sisters in El Manzano and throughout the Sierra Madre Mountains of Mexico.

The Lord has impressed on my heart the on-going needs of all the Western Tarahumara brothers and sisters of ours. The faithful ones, like Barbara and Teodulo, need encouragement to stay strong in the faith. The ones from El Manzano and the Rocoroibo area who have begun to return to "their old ways" need help and fellowship from the strong ones. The younger generation in Teodulo's church needs to exercise their spiritual gifts by teaching, evangelizing and supporting their weaker brethren. To that end we have initiated fund-raising to enable them to purchase gasoline and food so they can travel to the areas where the needs are. Ted and Sharon Wingo, still ministering for the Lord in South Carolina, are also contributing to this support for the outreach and discipleship of the Tarahumara believers. Praise God for Teodulo's enthusiasm to lead the way! He recently sent me a video taken with his new cell phone of an evangelism and fellowship trip he made with several of the younger believers to a remote, all-Tarahumara community of ranches!

You see, God is not finished doing His good work in a lot of us- in me, Teodulo, His Tarahumara church, and you.

Serving our Lord and Savior in Mexico was absolutely the greatest joy and adventure in my life. It also had some of the toughest challenges and lessons to be learned. My personal drifting away years later due to my shortcomings—and then getting back in a close relationship with the Lord—has sometimes not been easy to talk about. But I hope that you have seen parallels and lessons—both warnings and encouragement—for your own life from the pages of what I've written. If this account has not been a blessing to you, if you don't see how God can use a flawed but willing believer to become an ambassador for Him <u>anywhere</u>, if you can't find a few nuggets of wisdom to incorporate into your own life, then I have failed. But I bet I haven't. From the serious to the funny, from overcoming our human flaws to enjoying God's amazing grace, I hope you can be excited about how you <u>personally</u> fit into our Great God's master plan.

We only have one life to live, something that we all realize more profoundly as we get older. Our Lord summed up our choices in these words:

> **If anyone desires to come after Me, let him deny himself, and take up his cross, and follow Me. For whoever desires to save his life will lose it, but whoever loses his life for My sake will find it. For what profit is it to a man**

> **if he gains the whole world, and loses his own soul? Or what will a man give in exchange for his soul? For the Son of Man will come in the glory of His Father with His angels, and then He will reward each according to his works. (Matthew 16: 24–27)**

I did "desire" to follow Him. I did "lose" years and income-- probably good income-- by not becoming a pilot or general contractor (which I apparently later found out I actually had a good aptitude for). What if I had gained "the whole world" of a good income, a great house, nice cars, and lots of retirement money in the bank? I'll tell you what I would have "gained," as I can now look back on all of it: I would have <u>lost</u> my soul. I would have "exchanged it for my soul," in the Lord's words. My eternal soul would have been saved since Christ paid the price for it on the cross and I had become a born-again believer in Him. But I would have lost all that He wanted my one and only, personal soul to do for His glory and for His kingdom. I would not have been what He wanted me to be. Indeed, today-- every day-- I find that following these same principles gives me the deepest joy and fulfillment in life: desiring to follow Him, denying myself, taking up my cross, and following God's leading.

In a nutshell, that is what the Apostle Paul was so thankful for in his letter to the Philippians: those who were participating by their "fellowship in the gospel" (Phil. 1:5) were also committed in their "defense and confirmation of the gospel" and thus were "all partakers with [him] of [God's] grace" (Phil.1:7).

Where are you in the process of "His good work" in you? Looking forward to full-time Christian ministry? Wanting to serve Him better in your local church? Recovering from being wounded in His service, as I was for a time? Wondering how to get back into a truly vibrant, healthy relationship with Him?

I urge you to listen to God's "still, small voice" like Elijah did in his time of need. I challenge you to walk by His side and look where

He is looking, not having to be led with a bit and bridle like the stubborn mule but rather serving Him like the beautiful horse!

There are some other words of our Lord's that are still in my Bible and yours, two thousand years after He spoke them- those last words that He left with His disciples as He was about to ascend into heaven. He meant them then, and He wants us to take them to heart still today. Those words motivated someone-- actually many someones-- who eventually shared the Good News of salvation with you and me, and then helped us to become followers of our great God and Savior:

> **All authority has been given to Me in heaven and on earth. Go, therefore and make disciples of all the nations, baptizing them in the name of the Father and of the Son and of the Holy Spirit, teaching them to observe all things that I have commanded you; and lo, I am with you always, even to the end of the age. (Matthew 28: 18–20)**

He wants you.
We need you.
Go for it!
Follow Him!

Because of His infinite love,

Steve

Afterward

New Tribes Mission Becomes Ethnos360

New Tribes Mission began in 1942 as the vision of founder Paul Fleming and five other men to take the gospel to tribal people who had no access to it. In 2017 the Mission's name was changed to Ethnos360 to express a more all-encompassing definition of "unreached people groups." The focus is the same as the founders': To obey Jesus' command in Matthew 28:19 "to make disciples of all nations." That means going "wherever it is necessary to see a thriving church for every people." Thus the name change: Ethnos- nations, and 360- the entirety of the globe.

Today the training program still includes a college level Bible Institute that is two years in duration, cross-cultural training that includes developing and improving a close walk with God as well as with co-workers, and specialized language analysis training for those who qualify.

Career church planting and support ministries are the focus of Ethnos360, but there are also short-term programs offered annually: a three to seven day "familiarization" experience in Pennsylvania, two week trips to visit indigenous people groups, and six week trips to Papua New Guinea or Brazil to experience missionary life where an indigenous church has been established. By committing to an additional two to three weeks, it is possible to work in an internship in Papua New Guinea in Aviation, Missionary Medicine, Education of Missionary Children, IT Services, Business Administration or Property Maintenance.

For detailed information on opportunities, requirements for qualification and costs, go to Ethnos360.org.

About the Author

The author has lived in nine different states in diverse regions of the United States as well as one and a half years in Ontario, Canada, and nine years in Chihuahua, Mexico. He has enjoyed careers as a missionary and linguist in Mexico, followed by being a licensed general contractor in Illinois, California, and Hawaii. Along the way, he has pursued his part-time passions of being a writer and inventor. He currently lives on the Big Island of Hawaii with his wife, Cynthia, and ♫"two cats in the yard."♪

The author may be contacted at TaraMinistry23@yahoo.com